Nanotechnology for Electronic Materials and Devices

Nanotechnology for Electronic Materials and Devices

Editors

Patrick Fiorenza
Raffaella Lo Nigro
Béla Pécz
Jens Eriksson

MDPI • Basel • Beijing • Wuhan • Barcelona • Belgrade • Manchester • Tokyo • Cluj • Tianjin

Editors
Patrick Fiorenza
Consiglio Nazionale delle
Ricerche—Istituto per la
Microelettronica e
Microsistemi (CNR-IMM)
Italy

Raffaella Lo Nigro
Consiglio Nazionale delle
Ricerche—Istituto per la
Microelettronica e
Microsistemi (CNR-IMM)
Italy

Béla Pécz
Institute for Technical Physics
and Materials Science
Hungary

Jens Eriksson
Linköping University
Sweden

Editorial Office
MDPI
St. Alban-Anlage 66
4052 Basel, Switzerland

This is a reprint of articles from the Special Issue published online in the open access journal *Nanomaterials* (ISSN 2079-4991) (available at: https://www.mdpi.com/journal/nanomaterials/special_issues/nano_electronic_device).

For citation purposes, cite each article independently as indicated on the article page online and as indicated below:

LastName, A.A.; LastName, B.B.; LastName, C.C. Article Title. *Journal Name* **Year**, *Volume Number*, Page Range.

ISBN 978-3-0365-7352-6 (Hbk)
ISBN 978-3-0365-7353-3 (PDF)

© 2023 by the authors. Articles in this book are Open Access and distributed under the Creative Commons Attribution (CC BY) license, which allows users to download, copy and build upon published articles, as long as the author and publisher are properly credited, which ensures maximum dissemination and a wider impact of our publications.

The book as a whole is distributed by MDPI under the terms and conditions of the Creative Commons license CC BY-NC-ND.

Contents

About the Editors vii

Raffaella Lo Nigro, Patrick Fiorenza, Béla Pécz and Jens Eriksson
Nanotechnology for Electronic Materials and Devices
Reprinted from: *Nanomaterials* **2022**, *12*, 3319, doi:10.3390/nano12193319 1

Kristjan Kalam, Markus Otsus, Jekaterina Kozlova, Aivar Tarre, Aarne Kasikov, Raul Rammula, et al.
Memory Effects in Nanolaminates of Hafnium and Iron Oxide Films Structured by Atomic Layer Deposition
Reprinted from: *Nanomaterials* **2022**, *12*, 2593, doi:10.3390/nano12152593 3

Miklos Fried, Renato Bogar, Daniel Takacs, Zoltan Labadi, Zsolt Endre Horvath and Zsolt Zolnai
Investigation of Combinatorial WO_3-MoO_3 Mixed Layers by Spectroscopic Ellipsometry Using Different Optical Models
Reprinted from: *Nanomaterials* **2022**, *12*, 2421, doi:10.3390/nano12142421 21

Jihun Park, Changho Ra, Jaewon Lim and Jongwook Jeon
Device and Circuit Analysis of Double Gate Field Effect Transistor with Mono-Layer WS_2-Channel at Sub-2 nm Technology Node
Reprinted from: *Nanomaterials* **2022**, *12*, 2299, doi:10.3390/nano12132299 37

Kohei Yamasue and Yasuo Cho
Boxcar Averaging Scanning Nonlinear Dielectric Microscopy
Reprinted from: *Nanomaterials* **2022**, *12*, 794, doi:10.3390/nano12050794 47

Salvatore E. Panasci, Antal Koos, Emanuela Schilirò, Salvatore Di Franco, Giuseppe Greco, Patrick Fiorenza, et al.
Multiscale Investigation of the Structural, Electrical and Photoluminescence Properties of MoS_2 Obtained by MoO_3 Sulfurization
Reprinted from: *Nanomaterials* **2022**, *12*, 182, doi:10.3390/nano12020182 67

Emanuela Schilirò, Filippo Giannazzo, Salvatore Di Franco, Giuseppe Greco, Patrick Fiorenza, Fabrizio Roccaforte, et al.
Highly Homogeneous Current Transport in Ultra-Thin Aluminum Nitride (AlN) Epitaxial Films on Gallium Nitride (GaN) Deposited by Plasma Enhanced Atomic Layer Deposition
Reprinted from: *Nanomaterials* **2021**, *11*, 3316, doi:10.3390/nano11123316 83

Béla Pécz, Nikolaos Vouroutzis, György Zoltán Radnóczi, Nikolaos Frangis and John Stoemenos
Structural Characteristics of the Si Whiskers Grown by Ni-Metal-Induced-Lateral-Crystallization
Reprinted from: *Nanomaterials* **2021**, *11*, 1878, doi:10.3390/nano11081878 93

Patrick Fiorenza, Mario S. Alessandrino, Beatrice Carbone, Alfio Russo, Fabrizio Roccaforte and Filippo Giannazzo
High-Resolution Two-Dimensional Imaging of the 4H-SiC MOSFET Channel by Scanning Capacitance Microscopy
Reprinted from: *Nanomaterials* **2021**, *11*, 1626, doi:10.3390/nano11061626 107

Qingguo Gao, Chongfu Zhang, Ping Liu, Yunfeng Hu, Kaiqiang Yang, Zichuan Yi, et al.
Effect of Back-Gate Voltage on the High-Frequency Performance of Dual-Gate MoS_2 Transistors
Reprinted from: *Nanomaterials* **2021**, *11*, 1594, doi:10.3390/nano11061594 119

Shijie Li, Shidai Tian, Yuan Yao, Meng He, Li Chen, Yan Zhang and Junyi Zhai
Enhanced Electrical Performance of Monolayer MoS$_2$ with Rare Earth Element Sm Doping
Reprinted from: *Nanomaterials* **2021**, *11*, 769, doi:10.3390/nano11030769 . . . . **131**

László Pósa, György Molnár, Benjamin Kalas, Zsófia Baji, Zsolt Czigány, Péter Petrik, János Volk
A Rational Fabrication Method for Low Switching-Temperature VO$_2$
Reprinted from: *Nanomaterials* **2021**, *11*, 212, doi:10.3390/nano11010212 . . . . **143**

About the Editors

Patrick Fiorenza

Patrick Fiorenza (Dr.) received an M. Sc. in Physics and a PhD in Material Science from the University of Catania in 2003 and 2007, respectively. In 2005, he was a visiting scientist at IMEC (Belgium). Since 2011, he has worked as a researcher at CNR-IMM. His research activity is mainly focused on carrier transport, trapping phenomena, and reliability at Metal Insulator–Semiconductor and Metal–Semiconductor interfaces between SiC and GaN. He is a co-author of more than 150 papers and 3 book chapters.

Raffaella Lo Nigro

Raffaella Lo Nigro (Dr.) received her B.Sc. in Chemistry cum Laude in 1996, and in 2000, she received her Ph.D. from Catania University. From 1996 to 2000, she acquired an advanced knowledge in the field of MOCVD, and in 2001, she joined IMM-CNR as a permanent researcher, and since the 2020, she has been a Senior Researcher and responsible of the research group "Advanced Dielectric Materials for power devices". In 2009, she was named one of the "Best Young Scientists" by CNR for her research on Materials Science. Her current research interests include the synthesis of high-k dielectrics by Atomic Layer Deposition. She is an author of more than 140 papers and 5 book chapters.

Béla Pécz

Béla Pécz (Prof.) received a B.Sc. in Materials Science in 1993; in 2004, he received his Ph.D. from Hungarian Academy of Sciences, and in 2004, he was awarded a D.Sc. from the Hungarian Academy of Sciences. His current position is the Deputy Director of the Institute for Technical Physics and Materials Science, Budapest. His research topics are related to transmission electron microscopy analyses, SiC on Si and contact with SiC, III-nitrides, and defects in semiconductors. He has been a project leader of several national and European projects, he has received several awards, and his research activities have resulted in the publication of 140 papers in international journals and papers in conference proceedings.

Jens Eriksson

Jens Eriksson (Prof.) is currently working as a Senior Lecturer and head of the applied sensor science unit within the division of sensors and actuator systems at LiU. His research activities include the development and application of 2D materials, additive manufacturing, the implementation of sensors for environmental monitoring, and food safety. He is an author of about 30 papers.

 *nanomaterials*

Editorial

Nanotechnology for Electronic Materials and Devices

Raffaella Lo Nigro [1,*], Patrick Fiorenza [1], Béla Pécz [2] and Jens Eriksson [3]

1. Consiglio Nazionale della Ricerche (CNR), Istituto per la Microelettronica e Microsistemi (IMM), Strada VIII, 5, 95121 Catania, Italy
2. Centre for Energy Research, Institute for Technical Physics and Materials Science Research, Konkoly-Thege, 29-33, 1121 Budapest, Hungary
3. Department of Physics, Chemistry and Biology (IFM), University of Linkoping, Campus Valla, Fysikhuset, SE-581 83 Linkoping, Sweden
* Correspondence: raffaella.lonigro@imm.cnr.it

The historical scaling down of electronics devices is no longer the main goal of the International Roadmap for Devices and Systems [1], but the integration of electronic components at the nanoscale is an emerging focus, coupled with the need for novel nanomaterials, emerging characterization methods and device fabrication techniques at the nanoscale. The growing interest in nanomaterials [2] can be associated with their unique properties, which are not present in bulk or thick films, and they are currently finding rapid application in many technological areas (such as high-frequency electronics [3], power devices [4], displays, energy conversion systems, energy storage [5], photovoltaics and sensors). At the same time, fabrication methods based on novel processes and/or approaches must be developed for the synthesis of the nanostructured materials, as well as accurate characterization techniques at the nanoscale for the materials and their interfaces.

In this context, the aim of this Special Issue, entitled "**Nanotechnology for Electronic Materials and Devices**", is to collect dedicated papers in several nanotechnological fields. The issue consists of eleven selected regular papers focusing on the latest developments in nanomaterials and nanotechnologies for electronic devices and sensors. Thus, topics such as approaches to synthesis, advanced characterization methods and device fabrication techniques have been covered in the present issue.

We editors are aware that, due to the many topics related to the use of nanotechnology for electronics, the present issue cannot provide a comprehensive presentation of the arguments; however, we are confident that the main general areas have been discussed and can be summarized in the following research topics:

(i) Nanoscaled materials and their properties: several papers in this issue focus on nanolaminated oxide combinations (such as hafnium oxide/iron oxide [6] or tungsten oxide/molybdenum oxides [7]) as well as on 2D materials (molybdenum disulphides and its rare-earth-doped-thin layers [8]).
(ii) Moreover, innovative synthesis approaches have been described in some papers for nanomaterials and thin films, such as aluminium nitrides [9], silicon whiskers [10] or vanadium-oxide-rich layers [11].
(iii) Other paper focus on advanced nanoscale characterization, mainly based on scanning-probe methods (scanning non linear dielectric microscopy [12] and high-resolution scanning capacitance spectroscopy [13]), as well as on surface optical techniques (photoluminescence and spectroscopic ellipsometry) [14].
(iv) Finally, some papers are dedicated to device performances [15] and circuit analysis [16], providing evidence that it is crucial to move from research to technological development to control the quality of innovative products and functionalities.

We editors are grateful to all the authors for submitting their scientific results to the present Special Issue and we hope that *Nanomaterials* readership will find interesting imputs in the wider scenario of electronical applications of nanotechnology.

Citation: Lo Nigro, R.; Fiorenza, P.; Pécz, B.; Eriksson, J. Nanotechnology for Electronic Materials and Devices. *Nanomaterials* **2022**, *12*, 3319. https://doi.org/10.3390/nano12193319

Received: 7 September 2022
Accepted: 13 September 2022
Published: 23 September 2022

Publisher's Note: MDPI stays neutral with regard to jurisdictional claims in published maps and institutional affiliations.

Copyright: © 2022 by the authors. Licensee MDPI, Basel, Switzerland. This article is an open access article distributed under the terms and conditions of the Creative Commons Attribution (CC BY) license (https://creativecommons.org/licenses/by/4.0/).

Author Contributions: P.F., R.L.N., B.P. and J.E. contributed equally to the writing, review and editing of the manuscript. All authors have read and agreed to the published version of the manuscript.

Funding: This article received no external funding.

Acknowledgments: We are grateful to all the authors for submitting their scientific results to the present Special Issue and we deeply acknowledge Keyco Li for the kind assistance.

Conflicts of Interest: The authors declare no conflict of interest.

References

1. International Roadmap for Devices and Systems (IRDS™) 2021 Edition. Available online: https://irds.ieee.org/editions/2021/executive-summary (accessed on 21 September 2022).
2. Bytler, S.Z.; Hollen, S.M.; Cao, L.Y.; Cui, Y.; Gupta, J.A.; Gutierrez, H.R.; Heinz, T.F.; Hong, S.S.; Huang, J.X.; Ismach, A.F.; et al. Progress, Challenges, and Opportunities in Two-Dimensional Materials Beyond Graphene. *ACS Nano* **2013**, *7*, 2898. [CrossRef]
3. Lo Nigro, R.; Fiorenza, P.; Greco, G.; Schilirò, E.; Roccaforte, F. Structural and Insulating Behaviour of High-Permittivity Binary Oxide Thin Films for Silicon Carbide and Gallium Nitride Electronic Devices. *Materials* **2022**, *15*, 2898. [CrossRef] [PubMed]
4. Bose, B.K. Power electronics-an emerging technology. *IEEE Trans. Ind. Electron.* **1989**, *36*, 403. [CrossRef]
5. Koohi-Fayegh, S.; Rosen, M.A. A review of energy storage types, applications and recent developments. *J. Energy Storage* **2020**, *2*, 101047. [CrossRef]
6. Kalam, K.; Otsus, M.; Kozlova, J.; Tarre, A.; Kasikov, A.; Rammula, R.; Link, J.; Stern, R.; Vinuesa, G.; Lendinez, J.M.; et al. Memory Effects in Nanolaminates of Hafnium and Iron Oxide Films Structured by Atomic Layer Deposition. *Nanomaterials* **2022**, *12*, 2593. [CrossRef]
7. Fried, M.; Bogar, R.; Takacs, D.; Labadi, Z.; Horvath, Z.E.; Zoinai, Z. Investigation of Combinatorial WO_3-MoO_3 Mixed Layers by Spectroscopic Ellipsometry Using Different Optical Models. *Nanomaterials* **2022**, *12*, 2421. [CrossRef]
8. Li, S.; Tian, S.; Yao, Y.; He, M.; Chen, L.; Zhang, Y.; Zhai, J. Gallic Enhanced Electrical Performance of Monolayer MoS_2 with Rare Earth Element Sm Doping. *Nanomaterials* **2021**, *11*, 769. [CrossRef] [PubMed]
9. Schilirò, E.; Giannazzo, F.; Di Franco, S.; Greco, G.; Fiorenza, P.; Roccaforte, F.; Prystawko, P.; Kruszewski, P.; Leszczynski, M.; Cora, I.; et al. Highly Homogeneous Current Transport in Ultra-Thin Aluminum Nitride (AlN) Epitaxial Films on Gallium Nitride (GaN) Deposited by Plasma Enhanced Atomic Layer Deposition. *Nanomaterials* **2021**, *11*, 3316. [CrossRef] [PubMed]
10. Pecz, B.; Vouroutzis, N.; Radnoczi, G.Z.; Frangis, N.; Stoemenos, J. Structural Characteristics of the Si Whiskers Grown by Ni-Metal-Induced-Lateral-Crystallization. *Nanomaterials* **2021**, *11*, 1878. [CrossRef] [PubMed]
11. Posa, L.; Molnar, G.; Kalas, B.; Baji, Z.; Czigany, Z.; Petrik, P.; Volk, J. A Rational Fabrication Method for Low Switching-Temperature VO_2. *Nanomaterials* **2021**, *11*, 212. [CrossRef] [PubMed]
12. Yamasue, K.; Cho, Y. Boxcar Averaging Scanning Nonlinear Dielectric Microscopy. *Nanomaterials* **2022**, *12*, 794. [CrossRef] [PubMed]
13. Fiorenza, P.; Alessandrino, M.S.; Carbone, B.; Russo, A.; Roccaforte, F.; Giannazzo, F. High-Resolution Two-Dimensional Imaging of the 4H-SiC MOSFET Channel by Scanning Capacitance Microscopy. *Nanomaterials* **2021**, *11*, 1626. [CrossRef] [PubMed]
14. Panasci, S.E.; Koos, A.; Schilirò, E.; Di Franco, S.; Greco, G.; Fiorenza, P.; Roccaforte, F.; Agnello, S.; Cannas, M.; Gelardi, F.M.; et al. Multiscale Investigation of the Structural, Electrical and Photoluminescence Properties of MoS_2 Obtained by MoO_3 Sulfurization. *Nanomaterials* **2022**, *12*, 182. [CrossRef] [PubMed]
15. Gao, Q.; Zhang, C.; Liu, P.; Hu, Y.; Yang, K.; Yi, Z.; Lui, L.; Pan, X.; Zhang, Z.; Yang, J.; et al. Effect of Back-Gate Voltage on the High-Frequency Performance of Dual-Gate MoS_2 Transistors. *Nanomaterials* **2021**, *11*, 1594. [CrossRef] [PubMed]
16. Park, J.; Ra, C.; Lim, J.; Jeon, J. Device and Circuit Analysis of Double Gate Field Effect Transistor with Mono-Layer WS_2-Channel at Sub-2 nm Technology Node. *Nanomaterials* **2022**, *12*, 2299. [CrossRef] [PubMed]

Article

Memory Effects in Nanolaminates of Hafnium and Iron Oxide Films Structured by Atomic Layer Deposition

Kristjan Kalam [1,*], Markus Otsus [1], Jekaterina Kozlova [1], Aivar Tarre [1], Aarne Kasikov [1], Raul Rammula [1], Joosep Link [2], Raivo Stern [2], Guillermo Vinuesa [3], José Miguel Lendínez [3], Salvador Dueñas [3], Helena Castán [3], Aile Tamm [1] and Kaupo Kukli [1]

[1] Institute of Physics, University of Tartu, W. Ostwaldi 1, 50411 Tartu, Estonia; markus.otsus@ut.ee (M.O.); jekaterina.kozlova@ut.ee (J.K.); aivar.tarre@ut.ee (A.T.); aarne.kasikov@ut.ee (A.K.); raul.rammula@ut.ee (R.R.); aile.tamm@ut.ee (A.T.); kaupo.kukli@ut.ee (K.K.)
[2] Laboratory of Chemical Physics, National Institute of Chemical Physics and Biophysics, Akadeemia tee 23, 12618 Tallinn, Estonia; joosep.link@kbfi.ee (J.L.); raivo.stern@kbfi.ee (R.S.)
[3] Department of Electronics, University of Valladolid, Paseo Belén 15, 47011 Valladolid, Spain; guillermo.vinuesa@alumnos.uva.es (G.V.); josemilen99@gmail.com (J.M.L.); sduenas@ele.uva.es (S.D.); helcas@tel.uva.es (H.C.)
* Correspondence: kristjan.kalam@ut.ee

Abstract: HfO_2 and Fe_2O_3 thin films and laminated stacks were grown by atomic layer deposition at 350 °C from hafnium tetrachloride, ferrocene, and ozone. Nonlinear, saturating, and hysteretic magnetization was recorded in the films. Magnetization was expectedly dominated by increasing the content of Fe_2O_3. However, coercive force could also be enhanced by the choice of appropriate ratios of HfO_2 and Fe_2O_3 in nanolaminated structures. Saturation magnetization was observed in the measurement temperature range of 5–350 K, decreasing towards higher temperatures and increasing with the films' thicknesses and crystal growth. Coercive force tended to increase with a decrease in the thickness of crystallized layers. The films containing insulating HfO_2 layers grown alternately with magnetic Fe_2O_3 exhibited abilities to both switch resistively and magnetize at room temperature. Resistive switching was unipolar in all the oxides mounted between Ti and TiN electrodes.

Keywords: multilayers; atomic layer deposition; hafnium oxide; iron oxide; ferromagnetism; resistive switching; nanolaminates

Citation: Kalam, K.; Otsus, M.; Kozlova, J.; Tarre, A.; Kasikov, A.; Rammula, R.; Link, J.; Stern, R.; Vinuesa, G.; Lendínez, J.M.; et al. Memory Effects in Nanolaminates of Hafnium and Iron Oxide Films Structured by Atomic Layer Deposition. *Nanomaterials* **2022**, *12*, 2593. https://doi.org/10.3390/nano12152593

Academic Editors: Patrick Fiorenza, Raffaella Lo Nigro, Béla Pécz and Jens Eriksson

Received: 5 July 2022
Accepted: 25 July 2022
Published: 28 July 2022

Publisher's Note: MDPI stays neutral with regard to jurisdictional claims in published maps and institutional affiliations.

Copyright: © 2022 by the authors. Licensee MDPI, Basel, Switzerland. This article is an open access article distributed under the terms and conditions of the Creative Commons Attribution (CC BY) license (https://creativecommons.org/licenses/by/4.0/).

1. Introduction

Prospective applications to magnetoresistive [1] and resistive [2] memory effects, which were notified few decades ago, have extended the search for potentially multiferroic materials, whereby the list of such materials has continuously been updated. Studies on layered compound materials, concurrently exhibiting resistive switching (RS) and ferromagnetic (FM) characteristics, have been conducted. Both RS and FM properties could have simultaneously been registered in devices built on thin films of few different compounds, e.g., ZnO:Co [3], ZnO:Co/SiO$_2$:Co [4], copper oxides [5], or HfO$_2$ [6]. Aside from nonlinear, saturative, and hysteretic magnetization behavior, bipolar resistive switching behavior was recorded in devices built on these compounds, expressed by two distinct conduction current (resistivity) states stabilized during consecutive programming pulses upon changes in voltage polarity.

The films referred to above were formed by physical vapor deposition (PVD) techniques. The exploitation of PVD allows the formation of solid films with maximum chemical purity, as the purity of a deposited material is determined by that of the precursor sublimed. At the same time, PVD techniques may face challenges before the uniform deposition of thin films over substrates of arbitrary area and shape. Chemical vapor deposition routes to the multifunctional ferroic films are thus additionally sought in order to open complementary perspectives to tailor materials possessing useful, and differently manifested, physical properties. Amongst several materials that exhibit magnetoresistive performance, HfO$_2$ can be regarded as a material feasibly grown over large area substrates if appropriate routes, such as atomic layer deposition (ALD), were used. HfO$_2$ might further stand out as a compound exhibiting resistive switching behavior together with magnetic susceptibility, especially when supported by an additive or dopant-enhancing internal magnetization, particularly Fe$_2$O$_3$.

HfO$_2$, together with Ta$_2$O$_5$, has been considered one of the most intensely investigated thin film materials for application in nonvolatile, resistively switching (memristive) memories, which are based on the migration of either cations or oxygen vacancies into the lattice of a switching medium [7]. The resistive switching (RS) effect is a reversible and non-volatile change in the resistance of a material. By applying a certain electric field, a conductive filament (CF) is formed through the oxide, connecting the metals that surround it. Once the filament is formed for the first time (electroforming process), different electric field values will allow for repetitively disrupting (RESET process) and forming (SET process) the CF reversibly [2,8,9]. If the SET and RESET processes occur at different voltage polarities, the effect is known as bipolar resistive switching (BRS), which is usually due to oxygen anion migration and electron hopping through oxygen vacancies in the oxide media (valence change mechanism or VCM) whereby the metal electrodes are inert metals [2,8,10–13]. BRS can also be produced by the formation of a metallic filament (electrochemical metallization mechanism or ECM, also known as conductive bridge RAM or CBRAM). In the latter case, an electrochemically active metal electrode is needed as a source of the metal cations that will diffuse through the oxide, creating the CF [2,8,10–13]. On the other hand, unipolar resistive switching (URS) is attributed to thermochemical processes dominating over electrochemical ones (thermochemical memory or TCM) [14,15]. Thus, temperature gradients produced by Joule heating lead to redox reactions and local changes in the material (oxide) stoichiometry, which results in a change of the conductivity [10–13]. The switching mechanism in oxide film media, including HfO$_2$, has largely been described as that based on filamentary conduction [16]. Nonetheless, switching in HfO$_2$ has also been found to be dependent on electrode metals, whereby both bipolar and unipolar switching could be initiated [17]. Resistively switching HfO$_2$ films can be synthesized using different techniques, including metalorganic chemical vapor deposition [17] and atomic layer deposition (ALD) [18].

The application of external magnetic fields can influence the resistive switching performance of ALD-processed HfO$_2$ based cells [18]. Further, internal magnetization in HfO$_2$ films alone has been possible due to the presence of significant amounts of oxygen vacancies [19,20], which may also be related to the formation of metastable HfO$_2$ polymorphs. In general, the achievement and appearance of ferromagnetic-like behavior has been regarded as an inherent, although sometimes unexpected, property of nanocrystalline materials [21]. Nonlinear hysteretic magnetization is in such cases caused by defective crystallite boundaries involving vacancies and unsaturated coordination of metal atoms, i.e., the factors generally causing leakage and increasing conductivity. Thereby, the magnetization should take place in a medium that, at the same time, should also switch resistively. The prerequisite for the resistive switching process is insulation in the virgin, although defective, state of the medium. Thus, the demands for materials demonstrating both magnetization and resistive switching may appear controversial. Such materials should in principle simultaneously perform as wide-band-gap dielectrics and electrically rather conductive magnetic materials, which may be regarded as contradicting properties. Therefore, a tradeoff between insulating dielectric properties and the ability to hysteretically magnetize upon choosing the constituent materials is necessary. Engineering combinations of reliably resistively switching material layers, such as HfO$_2$, with complementary compounds reliably magnetizing and also growing, such as Fe$_2$O$_3$ [22–24], is justified and is to be purposefully examined in terms of both memory effects. Quite naturally, before the examination of coupling between hysteretic magnetization and electrical switching, it would be reasonable to examine the appearance of both effects separately, in order to attempt optimization of the deposition process and the forming structures. This is essentially the aim of the present study.

Studies on composites or solid solutions based on iron and hafnium oxides are scarce. Crystallization has been investigated in the HfO_2-Fe_2O_3 system [25] at temperatures more than two times higher than those applied in the present study. The enhancement of magnetization has been observed in Fe-doped HfO_2 [26] due to the phase segregation and formation of Fe_2O_3. Composite materials, especially in the form of functional thin films consisting of iron and hafnium oxides, are thus not quite explored yet.

Regarding layered materials containing either HfO_2 or Fe_2O_3, we have earlier observed both saturative hysteretic magnetization and bipolar resistive switching behavior in HfO_2-Al_2O_3 [27], HfO_2-ZrO_2 [28,29], and SiO_2-Fe_2O_3 [30] multilayers grown by atomic layer deposition. In the present study, nonlinear saturative and hysteretic magnetization in HfO_2-based thin solid films grown by ALD, enhanced by the contribution from Fe_2O_3 to HfO_2-based multistoried films, was examined. Here, HfO_2 and Fe_2O_3 layers were grown sequentially into stacks to tailor magnetic and insulating materials. The goal was to ensure nonlinear hysteretic magnetization as well as resistive switching in the same materials, yet without a detailed investigation of the coupling effects that remain beyond the scope of the present study. The objective was to examine whether it is possible to observe reliable switching behavior and hysteretic magnetization at room temperature in HfO_2-Fe_2O_3 nanolaminates grown using the same deposition cycle sequences.

2. Materials and Methods

The films studied in this work were grown in a low-pressure flow-type ALD reactor [31]. Hafnium tetrachloride ($HfCl_4$, 99.9%, Sigma Aldrich, Burlington, MA, USA), used as the hafnium precursor, and ferrocene ($Fe(C_5H_5)_2$, 99.5%, Alfa Aesar, Word Hill, MA, USA), used as an iron precursor, were evaporated at 160 and 83 °C, respectively, from a half-open glass boat inside the reactor. Nitrogen (N_2, 99.999%, AS Linde Gas, Tallinn, Estonia) was applied as the carrier and purging gas. Ozone produced from O_2 (99.999% purity, AS Linde Gas) was used as an oxidizer. The ALD reactions were carried out at 350 °C. Cycle times for Fe_2O_3 deposition were 5-5-5-5 s for the sequence: metal precursor pulse—N_2 purge—O_3 pulse—N_2 purge, respectively. Cycle times for HfO_2 were 5-2-5-5 s for an analogous sequence. Single HfO_2 and Fe_2O_3 films were grown to thicknesses ranging from 20 to 60 nm in order to acquire the reference data from composition analysis as well as resistive switching or magnetizing media. Further, a double-layered Fe_2O_3-HfO_2 stack as well as nanolaminates of HfO_2 and Fe_2O_3 were deposited, aiming at the formation of a series of stacks consisting of both iron-rich and hafnium-rich solid media, as presented in Table 1.

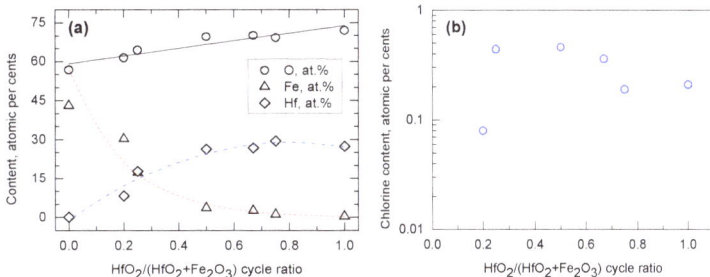

Figure 1. Contents of elements (**a**) and residual impurities (**b**) measured by XRF, constituting the HfO_2-Fe_2O_3 films, expressed in atomic% against relative amount of HfO_2 deposition cycles. The elements are indicated in the legends. Polynomial lines are guides for the eye.

Table 1. List of HfO_2, Fe_2O_3, and HfO_2-Fe_2O_3 samples revealing the deposition cycle sequences, relative $HfO_2/(HfO_2 + Fe_2O_3)$ deposition cycle ratio, total film thickness in accord with XRR, and relative Hf/(Hf + Fe) cation ratio measured by XRF and EDS. The samples are presented in the order of decreasing relative cycle ratio for HfO_2 and, concurrently, descending cation ratio for Hf, measured by XRF. For the contents of residual chlorine, also measured by XRF, see Figure 1.

Cycle Sequence	Cycle Ratio	t_{total}, nm	Hf/(Hf + Fe) by XRF	Hf/(Hf + Fe) by EDS
500 × HfO_2	1	54	1	1
2 × (150 × HfO_2 +50 × Fe_2O_3)	0.75	23	0.96 (0.03)	0.98
100 × HfO_2 + 100 × Fe_2O_3 + 100 × HfO_2	0.67	27	0.91 (0.04)	0.95
2 × (100 × HfO_2 +100 × Fe_2O_3)	0.5	26	0.88 (0.02)	0.91
2 × (50 × HfO_2 +150 × Fe_2O_3)	0.25	29	0.51 (0.01)	0.49
400 × Fe_2O_3 +100 × HfO_2	0.2	63	0.21 (0.01)	0.24
500 × Fe_2O_3	0	37	0	0

The films were grown on undoped Si(100) and, for the electrical evaluation, also on highly doped conductive Si substrates covered by a 10 nm TiN film. The conductive Si wafers were boron-doped to concentrations of $5 \times 10^{18} - 1 \times 10^{19}$ cm^{-3} and coated with crystalline TiN layer by pulsed chemical vapor deposition using a batch $TiCl_4/NH_3$ process [32,33] at temperatures of 450–500 °C in an ASM A412 Large Batch 300 mm reactor at Fraunhofer IPMS-CNT. The films, which were deposited on TiN substrates for electrical measurements, were also supplied with Ti/Au electron-beam evaporated electrodes on top of the films, with the Ti layer directly contacting the switching oxide medium and Au deposited in order to provide non-oxidizing electrical contact to the measurement circuit.

The crystal structure of the films was evaluated by grazing incidence X-ray diffraction (GIXRD) method using a SmartLab (Rigaku, Tokyo, Japan) X-ray diffractometer and the CuKα radiation with a wavelength of 0.15406 nm. The same apparatus was exploited to determine the thickness, density, and roughness of the films by X-ray reflectometry (XRR). Energy dispersive X-ray spectrometry (EDS) measurements were carried out at an accelerating voltage of 15 kV with a current of 0.69 nA using an INCA Energy 350 EDS spectrometer (Oxford Instruments, Abingdon, Oxfordshire, UK) connected to a Helios Nanolab 600 (FEI) scanning electron microscope. Scanning transmission electron microscopy (STEM) and elemental mapping of the films in cross-sectional orientation were performed in a Cs-corrected Titan Themis 200 microscope (FEI, Hillsboro, OR, USA). EDS maps were acquired using Esprit software version 1.9 (Bruker, Billerica, MA, USA). Thin cross-sectional samples for STEM observations were prepared using the in situ lift-out technique using a Helios Nanolab 600 scanning electron microscope/focused ion beam system (FEI, Hillsboro, OR, USA), equipped with a super-X EDX system (FEI/Bruker). In order to protect the surface from ion milling during the preparation of STEM samples, the area of interest was covered with a platinum protection layer. An X-ray fluorescence (XRF) analyzer ZSX400 (Rigaku) was complementarily used for the elemental composition analysis. Considering the feasibility of the measurements, the composition analysis was conducted on Fe_2O_3 and HfO_2 reference films grown to somewhat higher thicknesses using 500 ALD cycles, whereas thinner films grown using 200 cycles to thicknesses similar to those of nanolaminates were further subjected to electrical and magnetic measurements.

Electrical measurements were carried out in a probe station using a Keithley 4200-SCS semiconductor analyzer (Keysight Technologies, Cleveland, OH, USA). In the DC measurements, the bias voltage was applied to the top electrode, and the bottom electrode remained grounded. To initiate RS, every sample required an electroforming procedure that was carried out as a voltage sweep with positive bias and a current compliance of 10 μA to avoid irreversibly breaking the device. Capacitance measurements were performed by applying an AC signal of 30 mV along with a DC bias of 0.1 V in the frequency range 1–1000 kHz. Magnetic measurements were performed using the Vibrating Sample Magnetometer (VSM) option of the Physical Property Measurement System 14T (Quantum Design, San Diego, CA, USA) by scanning the magnetic field from −1.5 to 1.5 T parallel to the film surface in the temperature range of 5–350 K.

3. Results and Discussion

3.1. Growth and Structure

The metal oxide films constituting the nanolaminates were grown in processes under the same reactor conditions and exploiting the same precursor chemistry as those earlier suited to the growth of HfO_2 [34] and Fe_2O_3 [35] films. In the present study, the thickness of multilayered HfO_2-Fe_2O_3 films could be appreciably well controlled by adjusting the amounts of the growth cycles for constituent oxide layers (Table 1). In addition, the presence of iron and hafnium in the films was proven by both XRF and EDS analysis, whereby the relative contents of both metals were correlated to the relative amounts of their growth cycles applied (Table 1, Figure 1a). Further, chlorine and carbon were detected as impurities present in the films (Figure 1b). Both impurities can be regarded as natural residues arising from the ligands to the metal precursors. Within the accuracy limits of the analysis method, the content of Cl and C was not systematically dependent on the relative deposition cycle ratio.

The HfO_2-Fe_2O_3 multilayers were truly formed as nanolaminates, as proven by XRR results depicted in Figure 2. The X-ray reflection intensity curves allowed one to fit the measured data, in a good approximation, with the predicted thicknesses of the constituent layers of both metal oxides, roughly correlated to the amounts of deposition cycles applied in the case of both HfO_2 and Fe_2O_3. It is well known that in the case of ALD, the growth rates of materials on substrates of foreign composition may markedly differ at different growth stages, generally being essentially lower at the early stages of growth, i.e., at low thicknesses. The influence of the nucleation rate and the length of the so-called incubation period depends on temperature, substrate, and growing material, and should be explored separately, if required. In the present study, the growth rate of HfO_2 on Fe_2O_3 noticeably exceeded the growth rate of Fe_2O_3 on HfO_2. In the case of the growth of HfO_2 on crystallized Fe_2O_3 (Figure 2c), the growth rate of HfO_2 could reach as high as 0.18 nm/cycle, possibly supported by a larger specific surface area of underlying polycrystalline iron oxide layer.

STEM studies revealed sequential deposition of the hafnium and iron oxide layers, distinct in terms of structure (Figure 3) and elemental distribution (Figure 4), thus supporting the XRR results. One can see that the layers were crystallized throughout the film thickness (Figure 3a,b) without structurally sharp interfaces between the HfO_2 and Fe_2O_3 constituent layers, still enabling the distinction between metal oxides due to the differences in atomic numbers. At the same time, the interface between HfO_2 and the amorphous SiO_2 top layer on the Si substrate was sharply formed and distinct (Figure 3c). It is, however, to be noted that the growth rates and resulting thicknesses of component layers in nanolaminate structures are not to be compared to those of reference films. It is well-known that the films grown by ALD require an incubation time before achieving stable growth and structural formation. The length of the incubation period may vary considerably, depending on the material to be grown as well as the substrate material and structure. Nucleation at early stages, i.e., growth of HfO_2 on Fe_2O_3 and vice versa would require a separate study. Compositionally, the constituent layers became clearly distinguishable (Figure 4), allowing one to rely on the formation of nanomaterial composed of physically and chemically different oxides, further enabling the appearance of both magnetic and insulating materials' properties.

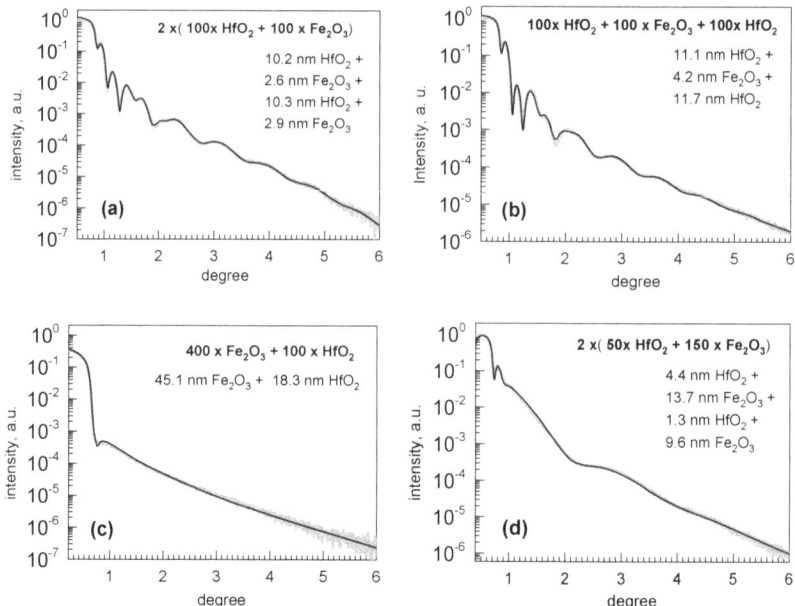

Figure 2. X-ray reflectivity results for selected stacks of Fe_2O_3 and HfO_2 layers grown on Si, denoted by the labels revealing the amounts of ALD cycles used for the deposition of constituent layers. The thicknesses of constituent layers as the results of the curve fittings are also given by labels. The curves with fitting results are presented for the four-layer laminate grown using equal amounts of cycles for both constituent oxides (**a**), the three-layer laminate grown using equal amounts of cycles for both constituent oxides (**b**), the double-layer consisting of relatively thicker Fe_2O_3 and thinner HfO_2 films (**c**), and the four-layer laminate containing Fe_2O_3 layers relatively thicker compared to the HfO_2 component (**d**).

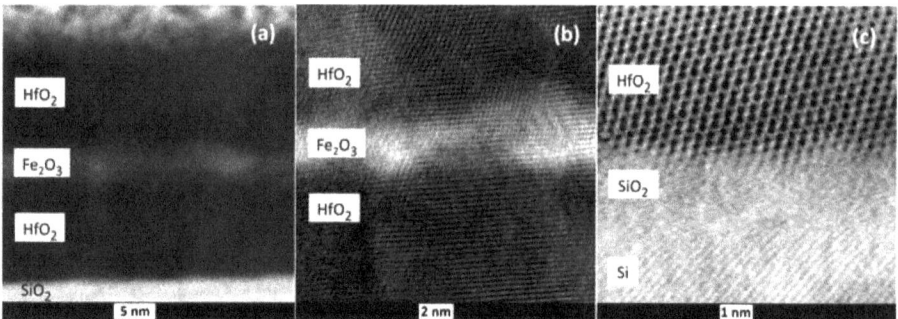

Figure 3. Bright field STEM images of HfO_2-Fe_2O_3-HfO_2 nanolaminate grown using 100 ALD cycles for each constituent layer, taken under different magnifications (**a**,**b**), and an image of the interface between silicon substrate and the first HfO_2 layer in the same laminate (**c**).

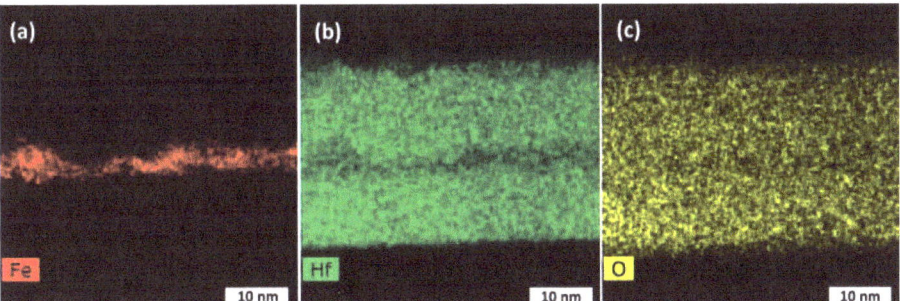

Figure 4. Elemental mapping for iron (**a**), hafnium (**b**), and oxygen (**c**) in the HfO_2-Fe_2O_3-HfO_2 nanolaminate grown using 100 ALD cycles for each constituent layer.

The Fe_2O_3 films grown alone without alternate layering with HfO_2 were moderately crystallized in their as-deposited states (Figure 5, the bottom pattern). Two weak but still distinct reflection peaks at 33.6 and 56.5° could be attributed to the 104 and 116 reflections of rhombohedral Fe_2O_3, that is, the hematite phase. At the same time, the HfO_2 films grown alone without alternate layering with Fe_2O_3 were relatively more crystallized in their as-deposited states (Figure 5, the 2nd pattern from bottom). The HfO_2 film grown using 200 deposition cycles could be described as a multiphase solid medium consisting of a stable monoclinic phase of HfO_2 and a metastable, quite likely tetragonal, polymorph of HfO_2. Whereas most of the reflection peaks remained very weak, the most distinct reflections unambiguously belonging to the −111 and 111 of monoclinic HfO_2 peaked at 28.3 and 31.5°, respectively. Between the latter reflections, a peak assigned as 101 of tetragonal HfO_2 was clearly detected at 30.3°. These three neighboring reflections can be regarded as proof of multiphase composition. Further and notably, after 500 ALD cycles, the metastable phases, if initially formed and present in HfO_2 films, were already almost insignificant in the diffraction patterns. The diffractogram from the HfO_2 film grown using 500 cycles comprised reflections attributed exclusively to monoclinic HfO_2 (Figure 5, the 3rd pattern from bottom).

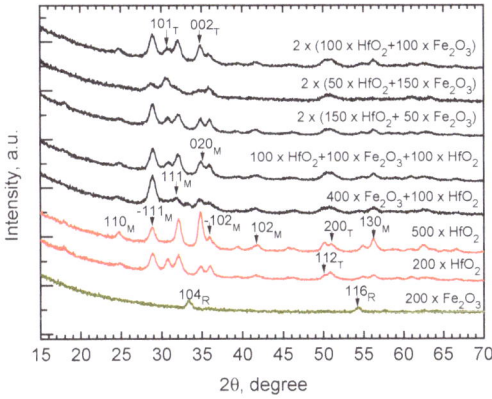

Figure 5. Grazing incidence X-ray diffraction patterns of Fe_2O_3-, HfO_2-, and HfO_2-Fe_2O_3-laminated films. The growth cycle sequences are denoted by labels. The reflections supplied with Miller indexes are assigned as those belonging to either monoclinic (M, ICDD PDF-2 card no 43-1017) or tetragonal (T, card 01-078-5756) HfO_2, whereby reflections from rhombohedral hematite Fe_2O_3 are denoted by R (card 01-1053).

Somewhat surprisingly, in the diffractograms taken from most of the films consisting of stacked HfO_2 and Fe_2O_3 layers, no reflections attributable to any of the known iron oxide phases could be recognized. At the same time, crystallization in the films was obvious and due to the crystal growth in the HfO_2 corresponding to the stacks or multilayers. With regard to the reflections characteristic of HfO_2, the significance of the ones attributable to −111 and 111 of monoclinic HfO_2, peaking at 28.3 and 31.5°, respectively, tended to increase with the relative amounts of HfO_2 deposition cycles (Figure 5). The relative significance of the reflection assigned as 101 of tetragonal HfO_2, at 30.3°, quite expectedly increased with the decrease in the relative amount of the HfO_2 deposition cycles (Figure 5). Notably, reflections characteristic of Fe_2O_3 did not appear in the stacked HfO_2 and Fe_2O_3 layers, with an exception of the sample grown using the cycle sequence of 400 × Fe_2O_3 + 100 × HfO_2, where a weak 104 peak of rhombohedral hematite phase could be recognized at 33.5°.

3.2. Magnetization Behavior

The reference Fe_2O_3 film grown on diamagnetic Si substrates expectedly demonstrated ferromagnetic-like magnetization behavior (Figure 6a) with the coercive force measured as strong as 2272 Oe at 5 K. The thinnest 24 nm-thick HfO_2 films grown in the present study using 200 ALD cycles were magnetized nonlinearly and saturatively in external fields (Figure 6a). Both the saturation magnetization and the coercive field remained low, although clearly measurable, in the 24 nm-thick HfO_2 film compared to those of the Fe_2O_3 films. At the same time, the saturation magnetization and coercivity in the 54 nm-thick HfO_2, grown using 500 cycles, became suppressed almost entirely. This is plausibly due to the obvious difference between phase compositions of 24 and 54 nm-thick HfO_2 films (Figure 5). The thinner HfO_2 film contained, besides stoichiometric monoclinic HfO_2, probably also oxygen-deficient metastable either tetragonal or cubic HfO_2, which would give rise to the magnetization. Upon an increase in the film thickness and crystal growth, the formation of dominant monoclinic dioxide caused a suppression of the magnetization in the solid material. At room temperature, the saturation magnetization values were not significantly decreased, differently from coercitivities. Upon increasing the measurement temperatures from 5 to 300 K, the coercivities were decreased nearly 10, 4, and 2 times in the Fe_2O_3 film grown using 200 and 500 cycles, and in HfO_2 film grown using 200 cycles, respectively (Figure 6b)

With regard to the HfO_2 films, undoped and crystallized hafnium dioxide is not supposed to magnetize in its bulk and stoichiometric form, and contamination by handling with stainless-steel tweezers may sometimes have led to measurable magnetic signals [36]. However, magnetization earlier unexpectedly detected in HfO_2 films [37] can intentionally be induced, as supported by the presence of defects, in the first place oxygen vacancies [19,20]. Oxygen vacancies are inevitable constituents in the metal oxide lattices, also considered as a cause of the filamentary switching mechanism [38–40] in the device cells.

In the samples in which Fe_2O_3 and HfO_2 films were grown into double, triple, or four-layered stacks, the saturation magnetization values obtained at both 5 and 300 K tended, somewhat expectedly, to be the highest in the samples where the amount of sequential Fe_2O_3 growth cycles exceeded those applied for the HfO_2 by 3–5 times (Figure 6c). However, in the case of laminated films, one should take into account that the microstructure of the individual Fe_2O_3 layers, most strongly affecting the magnetic properties, also varies due to the thickness variation (Figure 2). For instance, in the double-layered (400 × Fe_2O_3 + 100 × HfO_2) sample, the Fe_2O_3 was moderately crystallized, whereas in all other laminated samples, Fe_2O_3 was X-ray-amorphous (Figure 5). Notably, the thickness of Fe_2O_3 in the double layer was nearly 10 times higher compared to that in the three- and four-layer samples when 100 cycles of Fe_2O_3 was applied (see Figure 2a,b). Apparently, in the latter samples, smaller Fe_2O_3 nanocrystals could form and possibly agglomerate. The coercivity value measured at 5 K for the film consisting of two double layers of HfO_2 and Fe_2O_3 grown using 50 and 150 cycles, respectively, exceeded 1100 Oe. Coercivity in the double layer consisting of a Fe_2O_3 film grown at first using 400 cycles, followed by HfO_2 grown using

100 cycles, reached nearly 1500 Oe. At room temperature, these values were decreased down to 65 and 271 Oe, respectively.

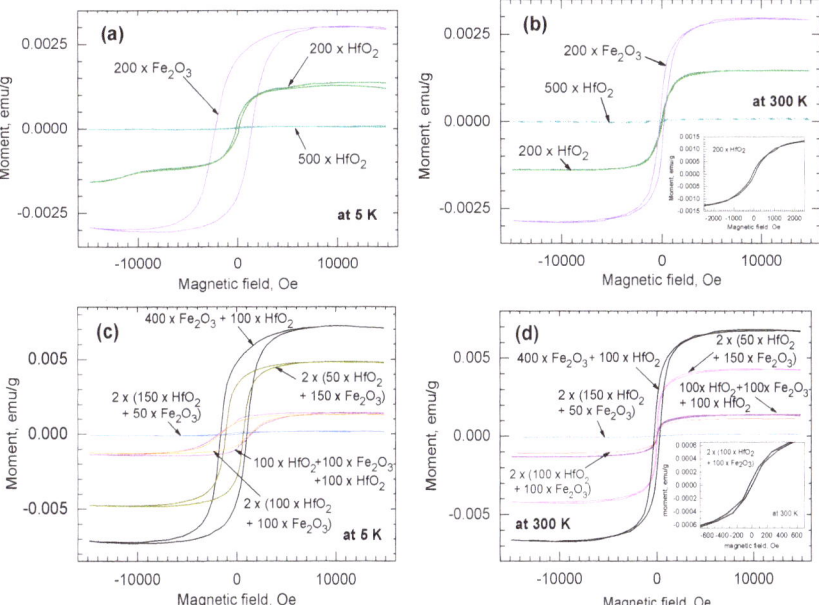

Figure 6. Magnetization-field curves from reference HfO_2 and Fe_2O_3 films measured at 5 K (**a**) and at 300 K (**b**), as compared to the curves from $HfO-Fe_2O_3$-laminated structures measured at 5 K (**c**) and 300 K (**d**). The films were grown on SiO_2/Si substrates using cycle sequences represented by labels.

Despite the ability of nanocrystalline HfO_2 to moderately magnetize, also revealing hysteretic performance, the magnetization in terms of both saturation and coercive force was quite naturally dominated by Fe_2O_3 constituting the nanolaminates. Higher amounts of iron in the iron-hafnium oxide multilayers certainly caused increments in both saturation magnetization (Figure 7a) and coercivity (Figure 7b). Interestingly, relatively strong coercivities among nanolaminate samples, reaching nearly 1850 Oe at 5 K and remaining below 50 Oe at 300 K, were obtained in the triple HfO_2-Fe_2O_3-HfO_2 layer and in four-layer film consisting of two HfO_2-Fe_2O_3 double layers (Figure 6c). These samples were characterized by Hf/(Hf + Fe) ratios of 0.91 and 0.88, respectively (Figure 7b, Table 1). In the latter two samples, all the constituent metal oxide layers were grown using 100 ALD cycles. At the same time, the saturation magnetization in the same samples was decreased about five times below the values characterizing the films containing Fe_2O_3 layers grown using 150 and 400 cycles, described above. It is thus possible that despite the relatively low Fe_2O_3 amount in such laminates and accompanying weak saturation magnetization, the growth of constituent oxides in such nanolaminates after application of sufficient amounts of deposition cycles has enabled the ordering and growth of nanocrystals enhancing structure or shape anisotropy and a simultaneous increment in coercivity. Further and more detailed studies including parametrization and scaling up the process would be required in order to clarify the interdependencies between deposition cycle numbers, crystallographic orientation, and magnetic performance.

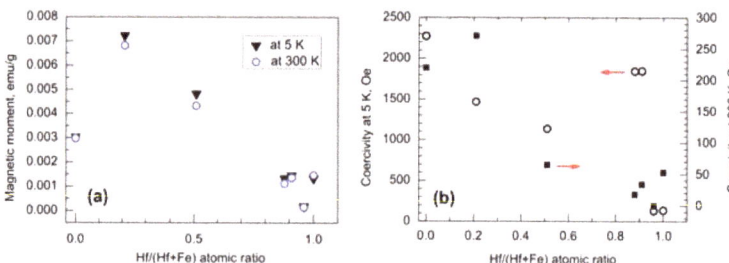

Figure 7. Magnetic moment (**a**) and coercivity (**b**) against relative content of hafnium, expressed by Hf/(Hf + Fe) cation ratio, in HfO$_2$-Fe$_2$O$_3$ nanolaminates. For the cycle ratios and sequences applied for the growth of the samples with the corresponding atomic ratios, see Table 1.

The samples based on triple HfO$_2$-Fe$_2$O$_3$-HfO$_2$-layer and four-layer film consisting of two HfO$_2$-Fe$_2$O$_3$ double layers are those worth further attention, because the same samples further exhibited defined resistive switching behavior, as will be described below. Superparamagnetic behavior was expected at first, and the same samples were additionally subjected to the temperature-dependent magnetization measurements. As was already implied by the magnetization-field curves recorded at 5 and 300 K (Figure 6c,d), the triple-layered film grown using the cycle sequence of 100 × HfO$_2$ + 100 × Fe$_2$O$_3$ + 100 × HfO$_2$ exhibited slightly higher saturation magnetization values compared to the four-layered film grown using the cycle sequence of 2 × (100 × HfO$_2$ + 100 × Fe$_2$O$_3$). This can plausibly be explained by the distribution of Fe$_2$O$_3$ differing in the latter two samples. In the four-layered sample, the thickness of the two Fe$_2$O$_3$ layers summarized was similar to that in the three-layer sample containing a single Fe$_2$O$_3$ layer in between two HfO$_2$ layers (Figure 2). Therefore, in the three-layer sample, the short-range order in Fe$_2$O$_3$, although not detectable by GIXRD, could possibly be better defined compared to that in the four-layer film, providing higher saturation magnetization. Further, field-cooling (FC) measurements were carried out in the temperature range of 355–5 K (Figure 8), recording the magnetization values at each temperature after the application of the external field of 1000 Oe. For both samples, the zero-field-cooling (ZFC) measurements were also carried out in order to estimate the blocking temperatures related to thermal energy, below which the magnetization in a material consisting of single-domain nanocrystallites would lose its preferred direction in a near-zero external field and relax. In the four-layer structure (Figure 8a), the blocking temperature, T_B, remained lower compared to that estimated for the three-layer structure (135 vs. 215 K, Figure 8b). This may be indicative of the effect of the lower amount of easily magnetized, and for this reason, also more easily reoriented, amount of iron-rich nanoparticles present in the three-layer film.

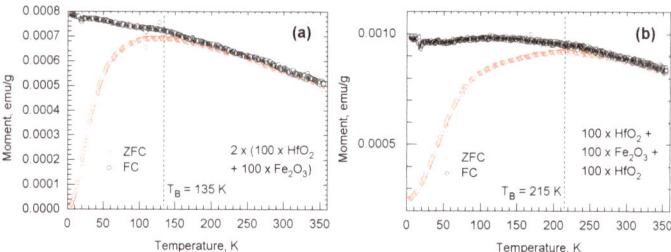

Figure 8. Magnetization-temperature curves measured in zero-field-cooling (ZFC) and field-cooling (FC) mode from representative structures consisting of two HfO$_2$-Fe$_2$O$_3$ double layers (**a**) and one HfO$_2$-Fe$_2$O$_3$-HfO$_2$ triple layer (**b**). The films were grown on diamagnetic SiO$_2$/Si substrates using cycle sequences represented by labels.

3.3. Electrical Behavior

The reference HfO_2 films behaved electrically as dielectric materials with defined insulating properties. Figure 9 represents the results of capacitance dispersion measurements, expressed as permittivity-frequency curves, after calculating the permittivity considering the simple parallel-plate capacitor configuration, containing dielectric film with thickness determined by XRR measurements. One can see that the permittivity-frequency dependencies represent appreciably flat plateaus, being indicative of the minor role for parasitic space charge and interfacial polarization in the frequency range of 10 kHz–1 MHz. The average permittivity value for the 24 nm-thick HfO_2 film grown using 200 deposition cycles remained at 18, whereas the permittivity of the 54 nm-thick film grown using 500 cycles exceeded 20. This difference was plausibly due to the more developed crystallinity in the thicker film. Since the HfO_2 films in the present study were characterized with multiphase composition (Figure 5), i.e., contained both metastable and stable polymorphs of HfO_2, the permittivity value remained even, quite expectedly, between those earlier calculated as those characteristic of corresponding phases [41]. One could also note that the permittivity values measured in the present study corresponded appreciably well to those measured earlier in a study reporting insulating properties of HfO_2-based nanolaminates and single HfO_2 films grown by ALD using $HfCl_4$ and H_2O as precursors [42].

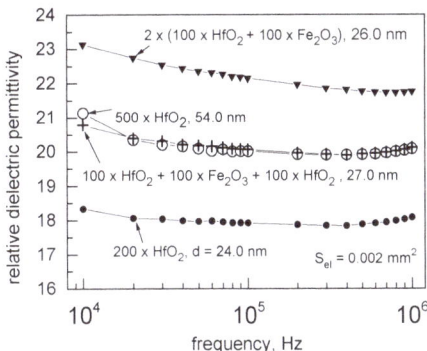

Figure 9. Permittivity versus measurement frequency dispersion test results for reference HfO_2 films as well as nanolaminate stacks grown using amounts of ALD cycles and to the thicknesses indicated by the labels. The capacitor electrode areas were 0.002 mm^2.

The HfO_2-Fe_2O_3-HfO_2 triple layer and the periodically deposited sample consisting of two HfO_2-Fe_2O_3 double layers grown using 100 deposition cycles for each component oxide behaved electrically reliable enough to enable stable capacitance measurements. The capacitance, and consequently the estimated permittivity values, appeared higher than those in the reference HfO_2 film grown to the comparable thickness (Figure 9), possibly due to the influence of interfacial polarization enabled by the relatively leaky intermediate Fe_2O_3 layers. Furthermore, even the iron-rich sample consisting of periodical nanolaminate deposited using the cycle sequence of $2 \times (50 \times HfO_2 + 150 \times Fe_2O_3)$ film grown to the total thickness of 29 nm occurred electrically stable enough, exhibiting permittivity values up to 50–60 (not shown) in the frequency range examined. Iron oxide films, deposited without complementary HfO_2 layers, could not be capacitively evaluated due to their high conductivity. One could clearly see that alternate layering of HfO_2 and Fe_2O_3 usefully assisted the trade-off between conductivity and capacitance increments, being indicative of the possibility to usefully tune the electrical resistivity in magnetic materials. The reliability of capacitance measurements, revealing the permittivity of the artificially structured HfO_2-Fe_2O_3 laminates, evidently governed by the properties of HfO_2, allows one to further expect stability of the resistive switching phenomena.

The HfO$_2$ reference films grown to the thicknesses of 24 and 54 nm after application of 200 and 500 deposition cycles, respectively, exhibited well-defined unipolar resistive switching behavior (Figure 10). The main RS parameters, such as low to high resistive state ratios and switching voltages, did not differ markedly for the films grown to different thicknesses, being indicative of the insensitivity of the polymorphic phase composition differing in these HfO$_2$ films (Figure 5). Switching parameters did not depend on the device area in those samples in which both 0.002 mm^2 and 0.052 mm^2 electrode surface areas delivered RS behavior. In the case of the HfO$_2$ films grown to the thickness of 54 nm, reliable switching behavior could be observed only upon measurements conducted on the electrodes of the smallest size, 0.002 mm^2 (Figure 10b), whereas in the case of the HfO$_2$ films grown to the thickness of 24 nm, electrodes with an area of 0.052 mm^2 also allowed one to acquire reliable switching characteristics (Figure 10a). Plausibly, growing film thickness enables the growth of larger crystallites accompanied by higher surface roughness, structural inhomogeneities, and voids, necessitating measurements on smaller sized electrodes in order to acquire reliable results. One has to note that an apparent dependence of switching reliability on electrode area is not necessarily to be related to the domination of the interfacial conduction mechanism over the filamentary one. Indeed, the unipolar switching produced by the thermochemical mechanism (TCM) is known to be filamentary [14,43], and the switching parameters, i.e., resistance in both the LRS and HRS as well as current values, are expected to be independent from the electrode area [14,44–46]. Under this thermochemical mechanism, thermochemical redox processes dominate the electrochemical ones. Local redox reactions occur due to a local temperature increase that energetically favors lower oxidation states. Thus, oxygen drifts out of this high-temperature region, producing a variation of the local conductivity due to stoichiometry variations, which are usually attributed to the formation of a lower oxidation state sub-oxide, or the metal itself if such sub-oxide does not exist [15,47]. The filaments can then be induced under the chosen voltage polarity and disrupted afterwards by the currents causing Joule heating, healing the defective channel under an applied voltage of the same polarity, but inducing much higher currents in the low resistivity state. As it is common in cells presenting unipolar resistive switching, the low to high resistivity state ratios could exceed three orders of magnitude, with a high cycle-to-cycle variability of the switching voltages and the resistance value of the HRS.

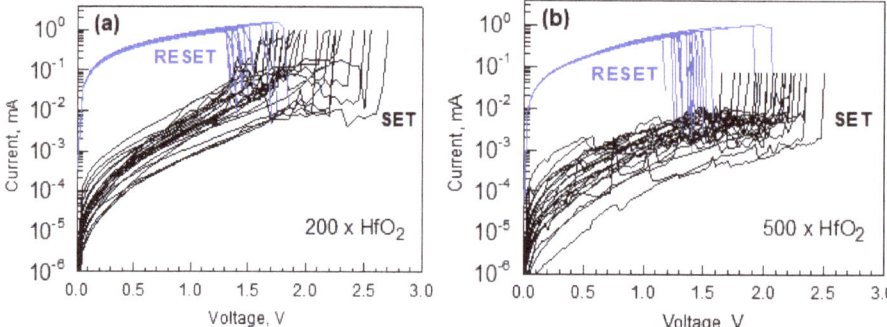

Figure 10. Current-voltage characteristics demonstrating unipolar switching in TiN/HfO$_2$/Ti devices containing HfO$_2$ films grown to thicknesses of 24 (**a**) and 54 nm (**b**) using 200 and 500 ALD cycles, respectively.

Figure 11 demonstrates defined switching behavior recorded in periodical HfO$_2$-Fe$_2$O$_3$ laminates (Figure 11a,b) as well as in the HfO$_2$-Fe$_2$O$_3$-HfO$_2$ triple-layer stack (Figure 11c). It is worth noting that in the periodically stacked HfO$_2$-Fe$_2$O$_3$ laminate grown using the cycle sequence of 2 × (150 × HfO$_2$ + 50 × Fe$_2$O$_3$), the low to high resistivity state ratios could reach even five orders of magnitude (Figure 11a). However, the repeatability of switching cycles in such films remained rather low, not allowing one to reliably record more than 8–10 switching cycles. To additionally recall, this sample was relatively weakly magnetized (Figures 6c,d and 7), demonstrating almost insignificant saturation magnetization and rather weak coercivity (below 200 Oe) already at 5 K compared to the rest of the samples grown using higher relative amounts of Fe_2O_3 deposition cycles. Thus, the deposition program applied to this particular sample could result in a material representing trade-off between magnetic and resistively switching performance, implying a possibility for optimization.

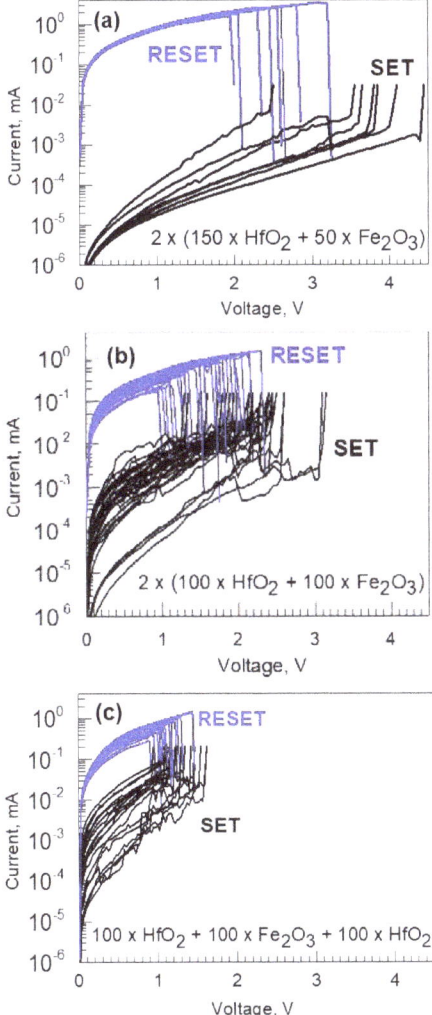

Figure 11. Current-voltage characteristics demonstrating unipolar switching in TiN/HfO_2-Fe_2O_3/Ti devices containing (**a**) periodically laminated media grown using relatively large amounts of HfO_2 deposition cycles, (**b**) periodically laminated media grown using the same cycle numbers for HfO_2 and Fe_2O_3, and (**c**) three-layer stack with Fe_2O_3 layer grown in between HfO_2 films. The deposition cycle sequences are indicated by labels.

The repeatability of current-voltage behavior upon resistive switching cycles after endurance tests was obvious in the reference HfO_2 films (Figure 12a,b). However, noticeable scattering in the current values in high-resistance states upon sequential switching cycles was recorded. One could suppose that the stability of switching the current level in the HRS after the RESET events is markedly dependent of the structural quality of the material restored after breaking filaments or quenching the conduction channels. At the same time, the resistivity levels in LRS after SET events might more significantly be determined by the current compliance limits. In this regard, the stability of HRS could serve as a structure-related descriptor of the crystalline switching medium and be worth depicting as an implication of the device functionality.

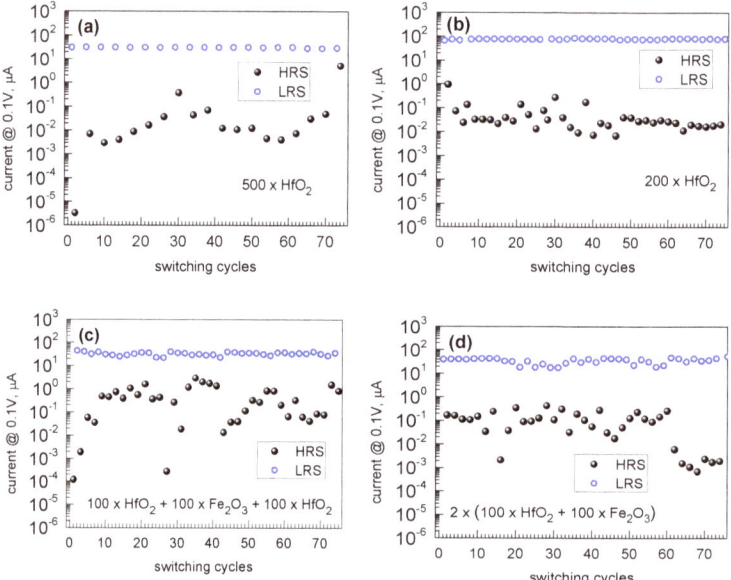

Figure 12. Current values measured after each RESET (HRS points) and SET (LRS points) processes at 0.1 V in TiN/HfO_2-Fe_2O_3/Ti devices containing (**a**) 500 and (**b**) 200 ALD cycles of HfO_2, (**c**) three-layer stack with Fe_2O_3 layer grown in between HfO_2 films, and (**d**) periodically laminated media grown using the same cycle numbers for HfO_2 and Fe_2O_3. The deposition cycle sequences are indicated by labels.

The decrement in the low to high resistivity ratio was detected simultaneously with increased variability in low resistivity states. The LRS:HRS ratios during endurance tests remained slightly higher and also somewhat more stable in the reference HfO_2 films (Figure 12a,b) compared to the results recorded in a device built on triple-layered HfO_2-Fe_2O_3-HfO_2 film (Figure 12c) as well as on four-layered HfO_2-Fe_2O_3-HfO_2-Fe_2O_3 (Figure 12d), all grown to comparable thicknesses. The increased variability in the LRS is most plausibly due to the iron oxide constituents in the films, increasing the material conductivity already in its virgin state before the SET event. This property may ease the formation of conductive channel but worsen the control over breaking it. The main outcome of the RS measurements was, thus, the recognition of a certain balance between growth cycles of constituent dielectric and magnetic materials while engineering the deposition process, before the achievement of both resistive switching and magnetic polarization at room temperature.

It should be emphasized that the unipolar resistive switching behavior of these samples has been of high interest when studying the physics behind RS. Although previous studies on HfO_2-based RRAM devices have also shown unipolar resistive switching, it was in some way always due to the metals chosen for the bottom and top electrodes [48]. It is known that RRAM cells that use the same metal for both electrodes will most likely show URS [13], as observed in the case of $Pt/HfO_2/Pt$ [49,50] and $TiN/HfO_2/TiN$ [51] MIM stacks. At the same time, $Pt/HfO_2/TiN$ cells can demonstrate both URS and BRS [52,53]. $Pt/HfO_2/Ti$ stacks have also shown bipolar switching [49], indicating better properties of Ti as an oxygen reservoir when compared to TiN, enabling and supporting the VCM. Thus, the use of a thin Ti cap in $TiN/HfO_2/Ti/TiN$ devices allows one to observe BRS [54], with unipolar switching appearing only under extreme programming conditions [55]. When looking at RRAM cells similar to the ones presented in this work, i.e., HfO_2-based RRAM with TiN and Ti as bottom and top electrodes (BE an TE), respectively, the literature strongly suggests that bipolar switching is expected [48–50], contrary to the results presented here. This could be attributed to the use of Au as the top electrode over to Ti. Bertaud et al. [56] showed that the use of a metal with low a enthalpy of formation of oxides, such as gold, for the TE, should lead to unipolar switching, and Walzcyk et al. [57] reported URS in $Au/HfO_2/TiN$ MIM stacks. Here, it is worth noting that a previous work on resistively switching media based on Fe_2O_3 has also reported URS [58], although their stack made use of somewhat symmetric Pt metal electrodes ($Pt/Fe_2O_3/Pt/Ti$). Nevertheless, a study conducted as early as 1969 [59] reports unipolar switching in thin iron oxide, associating increased conductivity (forming or SET processes) either with the formation of sub-oxides mentioned above [47] or with the expected decrease in transition metals' resistance with increasing temperature, known as metal-insulator transitions [60], which has been specifically proven for both thick [61] and thin Fe_2O_3 films [62].

4. Summary and Conclusions

Insulating HfO_2 and magnetic Fe_2O_3 were successfully tailored as nanolaminates of alternately layered films of hafnium and iron oxides. The relative contents of hafnium and iron were modified by changing the relative amounts of the deposition cycles for both constituent oxides. The films contained some amounts of chlorine and carbon as residual impurities. The structure of the films could be regarded as nanocrystalline, whereby a multiphase nature of nanolaminates, based on the simultaneous appearance of both stable and metastable polymorphs of HfO_2, was established.

Stable dielectric polarization and resistive switching properties expectedly characteristic of HfO_2 were achieved and recorded in the laminated stacks containing measurable amounts of relatively highly conducting Fe_2O_3. At the same time, the presence of Fe_2O_3 as well as formation of nanocrystalline phases of HfO_2 enabled the appearance and recording of nonlinear, saturative, and hysteretic magnetization in the laminates, somewhat correlated with the relative content of Fe_2O_3. The coercivity appeared the strongest in the films consisting of two sequentially grown HfO_2-Fe_2O_3 double layers as well as a triple HfO_2-Fe_2O_3-HfO_2 layer, measured at 5 K. The coercivity diminished drastically at room temperature, remaining, however, measurable below 100 Oe. Notably, the same structures, clearly also exhibited an ability to switch resistively, whereas samples containing relatively larger amounts of iron could not switch resistively due to increasing conductivity.

All samples deposited using 100 or less Fe_2O_3 cycles between HfO_2 layers demonstrated unipolar resistive switching. Higher amounts of Fe_2O_3 ALD cycles resulted in a decrease of the low to high resistance state ratio. Fe_2O_3 layers constituting the laminates probably did not allow for the formation of conductive filaments as efficiently as HfO_2, hindering the variability of the low resistance state. The appearance of the unipolar resistive switching of these samples may be regarded as notable in light of common knowledge suggesting that Ti and TiN used for the top and bottom electrodes, mounting HfO_2, should lead to bipolar resistive switching. This could be due to the dominance of a thermochemical process over an electrochemical one. Further studies could be devoted to the investigation of the effect of electrodes with variable enthalpy as well as coupling between conductivity and electromagnetic polarization.

Author Contributions: Conceptualization, K.K. (Kristjan Kalam) and K.K. (Kaupo Kukli); methodology, K.K. (Kristjan Kalam); software, G.V., J.L., J.M.L., R.R. and M.O.; formal analysis, G.V., J.L., R.R. and A.T. (Aivar Tarre); investigation, R.R., G.V., J.M.L., M.O., A.K. and J.K.; resources, R.S., S.D., H.C., A.T. (Aile Tamm) and K.K. (Kaupo Kukli); writing—original draft preparation, K.K. (Kristjan Kalam), K.K. (Kaupo Kukli), G.V. and J.L.; visualization, G.V. and A.T. (Aivar Tarre); project administration, K.K. (Kaupo Kukli), A.T. (Aile Tamm), S.D. and H.C.; funding acquisition, K.K. (Kaupo Kukli), A.T. (Aile Tamm), R.S. and H.C. All authors have read and agreed to the published version of the manuscript.

Funding: The present study was partially supported by the European Regional Development Fund project "Emerging orders in quantum and nanomaterials" (TK134), the Spanish Ministry of Economy and Competitiveness (TEC2017-84321-C4-2-R) with the support of Feder Funds, and the Estonian Research Agency (PRG753, PRG4).

Data Availability Statement: Not applicable.

Conflicts of Interest: The authors declare no conflict of interest. The funders had no role in the design of the study; in the collection, analyses, or interpretation of data; in the writing of the manuscript, or in the decision to publish the results.

References

1. Wolf, S.A.; Awschalom, D.D.; Buhrman, R.A.; Daughton, J.M.; von Molnár, S.; Roukes, M.L.; Chtchelkanova, A.Y.; Treger, D.M. Spintronics: A spin-based electronics vision for the future. *Science* **2001**, *294*, 1488–1495. [CrossRef] [PubMed]
2. Waser, R.; Aono, M. Nanoionics-based resistive switching memories. *Nat. Mater.* **2007**, *6*, 833–840. [CrossRef] [PubMed]
3. Li, S.-S.; Su, Y.-K. Conductive filaments controlled ferromagnetism in Co-doped ZnO resistive switching memory device. *Jpn. J. Appl. Phys.* **2019**, *58*, SBBI01. [CrossRef]
4. Du, F.; Li, Y.; Li, X.; Yang, J.; Bai, Y.; Quan, Z.; Liu, C.; Xu, X. Resistive switching and its modulating ferromagnetism and magnetoresistance of a ZnO:Co/SiO$_2$:Co film. *J. Magn. Magn. Mater.* **2019**, *489*, 165445. [CrossRef]
5. Xie, J.; Ren, S.; Bu, J.; Cheng, B.; Liu, W.; Liu, L.; Zhou, G.; Qin, H.; Hu, J. Resistive switching and ferromagnetism modulation in copper oxide film on Nb:SrTiO$_3$ substrate. *J. Magn. Magn. Mater.* **2018**, *465*, 295–299. [CrossRef]
6. Ren, S.; Zhu, G.; Xie, J.; Bu, J.; Qin, H.; Hu, J. Resistive switching and electrical control of ferromagnetism in a Ag/HfO$_2$/Nb:SrTiO$_3$/Ag resistive random access memory (RRAM) device at room temperature. *J. Phys. Condens. Matter* **2016**, *28*, 056001. [CrossRef] [PubMed]
7. Slesazeck, S.; Mikolajick, T. Nanoscale resistive switching memory devices: A review. *Nanotechnology* **2019**, *30*, 352003. [CrossRef] [PubMed]
8. Chen, A. A review of emerging non-volatile memory (NVM) technologies and applications. *Solid-State Electr.* **2016**, *125*, 25–38. [CrossRef]
9. Jasmin, A.C. Filamentary model in resistive switching materials. *AIP Conf. Proc.* **2017**, *1901*, 060004. [CrossRef]
10. Waser, R. Redox-based resistive switching memories. *J. Nanosci. Nanotech.* **2012**, *12*, 7628–7640. [CrossRef]
11. Menzel, S.; Waters, M.; Marchewka, A.; Böttger, U.; Dittmann, R.; Waser, R. Origin of the ultra-nonlinear switching kinetics in oxide-based resistive switches. *Adv. Funct. Mater.* **2011**, *21*, 4487–4492. [CrossRef]
12. Valov, I. Redox-based resistive switching memories (ReRAMs): Electrochemical systems at the atomic scale. *Chem. Electro. Chem.* **2014**, *1*, 26–36. [CrossRef]
13. Valov, I. Interfacial interactions and their impact on redox-based resistive switching memories (ReRAMs). *Semicond. Sci. Technol.* **2017**, *32*, 093006. [CrossRef]
14. Ielmini, D.; Bruchhaus, R.; Waser, R. Thermochemical resistive switching: Materials, mechanisms, and scaling projections. *Phase Trans.* **2011**, *84*, 570–602. [CrossRef]
15. Waser, R. Electrochemical and thermochemical memories. In Proceedings of the 2008 IEEE International Electron Devices Meeting, San Francisco, CA, USA, 15–17 December 2008. [CrossRef]
16. Bersuker, G.; Gilmer, D.C.; Veksler, D.; Kirsch, P.; Vandelli, L.; Padovani, A.; Larcher, L.; McKenna, K.; Shluger, A.; Iglesias, V.; et al. Metal oxide resistive memory switching mechanism based on conductive filament properties. *J. Appl. Phys.* **2011**, *110*, 124518. [CrossRef]
17. Lin, K.-L.; Hou, T.-H.; Shieh, J.; Lin, J.-H.; Chou, C.-T.; Lee, Y.-J. Electrode dependence of filament formation in HfO$_2$ resistive-switching memory. *J. Appl. Phys.* **2011**, *109*, 084104. [CrossRef]
18. Maldonado, D.; Roldán, A.M.; González, M.B.; Jiménez-Molinos, F.; Campabadal, F.; Roldán, J.B. Influence of magnetic field on the operation of TiN/Ti/HfO$_2$/W resistive memories. *Microel. Eng.* **2019**, *215*, 110983. [CrossRef]
19. Hong, N.H. Magnetism due to defects/oxygen vacancies in HfO$_2$ thin films. *Phys. Stat. Sol. c* **2007**, *4*, 1270–1275. [CrossRef]
20. Tereshchenko, O.E.; Golyashov, V.A.; Eremeev, S.V.; Maurin, I.; Bakulin, A.V.; Kulkova, S.E.; Aksenov, M.S.; Preobrazhenskii, V.V.; Putyato, M.A.; Semyagin, B.R.; et al. Ferromagnetic HfO$_2$/Si/GaAs interface for spin-polarimetry applications. *Appl. Phys. Lett.* **2015**, *107*, 123506. [CrossRef]

21. Singh, R. Unexpected magnetism in nanomaterials. *J. Mag. Mag. Mater.* **2013**, *346*, 58–73. [CrossRef]
22. Daub, M.; Bachmann, J.; Jing, J.; Knez, M.; Gösele, U.; Barth, S.; Mathur, S.; Escrig, J.; Altbir, D.; Nielsch, K. Ferromagnetic nanostructures by atomic layer deposition: From thin films towards core-shell nanotubes. *ECS Trans.* **2007**, *11*, 139–148. [CrossRef]
23. Schneider, J.R.; Baker, J.G.; Bent, S.F. The influence of ozone: Superstoichiometric oxygen in atomic layer deposition of Fe_2O_3 using tert-butylferrocene and O_3. *Adv. Mater. Interfaces* **2020**, *7*, 2000318. [CrossRef]
24. Márquez, P.; Alburquenque, D.; Celis, F.; Freire, R.M.; Escrig, J. Structural, morphological and magnetic properties of iron oxide thin films obtained by atomic layer deposition as a function of their thickness. *J. Magn. Magn. Mater.* **2021**, *530*, 167914. [CrossRef]
25. Štefanić, G.; Musić, S. Thermal behavior of the amorphous precursors of the Fe_2O_3-HfO_2 system. *Thermochim. Acta* **2001**, *373*, 59–67. [CrossRef]
26. Rao, M.S.R.; Kundaliya, D.C.; Dhar, S.; Cardoso, C.A.; Curtin, A.; Welz, S.J.; Erni, R.; Browning, N.D.; Lofland, S.E.; Metting, C.J.; et al. Search for magnetism in Co and Fe doped HfO_2 thin films for potential spintronic applications. *Mater. Res. Soc. Proc.* **2004**, *830*, 262–275. [CrossRef]
27. Kukli, K.; Kemell, M.; Castán, H.; Dueñas, S.; Seemen, H.; Rähn, M.; Link, J.; Stern, R.; Ritala, M.; Leskelä, M. Atomic layer deposition and properties of HfO_2-Al_2O_3 nanolaminates. *ECS J. Solid State Sci. Tech.* **2018**, *7*, P501–P508. [CrossRef]
28. Kalam, K.; Seemen, H.; Mikkor, M.; Ritslaid, P.; Stern, R.; Dueñas, S.; Castán, H.; Tamm, A.; Kukli, K. Electric and magnetic properties of atomic layer deposited ZrO_2-HfO_2 thin films. *ECS J. Solid State Sci. Technol.* **2018**, *7*, N117–N122. [CrossRef]
29. Ossorio, O.G.; Dueñas, S.; Castán, H.; Tamm, A.; Kalam, K.; Seemen, H.; Kukli, K. Resistive switching properties of atomic layer deposited ZrO_2-HfO_2 thin films. In Proceedings of the 2018 Spanish Conference on Electron Devices (CDE), Salamanca, Spain, 14–16 November 2018. [CrossRef]
30. Kukli, K.; Kemell, M.; Castán, H.; Dueñas, S.; Link, J.; Stern, R.; Heikkilä, M.J.; Jõgiaas, T.; Kozlova, J.; Rähn, M.; et al. Magnetic properties and resistive switching in mixture films and nanolaminates consisting of iron and silicon oxides grown by atomic layer deposition. *J. Vac. Sci. Technol. A* **2020**, *38*, 042405. [CrossRef]
31. Arroval, T.; Aarik, L.; Rammula, R.; Kruusla, V.; Aarik, J. Effect of substrate-enhanced and inhibited growth on atomic layer deposition and properties of aluminum–titanium oxide films. *Thin Solid Films* **2016**, *600*, 119–125. [CrossRef]
32. Granneman, E.; Fischer, P.; Pierreux, D.; Terhorst, H.; Zagwijn, P. Batch ALD: Characteristics, comparison with single wafer ALD, and examples. *Surf. Coat. Technol.* **2017**, *201*, 8899–8907. [CrossRef]
33. Zagwijn, P.; Verweij, W.; Pierreux, D.; Adjeroud, N.; Bankras, R.; Oosterlaken, E.; Snijders, G.J.; van den Hout, M.; Fischer, P.; Wilhelm, R.; et al. Novel batch titanium nitride CVD process for advanced metal electrodes. *ECS Transact.* **2008**, *13*, 459–464. [CrossRef]
34. Aarik, L.; Arroval, T.; Mändar, H.; Rammula, R.; Aarik, J. Influence of oxygen precursors on atomic layer deposition of HfO_2 and hafnium-titanium oxide films: Comparison of O_3- and H_2O-based processes. *Appl. Surf. Sci.* **2020**, *530*, 147229. [CrossRef]
35. Kalam, K.; Seemen, H.; Ritslaid, P.; Rähn, M.; Tamm, A.; Kukli, K.; Kasikov, A.; Link, J.; Stern, R.; Dueñas, S.; et al. Atomic layer deposition and properties of ZrO_2/Fe_2O_3 thin films. *Beilstein J. Nanotechnol.* **2018**, *9*, 119–128. [CrossRef] [PubMed]
36. Abraham, D.W.; Frank, M.M.; Guha, S. Absence of magnetism in hafnium oxide films. *Appl. Phys. Lett.* **2005**, *87*, 252502. [CrossRef]
37. Venkatesan, M.; Fitzgerald, C.B.; Coey, J.M.D. Unexpected magnetism in a dielectric oxide. *Nature* **2004**, *430*, 630. [CrossRef] [PubMed]
38. Xue, K.-H.; Miao, X.-S. Oxygen vacancy chain and conductive filament formation in hafnia. *J. Appl. Phys.* **2018**, *123*, 161505. [CrossRef]
39. Dai, Y.; Pan, Z.; Wang, F.; Li, X. Oxygen vacancy effects in HfO_2-based resistive switching memory: First principle study. *AIP Adv.* **2016**, *6*, 085209. [CrossRef]
40. Kumar, S.; Rath, C. Oxygen vacancy mediated stabilization of cubic phase at room temperature and resistive switching effect in Sm- and Dy-doped HfO_2 thin film. *Phys. Stat. Sol. A* **2020**, *217*, 1900756. [CrossRef]
41. Zhao, X.; Vanderbilt, D. First-principles study of structural, vibrational, and lattice dielectric properties of hafnium oxide. *Phys. Rev. B* **2002**, *65*, 233106. [CrossRef]
42. Kukli, K.; Ihanus, J.; Ritala, M.; Leskelä, M. Tailoring the dielectric properties of HfO_2–Ta_2O_5 nanolaminates. *Appl. Phys. Lett.* **1996**, *68*, 3737–3739. [CrossRef]
43. Chang, S.H.; Lee, J.S.; Chae, S.C.; Lee, S.B.; Liu, C.; Kahng, B.; Kim, D.-W.; Noh, T.W. Occurrence of both unipolar memory and threshold resistance switching in a NiO film. *Phys. Rev. Lett.* **2009**, *102*, 026801. [CrossRef] [PubMed]
44. Baek, I.G.; Lee, M.S.; Seo, S.; Lee, M.J.; Seo, D.H.; Suh, D.-S.; Park, J.C.; Park, S.O.; Kim, H.S.; Yoo, I.K.; et al. Highly scalable nonvolatile resistive memory using simple binary oxide driven by asymmetric unipolar voltage pulses. In Proceedings of the IEDM Technical Digest. IEEE International Electron Devices Meeting, San Francisco, CA, USA, 13–15 December 2004. [CrossRef]
45. Nardi, F.; Ielmini, D.; Cagli, C.; Spiga, S.; Fanciulli, M.; Goux, L.; Wouters, D.J. Sub-10 μA reset in NiO-based resistive switching memory (RRAM) cells. In Proceedings of the 2010 IEEE International Memory Workshop, Seoul, Korea, 16–19 May 2010. [CrossRef]
46. Ielmini, D.; Spiga, S.; Nardi, F.; Cagli, C.; Lamperti, A.; Cianci, E.; Fanciulli, M. Scaling analysis of submicrometer nickel-oxide-based resistive switching memory devices. *J. Appl. Phys.* **2011**, *109*, 034506. [CrossRef]
47. Chudnovskii, F.A.; Odynets, L.L.; Pergament, A.L.; Stefanovich, G.B. Electroforming and switching in oxides of transition metals: The role of metal–insulator transition in the switching mechanism. *J. Solid State Chem.* **1996**, *122*, 95–99. [CrossRef]

48. Mohammad, B.; Jaoude, M.A.; Kumar, V.; Al Homouz, D.M.; Nahla, H.A.; Al-Qutayri, M.; Christoforou, N. State of the art of metal oxide memristor devices. *Nanotechnol. Rev.* **2016**, *5*, 311–329. [CrossRef]
49. Traoré, B.; Xue, K.-H.; Vianello, E.; Molas, G.; Blaise, P.; De Salvo, B.; Padovani, A.; Pirrotta, O.; Larcher, L.; Fonseca, L.R.C.; et al. Investigation of the role of electrodes on the retention performance of HfO$_x$ based RRAM cells by experiments, atomistic simulations and device physical modeling. In Proceedings of the 2013 IEEE International Reliability Physics Symposium (IRPS), Monterey, CA, USA, 14–18 April 2013. [CrossRef]
50. Traoré, B.; Blaise, P.; Vianello, E.; Perniola, L.; De Salvo, B.; Nishi, Y. HfO$_2$ based RRAM: Electrode effects, Ti/HfO$_2$ interface, charge injection, and oxygen (O) defects diffusion through experiment and *Ab Initio* calculations. *IEEE Transact. Electron Dev.* **2016**, *63*, 360–368. [CrossRef]
51. Wang, X.P.; Chen, Y.Y.; Pantisano, L.; Goux, L.; Jurczak, M.; Groeseneken, G.; Wouters, D.J. Effect of anodic interface layers on the unipolar switching of HfO$_2$-based resistive RAM. In Proceedings of the 2010 International Symposium on VLSI Technology, System and Application, Hsinchu, Taiwan, 26–28 April 2010. [CrossRef]
52. Goux, L.; Czarnecki, P.; Chen, Y.Y.; Pantisano, L.; Wang, X.P.; Degraeve, R.; Govoreanu, B.; Jurczak, M.; Wouters, D.J.; Altimime, L. Evidences of oxygen-mediated resistive-switching mechanism in TiN\HfO$_2$\Pt cells. *Appl. Phys. Lett.* **2010**, *97*, 243509. [CrossRef]
53. Goux, L.; Chen, Y.-Y.; Pantisano, L.; Wang, X.-P.; Groeseneken, G.; Jurczak, M.; Wouters, D.J. On the gradual unipolar and bipolar resistive switching of TiN\HfO$_2$\Pt memory systems. *Electrochem. Solid-State Lett.* **2010**, *13*, G54–G56. [CrossRef]
54. Lee, H.Y.; Chen, Y.S.; Chen, P.S.; Wu, T.Y.; Chen, F.; Wang, C.C.; Tzeng, P.J.; Tsai, M.-J.; Lien, C. Low power and nanosecond switching in robust hafnium oxide resistive memory with a thin Ti cap. *IEEE Electron. Dev. Lett.* **2010**, *31*, 44–46. [CrossRef]
55. Chen, Y.S.; Lee, H.Y.; Chen, P.S.; Gu, P.Y.; Chen, C.W.; Lin, W.P.; Liu, W.H.; Hsu, Y.Y.; Sheu, S.S.; Chiang, P.C.; et al. Highly scalable hafnium oxide memory with improvements of resistive distribution and read disturb immunity. In Proceedings of the 2009 IEEE International Electron Devices Meeting (IEDM), Baltimore, MD, USA, 7–9 December 2009. [CrossRef]
56. Bertaud, T.; Walczyk, D.; Walczyk, C.; Kubotsch, S.; Sowinska, M.; Schroeder, T.; Wenger, C.; Vallée, C.; Gonon, P.; Mannequin, C.; et al. Resistive switching of HfO$_2$-based metal–insulator–metal diodes: Impact of the top electrode material. *Thin Solid Films* **2012**, *520*, 4551–4555. [CrossRef]
57. Walczyk, C.; Wenger, C.; Sohal, R.; Lukosius, M.; Fox, A.; Dąbrowski, J.; Wolansky, D.; Tillack, B.; Müssig, H.-J.; Schroeder, T. Pulse-induced low-power resistive switching in HfO$_2$ metal-insulator-metal diodes for nonvolatile memory applications. *J. Appl. Phys.* **2009**, *105*, 114103. [CrossRef]
58. Inoue, I.H.; Yasuda, S.; Akinaga, H.; Takagi, H. Nonpolar resistance switching of metal/binary-transition-metal oxides/metal sandwiches: Homogeneous/inhomogeneous transition of current distribution. *Phys. Rev. B* **2008**, *77*, 035105. [CrossRef]
59. Morris, R.C.; Christopher, J.E.; Coleman, R.V. Conduction phenomena in thin layers of iron oxide. *Phys. Rev.* **1969**, *84*, 565–573. [CrossRef]
60. Zimmers, A.; Aigouy, L.; Mortier, M.; Sharoni, A.; Wang, S.; West, K.G.; Ramirez, J.G.; Schuller, I.K. Role of thermal heating on the voltage induced insulator-metal transition in VO$_2$. *Phys. Rev. Lett.* **2013**, *110*, 056601. [CrossRef] [PubMed]
61. Mirzaei, A.; Janghorban, K.; Hashemi, B.; Hosseini, S.R.; Bonyani, M.; Leonardi, S.G.; Bonavita, A.; Neri, G. Synthesis and characterization of mesoporous α-Fe$_2$O$_3$ nanoparticles and investigation of electrical properties of fabricated thick films. *Process. Appl. Ceram.* **2016**, *10*, 209–217. [CrossRef]
62. Engel, J.; Tuller, H.L. The electrical conductivity of thin film donor doped hematite: From insulator to semiconductor by defect modulation. *Phys. Chem. Chem. Phys.* **2014**, *16*, 11374. [CrossRef] [PubMed]

Article

Investigation of Combinatorial WO$_3$-MoO$_3$ Mixed Layers by Spectroscopic Ellipsometry Using Different Optical Models

Miklos Fried [1,2,*], Renato Bogar [1], Daniel Takacs [1], Zoltan Labadi [2], Zsolt Endre Horvath [2] and Zsolt Zolnai [2]

[1] Institute of Microelectronics and Technology, Kando Kalman Faculty of Electrical Engineering, Óbuda University, H-1084 Budapest, Hungary; bogarrenato@gmail.com (R.B.); tdani98elektro@gmail.com (D.T.)
[2] Institute of Technical Physics and Materials Science (MFA), Centre for Energy Research, Hungarian Academy of Sciences, H-1525 Budapest, Hungary; labadi.zoltan@energia.mta.hu (Z.L.); horvath.zsolt.endre@energia.mta.hu (Z.E.H.); zolnai.zsolt@energia.mta.hu (Z.Z.)
* Correspondence: fried.miklos@energia.mta.hu

Abstract: Reactive (Ar-O$_2$ plasma) magnetron sputtered WO$_3$-MoO$_3$ (nanometer scaled) mixed layers were investigated and mapped by Spectroscopic Ellipsometry (SE). The W- and Mo-targets were placed separately, and 30 × 30 cm glass substrates were slowly moved under the two (W and Mo) separated targets. We used different (oscillator- and Effective Medium Approximation, EMA-based) optical models to obtain the thickness and composition maps of the sample layer relatively quickly and in a cost-effective and contactless way. In addition, we used Rutherford Backscattering Spectrometry to check the SE results. Herein, we compare the "goodness" of different optical models depending upon the sample preparation conditions, for instance, the speed and cycle number of the substrate motion. Finally, we can choose between appropriate optical models (2-Tauc-Lorentz oscillator model vs. the Bruggeman Effective Medium Approximation, BEMA) depending on the process parameters. If one has more than one "molecular layer" in the "sublayers", BEMA can be used. If one has an atomic mixture, the multiple oscillator model is better (more precise) for this type of layer structure.

Keywords: spectroscopic ellipsometry; combinatorial approach; metal oxides

Citation: Fried, M.; Bogar, R.; Takacs, D.; Labadi, Z.; Horvath, Z.E.; Zolnai, Z. Investigation of Combinatorial WO$_3$-MoO$_3$ Mixed Layers by Spectroscopic Ellipsometry Using Different Optical Models. *Nanomaterials* **2022**, *12*, 2421. https://doi.org/10.3390/nano12142421

Academic Editors: Patrick Fiorenza, Raffaella Lo Nigro, Béla Pécz and Jens Eriksson

Received: 16 May 2022
Accepted: 12 July 2022
Published: 14 July 2022

Publisher's Note: MDPI stays neutral with regard to jurisdictional claims in published maps and institutional affiliations.

Copyright: © 2022 by the authors. Licensee MDPI, Basel, Switzerland. This article is an open access article distributed under the terms and conditions of the Creative Commons Attribution (CC BY) license (https://creativecommons.org/licenses/by/4.0/).

1. Introduction

For protection against extra heat through glass windows, electrochromic film as a smart window [1] can be the most useful tool to reduce heat in buildings. A smart glass window consists of a layer of electrochromic material bounded by metal oxide layers. The special feature is the ability to modify the optical properties by supplying electric charge to the film system, which can be transformed from translucent glass into darker or more opaque glass and can be returned to the translucent state with low electric current. It also controls the transmitted amount of light. Electrochromic materials capable of heat radiation protection through glass consist of semiconductor metal oxide film coatings on glass, such as TiO$_2$, CrO, Nb$_2$O$_5$, SnO$_2$, NiO, IrO$_2$ [2], WO$_3$, and MoO$_3$ [3,4]. Researchers have different methods of deposition as sputtering [5], Atmospheric Pressure Chemical Vapor Deposition (APCVD) [6], dipping [7], sol-gel method [1,4], and sintering [8]. Authors of Ref. [8] investigated mixed materials, but only a limited number of compositions: (MoO$_3$)$_x$-(WO$_3$)$_{1-x}$ for x = 0, 0.2, 0.4, 0.6, 0.8. Pure WO$_3$ layers were also investigated [9–11] by spectroscopic ellipsometry.

During the present work, we used reactive magnetron sputtering (in Ar-O$_2$ plasma) to create all combinations of WO$_3$-MoO$_3$ mixed layers along a line/band. To prepare one sample in the vacuum chamber, we needed 4 h including the vacuum preparation. If we wanted to prepare 21 separate samples with compositions from 0 to 100% with 5% "resolution", we would need 21 × 4 h, minimum of 10 working days. Using the combinatorial approach, we achieved all of the compositions after one sputtering process in the same sputtering chamber. Furthermore, our aim was to investigate the goodness of WO_3-MoO_3 mixed layers as electrochromic materials for "smart" windows (transparency ratio, switching speed, coloration efficiency).

After sputtering, we investigated and mapped the samples by Spectroscopic Ellipsometry (SE), which is a relatively quick, cost-effective, and contactless method. We used different (oscillator- and Effective Medium Approximation, EMA-based) optical models to obtain the thickness and composition map of the sample layer. We checked the SE results using Rutherford Backscattering Spectrometry. In a set of experiments, we changed the position of the sputtering targets, as well as the speed and cycle number of the substrate motion. Our aim was to compare the "goodness" of the different optical models depending upon the sample preparation conditions.

2. Materials and Methods

Layer depositions were performed in a reactive (Ar + O_2) gas mixture in high vacuum (~2×10^{-6} and ~10^{-3} mbar process pressure). Additionally, 30 sccm/s Ar and 30 sccm/s O_2 volumetric flow rate were applied in the magnetron sputtering chamber. The substrates were 300×300 mm soda lime glasses. The starting process was the preparation of a W-mirror (W sputtered only in Ar-plasma) to avoid the back-reflection of the measuring light-beam during Spectroscopic Ellipsometry (SE) measurements. The plasma powers of the two targets were selected in the 0.75–1.5 kW range independently. We used 1, 5 or 25 cm/s of walking speed (back and forth), which was the speed of the 30×30 cm glass sample between the end positions (the edges of the targets). See the sample fabrication parameters in Table 1.

Table 1. Summary of the sample fabrication conditions.

Sample Name	Target (s)	Target Position	Plasma Powers [kW]	Walking Cycles	Walking Speed
W-target-only	W	center	0.75	500	5 cm/s
W-target-only	W	center	1	500	5 cm/s
W-target-only	W	center	1.5	500	5 cm/s
Mo-target-only	Mo	center	0.75	500	5 cm/s
Mo-target-only	Mo	center	1	500	5 cm/s
Mo-target-only	Mo	center	1.5	500	5 cm/s
Double-target in closer position	W-Mo	Left-center	0.75–1.5	300	5 cm/s
Double-target in distant position "Slow"	W-Mo	Left-right	0.75–1.5	75	1 cm/s
Double-target in distant position "Fast"	W-Mo	Left-right	0.75–1.5	1500	25 cm/s

Electron Dispersive Spectra (EDS) analysis of the layers showed that the Metal/Oxygen atomic ratio was 1:3 at the applied oxygen partial pressure. Significantly lower oxygen partial pressure is needed to prepare oxygen-deficient (non-transparent, "black") layer.

The sputtering targets were placed in two arrangements as it can be seen in Figure 1. In the first arrangement, the two targets were placed at 35 cm, in the second arrangement they were placed at 70 cm distance from each other. According to the measurements, in the first arrangement the two "material streams" overlapped around the center position, while in the second arrangement the two "material streams" were separated.

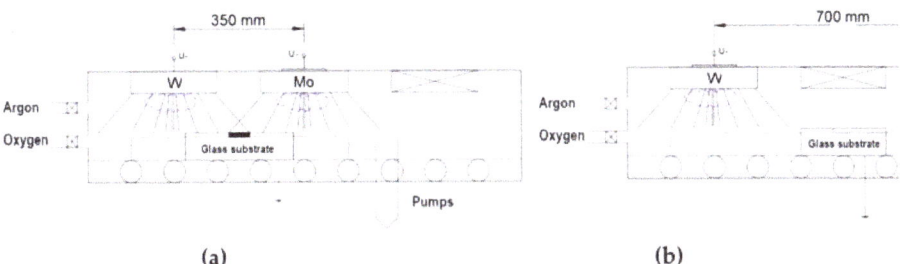

Figure 1. Two arrangements of the targets: (**a**) The two targets in closer position (35 cm from each other); (**b**) the two targets in distant position (70 cm from each other).

We have two possible optical mapping methods: Our Woollam M2000 SE device [12] or our "expanded beam" ellipsometer [13–15]. As a single-spot ellipsometer is more precise when both the thickness and the composition change "rapidly" (in our case ~50 nm and ~10% per cm), we used mainly the M2000 device. In addition, we used CompleteEASE program (from Woollam Co., https://www.jawoollam.com/ellipsometry-software/completeease, accessed 12 July 2022) to evaluate the mapping measurements using the built-in optical models and oscillator functions. Finding the best match between the model and the experiment is typically achieved through regression. An estimator, such as the Mean Squared Error (MSE), is used to quantify the difference between curves. The lower MSE indicates a better fit and better optical model. Notably, the maps from the M2000 measurements are compiled from four 15 × 15 cm parts. Our M2000 device can measure only one 15 × 15 cm part at once. The mapping measurements were performed using mm-sized beam-spot on a 15 × 15 grid with one spectra-pair per cm.

We used 5 × 50 mm Si-probes (6 pieces were placed at the center line of the substrate glass) for Rutherford Backscattering Spectrometry (RBS) and X-ray Diffractometry (XRD) measurements (see later in the "*3.3. Double-Target Samples*").

Moreover, 2.8 MeV ^{4}He$^+$ Rutherford Backscattering Spectrometry (RBS) have been performed in a scattering chamber with a two-axis goniometer at 7° tilt and 165° detector angles connected to the 5 MV EG-2R Van de Graaff accelerator of the Wigner FK RMI of the HAS. The ^{4}He$^+$ analyzing ion beam was collimated with two sets of four-sector slits to the spot size of 0.5 × 0.5 mm (width × height), while the beam divergence was maintained below 0.06°. The beam current was measured by a transmission Faraday cup. In the scattering chamber, the vacuum was about 10^{-4} Pa. Liquid N$_2$ cooled traps were used along the beam path and around the wall of the chamber to reduce the hydrocarbon deposition.

RBS spectra were detected using ORTEC silicon surface barrier detectors mounted at scattering angle of Θ = 165. The detector resolution was 20 keV for RBS. Spectra were recorded for sample tilt angles of both 7 and 60° to make a difference between the heavier and lighter atoms at the surface and in deeper regions. In this manner, the reliability of spectrum evaluation has been improved. The measured spectra were simulated with the RBX code [16].

XRD measurements were performed on a Bruker AXS D8 Discover device to determine the amount of amorphous fraction of the layers. We examined 4 Si-probes: One from the "W-side", two from the "mixed-part", and one from the "Mo-side" and found that our layers are highly amorphous. One example (from the mixed part) XRD measurement is shown in Figure 2. Only one significant broad peak in the 20–30° region can be seen as the sign of amorphous film. Crystalline peaks at higher angles can be identified as peaks of pure cubic (beta) tungsten, which was sputtered under the WO$_3$ and MoO$_3$ layers. The broad peak near 70° is from the silicon substrate. The vertical red lines show the calculated positions of beta tungsten, which is a thin (app. 100 nm) layer. We calculated the positions of monoclinic, triclinic, and orthorhombic WO$_3$ and hexagonal and orthorhombic MoO$_3$ peaks.

In addition, we cannot see any trace of crystalline WO$_3$ or MoO$_3$ material in the layers. Moreover, other authors found that independent of the deposition technique, the WO$_3$ thin films prepared at room temperature exhibited an amorphous structure (i.e., featureless XRD pattern) [10].

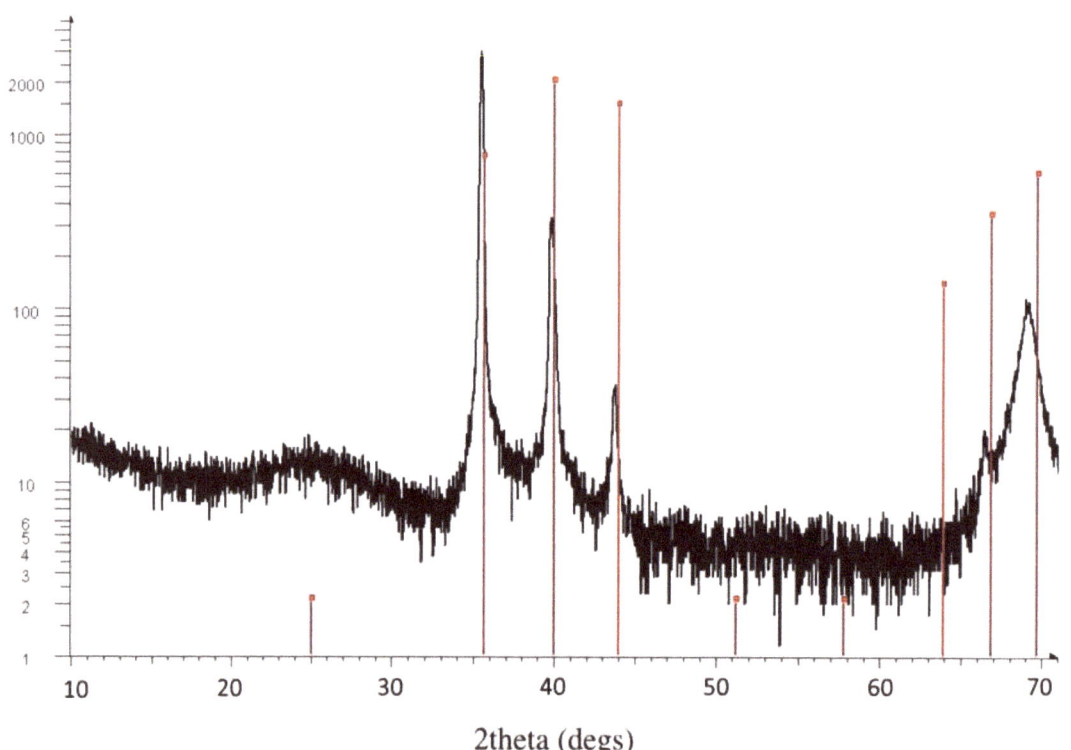

Figure 2. One example (from the mixed part) XRD measurement (note the logarithmic vertical scale) showing one significant broad peak in the 20-30° region as the sign of amorphous film. Crystalline peaks at higher angles can be identified as peaks of pure cubic (beta) tungsten, which was sputtered under the WO$_3$ and MoO$_3$ layers. In addition, the broad peak near 70° is from the silicon substrate. The vertical red lines show the calculated positions of beta tungsten. We calculated the positions of monoclinic, triclinic, and orthorhombic WO$_3$ and hexagonal and orthorhombic MoO$_3$ peaks. Moreover, we cannot see any trace of crystalline WO$_3$ or MoO$_3$ material in the layers.

Dispersion Relations

Magnetron sputtering results in amorphous materials (which is needed for good electrochromic performance) as the XRD measurements prove this (see Figure 2). We considered two different dispersion relations for the clean materials: Cauchy formula (Figure 3a) and Tauc-Lorentz oscillator model (Figure 3b). Both dispersion relations are built-in modules (CompleteEASE program) and can be used as a pre-determined component in Bruggeman Effective Medium Approximation (EMA or BEMA [17]).

Other authors used similar optical models for pure WO$_3$ [9–11]. In [9], the optical indexes, n and k, were determined by ellipsometric measurements, using various models, including Tauc-Lorentz [18], ensuring a good fit of tan(ψ) and cos(Δ) vs. the wavelength. In [11], the optical constants were measured with the film in the unintercalated and fully intercalated states using ellipsometry, transmission, and reflection data. Two Lorentz oscillators were used to model the dispersion in the 300 and 1700 nm wavelength region.

One oscillator in the UV was used to model the dispersion that takes place in dielectric materials for wavelengths larger than the band gap, and a second near 14 μm was used to represent structure in the optical constants due to the tungsten-oxygen network [11]. In the present paper, we do not use the infrared region over 1000 nm, thus we used only one Tauc-Lorentz per material.

In the EMA calculation, the mixed-layer is considered as a physical combination of two distinct phases formed by WO_3 and MoO_3 with an appropriate volume fraction. The constituents are considered equivalent; neither of the components is considered as a host material. In this case, it holds that

$$0 = \sum f_i(\varepsilon_i - \varepsilon)/(\varepsilon_i + 2\varepsilon), \tag{1}$$

where ε is the effective complex dielectric function of the composite layer; f_i and ε_i denote volume fraction and the complex dielectric function of the ith component. In the case of two components, WO_3 and MoO_3, the formula is a complex quadratic equation, where ε (the effective dielectric function) is the unknown and we can choose easily between the two solutions (the wrong one is physically meaningless). The used Bruggeman Effective Medium Approximation (EMA or BEMA) is relatively easy to calculate and can be extended simply to describe a material consisting of more than two phases. However, the generalized formula for a two-phase material is

$$\varepsilon = (\varepsilon_a \varepsilon_b + \kappa \varepsilon_h (f_a \varepsilon_a + f_b \varepsilon_b))/(\kappa \varepsilon_h + (f_a \varepsilon_b + f_b \varepsilon_a)) \tag{2}$$

Here, κ is defined by κ = (1 − q)/q using the screening factor q. In models that assume spherical dielectrics (i.e., the BEMA model), the screening factor is given by q = 1/3. We tried to use q = 1 (maximal screening) value, as well. However, it provides almost the same results for the compositions and the thickness within the fitting errors, with almost the same, but sometimes a little bit worse fitting quality (higher MSE).

Cauchy formula is good to describe the complex refractive index of low absorption materials: $N = n + ik$, where N is the complex refractive index, n is the real part of N, k is the imaginary part (extinction), i is the imaginary unit: $n(\lambda) = A + B/\lambda^2 + C/\lambda^4$; $k(\lambda) = U_1 e^{U_2(1239.84/\lambda - Eb)}$, where A, B, C, U_1, and U_2 are fitting parameters. The complex refractive index (N) and complex dielectric function ($\varepsilon = \varepsilon_1 + i\varepsilon_2$) are equivalents: $\varepsilon = N^2$; $\varepsilon_1 = n^2 - k^2$, $\varepsilon_2 = 2nk$. The main drawback of the Cauchy formula is that it is good only below the bandgap.

The Tauc-Lorentz (T-L) oscillator model is a combination of the Tauc and Lorentz models [18]. T-L model contains four parameters: Transition Amplitude, Broadening coefficient of the Lorentz oscillator, peak position for the Lorentz oscillator, and Bandgap Energy (E_g), which is taken to be the photon energy, where ε_2 (E) reaches zero. When the E photon energy is less than the bandgap energy, Eg, ε_2 (E) is zero. The real part of the dielectric function ε_1 (E) can be obtained from ε_2 (E) through the Kramers-Kronig relation.

We determined the dispersions for pure (100%) WO_3 and MoO_3 using both the Cauchy formula and the Tauc-Lorenz model. Considering the fitted SE spectra (for example, 100% WO_3 in Figure 4) using the Cauchy and Tauc-Lorentz (T-L) formulas, we can see, especially in the UV part, that the Tauc-Lorentz oscillator model is better (lower MSE) for these materials, even below 300 nm. Notably, the T-L formula has only 4 parameters. During the following optical models, we used the determined complex refractive indices (and complex dielectric functions) of the pure WO_3 and MoO_3 using the Tauc-Lorentz oscillator model, see Figure 3b. Finding the best match (see Figure 4) between the model and the experiment is typically achieved through regression. An estimator, such as the Mean Squared Error (MSE), is used to quantify the difference between curves.

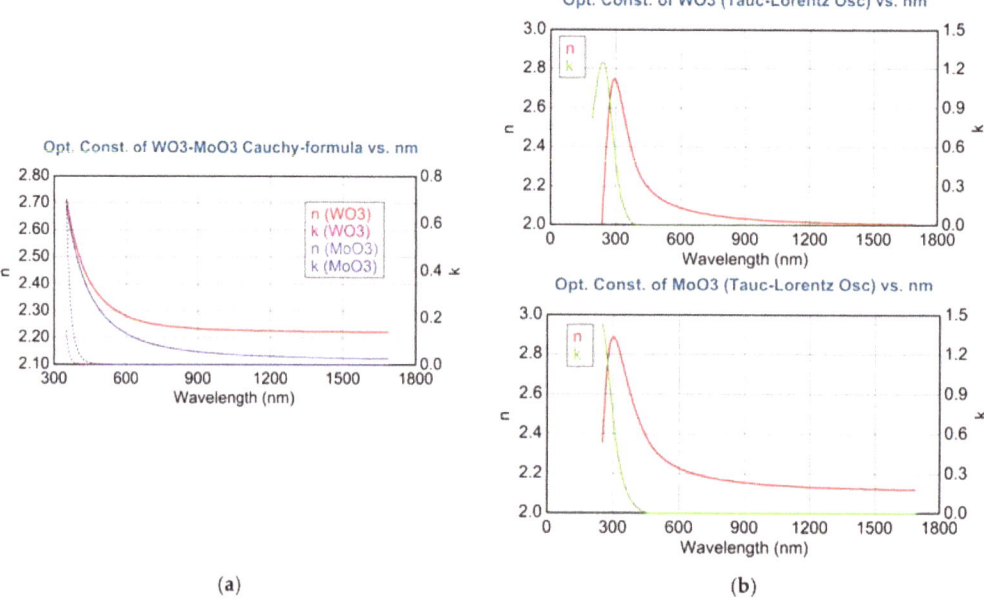

Figure 3. Determined complex refractive indices: (**a**) Using the Cauchy formula for the pure WO$_3$ and MoO$_3$; (**b**) using the Tauc-Lorentz oscillator model for pure WO$_3$ (upper) and MoO$_3$ (lower).

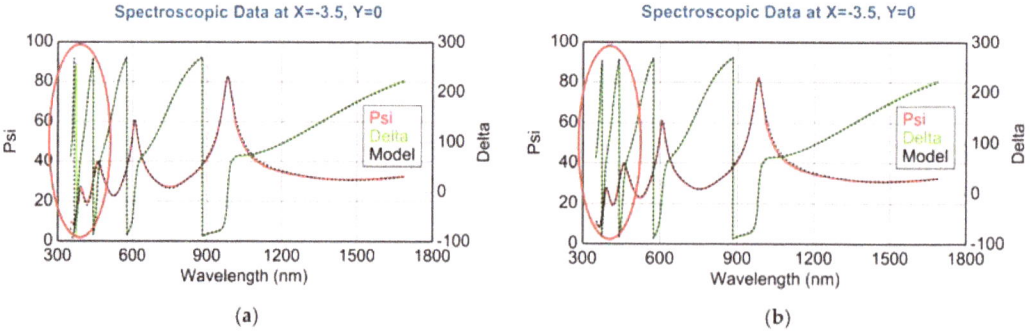

Figure 4. Measured (continuous lines) and fitted (dotted lines) SE spectra for the 100% WO$_3$ layer composition using Cauchy (**a**) and Tauc-Lorentz (T-L) (**b**) formulas. Red ellipses show the region where the quality of the fit is different, and is better using the Tauc-Lorentz formula.

3. Results and Discussion

3.1. Single-Target Samples

First, we performed single target depositions to assess the lateral distribution of sputtered material flux in the case of single W- and single Mo-targets at different electrical powers. When the composition is not changing, the expanded beam mapping is not bad, see Figure 5. Herein, we compare the results of expanded beam mapping (Figure 5a) and the Woollam M2000 map (Figure 5b). Notably, the M2000 map is compiled from four independently measured 15 × 15 cm parts and we tried to compose the whole map along the "iso-thickness" or "iso-color lines".

One can find a good summary regarding the "Mapping and imaging of thin films on large surfaces" in [19].

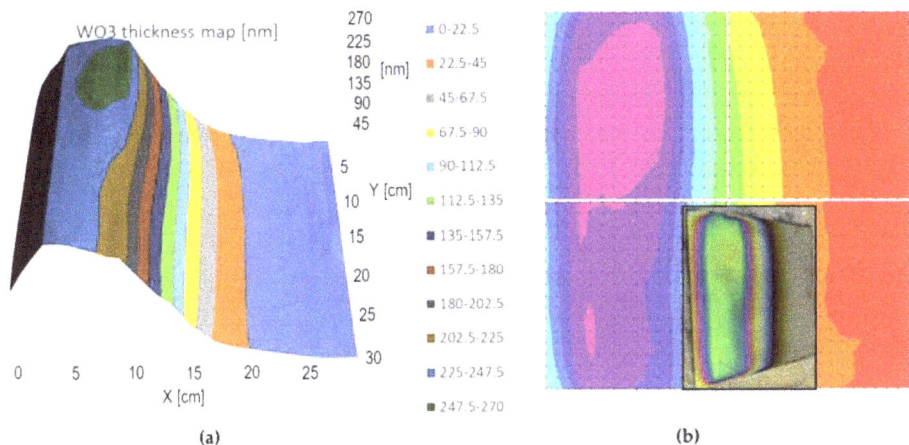

Figure 5. Thickness-maps (in nm) of a 30 × 30 cm sample. Maximum thickness value is 270 nm. One can compare (**a**) the results of expanded beam mapping and (**b**) the Woollam M2000 map. Notably, the M2000 map is compiled from four independently measured 15 × 15 cm parts. The photograph (inserted) shows the direct view of the sample.

3.2. Thickness vs. Power

We performed single-target experiments to assess the deposition rate dependence on the power and on the distance from the target. In this way, we determined the angle dependence of "the material stream". We used 1.5, 1, and 0.75 kW powers. The layer deposition rate is non-linear: Double power results in 7 times higher rate in the case of WO_3. Figures 6–8 are not fully relevant for the "double-target" experiments due to the different "walking" speeds and distances. "W-target only" and "Mo-target only" indicate that only the target was under electrical power during the deposition process. "Walking" speed indicates the speed of the 30 × 30 cm glass sample between the end positions (the edges of the targets). All these maps were measured by our Woollam M2000 SE device.

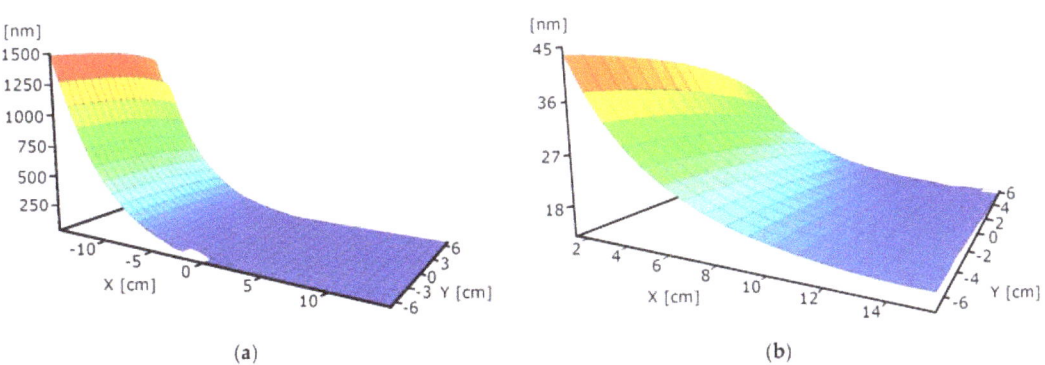

Figure 6. Thickness-maps (in nm) of "W-target only" sample at 1.5 kW power. Maximum thickness value is around 1500 nm. The left map (**a**) shows the middle 15 × 30 cm part, the right map (**b**) shows the thin part with magnified scale (maximum thickness value is around 45 nm).

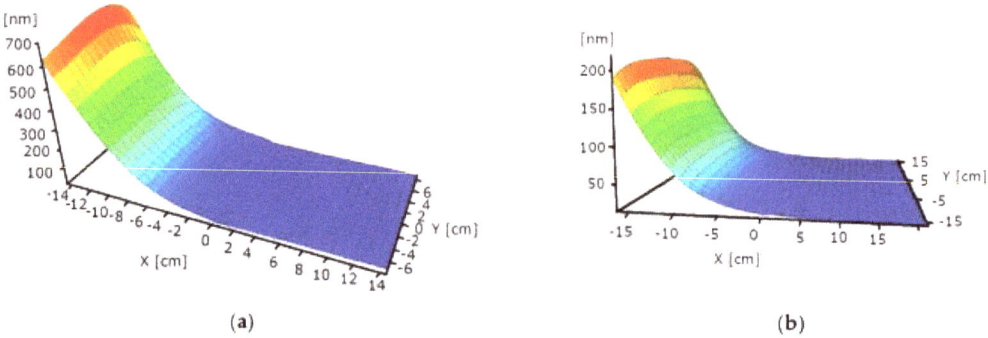

Figure 7. Thickness-maps (in nm) of "W-target only" samples at 1 (a) and 0.75 (b) kW power. Maximum thickness value is around 700 and 200 nm, respectively.

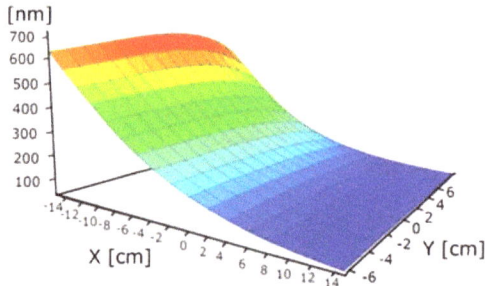

Figure 8. Thickness-map (in nm) of "Mo-target only" sample at 1 kW power. Maximum thickness value is around 700 nm, which corresponds to the W maximum thickness.

Similar measurements were performed for the Mo-target, as well. We show here only the 1 kW case, since it provides similar results to the "W-target only" case. Additionally, we used the small Si-probes (at the center lines of the 30 × 30 cm glass sheets, see later in the "3.3. Double-Target Samples") to determine the thickness by RBS as an independent method.

3.3. Double-Target Samples

3.3.1. Targets in Closer Position

The first (combinatorial) experiment was performed in the "targets in closer position" (Figure 1a); the power of the W-target was 0.75 kW and the power of the Mo-target was 1.5 kW. The choice of the W/Mo power ratio was based on the individual thickness profiles and was created to ensure that the 50% composition falls in the middle of the sample. Additionally, 300 walking cycles were applied with 5 cm/s walking speed. (We can calculate ~1 nm of sublayer thickness around the center part, where the 50% mixture is expected).

We used a 2-Tauc-Lorentz (2-T-L) oscillator optical model: W-substrate/interface-layer/T-L(WO_3)+T-L(MoO_3)-mixed-layer/surface-roughness-layer. (This model layer is better for atomic mixture). Additionally, five fitted parameters were used: Layer thickness and the two Amplitudes (oscillator strengths). The basic parameters (the Broadenings, the Peak positions, and the Bandgap Energies) of the clean materials were determined from the measurements near the edges of the samples. The typical values of surface roughness and interface thickness are not more than 10 and 20 nm, see, for example, Figure 9b.

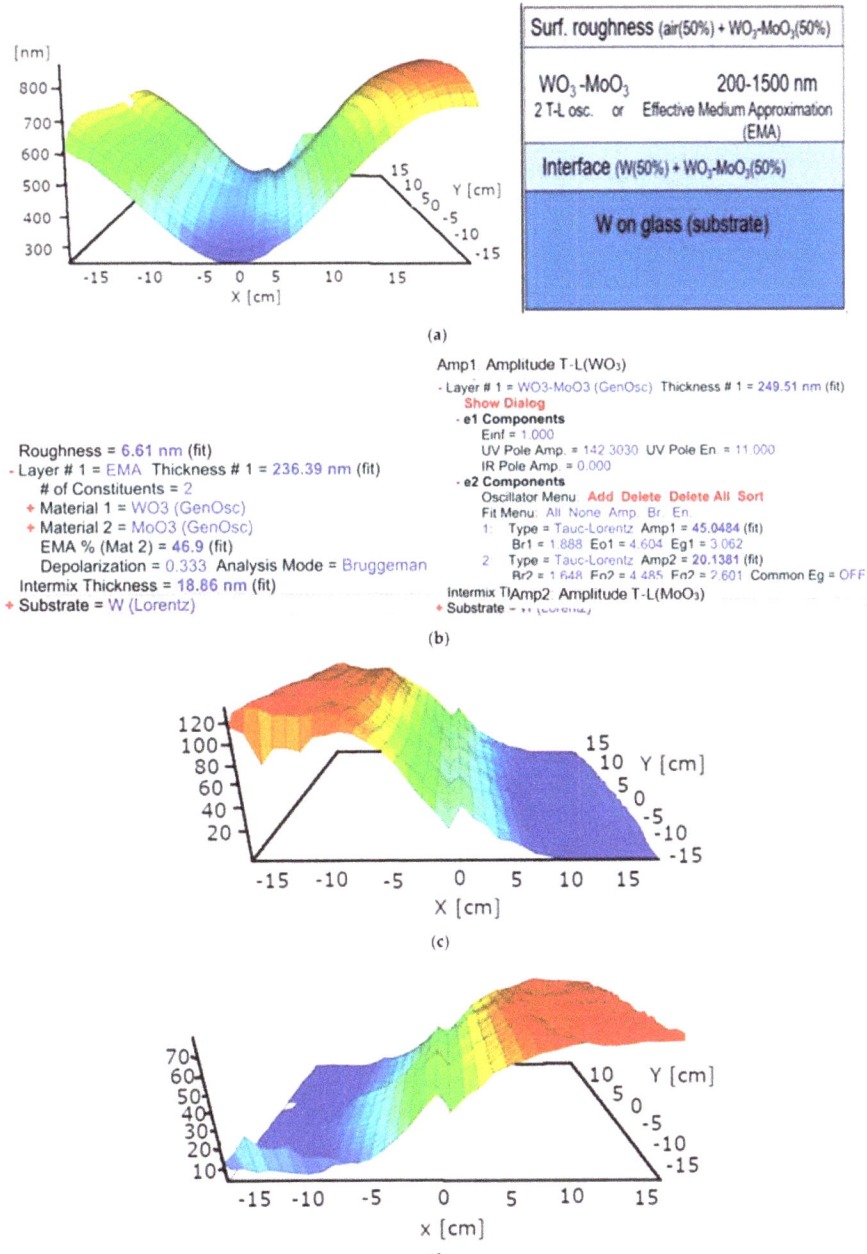

Figure 9. (a) Thickness-map and the schematic optical model; (b) two versions of the optical model: The Bruggeman Effective Medium Model (left), the 2-Tauc-Lorentz (2-T-L) oscillator model (right), "(fit)" show the fitted parameters; (c) Amp1: Amplitude-of-T-L(WO$_3$)–map; (d) Amp2: Amplitude-of-T-L(MoO$_3$)–map (the wrinkles at the center lines are artefacts caused by the manual "rotation" during the SE measurement).

Figure 9 shows the resulted maps (with the schematic optical model): Thickness-map and two Amplitude-maps (T-L(WO$_3$)–map and T-L(MoO$_3$)–map). One can see that the composition (Amplitudes) changes from 0 to 100% in the middle of 10–15 cm wide range.

The Amp$_{WO3}$/Amp$_{WO3-100\%}$ and Amp$_{MoO3}$/Amp $_{MoO3-100\%}$ ratios "move" to the opposite direction (Amp$_{WO3}$ = Amp1 and Amp$_{MoO3}$ = Amp2 the fitted parameters, see Figure 9b–d) and these Amplitude ratios are good estimators (within the fitted errors) for the W/Mo atomic ratio. We validated the results with the RBS results shown in Figure 10.

The composition at the different lateral positions were checked by RBS measurements, as well (see Figures 10 and 11), which shows a good agreement between the results of the two methods. Notably, the yield counts of the background free oxygen signal (channels #200–320) in the RBS spectra provides an uncertainty less than 8% for the stoichiometric ratio of oxygen in the (W$_x$Mo$_y$)O$_3$ layer, while for Mo and W, the error of x and y is less than 2% due to their significantly higher RBS yields. Nevertheless, the three components are fitted together, thus their atomic ratios are coupled in the simulation when looking for the best fit of measured data (red line). This provides a lower limit for the error of the oxygen content, as well. Therefore, the highest error 2% (±0.06) can be considered for the stoichiometric index of O.

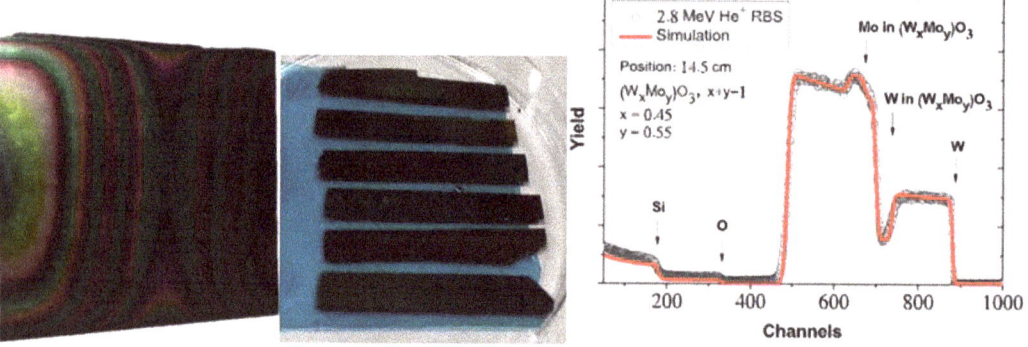

Figure 10. Photograph of one sample (left). Photograph of the Si-probes, which were placed at the center line of some samples for RBS and XRD (center). One Rutherford Backscattering Spectrometry example near the center position.

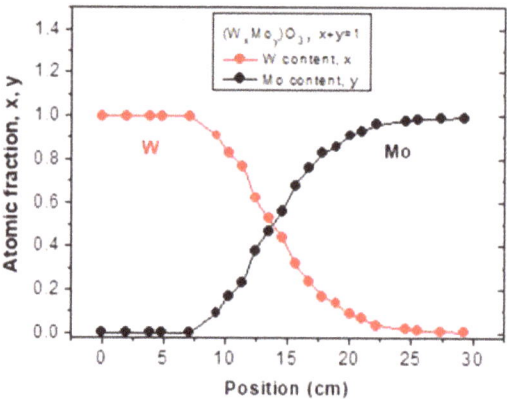

Figure 11. Composition-map along a central line by Rutherford Backscattering Spectrometry.

3.3.2. Atomic (or "Molecular") Mixture vs. "Superlattice"

We prepared two different samples in the "targets at distant position" mode (Figure 1b). The difference was the walking speed (and the number of the walking cycles): One "Fast" (walking speed: 25 cm/s) and one "Slow" (walking speed: 1 cm/s) sample. The different speeds resulted in different "sublayer thickness" of ~0.5 nm for the "Fast" sample and 3–5 nm for the "Slow" sample, calculated from the final thickness and the number of the walking cycles around the center part, where the 50–50% mixture is expected. We used two types of optical models: 2-T-L oscillator model and Effective Medium Approximation (EMA [17]) model (see Figure 9, upper right). Finding the best match between the model and the experiment is typically achieved through regression. An estimator, such as the Mean Squared Error (MSE), is used to quantify the difference between curves. We can choose between the optical models with the MSE-maps: The model is better if the MSE values are significantly lower at the relevant (around 50–50% composition) positions (see for example Figure 12). These figures show only the interesting quarters of the maps where the composition is changing faster.

"Fast" Sample, 25 cm/s Walking: ~0.5 nm "Sublayer Thickness"

The thickness of the layer around the center part is app. 1000 nm. We can calculate a "sublayer thickness" of ~0.5 nm for this "Fast" sample from the number of the walking cycles (1500) and we can consider it an atomic mixture. Thickness-maps (Figure 13) show nearly the same results for both optical models. The Amplitude-of-T-L (only WO$_3$)–map and the EMA (volume percent of WO$_3$)–map (Figure 14) and MSE-maps (Figure 12) show similar tendencies. However, the 2-T-L oscillator model shows significantly lower MSE values against the Effective Medium Approximation model, see the red ellipses in Figure 12. The significantly lower MSE values (around the 50–50% ratio) show that the 2-T-L oscillator model is better for this type (atomic mixture) of layer structure.

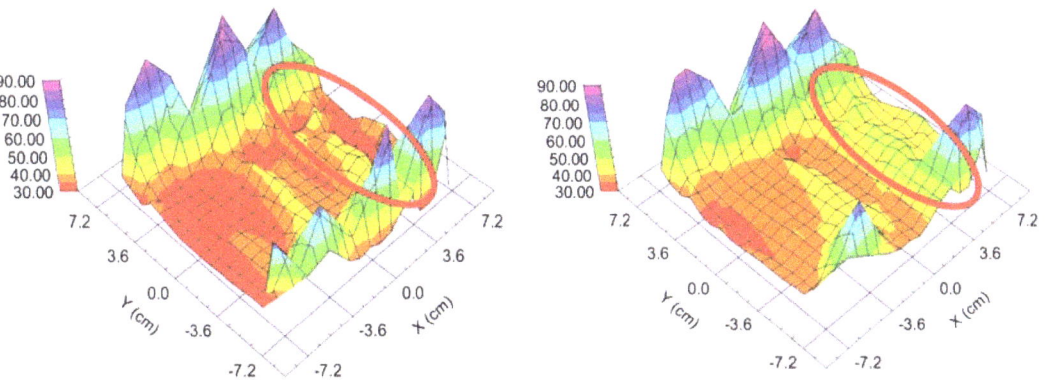

(a) MSE-map from the "2-T-L oscillator model" (b) From the "Effective Medium Approximation model"

Figure 12. Mean Squared Error (MSE)-maps (**a**) using the 2-Tauc-Lorentz (2-T-L) oscillator model (**b**) and the Effective Medium Approximation model. Red ellipses show the interesting area, where the composition changes the most. We show only one 15 × 15 cm part, all other parts show the same tendencies.

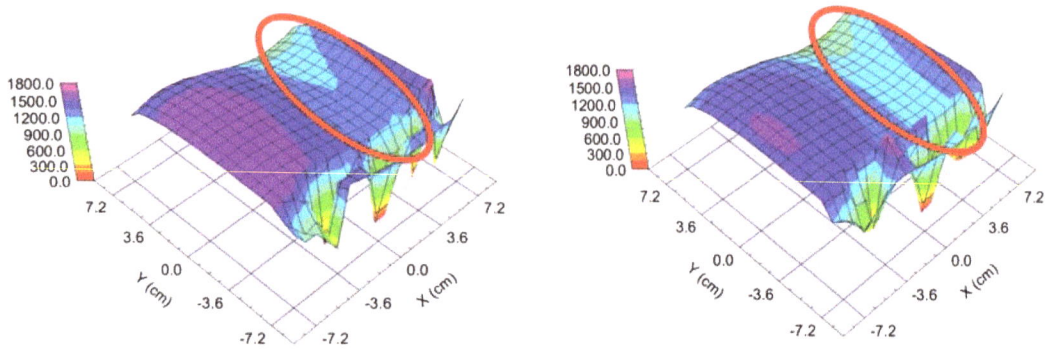

(a) Thickness-map [nm] from the "2-T-L oscillator model"   (b) From the "Effective Medium Approximation model"

Figure 13. Thickness-maps (a) using the 2-Tauc-Lorentz (2-T-L) oscillator model (b) and the Effective Medium Approximation model. Red ellipses show the interesting area, where the composition changes the most. We show only one 15 × 15 cm part, all other parts show the same tendencies.

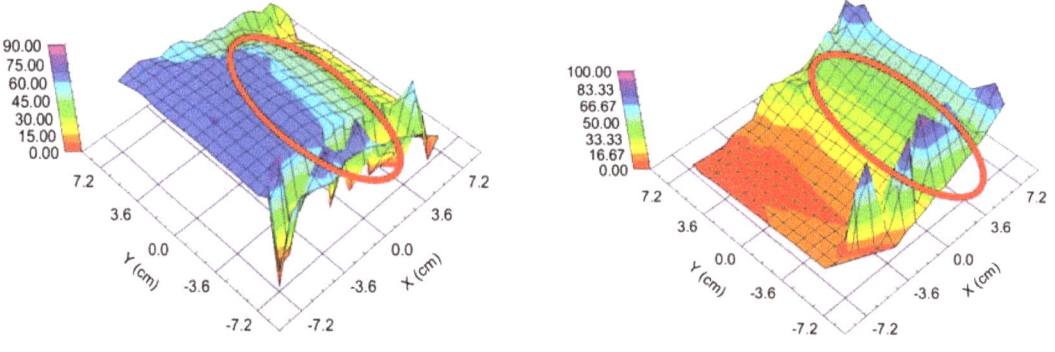

(a) Composition-map: Oscillator amplitude from the "2-T-L oscillator model"   (b) % From the "Effective Medium Approximation model"

Figure 14. Amplitude-of-T-L (only WO_3)–map (a) and EMA% (MoO_3)–map (b). Red ellipses show the interesting area, where the composition changes the most. We show only one 15 × 15 cm part, all other parts show the same tendencies.

The measured and fitted example spectra in Figure 15 show that the 2-T-L model is better, especially under the 450 nm wavelength region (see red ellipses) where the light absorption is significant.

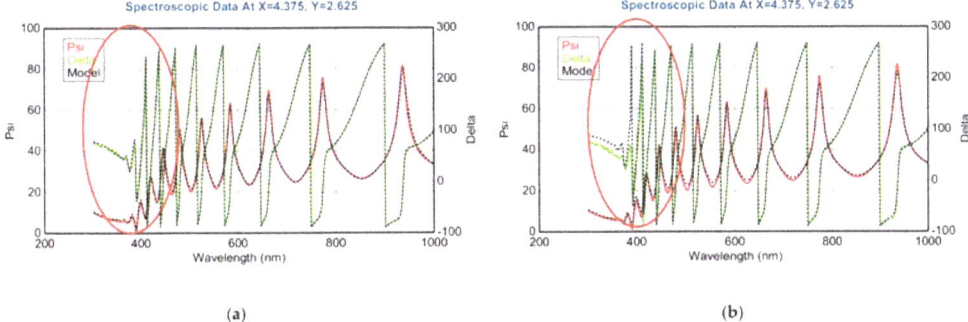

Figure 15. Measured and fitted spectra at one sample point: 2-Tauc-Lorentz (2-T-L) oscillator model. (**a**) Fit error (MSE) = 30.4, Thickness = 1159.6 ± 2.9 nm, Amp1 = 39.2 ± 1.1, Amp2 = 26.7 ± 0.4), and Effective Medium Approximation model; (**b**) fit error (MSE) = 40.1, Thickness = 1081.7 ± 2.8 nm, EMA% (Mat2) = 41.8 ± 0.8).

"Slow" Sample, 1 cm/s Walking: 3–5 nm Sublayer Thickness

The thickness of the layer around the center part is app. 280 nm. We can calculate a "sublayer thickness" of ~4 nm for this "Slow" sample from the number of the walking cycles (70) and we can consider it as a "superlattice". (We can call it is superlattice only at 50–50%, otherwise we could call it a type of superlattice).

The Amplitude-of-T-L (only WO$_3$)–map, MSE-maps (Figure 16), thickness-maps (Figure 17) and the EMA (volume percent of MoO$_3$)–map (Figure 18) show similar tendencies. However, the Effective Medium Approximation model shows significantly lower MSE values against the 2-T-L-oscillator-model, see the red ellipses in Figure 16. The significantly lower values around the center part, especially around the 50–50% ratio, show that the Effective Medium Approximation oscillator model is better for this "superlattice" type of layer structure. The measured and fitted example spectra in Figure 18 show that the Effective Medium Approximation model is better with a 1.3% precision of the composition (volume fraction) parameter.

The measured and fitted example spectra in Figure 19 show that the EMA model is better for the "superlattice" type of layer structure.

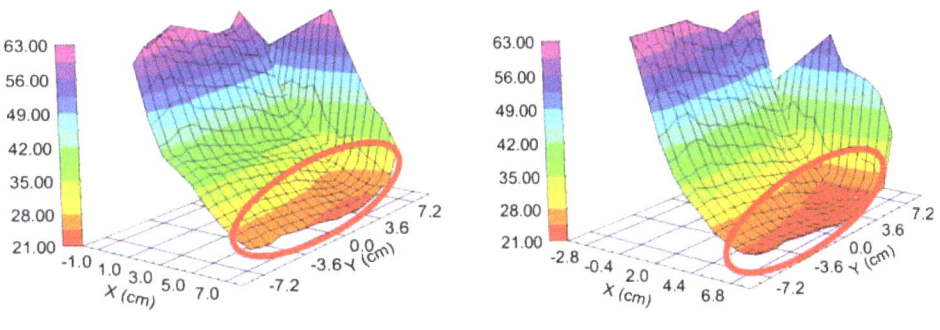

(**a**) MSE-map from the "2-T-L oscillator model"   (**b**) From the "Effective Medium Approximation model"

Figure 16. Mean Squared Error (MSE)-maps (**a**) using the 2-Tauc-Lorentz (2-T-L) oscillator model (**b**) and the Effective Medium Approximation model. Red ellipses show the interesting area, where the composition changes the most. We show only one 15 × 15 cm part, all other parts show the same tendencies.

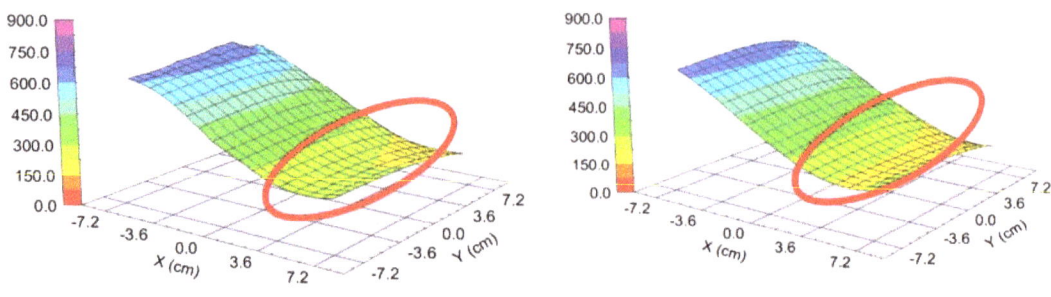

(a) Thickness-map [nm] from the "2-T-L oscillator model" (b) From the "Effective Medium Approximation model"

Figure 17. Thickness-maps (a) using the 2-Tauc-Lorentz (2-T-L) oscillator model (b) and the Effective Medium Approximation model. Red ellipses show the interesting area, where the composition changes the most. We show only one 15 × 15 cm part, all other parts show the same tendencies.

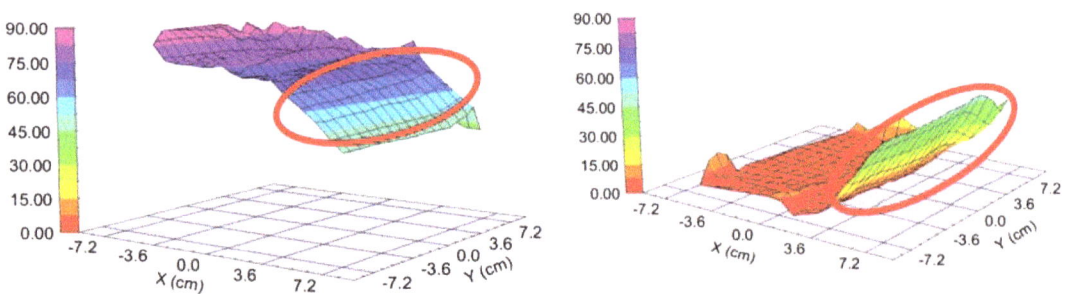

(a) Composition-map: Amplitude from the "2-T-L oscillator model" (b) % From the "Effective Medium Approximation model"

Figure 18. Amplitude-of-T-L (only WO_3)–map (a) and EMA% (MoO_3)–map (b). Red ellipses show the interesting area, where the composition changes the most. We show only one 15 × 15 cm part, all other parts show the same tendencies.

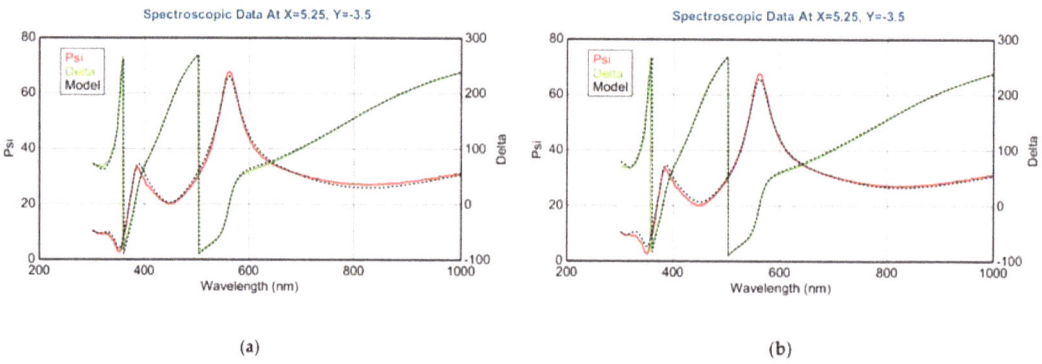

(a) (b)

Figure 19. Measured and fitted spectra at one sample point: 2-Tauc-Lorentz (2-T-L) oscillator model. (a) Fit error (MSE) = 29.2, Thickness = 230.4 ± 0.8 nm, Amp1 = 58.0 ± 1.5, Amp2 = 11.4 ± 0.7, and Effective Medium Approximation model; (b) fit error (MSE) = 24.8, Thickness = 218.0 ± 0.1 nm, EMA% (Mat2) = 28.5 ± 1.3.

4. Conclusions

In summary, we can produce combinatorial samples on large scale in a magnetron sputtering system. These samples can be mapped (thickness and composition maps, as well) in a fast and non-destructive manner by Spectroscopic Ellipsometry. Moreover, we can choose between appropriate optical models (2-Tauc-Lorentz oscillator model vs. the Bruggeman Effective Medium Approximation, BEMA) depending on the process parameters. In conclusion, if one has more than one "molecular layer" in the "sublayers", BEMA can be used. If one has an atomic mixture, the multiple oscillator model is better (more precise) for this type of layer structure.Moreover, our conclusion is that in the case of "atomic mixing", the two Amplitudes of the 2-Tauc-Lorentz oscillator (one T-L oscillator for the WO_3 component and one T-L oscillator for the MoO_3 component) is a better estimator for the atomic ratio of the W/Mo ratio.

In this way, we have a fast and non-destructive (contactless) method to determine the position dependent composition of our combinatorial samples when we measure the optimal electrochromic behavior of these samples [20].

Author Contributions: Conceptualization, M.F. and Z.L.; methodology, M.F. and Z.L.; validation, Z.E.H. (XRD) and Z.Z. (RBS); formal analysis, M.F., R.B. and D.T.; investigation, M.F. and Z.L.; writing and editing, M.F. All authors have read and agreed to the published version of the manuscript.

Funding: This research was funded by NKFIH OTKA NN 131269 (VOC-DETECT M-ERA.NET Transnational Call 2018) and NKFIH OTKA K129009 projects.

Institutional Review Board Statement: Not applicable.

Informed Consent Statement: Not applicable.

Data Availability Statement: Not applicable.

Conflicts of Interest: The authors declare no conflict of interest.

References

1. Granqvist, C.G. *Handbook of Inorganic Electrochromic Materials*; Elsevier: Amsterdam, The Netherlands, 1995.
2. Livage, J.; Ganguli, D. Sol-gel electrochromic coatings and devices: A review. *Sol. Energy Mater. Sol. Cells.* **2001**, *68*, 365–381. [CrossRef]
3. Hsu, C.S.; Chan, C.C.; Huang, H.T.; Peng, C.H.; Hsu, W.C. Electrochromic properties of nanocrystalline MoO3 thin films. *Thin Solid Film.* **2008**, *516*, 4839–4844. [CrossRef]
4. Lin, S.-Y.; Wang, C.-M.; Kao, K.-S.; Chen, Y.-C.; Liu, C.-C. Electrochromic properties of MoO3 thin films derived by a sol–gel process. *J. Sol Gel Sci. Technol.* **2010**, *53*, 51–58. [CrossRef]
5. Madhavi, V.; Jeevan Kumar, P.; Kondaiah, P.; Hussain, O.M.; Uthanna, S. Effect of molybdenum doping on the electrochromic properties of tungsten oxide thin films by RF magnetron sputtering. *Ionics* **2014**, *20*, 1737–1745. [CrossRef]
6. Ivanova, T.; Gesheva, K.A.; Kalitzova, M.; Hamelmann, F.; Luekermann, F.; Heinzmann, U. Electrochromic mixed films based on WO3 and MoO3, obtained by an APCVD method. *J. Optoelectron. Adv. Mater.* **2009**, *11*, 1513–1516.
7. Novinrooz, A.; Sharbatdaran, M.; Noorkojouri, H. Structural and optical properties of WO3 electrochromic layers prepared by the sol-gel method. *Cent. Eur. Sci. J.* **2005**, *3*, 456–466. [CrossRef]
8. Prameelaand, C.; Srinivasarao, K. Characterization of (MoO3)x-(Wo3)1-x composites. *Int. J. Appl. Eng. Res.* **2015**, *10*, 9865–9875.
9. Zimmer, A.; Gilliot, M.; Broch, L.; Boulanger, C.; Stein, N.; Horwat, D. Morphological and chemical dynamics upon electrochemical cyclic sodiation of electrochromic tungsten oxide coatings extracted by in situ ellipsometry. *Appl. Opt.* **2020**, *59*, 3766–3772. [CrossRef] [PubMed]
10. Sauvet, K.; Rougier, A.; Sauques, L. Electrochromic WO3 thin films active in the IR region. *Sol. Energy Mater. Sol. Cells* **2008**, *92*, 209–215. [CrossRef]
11. Hales, J.S.; DeVries, M.; Dworak, B.; Woollam, J.A. Visible and infrared optical constants of electrochromic materials for emissivity modulation applications. *Thin Solid Film.* **1998**, *313–314*, 205. [CrossRef]
12. Available online: https://www.jawoollam.com/products/m-2000-ellipsometer (accessed on 15 May 2022).
13. Fried, M. On-line monitoring of solar cell module production by ellipsometry technique. *Thin Solid Film.* **2014**, *571*, 345–355. [CrossRef]
14. Major, C.; Juhasz, G.; Labadi, Z.; Fried, M. High speed spectroscopic ellipsometry technique for on-line monitoring in large area thin layer production. In Proceedings of the IEEE 42nd Photovoltaic Specialist Conference, PVSC, New Orleans, LA, USA, 14–19 June 2015; pp. 1–6. Available online: https://ieeexplore.ieee.org/document/7355640 (accessed on 15 May 2022). [CrossRef]

15. Horváth, Z.G.; Juhász, G.; Fried, M.; Major, C.; Petrik, P. Imaging Optical Inspection Device with a Pinhole Camera U.S. Patent 8437002 B2, 23 May 2007.
16. Kótai, E. Computer Methods for Analysis and Simulation of RBS and ERDA spectra. *Nucl. Instr. Meth. B* **1994**, *85*, 588–596. [CrossRef]
17. Bruggeman, D.A.G. Dielectric constant and conductivity of mixtures of isotropic materials. *Ann. Phys.* **1935**, *24*, 636–664. [CrossRef]
18. Jellison, G.E., Jr.; Modine, F.A. Parameterization of the optical functions of amorphous materials in the interband region. *Appl. Phys. Lett.* **1996**, *69*, 371. [CrossRef]
19. Petrik, P.; Fried, M. Mapping and imaging of thin films on large surfaces. *Phys. Status Solidi* **2022**, *219*, 2100800. [CrossRef]
20. Labadi, Z.; Takács, D.; Zolnai, Z.; Petrik, P.; Fried, M. Electrochromic properties of mixed-oxide WO3/MoO3 films deposited by reactive sputtering. *Appl. Surf. Sci.* 2022. *submitted*

Article

Device and Circuit Analysis of Double Gate Field Effect Transistor with Mono-Layer WS$_2$-Channel at Sub-2 nm Technology Node

Jihun Park [†], Changho Ra [†], Jaewon Lim and Jongwook Jeon *

Department of Electrical and Electronics, Konkuk University, Seoul 05029, Korea; gns6702@konkuk.ac.kr (J.P.); wocwoc3@gmail.com (C.R.); ljw1611@konkuk.ac.kr (J.L.)
* Correspondence: jwjeon@konkuk.ac.kr; Tel.: +82-2-450-3494
† These authors contributed equally to this work.

Abstract: In this work, WS$_2$ was adopted as a channel material among transition metal dichalcogenides (TMD) materials that have recently been in the spotlight, and the circuit power performance (power consumption, operating frequency) of the monolayer WS$_2$ field-effect transistor with a double gate structure (DG WS$_2$-FET) was analyzed. It was confirmed that the effective capacitance, which is circuit power performance, was greatly changed by the extrinsic capacitance components of DG WS$_2$-FET, and the spacer region length (L$_{SPC}$) and dielectric constant (K$_{SPC}$) values of the spacer that could affect the extrinsic capacitance components were analyzed to identify the circuit power performance. As a result, when L$_{SPC}$ is increased by 1.5 nm with the typical spacer material (K$_{SPC}$ = 7.5), increased operating speed (+4.9%) and reduced active power (−6.8%) are expected. In addition, it is expected that the spacer material improvement by developing the low-k spacer from K$_{SPC}$ = 7.5 to K$_{SPC}$ = 2 at typical L$_{SPC}$ = 8 nm can increase the operating speed by 36.8% while maintaining similar active power consumption. Considering back-end-of-line (BEOL), the change in circuit power performance according to wire length was also analyzed. From these results, it can be seen that reducing the capacitance components of the extrinsic region is very important for improving the circuit power performance of the DG WS$_2$-FET.

Keywords: WS$_2$; TMD; Sub-2 nm technology; double gate

1. Introduction

Over the past few decades, semiconductor technology has made progress through scaling down and performance improvements of semiconductors according to Moore's Law [1] and the Dennard scaling rule [2]. The planar MOSFET process was successfully replaced and commercialized because the so-called FinFET had better electrostatic control. This success of FinFET has led to the 5 nm technology node and is expected to reach beyond the technology node with the introduction of EUV [3,4]. Thanks to these structural changes and the success of FinFET through process optimization, the introduction of a gate-all-around (GAA) structure has recently been actively attempted in academia and industry. Among them, the nanosheet structure is in the spotlight as a strong candidate because it has gate controllability for channels superior to FinFET and more immunity for short channels [5–7]. It is expected that scaling due to such a structural change will have a limitation of less than or equal to 3 nm technology node, and a new channel material is attracting attention. Germanium and various III-V material-based channels have better carrier mobility than silicon channels and thus have better electrical properties [8,9]. Additionally, the channel application of two-dimensional materials is actively being studied [10]. Among them, it is noted that a TMD material is thin and thus may effectively reduce a short channel effect and replace silicon due to its excellent interface characteristics and excellent mobility characteristics due to an absence of dangling bond due to Van der Waals bonding [11,12]. In addition, the results of device characteristic analysis through process developments such as contact resistance and doping technology and atomic level analysis have recently been announced [13]. In addition, recently, research on TMD materials has been actively conducted, and research on a FinFET device in which a single-layer TMD material is vertically aligned has been conducted [14–18]. Recently, Z.Ahmed presented DG FET with mono-layer WS_2 channels and device and circuit power performance that multi-stacked them, showing the possibility of using TMD in sub-2 nm technology node [19]. In this work, the quantitatively analyzed effect of extrinsic components of DG WS_2-FET on circuit power performance to optimize circuit power performance based on these research results was performed, and a device design guideline for scaling down to improve circuit performance based on DG WS_2-FET is presented. In addition, the changes in circuit power performance according to various circuit layout types were analyzed.

In this work, based on the DG WS_2-FET proposed by Z.Ahmed [19], a circuit model library was developed, and device and circuit co-analysis was performed. Through this, the effect of front-end-of-line (FEOL), middle-of-line (MOL), and BEOL on the circuit in DG WS_2-FET technology is analyzed, and optimization through changes in the performance of the circuit by various K_{SPC} and contacted gate pitch (CGP) by spacer length is analyzed (CGP = L_{CH} + L_{CNT} + 2 L_{SPC}). Through this, we present a circuit process development guide for TMD materials that are spotlighted as next-generation materials beyond silicon.

2. Device and Circuit Co-Analysis of DG WS_2-FET

The scaling-down technology based on the CGP and metal pitch (MP) becomes the core of the semiconductor scaling technology, enabling low power and high operating speed. However, silicon technology is facing limitations, and TMD continues to scale down beyond its limitations due to its material characteristics. Figure 1 shows the DG WS_2-FET used in this work. Based on the CGP for the 2 nm technology node [19], CGP by various spacer lengths is presented and summarized as a physical parameter in Table 1. The source/drain extension region below the spacer was considered a heavily doped region with a carrier density (N_{SD}) of 1.6×10^{13} cm^{-2}, and the resistance of the extension region is 16 $\Omega \cdot \mu m$.

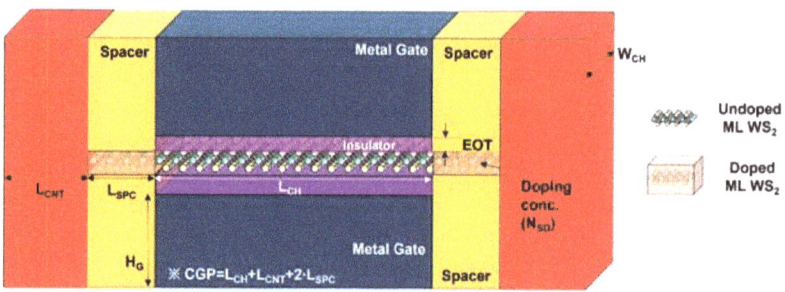

Figure 1. Structure of DG WS_2-FET used in this work.

Table 1. Key device geometric parameters of DG WS_2-FET.

	Geometric Parameter			
CGP (nm)	42	43	44	45
L_{SPC} (nm)	8	8.5	9	9.5
L_G (nm)	14	14	14	14
MP (nm)	16	16	16	16
L_{CNT} (nm)	12	12	12	12
EOT (nm)	0.5	0.5	0.5	0.5
W_{CH} (nm)	52	52	52	52
H_G (nm)	20	20	20	20

W_{CH}: width of the channel of DG WS_2-FET.

The electrical properties of DG WS$_2$-FET were obtained using atomistic analysis and the calibrated commercial TCAD simulator. The calibration process of DG WS$_2$-FET in Figure 1 was performed using the I-V transfer curve based on the atomistic level simulation of Ref. [19], and through this process, the C-V characteristic curve was obtained to secure the electrical characteristics of DG WS$_2$-FET. Note that an effective mobility (= 200 cm^2/V·s) of the monolayer WS$_2$ channel was estimated in previous work [19] through atomistic calculation, and we take this value in I-V characteristics. Based on the obtained I-V and C-V data, circuit model library generation was performed by using BSIM-IMG [20]. Figure 2 shows the overall BSIM-IMG model parameter extraction flow used in this work. Figure 3a is I-V transfer curve that can confirm the consistency of reference device simulation and performed circuit simulation. The off current (I_{OFF}) was the current flowing through the channel when $V_{GS} = 0$ V and $V_{DS} = 0.6$ V (supply voltage), and it was targeted at 2 nA. Figure 3b,c are the drain current change and gate capacitance change according to the change of L_{SPC}, respectively. As shown in Figure 3b, when the L_{SPC} increases, the current of the DG WS$_2$-FET decreases because of the resistance component in the extension.

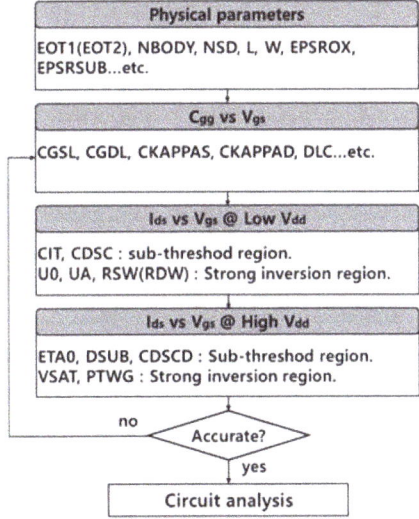

Figure 2. BSIM-IMG model parameter extraction flow used in this work.

Region (R_{EXT}) increases. This phenomenon is the same as the general phenomenon that appears in devices such as silicon FinFET [21]. However, although the I_{ON}/I_{OFF} ratio and subthreshold swing (SS) are noticeably changed in silicon FinFET, there is little I_{ON}/I_{OFF} ratio and SS change because the L_{SPC} change is very small in this work (in all cases of $L_{SPC} = 8$ nm ~ 9.5 nm of DG WS$_2$-FET, the I_{ON}/I_{OFF} ratio is about 1.33×10^5, and SS is about 69 mV/dec). As L_{SPC} increases in Figure 3c, the gate capacitance decreases because the capacitance component by the gate fringe field (C_{EXT}) and the capacitance component between the gate and MOL contact (C_{MOL}) are affected by the L_{SPC}. That is, it can be seen that L_{SPC} is a key parameter that scales R_{EXT} and C_{MOL}, which are parasitic components excluding the intrinsic components of the device. In addition, it can be expected that there will be a change in the extrinsic component not only in the L_{SPC} but also in the change in the spacer material. Therefore, the influence of the lower dielectric constant of the spacer (K_{SPC}) was also investigated. As shown in Figure 3d, the gate capacitance is significantly reduced by reducing K_{SPC} as C_{EXT} and C_{MOL} are reduced by the influence of K_{SPC}.

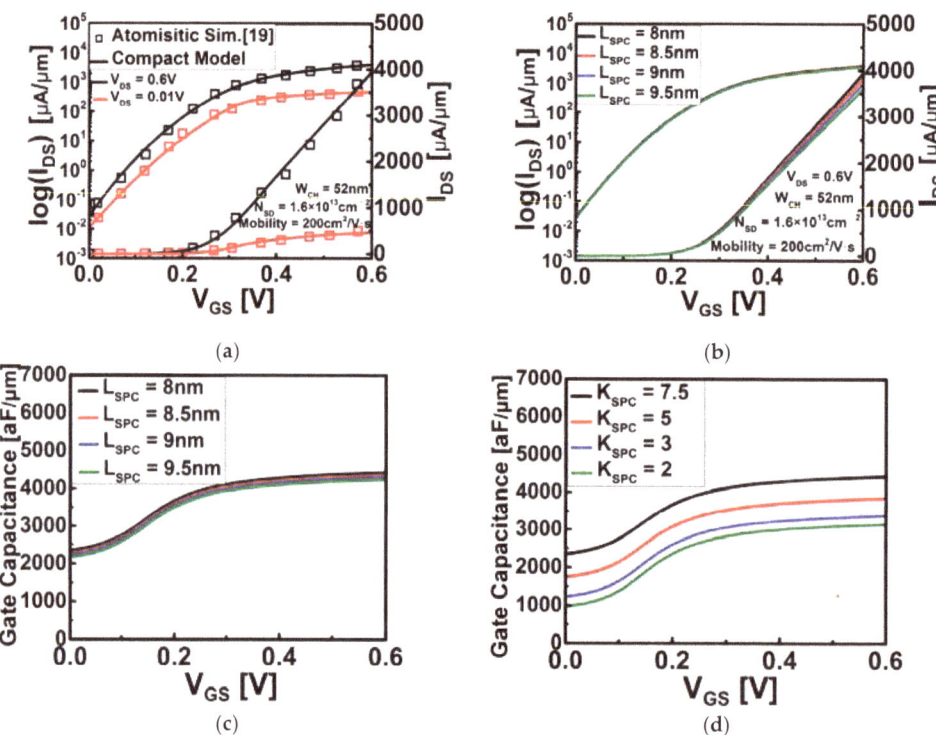

Figure 3. (a) I–V transfer curve of DG WS$_2$-FET. The black line is when high voltage (V$_{DS}$ = 0.6 V) is applied, and the red line is when the low voltage (V$_{DS}$ = 0.01 V) is applied; (b) I–V transfer curve according to L$_{SPC}$ when high voltage applied; (c) gate capacitance according to L$_{SPC}$; and (d) gate capacitance according to K$_{SPC}$.

The circuit simulator and circuit scheme used in this work are Synopsys' HSPICE and inverter ring-oscillator with fan-out = 3 (FO3 INV RO), respectively, which are widely used in the industry. The FO3 INV RO circuit is depicted in Figure 4a and consists of 15 stages. The R/C component of the BEOL load was attached between the output of one inverter and the input of the next stage. From the INV RO circuit simulation results as shown in Figure 4b, the average signal delay can be extracted to obtain a frequency representing the speed of the operation, and the active dynamic power at the same static power can be extracted.

Figure 5a illustrates the change in circuit power performance when considering contact resistance (R$_{CNT}$) and MOL R/C components (R$_{MOL}$, C$_{MOL}$) with intrinsic channel. A contact resistance of 80 Ω·μm, the target value of Ref. [19], was adopted. In the developed circuit model, R$_{CNT}$, R$_{MOL}$, and C$_{MOL}$ were considered by attaching these components to both ends of the source and drain of BSIM-IMG model for the DG WS$_2$-FET. Based on V$_{DD}$ (supply voltage) = 0.7 V, when R$_{CNT}$ was considered under the same power condition, the operation frequency was decreased by 35.6%, and in addition, considering R$_{MOL}$, it was confirmed that there was a decrease of 2.6%, and when C$_{MOL}$ is added, it is decreased by 35.1%.

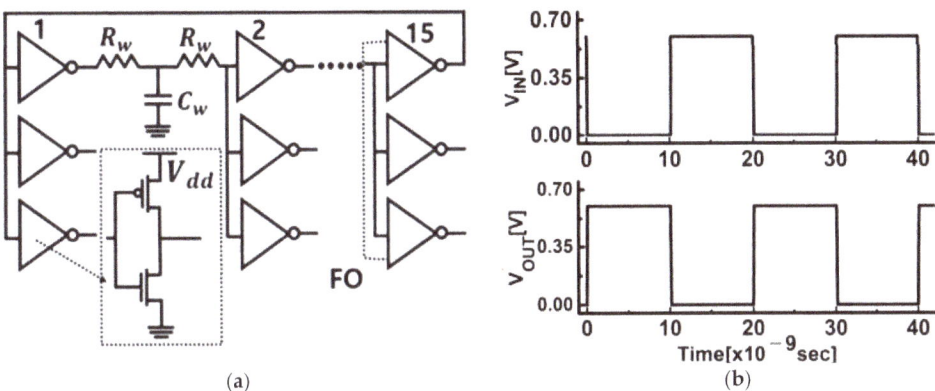

Figure 4. (**a**) Schematic of inverter ring oscillator with fan−out 3, which includes distributed interconnect RC components; (**b**) the transient simulation results of designed inverter ring oscillator.

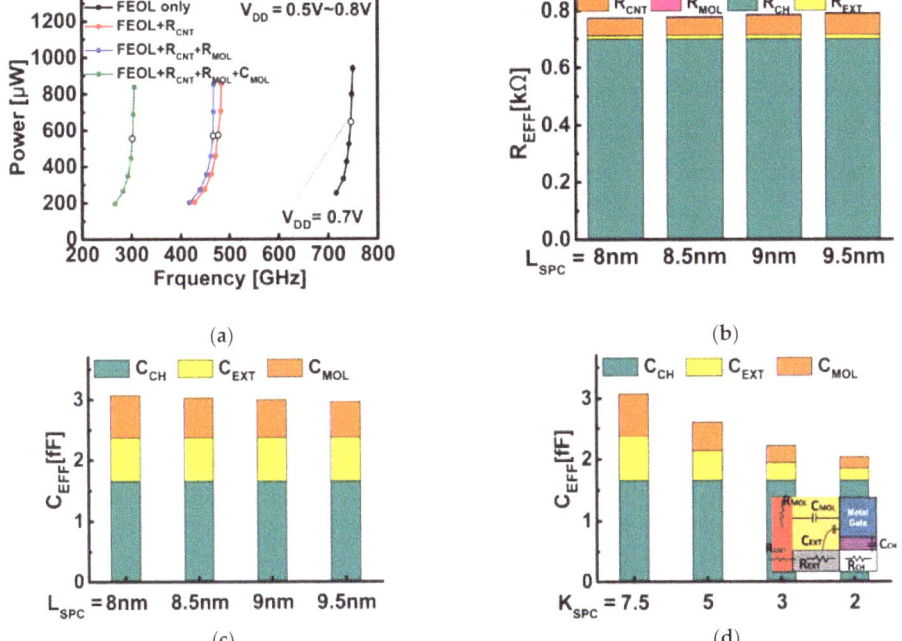

Figure 5. (**a**) Circuit power performance (power consumption, operating frequency) when contact resistance and MOL components are added to the intrinsic channel; (**b**) analysis of results of the effect of various components on circuit using R_{EFF}; (**c**) analysis of results of the effect of various components on circuit according to L_{SPC} using C_{EFF}; (**d**) analysis of results of the effect of various components on circuit according to K_{SPC} using C_{EFF}. The figure inserted in (**d**) shows resistances for channel (R_{CH}), extension (R_{EXT}), contact (R_{CNT}), and MOL (R_{MOL}) and capacitances for channel (C_{CH}), extension (C_{EXT}), and MOL (C_{MOL}), respectively.

The elements that determine the circuit operation characteristics were analyzed using the segmentation technique. This is possible by extracting the operating frequency, the IDDA (active current), and the IDDQ (leakage current) from the inverter ring oscillator circuit.

The operating behavior, and the calculating effective resistance (R_{EFF}) and capacitance (C_{EFF}), represent the circuit operating speed and power consumption [22]. The circuit characteristics were analyzed by adjusting the WS$_2$ channel, contact resistance, and MOL of the circuit model during circuit simulation, and the effects of each component were observed in R_{EFF} and C_{EFF}.

The R_{CH} characteristics that vary with the gate voltage of the device are all reflected in the R_{EFF} obtained from the simulation, including the dynamic behavior characteristics of the circuit, which are shown in Figure 5b. The ratio in which the channel and the extension region form the resistance was extracted from V_{DS} = 0.6 V and V_{GS} = 0.6 V under the condition that only FEOL is considered. In Figure 5b, it can be seen that as the L_{SPC} becomes larger, the R_{EFF} also increases. In particular, the effect of the channel, the contact resistance, and the MOL resistance on circuits is almost constant, even if L_{SPC} changes, and it can be seen that R_{EXT} increases. R_{EXT} increased by about 24% as L_{SPC} increased from 8 nm to 9.5 nm. This fact can be explained in Figure 3b as the L_{SPC} increases and the current decreases. In Figure 5c, it can be observed that as L_{SPC} increases, C_{MOL} mainly decreases and the total C_{EFF} decreases. It can be seen from Figure 5d that the C_{EFF} decreases as the K_{SPC} decreases. C_{EXT} and C_{MOL} can be called the parasitic capacitance components, and as the K_{SPC} decreases, it can be seen that the C_{EXT} and C_{MOL} gradually decrease. Through Figure 5b–d, the R_{EFF} can be improved through L_{SPC} scaling, and the importance of the C_{EFF} can be understood through the change of the spacer material.

Figures 6 and 7 show the results of inverter ring oscillator circuit simulation according to the changes in K_{SPC} and L_{SPC}. Figure 6 shows that the operating frequency is improved by 13% to 37% at V_{DD} = 0.7 V based on the default K_{SPC} (=7.5). As confirmed in Figure 5c, the operating speed of the circuit was improved through the reduction of the capacitance by the K_{SPC}.

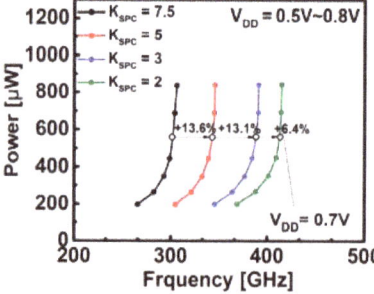

Figure 6. Power versus frequency for DG WS$_2$-FET according to K_{SPC}.

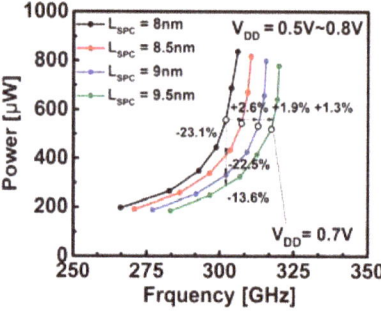

Figure 7. Power versus frequency for DG WS$_2$-FET according to L_{SPC}.

As a result of Figure 7, which shows that the performance increases as the L_{SPC} increases, it can be seen that even if the R_{EXT} increases and the overall resistance increases, the performance is improved due to the capacitance component reduced by the L_{SPC}. At $V_{DD} = 0.7$ V, the frequency increases by 2% to 5% and the power decreases by 3% to 7% based on the default L_{SPC} (=8 nm). Since the increased L_{SPC} from the point of view of area scaling is not positive, the improvement of the K_{SPC} is more effective.

Through Figure 8, the effect of the wiring length and BEOL load on the circuit can be analyzed. The wire resistance of the BEOL load was applied as $R_W = 1447\ \Omega/\mu m$, and the wire capacitance was applied as $C_W = 208\ aF/\mu m$ [23]. As the L_{SPC} changes from 8 nm to 9.5 nm, the CGP changes from 42 nm to 45 nm. Figure 8a shows a power-frequency curve by a BEOL interconnect according to two wiring lengths of 25 CGP and 10 CGP. In each CGP case, it can be seen that the speed change according to the wiring length is 32% to 34%, and the effect of the BEOL component on the circuit is significant. In Figure 8b, the effect of the BEOL load on delay was analyzed by dividing the wiring length into 5 CGP, 25 CGP, and 100 CGP, into short, medium, and long cases, respectively. Based on 25 CGP, the delay decreased by 32% at 5 CGP, and at 100 CGP, the delay increased by 2.5 times. Figure 8c is an analysis of the delay of the circuit according to fan-out dependency when considering the BEOL load. As the fan-out number increases and the total number of inverters in the circuit increases, the delay increases. In addition, it can be seen that not only the delay by the fan-out number increases but also the delay by each component (FEOL, MOL, and BEOL) increases. Figure 8 shows that while the FEOL and MOL processes are of course important, the performance improvements through the BEOL process optimization are essential.

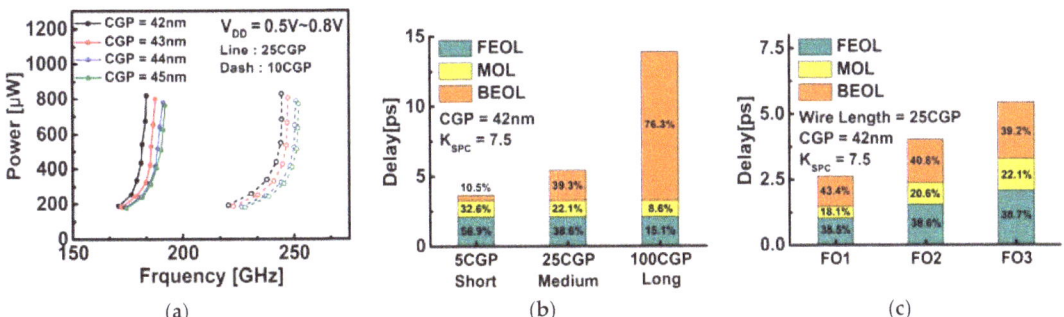

Figure 8. (a) Power versus frequency for DG WS$_2$-FET according to CGP due to changes in L_{SPC} with BEOL load ($K_{SPC} = 7.5$). The wire length is 25 CGP, 10 CGP. (b) Analysis of delay of designed inverter ring oscillator with BEOL load. The wire length was considered in three cases (5 CGP, 25 CGP, and 100 CGP) in the BEOL load. (c) Analysis of delay of designed inverter ring oscillator with BEOL considering fan-out dependency.

3. Conclusions

This work analyzes the effect of performance change through L_{SPC} scaling and K_{SPC} change and the FEOL, MOL, and BEOL components of TMDC FET technology on the circuit based on the previous work using the WS$_2$ channel transistor of the double gate structure. In particular, it was confirmed that increasing L_{SPC} is more beneficial to circuit power performance, but there is a trade-off from the viewpoint of area, and it was also seen that the change in K_{SPC} has a great influence on speed improvement. This work confirmed that BEOL optimization is very important, as well as FEOL and MOL, through the effect of the BEOL load by various CGP cases and wiring lengths and the fan-out number on the circuit.

Author Contributions: J.P. and C.R. contributed to the main idea and writing of this research. J.L. performed the ring oscillator simulations. This research was planned and executed under the supervision of J.J. All authors have read and agreed to the published version of the manuscript.

Funding: This work was supported the National Foundation of Korea (NRF) grant funded by the Korea government (MIST) (No.2020M3F3A2A01081595) and partly by the National Foundation of Korea (NRF) grant funded by the Korea government (MIST) (No.2020M3F3A2A01082326).

Institutional Review Board Statement: Not applicable.

Data Availability Statement: Not applicable.

Acknowledgments: The EDA tool was supported by the IC Design Education Center (IDEC), Korea.

Conflicts of Interest: The authors declare no conflict of interest.

References

1. Moore, G. Cramming More Components Onto Integrated Circuits. *Proc. IEEE* **1998**, *86*, 82–85. [CrossRef]
2. Dennard, R.H.; Gaensslen, F.H.; Yu, H.; Rideout, V.L.; Bassous, E.; LeBlanc, A.R. Design of ion-implanted MOSFET's with very small physical dimensions. *IEEE Solid-State Circuits Soc. Newsl.* **2007**, *12*, 38–50. [CrossRef]
3. Colinge, J.P. (Ed.) *FinFETs and Other Multi-Gate Transistors*; Springer: New York, NY, USA, 2008.
4. Xie, R.; Montanini, P.; Akarvardar, K.; Tripathi, N.; Haran, B.; Johnson, S.; Hook, T.; Hamieh, B.; Corliss, D.; Wang, J.; et al. A 7nm FinFET Technology Featuring EUV Patterning and dual strained high mobility channels. In Proceedings of the 2016 IEEE International Electron Devices Meeting (IEDM), San Francisco, CA, USA, 3–7 December 2016; pp. 1–4.
5. Lee, Y.; Park, G.-H.; Choi, B.; Yoon, J.; Kim, H.-J.; Kim, D.H.; Kim, D.M.; Kang, M.-H.; Choi, S.-J. Design study of the gate-all-around silicon nanosheet MOSFETs. *Semicond. Sci. Technol.* **2020**, *35*, 03LT01. [CrossRef]
6. Jang, D.; Yakimets, D.; Eneman, G.; Schuddinck, P.; Bardon, M.G.; Raghavan, P.; Spessot, A.; Verkest, D.; Mocuta, A. Device exploration of nanosheet transistors for sub-7-nm technology node. *IEEE Trans. Electron. Devices* **2017**, *64*, 2707–2713. [CrossRef]
7. Thomas, S. Gate-all-around transistors stack up. *Nat. Electron.* **2020**, *3*, 728. [CrossRef]
8. Yeo, Y.-C.; Gong, X.; van Dal, M.J.H.; Vellianitis, G.; Passlack, M. Germanium-based transistors for future high performance and low power logic applications. In Proceedings of the 2015 IEEE International Electron Devices Meeting (IEDM), Washington, DC, USA, 7–9 December 2015; pp. 1–4.
9. Chen, Y.; Liu, J.; Zeng, M.; Lu, F.; Lv, T.; Chang, Y.; Lan, H.; Wei, B.; Sun, R.; Gao, J.; et al. Universal growth of ultra-thin III–V semiconductor single crystals. *Nat. Commun.* **2020**, *11*, 3979. [CrossRef] [PubMed]
10. Chhowalla, M.; Jena, D.; Zhang, H. Two-dimensional semiconductors for transistors. *Nat. Rev. Mater.* **2016**, *1*, 16052. [CrossRef]
11. Agarwal, T.; Yakimets, D.; Raghavan, P.; Radu, I.; Thean, A.; Heyns, M.; Dehaene, W. Benchmarking of MoS_2 FETs With Multigate Si-FET Options for 5 nm and Beyond. *IEEE Trans. Electron. Devices* **2015**, *62*, 4051–4056. [CrossRef]
12. Rai, A.; Movva, H.C.P.; Roy, A.; Taneja, D.; Chowdhury, S.; Banerjee, S.K. Progress in Contact, Doping and Mobility Engineering of $MoS2$: An Atomically Thin 2D Semiconductor. *Crystals* **2018**, *8*, 316. [CrossRef]
13. Shen, P.-C.; Su, C.; Lin, Y.; Chou, A.-S.; Cheng, C.-C.; Park, J.-H.; Chiu, M.-H.; Lu, A.-Y.; Tang, H.-L.; Tavakoli, M.M.; et al. Ultralow contact resistance between semimetal and monolayer semiconductors. *Nature* **2021**, *593*, 211–217. [CrossRef] [PubMed]
14. Chen, M.-L.; Sun, X.; Liu, H.; Wang, H.; Zhu, Q.; Wang, S.; Du, H.; Dong, B.; Zhang, J.; Sun, Y.; et al. A FinFET with one atomic layer channel. *Nat. Commun.* **2020**, *11*, 1205. [CrossRef] [PubMed]
15. Afzalian, A. Ab initio perspective of ultra-scaled CMOS from 2D-material fundamentals to dynamically doped transistors. *npj 2D Mater. Appl.* **2021**, *5*, 5. [CrossRef]
16. Mitta, S.B.; Choi, M.S.; Nipane, A.; Ali, F.; Kim, C.; Teherani, J.T.; Hone, J.; Yoo, W.J. Electrical characterization of 2D materials-based field-effect transistors. *2D Mater.* **2020**, *8*, 012002. [CrossRef]
17. Sebastian, A.; Pendurthi, R.; Choudhury, T.H.; Redwing, J.M.; Das, S. Benchmarking monolayer $MoS2$ and $WS2$ field-effect transistors. *Nat. Commun.* **2021**, *12*, 693. [CrossRef] [PubMed]
18. Arutchelvan, G.; Smets, Q.; Verreck, D.; Ahmed, Z.; Gaur, A.; Sutar, S.; Jussot, J.; Groven, B.; Heyns, M.; Lin, D.; et al. Impact of device scaling on the electrical properties of $MoS2$ field-effect transistors. *Sci. Rep.* **2021**, *12*, 6610. [CrossRef] [PubMed]
19. Ahmed, Z.; Afzalian, A.; Schram, T.; Jang, D.; Verreck, D.; Smets, Q.; Schuddinck, P.; Chehab, B.; Sutar, S.; Arutchelvan, G.; et al. Introducing 2D-FETs in Device Scaling Roadmap using DTCO. In Proceedings of the 2020 IEEE International Electron Devices Meeting (IEDM), San Francisco, CA, USA, 12–18 December 2020; pp. 1–4.
20. Hu, C.; Niknejad, A.; Sriramkumar, V.; Lu, D.; Chauhan, Y.; Kahm, M.; Sachid, A. BSIM-IMG: A Turnkey compact model for fully depleted technologies. In Proceedings of the 2012 IEEE International SOI Conference (SOI), Napa, CA, USA, 1–4 October 2012; pp. 1–24.
21. Park, J.; Kim, J.; Showdhury, S.; Shin, C.; Rhee, H.; Yeo, M.; Cho, E.-C.; Yi, J. Electrical Characteristics of Bulk FinFET According to Spacer Length. *Electronics* **2020**, *9*, 1283. [CrossRef]

22. Yu, X.; Han, S.; Zamdmer, N.; Deng, J.; Nowak, E.J.; Rim, K. Improved effective switching current (IEFF+) and capacitance methodology for CMOS circuit performance prediction and model-to-hardware correlation. In Proceedings of the 2008 IEEE International Electron Devices Meeting, San Francisco, CA, USA, 15–17 December 2008; pp. 1–4.
23. International Roadmap for Devices and Systems (IRDS™). 2020. Available online: https://irds.ieee.org/editions/2020 (accessed on 23 July 2020).

Boxcar Averaging Scanning Nonlinear Dielectric Microscopy

Kohei Yamasue * and Yasuo Cho

Research Institute of Electrical Communication, Tohoku University, 2-1-1 Katahira, Aoba, Sendai 980-8577, Japan; yasuocho@riec.tohoku.ac.jp
* Correspondence: yamasue@riec.tohoku.ac.jp

Abstract: Scanning nonlinear dielectric microscopy (SNDM) is a near-field microwave-based scanning probe microscopy method with a wide variety of applications, especially in the fields of dielectrics and semiconductors. This microscopy method has often been combined with contact-mode atomic force microscopy (AFM) for simultaneous topography imaging and contact force regulation. The combination SNDM with intermittent contact AFM is also beneficial for imaging a sample prone to damage and using a sharp microscopy tip for improving spatial resolution. However, SNDM with intermittent contact AFM can suffer from a lower signal-to-noise (S/N) ratio than that with contact-mode AFM because of the shorter contact time for a given measurement time. In order to improve the S/N ratio, we apply boxcar averaging based signal acquisition suitable for SNDM with intermittent contact AFM. We develop a theory for the S/N ratio of SNDM and experimentally demonstrate the enhancement of the S/N ratio in SNDM combined with peak-force tapping (a trademark of Bruker) AFM. In addition, we apply the proposed method to the carrier concentration distribution imaging of atomically thin van der Waals semiconductors. The proposed method clearly visualizes an anomalous electron doping effect on few-layer Nb-doped MoS_2. The proposed method is also applicable to other scanning near-field microwave microscopes combined with peak-force tapping AFM such as scanning microwave impedance microscopy. Our results indicate the possibility of simultaneous nanoscale topographic, electrical, and mechanical imaging even on delicate samples.

Keywords: scanning nonlinear dielectric microscopy; boxcar averaging; scanning probe microscopy; scanning near-field microwave microscopy; scanning microwave impedance microscopy

1. Introduction

Scanning nonlinear dielectric microscopy (SNDM) is a scanning probe microscopy (SPM) method using near-field microwaves and frequency modulation (FM) [1]. Owing to an exceptionally high sensitivity to local capacitance variation below the tip, this microscopy has versatile applications in science and engineering of dielectrics and semiconductors [2,3]. SNDM was originally devised for imaging electric anisotropy of dielectrics such as ferroelectric domains [4] and has the potential to become a key technology for ferroelectric probe data storage enabling Tbit/inch^2 recording density [5,6]. The scope of applications has also extended to the nanoscale evaluation of semiconductor materials and devices, including dopant profiling in miniaturized transistors [7,8], imaging the stored charges in flash memories [9], carrier distribution imaging on SiC power transistors [10], amorphous and monocrystalline Si solar cells [11,12], and atomically-thin layered semiconductors [13,14]. SNDM and its potentiometric extension can show true atomic resolution in surface dipole imaging on a Si (111)-(7 × 7) surface [15,16] and single-layer graphene on SiC [17]. Furthermore, new classes of SNDM called super-higher-order SNDM [10] and time-resolved SNDM [18] have recently emerged, enabling local deep level transient spectroscopy [18,19] and local capacitance-voltage profiling for semiconductors [20,21].

Among the members of the SNDM family, SNDM combined with atomic force microscopy (AFM) has been of importance for various applications. So far, SNDM has been mainly combined with contact-mode AFM (C-AFM), which permits topographic imaging by maintaining the contact force between a microscopy tip and the sample surface during the lateral scan of the surface [22]. However, C-AFM has a well-known drawback of higher probability for damaging the tip and the sample because of strong lateral forces [23]. For instance, atomically-thin van der Waals materials such as graphene and few-layer MoS$_2$ can be peeled off during imaging, in our experience [13]. The tip is likely to deform, especially when using an expensive ultra-sharp tip for attempting the improvement of spatial resolution. In such a case, we need to make significant effort to carefully optimize measurement conditions to suppress the probability of the tip deformation as much as possible.

One possible way to overcome these problems is to combine SNDM with intermittent-contact AFM (IC-AFM), following the development history of AFM [24]. There were several IC-AFM methods such as so-called tapping mode AFM [23], peak-force tapping (a trademark of Bruker) AFM [25], and force volume (a trademark of Bruker) imaging [26] differing by typical contact frequency. However, intermittent contact operation can cause a significant reduction of the signal-to-noise (S/N) ratio or an increase of measurement time in SNDM imaging [13,27]. This is because the signal from the SNDM channel is normally generated only when the tip is in contact with or in very close proximity to the sample surface [28]. Signal intensity is highest on the surface but rapidly decreases below the noise level as the tip moves slightly away from the surface. This indicates that the achievable S/N ratio of SNDM is basically limited by the total contact time for a given measurement time and, therefore, SNDM combined with IC-AFM (IC-SNDM) essentially has a lower achievable S/N ratio than that combined with C-AFM because of the shorter total contact time. In addition, as previously pointed out, an actual S/N ratio can be further reduced from the achievable level, unless the detection bandwidth of the SNDM signal is appropriately chosen for the given contact time [27]. In particular, SNDM combined with peak-force tapping AFM (PFT-SNDM) is beneficial but suffers from a much lower signal intensity than that combined with C-AFM (C-SNDM), because the bandwidth of the signal acquisition is hardly optimized for intermittent contact operations [13].

In order to improve the S/N ratio of PFT-SNDM, here, we apply the idea of boxcar averaging to PFT-SNDM. By significantly extending the consideration and results given in the previous brief report [29], we develop a more sophisticated theory of PFT-SNDM to quantitatively explain the S/N ratio of SNDM including C-SNDM and PFT-SNDM. We show that, by utilizing gated signal acquisition followed by averaging, the optimal S/N ratio can be achieved even for PFT-SNDM. The measurement parameters required to maximize the S/N ratio can be quantitatively determined by the developed theory. In addition, along with the practical aspects on the implementation of the proposed method, we experimentally demonstrate and discuss actual improvement in the S/N ratio by measuring a test semiconductor sample. Furthermore, we address a recent application of the proposed method to the imaging of the dominant carrier concentration distribution in atomically thin van der Waals semiconductors. As reported in greater detail in our recent paper [14], we were able to observe an anomalous doping effect on few-layer MoS$_2$ by utilizing the proposed method. Because of the similar imaging mechanism, the idea presented here can also be applied to the optimization of S/N ratios in other scanning near-field microwave microscopy such as scanning microwave impedance microscopy (SMIM) [30] combined with peak-force tapping AFM [25].

2. Principle of SNDM and Combination with IC-AFM

SNDM is an FM based SPM method using an electric self-oscillator for sensing the variations in the capacitance between the conductive sharp tip and the sample [1]. A fingertip-sized LC oscillator oscillating in a gigahertz range is often employed as a self-oscillating capacitance sensor called a SNDM probe. Figure 1 shows a schematic diagram of SNDM [13]. Here, the diagram illustrates PFT-SNDM with vertical periodic cantilever motion for the later description but the explanation below also applies to C-SNDM except that the tip keeps in contact with the sample surface in C-SNDM. If the duty ratio in PFT-SNDM is defined as the rate of the contact time to the repeating period, C-SNDM can be regarded as PFT-SNDM with a 100% duty ratio in terms of S/N ratio. In SNDM combined with AFM, a conductive cantilever with a sharp tip is attached to the LC oscillator, which makes the tip-sample capacitance C_{ts} electrically connected in parallel with a built-in LC tank circuit. Because the variations in the tip-sample capacitance ΔC_{ts} change the resonance frequency of the circuit, we can detect ΔC_{ts} from the shift of oscillation frequency Δf from the center frequency f_0. In a typical condition, Δf is approximately proportional to ΔC_{ts} with the proportionality constant of $-f_0/\{2(C+C_{ts0})\}$, as ΔC_{ts} is several orders of magnitude smaller than the built-in capacitance C. C_{ts0} denotes the static component of C_{ts}. As a result of the relationship between Δf and ΔC_{ts}, the FM signal can be obtained by applying a sinusoidal modulation voltage across the tip and the sample. The modulation frequency is typically 10 kHz for C-SNDM and 100 kHz~1 MHz for PFT-SNDM. FM in SNDM can be normally regarded as narrow band FM because of the very low modulation index. We use a frequency demodulator in a microwave range for the demodulation of ΔC_{ts} and a lock-in amplifier to obtain the first order capacitance variations, or a voltage derivative of capacitance, here called a dC/dV signal. The dC/dV signal is also called a ε_{333} signal in the measurement of dielectrics, because the dC/dV signal is proportional to a nonlinear third-order dielectric constant described by a third-rank tensor [1]. The minimum detectable ΔC_{ts} is typically as low as 2×10^{-22} F for a unity measurement bandwidth [16].

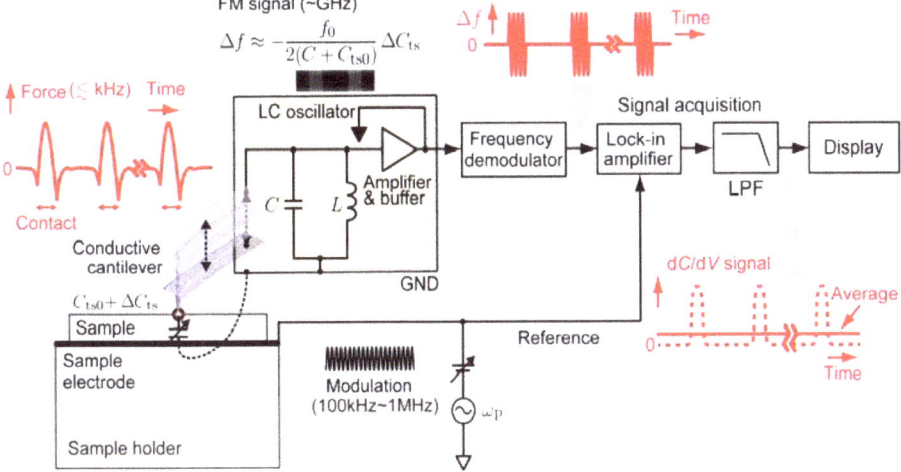

Figure 1. Schematic diagram of PFT-SNDM. The periodic contact of the tip with the sample surface generates a pulse train of frequency shift at the output of a frequency demodulator. The period and duty cycle of the pulse train are the same as those of the periodic contact. Because of the averaging effect on the pulse train in the signal acquisition, the signal intensity can significantly decrease. C-SNDM can be regarded as PFT-SNDM with a 100% duty cycle in terms of the S/N ratio.

dC/dV signals arise from different mechanisms on different materials. One of the main mechanisms is an electric anisotropic property of a material such as ferroelectric polarization below the tip [1]. The polarity of a dC/dV, or ε_{333}, signal is inverted depending on the polarity of a ferroelectric domain. The second is the change in the depletion layer capacitance in a semiconductor material. As is often done using scanning capacitance microscopy [31], we can determine the polarity of dominant carriers, p- or n-type, on a local area of a semiconductor from the polarity of the dC/dV signal, and the signal intensity gives local information of carrier concentration with superior sensitivity. If reference samples for calibration can be prepared, the dC/dV imaging can be used for the nanoscale quantitative measurement of non-linear permittivity on dielectrics [32] and dopant profiling on semiconductors [8,12].

SNDM is combined with AFM for controlling the force between the tip and the sample and obtaining a simultaneous topographic image. Odagawa and Cho first demonstrated SNDM combined with C-AFM [22]. Recently, Yamasue and Cho integrated SNDM with PFT-AFM in a commercial SPM system (Bruker Dimension Icon, Billerica, MA, USA) to image atomically thin van der Waals semiconductors [13]. PFT-SNDM was able to visualize the distributions of dominant carrier concentration on atomically thin MoS_2 including single-layer structures. In addition to the capability of avoiding damaging the tip and the sample, the imaging stability of the SNDM channel is improved by suppressing the probability of charge injection from the tip to the sample, which can accidentally cause abrupt changes to the signal intensity [14]. Another benefit is that PFT-AFM had much better reproducibility in the measurement of topographic height differences in different stacking layers, which helps the identification of the layer number. PFT-AFM also allows us to investigate the mechanical properties of sample [25], even on fragile biological samples [33,34]. Since SNDM is useful for imaging the local electric properties, its combination with PFT-AFM will permit the nanoscale investigation on the correlation between local electric and mechanical properties.

The problem is that PFT-SNDM has one order of magnitude higher contact frequency (typically at 2 kHz) than the typical frequency bandwidth of signal acquisition (~100 Hz). This results in much shorter contact time (~50 µs) than the typical time constants of signal acquisition (~1 ms). As shown in Figure 1, because the signal in the conventional PFT-SNDM is averaged through the signal acquisition regardless of whether the tip is in contact with the surface or not, that is, whether the signal is present or absent, an averaging effect drastically reduces signal intensity. The signal intensity decreased by a factor of the duty cycle (~0.1). The averaging effect can be avoided by gated signal acquisition and averaging with a tuned bandwidth, which enables a much higher S/N ratio for a given contact time and measurement time, as shown in the next section.

It is noted that, historically, the first IC-SNDM was developed by Hiranaga and Cho [24]. They proposed a measurement method that repeats a cycle of approaching, maintaining the contact, acquiring the dC/dV signal, and withdrawing for every measurement point. They reported that, compared to C-SNDM, their lab-made IC-SNDM achieved higher stability and better reproducibility in SNDM imaging on a ferroelectric material. The difference from PFT-SNDM treated in this paper is that the contact frequency and contact time in their method were about 25 Hz and 10 ms, respectively, which are two orders of magnitude lower and longer than those in PFT-SNDM. The contact time is taken long enough to wait for the signal to reach an intensity as high as that in C-SNDM, which results in a longer measurement time. In this case, no averaging effect occurred in the signal acquisition. Detailed discussion on S/N ratio has not been given in the literature. A similar IC-SNDM method has recently been implemented by Yamasue and Cho to a commercial SPM system utilizing force volume imaging rather than PFT imaging [27]. In their paper, they discussed the S/N ratio of IC-SNDM, which gave us a clue to the improvement of the S/N ratio by the boxcar averaging based scheme presented here. They pointed out that the balance between the bandwidth, or time constant of the signal acquisition, and the contact time of IC-SNDM needs to be optimized to obtain the highest S/N ratio in a given measurement time.

3. S/N Ratio of SNDM

In IC-SNDM, the intensity of a dC/dV signal typically becomes highest only when the tip is in contact with the sample but rapidly decreases below the noise level as the tip-sample separation increases. Therefore, the dC/dV signal is regarded as a pulse train with a duty cycle $D = T_c/T$, where T_c and T denote the contact time and the contact period, respectively. A typical duty cycle in PFT-SNDM is as low as $D = 0.1$, which has a significant impact on the conventional signal acquisition. Figure 2a,b compare the difference between a 100% duty ratio equivalent to C-SNDM and a low duty ratio corresponding to PFT-SNDM. For a 100% duty ratio, the signal continuously takes the highest level with no averaging effect, while the noise level decreases by a factor depending the detection bandwidth of the signal acquisition. On the other hand, in the case of the low duty ratio, the signal intensity decreases by a factor of D, as illustrated in Figure 2b. This is because the signal with a pulse train is averaged though continuous signal acquisition with a much narrower bandwidth than contact frequency. The noise level is the same as that in C-SNDM as long as the noise densities are the same regardless of whether the tip is in contact with the surface or not. Thus, PFT-SNDM has a significantly lower S/N ratio than C-SNDM.

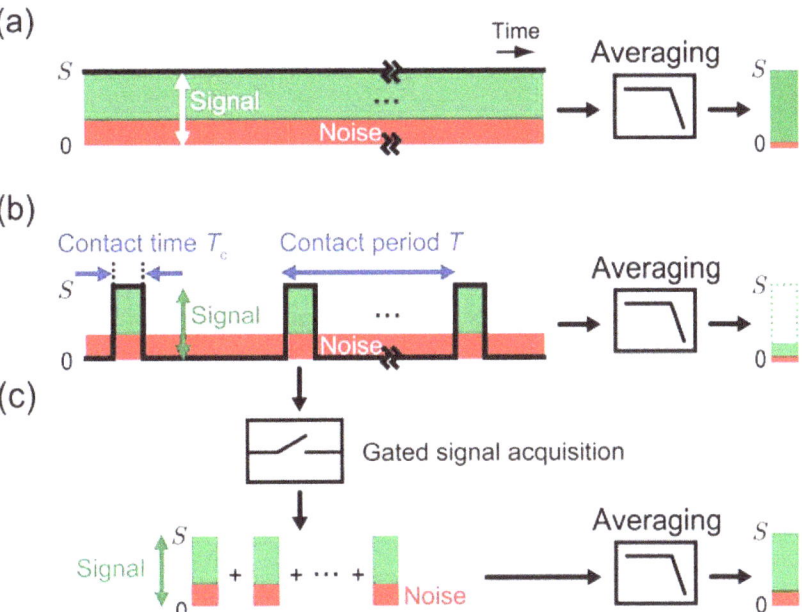

Figure 2. Schematic illustration of signal acquisition and the achievable S/N ratio in (**a**) C-SNDM, (**b**) PFT-SNDM, and (**c**) BA-PFT-SNDM. Green parts indicate the intensity of dC/dV signals, or the amplitude of frequency shift, in the capacitance sensor. Red parts depict noise levels.

The idea is to eliminate the periods that contain no signal but only the noise from the signal averaging stage. As shown in Figure 2c, we can utilize gated signal acquisition to extract the signal only when the tip is in contact with the surface. The extracted signal can be then regarded as a continuous signal like that in C-SNDM. The signal becomes suitable for averaging because the intensity remains highest. The idea here has been called boxcar averaging [35,36] and the proposed method here is called boxcar averaging PFT-SNDM (BA-PFT-SNDM). It is noted that the noise level becomes higher than that in C-SNDM because of the shorter total contact time for a given measurement time. In fact, we need to increase the bandwidth of a lock-in amplifier to acquire the signal at the highest intensity. If the bandwidth is tuned, the signal is expected to rise from the noise level to the highest level during contact time without causing the averaging affect. The increase of the bandwidth results in the increase of noise included in the output of the lock-in amplifier, while the noise level is further reduced through the subsequent averaging stage without reducing the signal intensity.

Here, we develop a theory to predict the optimal detection bandwidth and S/N ratio in BA-PFT-SNDM by extending the discussion given in the previous brief report [29]. To increase the level of the dC/dV signal acquired during contact, the output of a low-pass filter (LPF) in the lock-in amplifier needs to follow a pulse train of Δf signal fast enough and reach the vicinity of the highest value S, before the tip is away from the surface. Settling time and its methodology treated in a classical control theory help to describe this situation.

Settling time T_S is the time required for the output of a system to reach and stay within a given range in the vicinity of the final value after a step input. To maximize the signal level, T_S needs to be smaller than T_c. In addition, T_S should be smaller than T_p, which denotes the average time elapsed for constructing one pixel of a dC/dV image. If T_S is determined for a given T_c (or D) and T_p, we can calculate the minimum bandwidth of the signal acquisition required to obtain the highest signal intensity, which also minimizes the noise level. It is noted that the time constant of the LPF is related to T_S but deviates from it in a high-order system like the LPF stage of a lock-in amplifier.

We discuss the S/N ratio in IC-SNDM based on the settling time. However, to exactly obtain the settling time for a given specific system, it is necessary to derive the step response of the system, or the transient output response to a step input. Thus, we employ the traditional simple methodology proposed by Elmore to treat the transient output response of a linear system [37]. In this methodology, the impulse response of a given system, or the time-derivative of the step response, is approximated by the impulse response of a Gaussian transfer function system that can be mathematically more tractable. The approximation is justified because the impulse response of a linear time-invariant system becomes closer to that of a Gaussian transfer function system, as the order of the system increases, under reasonable assumptions. The impulse response of the Gaussian transfer function system becomes a Gaussian function of time again. This implies that we can approximate the step response of interest by the time-integration of the impulse response from the Gaussian transfer function. As shown in Figure 3, the step input to a signal acquisition system (Figure 3a) causes the step response with a settling time depending on the bandwidth (Figure 3b). The step response is given by the integration of impulse response approximated by the cumulative distribution function of the Gaussian function (Figure 3c). Thus, we can define the rise time T_R by the cumulative frequency of the Gaussian function. Note that Gaussian transfer function systems are not causal. Unlike the original system of interest, the output of the corresponding Gaussian system arises before the input is applied. The impulse response already reaches the maximum at $t = 0$. To adjust the time of the maximum output from the Gaussian system to that from the original system, a delay time T_D is further introduced in this methodology. This methodology works well for the filters without significant overshoot in the step response, as realized in a typical LPF stage of a lock-in amplifier.

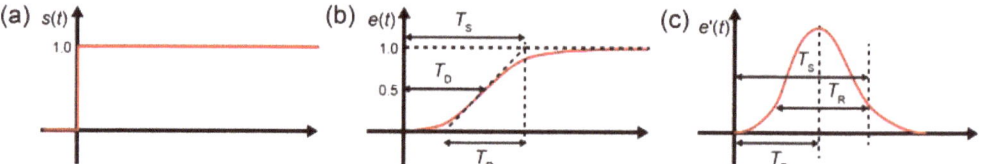

Figure 3. Step response of a system and the definition of settling time (T_S) based on the delay time (T_D) and the rise time (T_R). (**a**) step input (**b**) step response (**c**) impulse response. The step response [(**b**)] is given by integrating the impulse response [(**c**)] approximated by a Gaussian function.

According to the work by Elmore, T_D and T_R are approximated using the impulse response of interest $e'(t)$, respectively.

$$T_D = \int_0^\infty t e'(t) dt, \quad (1)$$

$$T_R = \sqrt{2\pi} \sqrt{\left(\int_0^\infty t^2 e'(t) dt\right) - T_D^2} \quad (2)$$

Equations (1) and (2) give the first order and second order moments of $e'(t)$ when $e'(t)$ is approximated by a Gaussian function in the time domain. The first and second order moments correspond to the average and variation of the Gaussian function, respectively. Then, we define the settling time as follows:

$$T_S = T_D + \alpha(\gamma)\frac{T_R}{2}, \tag{3}$$

where α denotes a constant depending on the parameter γ, which indicates how close to the maximum intensity the signal level is required to be at the settling time. γ is typically chosen to be $\gamma = 90\%$ or 95% relative to the maximum intensity, or the final value of the output at the steady state. If the signal acquisition system is decomposed into m lower order cascaded systems connected in the series, it can be shown that T_D and T_R are given by the sum of the delay time and the root of the square sum of the rise time in each system.

$$T_D = \sum_{i=1}^{m} T_{D_i}, \tag{4}$$

$$T_R = \sqrt{\sum_{i=1}^{m} T_{R_i}^2}. \tag{5}$$

To obtain the signal with the $\gamma\%$ level to the maximum intensity at the settling time, the following condition should be satisfied.

$$T_S \leq T_c = DT. \tag{6}$$

In addition, we require T_S to be smaller than T_p, denoting the time allowed for the tip to stay for one pixel of a dC/dV image.

$$T_S \leq T_p. \tag{7}$$

In PFT-SNDM, we acquire a dC/dV signal from Δf by using a lock-in amplifier with a high order LPF. Let us assume that the filter consists of m-cascaded first-order filters with a time constant of τ_1 shared for each stage, as is the case in typical commercial lock-in amplifiers. Then, the delay time T_{D_i} and rise time T_{R_i} for the i-th stage is equivalent to τ_1 and $\tau_1\sqrt{2\pi}$, respectively. As shown in Figure 3, the settling time can be defined as the sum of the delay time and half rise time. From Equations (4) and (5), the settling time for the m-th order LPF stage is calculated as follows:

$$\begin{aligned} T_S = T_D + \alpha(\gamma)\frac{T_R}{2} &= mT_{D_1} + \frac{\alpha(\gamma)}{2}\left(\sum_{i=1}^{m} T_{R_i}^2\right)^{\frac{1}{2}} \\ &= \left(m + \alpha(\gamma)\sqrt{\frac{m\pi}{2}}\right)\tau_1. \\ &= \tau_1/\beta(m,\gamma), \end{aligned} \tag{8}$$

where $\beta(m,\gamma)$ is defined by

$$\beta(m,\gamma) = \left(m + \alpha(\gamma)\sqrt{\frac{m\pi}{2}}\right)^{-1}. \tag{9}$$

For 90% and 95% settling time, $\alpha \approx 1.3$ and $\alpha \approx 1.6$ are respectively determined from $\alpha(\gamma) = \sqrt{2}\mathrm{erf}^{-1}(2\gamma - 1)$. From Equation (6), τ_1 needs to be limited to obtain the signal level at $\gamma\%$ before the tip starts to be off the surface:

$$\tau_1 \leq \beta(m,\gamma)DT. \tag{10}$$

In addition, τ_1 should satisfy the next condition equivalent to Equation (7), because the signal also needs to increase up to the required level before the tip moves to the location corresponding to the next pixel of the image, as follows:

$$\tau_1 \leq \beta(m, \gamma)T_p. \tag{11}$$

Since we can assume $T \leq T_p$ in a normal operation, if τ_1 satisfies the first condition, it also satisfies the second one. The second condition is utilized for obtaining the S/N ratio in the conventional PFT-SNDM.

In order to calculate the S/N ratio, we consider the noise level at the output of the lock-in amplifier. Here, we assume that noise density is constant within the measurement bandwidth and does not change regardless of whether the tip is in contact with the surface or not. The -3 dB cut-off frequency or the measurement bandwidth is connected to the rise time by the following relationship:

$$B_{-3dB} \approx \frac{\zeta(\gamma)}{T_R}. \tag{12}$$

Here, ζ denotes a constant depending on γ. For $\gamma = 90\%$ and 95%, $\zeta \approx 0.34$ and 0.43, respectively. In addition, the equivalent noise bandwidth B_N is determined by B_{-3dB}.

$$B_N \approx \tilde{\zeta}(m)B_{-3dB}, \tag{13}$$

where $\tilde{\zeta}$ is a constant determined by the order of the LPF stage. For the m-th order detector, we obtain more specific representation, as follows:

$$B_N \approx \frac{\zeta(\gamma)}{\tau_1\sqrt{2m\pi}}\tilde{\zeta}(m). \tag{14}$$

Then, we give the S/N ratio at the output of the lock-in amplifier by

$$\left(\frac{S}{N}\right) = \frac{\gamma S}{n\sqrt{B_N}} \approx \frac{\gamma S}{n}\sqrt{\frac{\sqrt{2m\pi}}{\zeta(\gamma)\tilde{\zeta}(m)}}\sqrt{\tau_1} \tag{15}$$

Here, S denotes the maximum intensity of the dC/dV signal at a given location or pixel. For the m-th order LPF stage, we obtain the following representation from Equation (10):

$$\left(\frac{S}{N}\right) \leq \frac{\gamma\kappa(m,\gamma)S}{n}\sqrt{DT}, \tag{16}$$

where κ denotes a constant determined by a given m and γ as follows:

$$\kappa(m, \gamma) = \sqrt{\frac{\sqrt{2m\pi}\beta(m,\gamma)}{\zeta(\gamma)\tilde{\zeta}(m)}} \tag{17}$$

The right-hand side of Equation (16) is obtained for $\tau_1 = \beta DT$ and gives the achievable S/N ratio at the output of the lock-in amplifier. In BA-PFT-SNDM, the output of the lock-in amplifier is further averaged over the number of the contact cycles per one pixel to give the dC/dV signal at the pixel. Since the average number of the samples per one pixel can be given by T_p/T, the averaging reduces the noise by a factor of $\sqrt{T_p/T}$. This implies that the equivalent noise bandwidth for BA-PFT-SNDM is given by $B_{N,BA} = B_N/(T_p/T)$. Then, the S/N ratio of BA-PF-SNDM is described as follows:

$$\left(\frac{S}{N}\right)_{BA} \leq \frac{\gamma\kappa(m,\gamma)S}{n}\sqrt{DT_p}. \tag{18}$$

For the conventional PFT-SNDM, because of signal reduction by a factor of D, the S/N ratio is given by

$$\left(\frac{S}{N}\right)_{\text{PFT}} = \frac{\gamma DS}{n\sqrt{B_{N,\text{PFT}}}}. \tag{19}$$

$B_{N,\text{PFT}}$ denotes the equivalent noise bandwidth of PFT-SNDM. For obtaining the S/N ratio improvement rate (SNIR), the filter order is assumed to be the same both in BA-PFT-SNDM and PFT-SNDM. Since $B_{N,\text{PFT}}$ is determined by τ_1 satisfying Equation (11) in PFT-SNDM, the S/N ratio is described as follows:

$$\left(\frac{S}{N}\right)_{\text{PFT}} \leq \frac{\gamma \kappa(m,\gamma)DS}{n}\sqrt{T_p}. \tag{20}$$

The achievable S/N ratio is given by the right-hand side in Equation (20) derived from $\tau_1 = \beta T_p$. It is noted that Equations (19) and (20) are derived under the assumption that τ_1 is comparable or higher than T, which implies that the output of the lock-in amplifier to the input pulse train can be well approximated by the step response with the input height equivalent to D (See, Appendix A). This assumption is normally satisfied for PFT-SNDM, because τ_1 is set to be higher or equivalent to T. Equations (18) and (20) yield the achievable SNIR as follows:

$$(\text{SNIR})_{\text{BA/PFT}} = \frac{1}{\sqrt{D}} \tag{21}$$

Therefore, BA-PFT-SNDM can improve the S/N ratio by a factor of $1/\sqrt{D}$, as mentioned in the previous brief report [29]. Equation (20) for $D = 1$ yields the S/N ratio for C-SNDM:

$$\left(\frac{S}{N}\right)_C \leq \frac{\gamma \kappa(m,\gamma)S}{n}\sqrt{T_p} \tag{22}$$

By comparing Equation (22) to Equation (16), the S/N ratio in BA-PFT-SNDM is equivalent to that in C-SNDM, staying DT_p for one pixel rather than T_p, which results from the fact that the achievable S/N ratio is essentially determined by the total contact time for a given measurement time under the assumptions here. In conclusion, the achievable S/N ratio is highest in C-SNDM, followed by BA-PFT-SNDM and the conventional PFT-SNDM in order, with a ratio of $1 : \sqrt{D} : D$ for a given measurement time.

Figure 4 shows SNIR by BA-PFT-SNDM and the comparison of S/N ratios as a function of duty cycle under a typical condition. Here, we assume $T = 0.5$ ms, $T_p = 4.0$ ms, S = 0.3 aF, and $n = 0.3$ zF/$\sqrt{\text{Hz}}$. In addition, we take the signal at the settling level as $\gamma = 95\%$ and $m = 4$, which yields $\alpha(95\%) \approx 1.6$, $\xi(4) \approx 1.1$ and $\zeta(95\%) = 0.43$. The achievable SNIR is shown by a blue thick solid curve, which is inversely proportional to the square root of the duty cycle. As given by Equation (21), the achievable SNIR is independent of specific parameters except duty cycle and rapidly increases with the decrease of the duty cycle. Figure 5 shows the dependence of τ_1, B_N, and $B_{-3\text{dB}}$ on the duty cycle to obtain the highest signal level at $\gamma = 95\%$ settling time. For $D = 0.1$ and $m = 4$, τ_1 needs to be less than 6.3 µs, which results in the wider detection bandwidth of $B_{-3\text{dB}} = 14$ kHz corresponding to $B_N = 15$ kHz at the LPF stage of the lock-in amplifier. At the final stage of signal acquisition, we can average eight samples per one pixel of the image, because the average number of contacts for one pixel is obtained from $T = 0.5$ ms and $T_p = 4.0$ ms. Then, the total equivalent noise bandwidth is to be $B_{N,\text{BA}} \approx 1.9$ kHz.

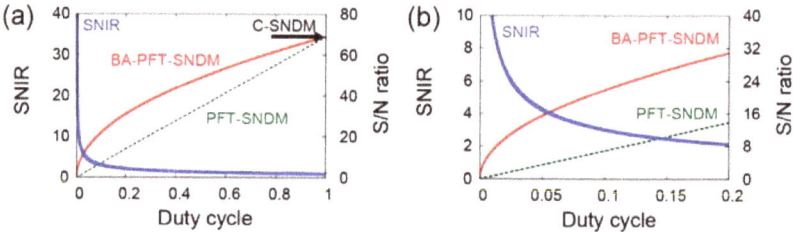

Figure 4. SNIR and comparison of S/N ratios in BA-PFT-SNDM and PFT-SNDM under typical measurement parameters. (**b**) magnifies (**a**) in the range of duty cycle from 0 to 0.2.

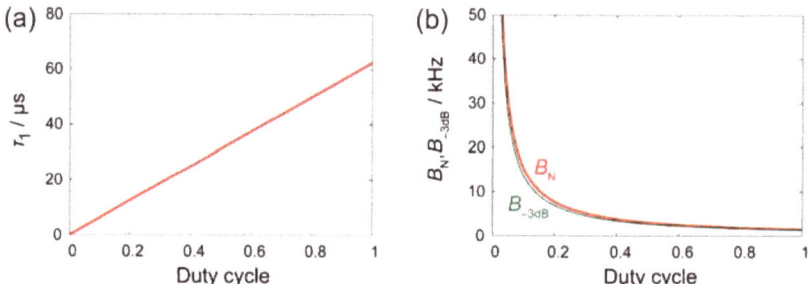

Figure 5. Time constant and bandwidth of the LPF stage at the lock-in amplifier to obtain the highest signal level in BA-PFT-SNDM. (**a**) Time constant of the LPF per one-order (**b**) −3 dB cut-off (green curve) and equivalent noise bandwidth (red curve).

4. Experimental Demonstration

We experimentally demonstrate that BA-PFT-SNDM achieves a higher S/N ratio than PFT-SNDM. Figure 6a shows a schematic diagram of BA-PFT-SNDM. We realized the proposed scheme by combining a commercial scanning probe microscopy system (Bruker Dimension Icon, Billerica, MA, USA) operating in PFT-AFM, a frequency demodulator (Anritsu MS616B, Atsugi, Japan), a lock-in amplifier (Zurich Instruments HF2-LI, Zurich, Switzerland) with a triggered (gated) sampling mode, a function generator (NF Corp. WF1948, Yokohama, Japan) generating the triggers, and a lab-made software offline signal averager. A trigger pulse train was generated by utilizing the function generator synchronized with the cantilever excitation signal available from the SPM system. For signal conditioning, we additionally inserted a band-pass filter (NF Corp. MF3611, Yokohama, Japan) between the function generator and the SPM system. The pulse train was then appropriately delayed for triggering the data sampling by the lock-in amplifier at the timing of the highest signal from the frequency demodulator. The data were stored in a personal computer and processed by the lab-made software created by Python language.

For demonstration, we measured a test Si sample, which had patterned p-, n-, n+ doped areas [38]. We mounted a micro-cantilever coated with Pt-Ir (Nanosensors PPP-EFM, Neuchâtel, Switzerland) with a nominal force constant of 2.8 N/m and resonance frequency of 75 kHz on a SNDM probe oscillating at about 1 GHz. The SNDM probe was specially designed in our laboratory and can be attached to the scanner head of the Icon SPM system, as shown in Figure 6b,c. The SNDM probe is made of a custom-made LC oscillator working as a capacitance sensor mounted on a hand-made fixture board. The cantilever was glued on a particular electrode of the LC oscillator with a conductive paste. The cantilever on the SNDM probe can be located at a position compatible with the laser and optical microscopy in the head. The measurement was done in air at room temperature. For comparison, we acquired images with three different modes: C-SNDM, PFT-SNDM, and BA-PFT-SNDM. The PFT- and BA-PFT-SNDM images were obtained simultaneously. Then, a C-SNDM image was taken separately under the same experimental conditions, except the imaging mode. In PFT- and BA-PFT-SNDM, the contact frequency was set at 2 kHz, which is typical for PFT-AFM. We applied a sinusoidal voltage of 0.2 V_{pk} at a frequency of 200 kHz to the test sample. All images were processed by Gwyddion software [39], because the software can handle BA-PFT-SNDM image files saved in a file format different from the Bruker's standard SPM format. The raw data from BA-PFT-SNDM included time sequences of peak dC/dV values and corresponding lateral tip positions, or X and Y scan voltages. The peak dC/dV values were sampled by the HF2LI lock-in amplifier in the triggered sampling mode. Simultaneously, the X and Y monitor voltages were acquired using two auxiliary analog inputs of the lock-in amplifier, which were wired to a signal access module of the Nanoscope V controller. By using the lab-made Python software, the raw-data were converted to the image data in a so-called XYZ text format ('Z' is assigned to dC/dV). Gwyddion can read both XYZ and SPM files and apply a large number of processing functions to the image data in a unified manner.

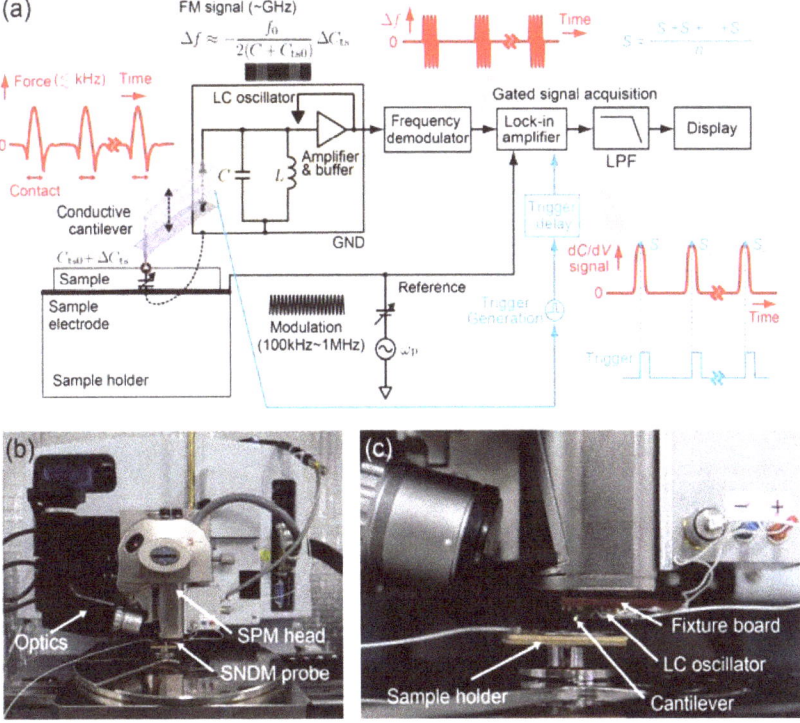

Figure 6. (**a**) Schematic diagram of BA-PFT-SNDM. Gated signal acquisition is realized by triggered signal sampling at the lock-in amplifier. The generated trigger pulse train is synchronized with periodic cantilever motion and appropriately delayed to obtain the highest signal intensity. The signal is further averaged by offline software averaging. (**b**) Overview photograph of the SPM system (Bruker Dimension Icon) with a SNDM probe. (**c**) Close-up picture of the SNDM probe attached to the SPM head.

Prior to the imaging, we observed the time-series of the signals in PFT-SNDM, keeping the tip lateral position fixed on a specific point of the sample surface to adjust the delay of the trigger and the time constant of the lock-in amplifier. Figure 7 shows the typical time-series data of the cantilever excitation (denoted by a red solid curve), cantilever deflection (green), trigger (blue), and dC/dV signal (pink) observed for different time constants of the lock-in amplifier by an oscilloscope. As the tip vertically approached and retracted in a periodic manner, it was in intermittent contact with the surface. The cantilever deflection peaked during each contact time and subsequently showed a free oscillation at the natural frequency away from the surface until the contact started again. The trigger signal was synchronized with 2 kHz excitation and deflection signals. The dC/dV signal showed a negative peak during the contact, which indicates that the tip was located on an n-doping area of the sample. For the time constant much longer than the contact time, the dC/dV signal had a low constant level because of the averaging effect, as shown in Figure 7a for $\tau_1 = 435$ µs. With lower time constants, the dC/dV signal exhibited more pronounced negative peaks during the contact, as indicated by Figure 7b for $\tau_1 = 43.5$ µs, Figure 7c for $\tau_1 = 21.7$ µs, and Figure 7d for $\tau_1 = 4.35$ µs. Based on the observation, we could adjust the filter setting of the lock-in amplifier. In addition, we estimated a duty cycle and determined the trigger delay. It is noted that the actual dC/dV signal had much noise rejected here by an averaging acquisition mode of the oscilloscope to make the preliminary adjustment easier.

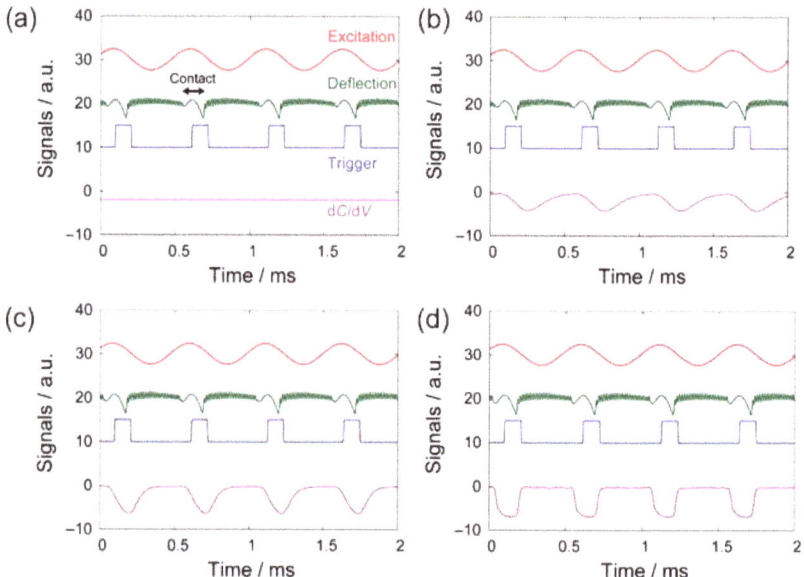

Figure 7. Time series data of the cantilever excitation (solid red curve), cantilever deflection (green), trigger (blue), and dC/dV signal (pink) for different time constants of the lock-in amplifier (a) $\tau_1 = 435$ µs (b) $\tau_1 = 43.5$ µs (c) $\tau_1 = 21.7$ µs (d) $\tau_1 = 4.35$ µs.

Figure 8 shows a topographic image (Figure 8a) and dC/dV images of the Si test sample by C-SNDM (Figure 8b), PFT-SNDM (Figure 8c,d), and BA-PFT-SNDM (Figure 8e). All images were taken with a resolution of 512 × 128 pixels, a scan rate of 0.238 Hz, and measurement time of about 9 min. In these dC/dV images, n- and p-type areas had negative and positive signals, respectively. Figure 8d is obtained from the same data as Figure 8c but has an enhanced contrast by changing the full range of the color scale. For PFT-SNDM and BA-PFT-SNDM, we determined the contact time and duty ratio to be $T_c = 62$ µs and $D = 0.12$, respectively, based on the preliminary observation of time-series data similar to those in Figure 7. We used the fourth order LPF built in the lock-in amplifier for all imaging modes. The time constant per one order, denoted by τ_1 in the previous section, was adjusted to $\tau_1 = 435$ µs ($B_N = 180$ Hz) for C-SNDM and PFT-SNDM and $\tau_1 = 6.5$ µs ($B_N = 12$ kHz) for BA-PFT-SNDM. τ_1 and B_N for BA-PFT-SNDM determined experimentally is in good agreement with the calculated values of $\tau_1 = 7.7$ µs and $B_N = 13$ kHz for $D = 0.12$, $\gamma = 95\%$, $m = 4$, and $T = 512$ μs, according to the theory in Section 3. For C-SNDM and PFT-SNDM, the output of the LPF at the lock-in amplifier was input to an external signal acquisition of the SPM controller. As for BA-PFT-SNDM, every peak value of the dC/dV signal was sampled using the lock-in amplifier under a gated triggered mode and stored as digital data in the personal computer. The stored data of the peak values were further treated by the lab-made software. We obtained an averaged dC/dV image with 512 × 128 pixels from eight different images, each of which was reconstructed from every eight peak values. This is because the number of peak values per one pixel was eight for the scan rate of 0.238 Hz and the resolution of 512 × 128 pixels. This reduces the bandwidth for BA-PFT-SNDM from 12 to 1.5 kHz, which results in the reduction of noise by a factor of $2\sqrt{2}$. As a result, the predicted increase of the S/N ratio was by a factor of about 2.9. The difference from PFT-SNDM [Figure 8c] shows a much lower signal intensity than C-SNDM (Figure 8b). One can see that the noise is much pronounced when the contrast is enhanced, as shown in Figure 8d. In stark contrast, we found that BA-PFT-SNDM (Figure 8e) exhibits higher signal intensity and improved image quality, as expected.

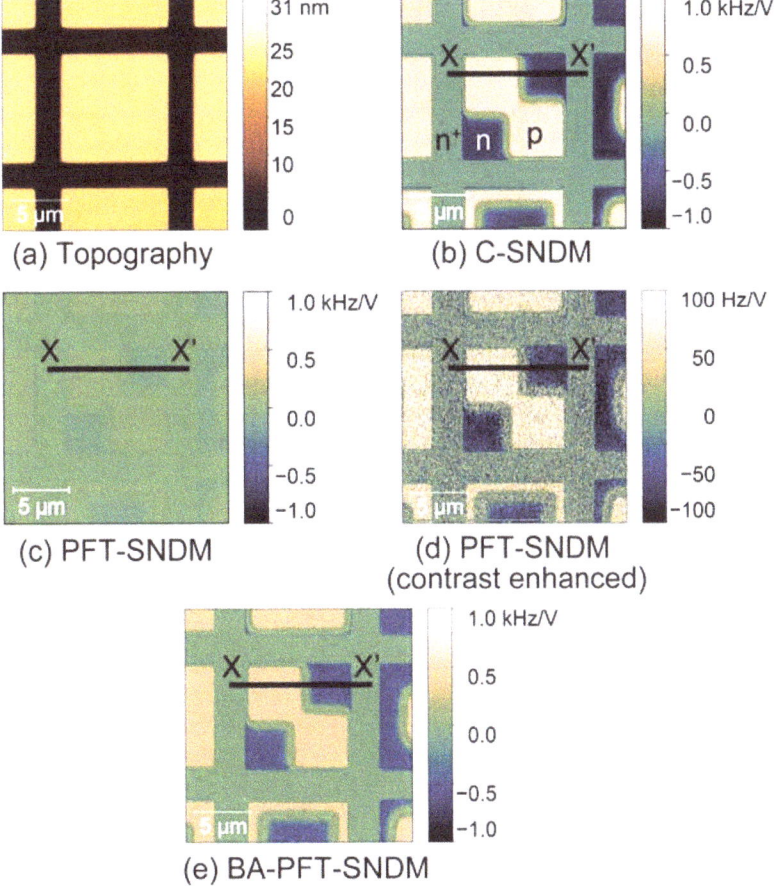

Figure 8. Topographic (**a**), C-SNDM (**b**), PFT-SNDM (**c**,**d**), and BA-PFT-SNDM (**e**) images for the Si test sample with p-, n-, and n⁺ doped areas. (**d**) is a contrast-enhanced image of (**c**). Profiles across the lines from X to X' in the images are shown in Figure 9.

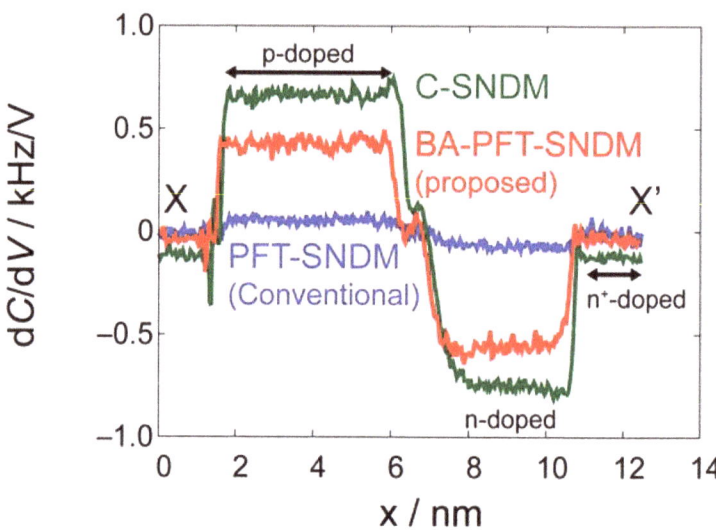

Figure 9. Comparison of the line profiles extracted from the C-SNDM [Figure 8b], PFT-SNDM [Figure 8c], and BA-PFT-SNDM (Figure 8e) images. The profiles are taken along the line from X to X' in Figure 8.

To discuss the effect of the proposed method quantitatively, we extracted profiles of these dC/dV images along the lines from X to X' in Figure 8b–e, as shown in Figure 9. In addition, we compared the signal intensity, noise levels, and S/N ratios among different imaging modes in Table 1 with SNIR. Signal and noise in Table 1 indicate the average of signal intensity and root-mean-squares of signal variations in different areas under the assumption that the fluctuations of dopant concentrations give negligible contribution to the variations of the signal in each area. In comparison to PFT-SNDM, BA-PFT-SNDM showed significantly higher signal intensity on n- and p-type areas, by a factor of 8.3 and 7.9, respectively. These improvement rates of the signal intensity on the n- and p-type areas were in good agreement with the predicted rate of $1/D \approx 8.3$. In addition, we achieved the experimental SNIRs of 4.5 and 4.0 for n and p-type areas, respectively, which are also comparable with the predicted SNIR $1/\sqrt{D} \approx 2.9$. C-SNDM had the best S/N ratios because of the longest contact time per the given measurement time. SNIRs were 8.3 and 6.5 for p- and n-type areas, respectively, which is also consistent with the predicted value of $1/D = 8.3$. The SNIRs tended to be smaller than the predicted rates, probably because C-SNDM is more affected by the noise than PFT-SNDM. Although we assumed that the noise level is equivalent regardless of contact, it actually becomes higher when the tip is in contact with the surface. In fact, C-SNDM had higher fluctuation than PFT-SNDM, as observed in Figure 9. As PFT-SNDM had lower contact time, the noise also becomes lower along with the signal intensity. Regarding n^+-area, there is a discrepancy that cannot be explained by our theory, while BA-PFT-SNDM gives much better results than PFT-SNDM. The signal intensity was improved only by a factor of 5.0, but the noise level was lower than expected. One of the possible reasons is that the dC/dV signal can include a slight offset on the areas of high dopant concentration, where the signal intensity can become very small, causing errors in the comparison. It is also noted that BA-PFT-SNDM basically had lower signal intensity than C-SNDM, while we assume that BA-PFT-SNDM achieves the same signal intensity as C-SNDM in our theory. We have not identified the cause of the different signal levels, but similar phenomenon is observed in other IC-SNDM using force volume imaging [27]. We speculate that the contact state of the tip on the surface in IC-SNDM is different from that in C-SNDM with much higher lateral forces. Nevertheless, our results demonstrate that BA-PFT-SNDM actually has much higher S/N ratios than the conventional PFT-SNDM in an almost predicted way.

Table 1. Signal intensity in Hz_{pk}/V_{pk}, noise levels in Hz_{rms}/V_{pk}, and S/N ratios in different imaging modes. SNIRs indicates S/N ratio normalized by those in PFT-SNDM.

	PFT-SNDM			BA-PFT-SNDM				C-SNDM			
Region	Signal	Noise	S/N Ratio	Signal	Noise	S/N Ratio	SNIR	Signal	Noise	S/N Ratio	SNIR
p	52	17	3.1	431	31	14	4.5	662	26	25	8.3
n	−70	17	4.1	−554	34	16	4.0	−748	28	27	6.5
n⁺	−7.4	23	0.32	−37	24	1.5	4.8	−112	14	8.0	25

5. Application to Imaging Atomically Thin van der Waals Semiconductors

BA-PFT-SNDM is particularly useful for samples prone to the damage. Atomically thin van der Waals materials [40], also called two-dimensional materials, are such materials that can be damaged by C-SNDM [13]. One of the materials is few-layer MoS_2, which has recently been under intensive research because of the material properties suitable for electronic device applications such as miniaturized transistors [41] and optoelectronics devices [42,43]. However, the electrical characteristics of these ultimately thin materials, consisting almost exclusively of surfaces, are often difficult to control because of the high susceptibility to external influences. One of the important characteristics to be precisely controlled is doping levels on the materials for semiconductor device applications [44–46]. However, it is not obvious whether the doping level in an ultra-thin material is the same as that in the bulk counterpart [45].

As already shown by the authors, SNDM is useful for the investigation of the anomalies in the doping levels on atomically thin van der Waals semiconductors [13,14]. Here, we introduce the application of the proposed BA-PFT-SNDM to the measurement of atomically thin natural and Nb-doped MoS_2. Bulk natural MoS_2 is typically n-doped. MoS_2 can also be p-doped by Nb acceptors [47]. We measured ultra-thin natural (SPI Supplies) and Nb-doped MoS_2 (HQ Graphene) mechanically exfoliated on thermally oxidized Si substrates. The samples were prepared by the so-called Scotch-tape method [48]. We used highly doped Si substrates with a resistivity of 0.001~0.005 Ωcm and a 300 nm-thick thermal oxide layer. We simultaneously obtained PFT-SNDM images as well as BA-PFT-SNDM images. The amplitudes of the applied voltages were 0.5 V_{pk} and 1.0 V_{pk} for natural and Nb-doped MoS_2, respectively, and the frequency was 200 kHz for both samples.

Figure 10 shows topographic (Figure 10a), PFT-SNDM (Figure 10b), and BA-PFT-SNDM images (Figure 10c) for few-layer natural MoS_2. We determined the number of stacking layers from the topographic heights of the observed MoS_2 layers. The sample had single- and three-layer MoS_2 with negative dC/dV signals, which indicates that these layers were n-doped. In comparison to the PFT-SNDM image (Figure 10b), the BA-PFT-SNDM image (Figure 10c) clearly resolved n-doping on the single-layer area. The results here showed that natural MoS_2 layers remained n-type semiconductors even in single-layer structures. On the other hand, Nb-doped MoS_2 showed different characteristics when the number of layers decreased. Figure 11 shows topographic (Figure 11a), PFT-SNDM (Figure 11b), and BA-PFT-SNDM (Figure 11c) images for atomically thin Nb-doped MoS_2. The Arabic numbers on the images denote the number of stacking layers on the indicated area. One can see that the sample included 1- to 6-layer MoS_2 layers in the field of view. We could confirm that the 4- to 6-layer MoS_2 showed positive dC/dV signals, indicating p-doping on these layers, as expected from Nb-doping. However, as the layer number decreased from 4 to 1, the signal intensity decreased and the polarity changed from positive to negative. We find that this unexpected p- to n-type transition became clearly visible by BA-PFT-SNDM rather than PFT-SNDM, as shown in Figure 11b,c.

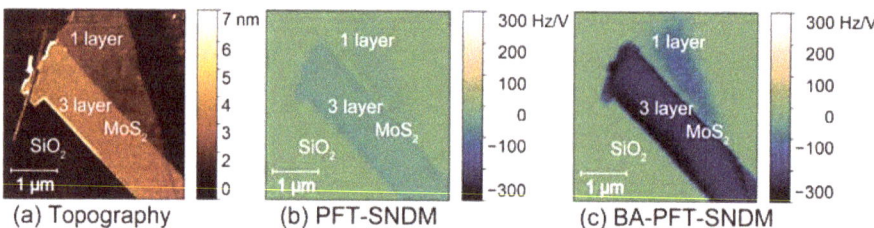

Figure 10. Topographic (**a**), PFT-SNDM (**b**), and BA-PFT-SNDM (**c**) images of few-layer natural MoS$_2$ mechanically exfoliated on a thermally oxidized Si substrate.

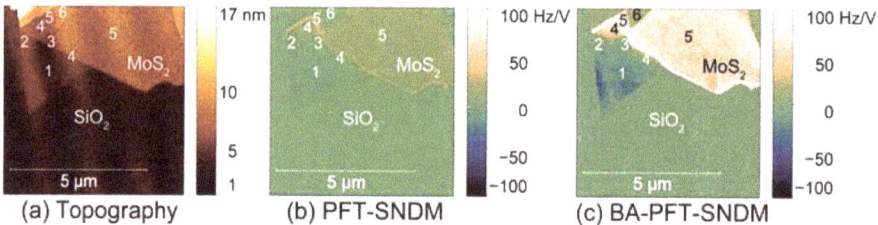

Figure 11. Topographic (**a**), PFT-SNDM (**b**), and BA-PFT-SNDM (**c**) images of atomically thin Nb-doped MoS$_2$ mechanically exfoliated on a thermally oxidized Si substrate. Each Arabic number in the figures denotes the number of stacking layers on the corresponding area.

It is noted that the unintentional n-doping on MoS$_2$ layers has also been reported by different groups recently [45,46]. Siao et al. suggested that sulfur vacancies on the surface layer of MoS$_2$ causes n-doping, which is high enough for overcompensating the artificial p-doping on few-layer MoS$_2$ [45]. In addition, Fang et al. have reported a p- to n-type transition in few-layer Nb-doped MoS$_2$ field effect transistors, with reference to the work by Siao et al. [46]. We think that the enhanced sensitivity of BA-PFT-SNDM established in this paper permitted real-space and nanoscale imaging of the anomalous doping effect on the atomically thin van der Waals semiconductor. The experimental results presented here demonstrate that BA-PFT-SNDM has superior imaging performance to PFT-SNDM. The detailed analysis and discussion on the measurement results are shown in greater detail in Ref. [14]. It is noted that PFT-AFM combined with SNDM has been known for its capability of quantitative nanomechanical mapping such as adhesion, modulus, and dissipation as well as topographic imaging [25]. Our results indicate that BA-PFT-SNDM allows for the possibility of simultaneous nanoelectrical and nanomechanical mapping along with topographic imaging, which will give a clue as to the comprehensive understanding of the material properties.

6. Conclusions

In this paper, we proposed BA-PFT-SNDM based on the theory extended here for giving quantitative insights into the S/N ratio of SNDM. In comparison to PFT-SNDM, BA-PFT-SNDM, which is based on gated signal acquisition and averaging, can increase the S/N ratio by a factor of the inverse square root of the duty cycle, or the rate of the contact time to the contact period in PFT-SNDM. Our theory gives the time constant to be chosen for the gated signal acquisition and allows us to predict SNIR in actual BA-PFT-SNDM measurement in a quantitative way. In addition, we experimentally showed that BA-PFT-SNDM improves the S/N ratios at the rate consistent with the predicted SNIR. The SNIR achievable by BA-PFT-SNDM is two to several times in a typical measurement condition. Furthermore, as an application of BA-PFT-SNDM, we presented the imaging of dominant carrier concentration distribution on atomically thin van der Waals semiconductors. We found that, in comparison to PFT-SNDM, BF-PFT-SNDM has significantly higher imaging capability, enabling clear visualization of the p- to n-type transition on few-layer Nb-doped MoS$_2$. We believe that the field of SNDM will further extend by the emergence of BA-PFT-SNDM, because it enables damage-less, higher sensitivity, and simultaneous nanoelectrical and nanomechanical imaging even on soft and fragile samples. The idea here can also be applied to the optimization of the S/N ratios in other scanning near-field microwave microscopy such as SMIM [30] operating in peak-force tapping mode [25].

Author Contributions: Conceptualization, data curation, formal analysis, investigation, software, writing—original draft preparation: K.Y.; resources, project administration, writing—review and editing, supervision: Y.C.; methodology, funding acquisition: K.Y. and Y.C. All authors have read and agreed to the published version of the manuscript.

Funding: This research was funded by the Japan Society for the Promotion of Science, grant numbers 16H06360 and 20H02613.

Data Availability Statement: The data that support the findings of this study are available from the corresponding author upon reasonable request.

Acknowledgments: We would like to thank Toshihiko Iwai, Tohoku University, for providing support in the development of high-sensitivity probes.

Conflicts of Interest: The authors declare no conflict of interest.

Appendix A

In BA-PFT-SNDM, where the individual peaks of the dC/dV signal are acquired with a lower time constant of the LPF stage, only the response to the step input needs to be considered to obtain the S/N ratio given to one pixel of the dC/dV image. On the other hand, in PFT-SNDM, strictly speaking, we need to consider the response to an input pulse train rather than the single step input. This is because the time constant of the LPF in the lock-in amplifier, denoted by τ_1 in Section 3, is normally set to be comparable with or higher than the contact time. As a result, the response of the LPF becomes much slower than the contact time (even if $\tau_1 \sim T$, due to the high order of the LPF in typical conditions). However, the response to the pulse train can still be approximated by a step response with a height of D as follows.

In general, the output $Y(s)$ to the input $U(s)$ is connected by the transfer function $G(s)$ of the LPF stage:

$$Y(s) = G(s)U(s). \tag{A1}$$

For the pulse train of the dC/dV signal starting at $t=0$, $U(s)$ is described by

$$U(s) = \frac{1 - e^{-DTs}}{1 - e^{-Ts}} \cdot \frac{1}{s}. \tag{A2}$$

Thus, from Equations (A1) and (A2), the output can be given by

$$Y(s) = G(s) \frac{1 - e^{-DTs}}{1 - e^{-Ts}} \cdot \frac{1}{s}. \tag{A3}$$

Here, let us assume $\tau_1 \sim T$ or $\tau_1 > T$. This implies that $|G(s)| \approx 1$ for $|s| \ll 1/T$ and $|G(s)| \ll 1$ for $|s| \sim 1/T$ or $|s| > 1/T$ is especially well satisfied in the high order LPF. In other words, the LPF passes only s satisfying $|s| \ll 1/T$ to the output, which allows for the following approximation of $U(s)$ within $|s| \ll 1/T$:

$$Y(s) = G(s) \frac{-DTs\left\{1 - \frac{DTs}{2!} + \frac{(DTs)^2}{3!} - \cdots\right\}}{-Ts\left\{1 - \frac{Ts}{2!} + \frac{(Ts)^2}{3!} - \cdots\right\}} \cdot \frac{1}{s} \approx G(s)\frac{D}{s} \tag{A4}$$

Equation (A4) implies that the response to the pulse train is approximated by the response to the step input starting at $t = 0$ in a typical measurement setup of PFT-SNDM.

References

1. Cho, Y.; Kirihara, A.; Saeki, T. Scanning nonlinear dielectric microscope. *Rev. Sci. Instrum.* **1996**, *67*, 2297–2303. [CrossRef]
2. Cho, Y. High resolution characterizations of fine structure of semiconductor device and material using scanning nonlinear dielectric microscopy. *Jpn. J. Appl. Phys.* **2017**, *56*, 100101. [CrossRef]
3. Cho, Y. *Scanning Nonlinear Dielectric Microscopy: Investigation of Ferroelectric, Dielectric, and Semiconductor Materials and Devices*; Elsevier: Amsterdam, The Netherlands, 2020; ISBN 978-0-08-102803-2.
4. Matsuura, K.; Cho, Y.; Odagawa, H. Fundamental Study on Nano Domain Engineering Using Scanning Nonlinear Dielectric Microscopy. *Jpn. J. Appl. Phys.* **2001**, *40*, 4354–4356. [CrossRef]
5. Cho, Y.; Fujimoto, K.; Hiranaga, Y.; Wagatsuma, Y.; Onoe, A.; Terabe, K.; Kitamura, K. Tbit/inch^2 ferroelectric data storage based on scanning nonlinear dielectric microscopy. *Appl. Phys. Lett.* **2002**, *81*, 4401–4403. [CrossRef]
6. Tanaka, K.; Cho, Y. Actual information storage with a recording density of 4 Tbit/in.^{2} in a ferroelectric recording medium. *Appl. Phys. Lett.* **2010**, *97*, 092901. [CrossRef] [PubMed]
7. Masahara, M.; Hosokawa, S.; Matsukawa, T.; Endo, K.; Naitou, Y.; Tanoue, H.; Suzuki, E. Dopant profiling in vertical ultrathin channels of double-gate metal–oxide–semiconductor field-effect transistors by using scanning nonlinear dielectric microscopy. *Appl. Phys. Lett.* **2004**, *85*, 4139–4141. [CrossRef]
8. Honda, K.; Ishikawa, K.; Cho, Y. Observation of dopant profile of transistors using scanning nonlinear dielectric microscopy. *J. Phys. Conf. Ser.* **2010**, *209*, 012050. [CrossRef]
9. Honda, K.; Cho, Y. Visualization of Electrons Localized in Metal–Oxide–Nitride–Oxide–Semiconductor Flash Memory Thin Gate Films by Detecting High-Order Nonlinear Permittivity Using Scanning Nonlinear Dielectric Microscopy. *Appl. Phys. Express* **2012**, *5*, 36602. [CrossRef]
10. Chinone, N.; Nakamura, T.; Cho, Y. Cross-sectional dopant profiling and depletion layer visualization of SiC power double diffused metal-oxide-semiconductor field effect transistor using super-higher-order nonlinear dielectric microscopy. *J. Appl. Phys.* **2014**, *116*, 84509. [CrossRef]
11. Hirose, K.; Chinone, N.; Cho, Y. Visualization and analysis of active dopant distribution in a p-i-n structured amorphous silicon solar cell using scanning nonlinear dielectric microscopy. *AIP Adv.* **2015**, *5*, 97136. [CrossRef]
12. Hirose, K.; Tanahashi, K.; Takato, H.; Cho, Y. Quantitative measurement of active dopant density distribution in phosphorus-implanted monocrystalline silicon solar cell using scanning nonlinear dielectric microscopy. *Appl. Phys. Lett.* **2017**, *111*, 32101. [CrossRef]
13. Yamasue, K.; Cho, Y. Local carrier distribution imaging on few-layer MoS$_2$ exfoliated on SiO$_2$ by scanning nonlinear dielectric microscopy. *Appl. Phys. Lett.* **2018**, *112*, 243102. [CrossRef]
14. Yamasue, K.; Cho, Y. Nanoscale characterization of unintentional doping of atomically thin layered semiconductors by scanning nonlinear dielectric microscopy. *J. Appl. Phys.* **2020**, *128*, 074301. [CrossRef]
15. Cho, Y.; Hirose, R. Atomic Dipole Moment Distribution of Si Atoms on a Si(111)−(7×7) Surface Studied Using Noncontact Scanning Nonlinear Dielectric Microscopy. *Phys. Rev. Lett.* **2007**, *99*, 186101. [CrossRef] [PubMed]
16. Yamasue, K.; Cho, Y. Scanning nonlinear dielectric potentiometry. *Rev. Sci. Instrum.* **2015**, *86*, 093704. [CrossRef] [PubMed]
17. Yamasue, K.; Fukidome, H.; Funakubo, K.; Suemitsu, M.; Cho, Y. Interfacial Charge States in Graphene on SiC Studied by Noncontact Scanning Nonlinear Dielectric Potentiometry. *Phys. Rev. Lett.* **2015**, *114*, 226103. [CrossRef]
18. Yamagishi, Y.; Cho, Y. Nanosecond microscopy of capacitance at SiO$_2$/4H-SiC interfaces by time-resolved scanning nonlinear dielectric microscopy. *Appl. Phys. Lett.* **2017**, *111*, 163103. [CrossRef]
19. Chinone, N.; Cho, Y. Local deep level transient spectroscopy using super-higher-order scanning nonlinear dielectric microscopy and its application to imaging two-dimensional distribution of SiO$_2$/SiC interface traps. *J. Appl. Phys.* **2017**, *122*, 105701. [CrossRef]
20. Suzuki, K.; Yamasue, K.; Cho, Y. A Study on Evaluation of Interface Defect Density on High-κ/SiO$_2$/Si and SiO$_2$/Si Gate Stacks Using Scanning Nonlinear Dielectric Microscopy. In Proceedings of the 2019 IEEE International Integrated Reliability Workshop (IIRW), South Lake Tahoe, CA, USA, 13–17 October 2019.
21. Yamasue, K.; Cho, Y. Local capacitance-voltage profiling and high voltage stress effect study of SiO$_2$/SiC structures by time-resolved scanning nonlinear dielectric microscopy. *Microelectron. Reliab.* **2021**, *126*, 114284. [CrossRef]
22. Odagawa, H.; Cho, Y. Simultaneous observation of nano-sized ferroelectric domains and surface morphology using scanning nonlinear dielectric microscopy. *Surf. Sci.* **2000**, *463*, L621–L625. [CrossRef]
23. Zhong, Q.; Inniss, D.; Kjoller, K.; Elings, V. Fractured polymer/silica fiber surface studied by tapping mode atomic force microscopy. *Surf. Sci.* **1993**, *290*, L688–L692. [CrossRef]
24. Hiranaga, Y.; Cho, Y. Intermittent contact scanning nonlinear dielectric microscopy. *Rev. Sci. Instrum.* **2010**, *81*, 23705. [CrossRef] [PubMed]
25. Hu, Y.; Hu, S.; Su, C. Method and Apparatus of Operating a Scanning Probe Microscope. U.S. Patent No. 8,739,309 B2, 27 May 2014.

26. Radmacher, M.; Cleveland, J.P.; Fritz, M.; Hansma, H.G.; Hansma, P.K. Mapping interaction forces with the atomic force microscope. *Biophys. J.* **1994**, *66*, 2159–2165. [CrossRef]
27. Yamasue, K.; Cho, Y. Optimization of signal intensity in intermittent contact scanning nonlinear dielectric microscopy. *Microelectron. Reliab.* **2019**, *100-101*, 113345. [CrossRef]
28. Ohara, K.; Cho, Y. Non-contact scanning nonlinear dielectric microscopy. *Nanotechnology* **2005**, *16*, S54–S58. [CrossRef]
29. Yamasue, K.; Cho, Y. Boxcar Averaging Based Scanning Nonlinear Dielectric Microscopy and Its Application to Carrier Distribution Imaging on 2D Semiconductors. In Proceedings of the 2019 IEEE International Integrated Reliability Workshop (IIRW), South Lake Tahoe, CA, USA, 13–17 October 2019. [CrossRef]
30. Lai, K.; Ji, M.B.; Leindecker, N.; Kelly, M.A.; Shen, Z.X. Atomic-force-microscope-compatible near-field scanning microwave microscope with separated excitation and sensing probes. *Rev. Sci. Instrum.* **2007**, *78*, 63702. [CrossRef] [PubMed]
31. Williams, C.C.; Slinkman, J.; Hough, W.P.; Wickramasinghe, H.K. Lateral dopant profiling with 200 nm resolution by scanning capacitance microscopy. *Appl. Phys. Lett.* **1989**, *55*, 1662–1664. [CrossRef]
32. Cho, Y.; Kazuta, S.; Ohara, K.; Odagawa, H. Quantitative Measurement of Linear and Nonlinear Dielectric Characteristics Using Scanning Nonlinear Dielectric Microscopy. *Jpn. J. Appl. Phys.* **2000**, *39*, 3086–3089. [CrossRef]
33. Akhatova, F.; Ishmukhametov, I.; Fakhrullina, G.; Fakhrullin, R. Nanomechanical Atomic Force Microscopy to Probe Cellular Microplastics Uptake and Distribution. *Int. J. Mol. Sci.* **2022**, *23*, 806. [CrossRef] [PubMed]
34. Costa-Junior, L.M.; Silva, C.R.; Soares, A.M.S.; Menezes, A.S.; Silva, M.R.L.; Amarante, A.F.T.; Costa, E.F.; Alencar, L.M.R. Assessment of biophysical properties of Haemonchus contortus from different life cycle stages with atomic force microscopy. *Ultramicroscopy* **2020**, *209*, 112862. [CrossRef] [PubMed]
35. Lawson, J.L.; Uhlenbeck, G.E. *Threshold Signals*; McGraw-Hill: New York, NY, USA, 1950.
36. Holcomb, D.F.; Norberg, R.E. Nuclear Spin Relaxation in Alkali Metals. *Phys. Rev. (Series I)* **1955**, *98*, 1074–1091. [CrossRef]
37. Elmore, W.C. The Transient Response of Damped Linear Networks with Particular Regard to Wideband Amplifiers. *J. Appl. Phys.* **1948**, *19*, 55–63. [CrossRef]
38. Sugimura, H.; Ishida, Y.; Hayashi, K.; Takai, O.; Nakagiri, N. Potential shielding by the surface water layer in Kelvin probe force microscopy. *Appl. Phys. Lett.* **2002**, *80*, 1459–1461. [CrossRef]
39. Nečas, D.; Klapetek, P. Gwyddion: An open-source software for SPM data analysis. *Cent. Eur. J. Phys.* **2012**, *10*, 181–188. [CrossRef]
40. Geim, A.K.; Grigorieva, I.V. Van der Waals heterostructures. *Nature* **2013**, *499*, 419–425. [CrossRef] [PubMed]
41. Radisavljevic, B.; Radenovic, A.; Brivio, J.; Giacometti, V.; Kis, A. Single-layer MoS_2 transistors. *Nat. Nanotechnol.* **2011**, *6*, 147–150. [CrossRef] [PubMed]
42. Mak, K.F.; Lee, C.; Hone, J.; Shan, J.; Heinz, T.F. Atomically Thin MoS_2: A New Direct-Gap Semiconductor. *Phys. Rev. Lett.* **2010**, *105*, 136805. [CrossRef] [PubMed]
43. Yin, Z.; Li, H.; Li, H.; Jiang, L.; Shi, Y.; Sun, Y.; Lu, G.; Zhang, Q.; Chen, X.; Zhang, H. Single-Layer MoS_2 Phototransistors. *ACS Nano* **2012**, *6*, 74–80. [CrossRef] [PubMed]
44. Lee, C.-H.; Lee, G.-H.; van der Zande, A.M.; Chen, W.; Li, Y.; Han, M.; Cui, X.; Arefe, G.; Nuckolls, C.; Heinz, T.F.; et al. Atomically thin p–n junctions with van der Waals heterointerfaces. *Nat. Nanotechnol.* **2014**, *9*, 676–681. [CrossRef]
45. Siao, M.D.; Shen, W.C.; Chen, R.S.; Chang, Z.W.; Shih, M.C.; Chiu, Y.P.; Cheng, C.-M. Two-dimensional electronic transport and surface electron accumulation in MoS_2. *Nat. Commun.* **2018**, *9*, 1442. [CrossRef] [PubMed]
46. Fang, N.; Toyoda, S.; Taniguchi, T.; Watanabe, K.; Nagashio, K. Full Energy Spectra of Interface State Densities for n- and p-type MoS_2 Field-Effect Transistors. *Adv. Funct. Mater.* **2019**, *29*, 1904465. [CrossRef]
47. Laskar, M.R.; Nath, D.N.; Ma, L.; Lee, E.W.; Lee, C.H.; Kent, T.; Yang, Z.; Mishra, R.; Roldan, M.A.; Idrobo, J.-C.; et al. p-type doping of MoS_2 thin films using Nb. *Appl. Phys. Lett.* **2014**, *104*, 092104. [CrossRef]
48. Novoselov, K.S.; Jiang, D.; Schedin, F.; Booth, T.J.; Khotkevich, V.V.; Morozov, S.V.; Geim, A.K. Two-dimensional atomic crystals. *Proc. Natl. Acad. Sci. USA* **2005**, *102*, 10451–10453. [CrossRef] [PubMed]

Article

Multiscale Investigation of the Structural, Electrical and Photoluminescence Properties of MoS₂ Obtained by MoO₃ Sulfurization

Salvatore E. Panasci [1,2], Antal Koos [3], Emanuela Schilirò [1], Salvatore Di Franco [1], Giuseppe Greco [1], Patrick Fiorenza [1], Fabrizio Roccaforte [1], Simonpietro Agnello [1,4,5], Marco Cannas [4], Franco M. Gelardi [4], Attila Sulyok [3], Miklos Nemeth [3], Béla Pécz [3,*] and Filippo Giannazzo [1,*]

1. Consiglio Nazionale delle Ricerche—Istituto per la Microelettronica e Microsistemi (CNR-IMM), Strada VIII 5, 95121 Catania, Italy; SalvatoreEthan.Panasci@imm.cnr.it (S.E.P.); Emanuela.Schiliro@imm.cnr.it (E.S.); salvatore.difranco@imm.cnr.it (S.D.F.); giuseppe.greco@imm.cnr.it (G.G.); Patrick.Fiorenza@imm.cnr.it (P.F.); fabrizio.roccaforte@imm.cnr.it (F.R.); simonpietro.agnello@unipa.it (S.A.)
2. Department of Physics and Astronomy, University of Catania, 95123 Catania, Italy
3. Centre for Energy Research, Institute of Technical Physics and Materials Science, Konkoly-Thege ut 29-33, 1121 Budapest, Hungary; koos.antal@ek-cer.hu (A.K.); sulyok.attila@ek-cer.hu (A.S.); nemeth.miklos@ek-cer.hu (M.N.)
4. Department of Physics and Chemistry Emilio Segrè, University of Palermo, 90123 Palermo, Italy; marco.cannas@unipa.it (M.C.); franco.gelardi@unipa.it (F.M.G.)
5. ATEN Center, University of Palermo, 90123 Palermo, Italy
* Correspondence: pecz.bela@ek-cer.hu (B.P.); filippo.giannazzo@imm.cnr.it (F.G)

Abstract: In this paper, we report a multiscale investigation of the compositional, morphological, structural, electrical, and optical emission properties of 2H-MoS₂ obtained by sulfurization at 800 °C of very thin MoO₃ films (with thickness ranging from ~2.8 nm to ~4.2 nm) on a SiO₂/Si substrate. XPS analyses confirmed that the sulfurization was very effective in the reduction of the oxide to MoS₂, with only a small percentage of residual MoO₃ present in the final film. High-resolution TEM/STEM analyses revealed the formation of few (i.e., 2–3 layers) of MoS₂ nearly aligned with the SiO₂ surface in the case of the thinnest (~2.8 nm) MoO₃ film, whereas multilayers of MoS₂ partially standing up with respect to the substrate were observed for the ~4.2 nm one. Such different configurations indicate the prevalence of different mechanisms (i.e., vapour-solid surface reaction or S diffusion within the film) as a function of the thickness. The uniform thickness distribution of the few-layer and multilayer MoS₂ was confirmed by Raman mapping. Furthermore, the correlative plot of the characteristic A_{1g}-E_{2g} Raman modes revealed a compressive strain ($\varepsilon \approx -0.78 \pm 0.18\%$) and the coexistence of n- and p-type doped areas in the few-layer MoS₂ on SiO₂, where the p-type doping is probably due to the presence of residual MoO₃. Nanoscale resolution current mapping by C-AFM showed local inhomogeneities in the conductivity of the few-layer MoS₂, which are well correlated to the lateral changes in the strain detected by Raman. Finally, characteristic spectroscopic signatures of the defects/disorder in MoS₂ films produced by sulfurization were identified by a comparative analysis of Raman and photoluminescence (PL) spectra with CVD grown MoS₂ flakes.

Keywords: MoS₂; sulfurization; XPS; Raman; TEM; C-AFM; photoluminescence

1. Introduction

Transition metal dichalcogenides (TMDs) are a wide family of layered van der Waals (vdW) materials with the general chemical formula MX_2, M being a transition metal (Ti, Zr, Hf, V, Nb, Ta, Mo, W, Re, Pd, or Pt) and X a chalcogen atom (S, Se, or Te) [1]. Most of them exhibit metallic or semiconducting phases. In particular, semiconducting TMDs have been the object of increasing scientific interest in the last decade, due to their huge potential for applications in several fields, including electronics, optoelectronics, spintronics, valleytronics, chemical/environmental sensing, energy generation, and catalysis [2–10]. Molybdenum disulfide (MoS_2) is the most investigated among TMDs, due to the natural abundance and good chemical/mechanical stability of its 2H semiconductor phase under ambient conditions. The bandgap tunability as a function of the thickness, with a transition from an indirect bandgap of ~1.2 eV for bulk or few-layer MoS_2 to a direct bandgap of ~1.8 eV for monolayer MoS_2 [11,12], makes this material appealing for optoelectronic and electronic applications. In fact, the first robust 2D transistor with a large on/off ratio and good field-effect mobility was demonstrated using monolayer 2H-MoS_2 flakes as the semiconducting channel [13,14]. This material and other TMDs are currently considered a potential replacement of Si for the next generation of complementary metal oxide semiconductor (CMOS) devices allowing the continuation of Moore's law [15]. Furthermore, they can represent the basis for new concept (More-than-Moore) devices [16,17].

Due to this wide application potential, scalable and reproducible growth methods for thin films of TMDs are strongly required for their future implementation in manufacturing lines. In this context, research on MoS_2 wafer-scale growth and device integration is relatively more mature than for other 2D TMDs.

Top-down synthesis approaches used to separate MoS_2 from bulk crystals, such as mechanical exfoliation [18,19], gold-assisted exfoliation [20–24], and liquid exfoliation [25], are not suitable to ensure the reproducibility and thickness control on a wafer scale required for high-end electronic applications. For this reason, bottom-up approaches as Chemical Vapour Deposition (CVD) [26,27], Pulsed Laser Deposition (PLD) [28], Molecular Beam Epitaxy (MBE) [29], and Atomic Layer Deposition (ALD) [30] represent the most promising methods to obtain a reproducible thin film of TMDs on a large area.

In particular, CVD using vapours from S and MoO_3 powders has been widely explored by several research groups, since it is a cost-effective method to produce MoS_2 domains with good crystalline quality on different substrates [31–33]. Although monolayer flakes with a triangular or hexagonal shape and lateral extension from tens to hundreds of micrometres have been obtained under optimized CVD conditions [34], achieving coverage and thickness uniformity on the wafer scale still represents a huge challenge, due to the difficulty of controlling all the parameters involved in the process (including the substrate temperature, the evaporation rates of the S and Mo precursors, the pressure in the chamber, and the carrier gas flow rate) [35–39].

As an alternative to the single-step CVD approach, sulfurization of a Mo (or Mo-oxide) film pre-deposited on a substrate (e.g., by evaporation or sputtering) allows superior control of MoS_2 coverage and uniformity by controlling the initial film thickness [40–43]. Different to CVD (where the Mo–S bonds are mostly formed by vapour phase reaction and the MoS_2 lands on the substrate), the sulfurization process is a heterogeneous vapour-solid reaction between the S vapour and the pre-deposited film [44]. The conversion of MoO_x to MoS_2 by sulfurization has been demonstrated to occur in a wide temperature range, from 500 °C to 1000 °C, although the best quality films are typically obtained at temperatures > 750 °C [44]. Besides the vapour-solid surface reaction, the initial Mo or MoO_x film thickness also plays an important role in the process. In fact, with increasing its thickness, the diffusion of S in the film represents the limiting mechanism for the formation of MoS_2 layers and determines their alignment with respect to the substrate [45,46]. In particular, at typical sulfurization temperatures of 750–800 °C, single or few-layers of MoS_2 horizontally aligned to the substrate plane are obtained for very thin (<3 nm) Mo films, whereas vertically aligned growth occurs for thicker Mo films [47]. This is due to the favoured sulphur diffusion along the vdW gaps between the vertically oriented MoS_2 layers [45,47,48]. Besides the initial Mo (or Mo-oxide) thickness, other key factors controlling MoS_2 formation include the substrate heating rate, pressure, and local S concentration on the sample surface [49–51]. Furthermore, the underlying substrate can play an important role in MoS_2 formation during sulfurization of pre-deposited MoO_3. In fact, while a higher temperature may enhance the sulfurization degree, on the other hand, it can also result in increased MoO_3 evaporation and diffusion of Mo atoms on the substrate surface. This latter phenomenon strongly depends on the adhesion energy and surface diffusivity of Mo atoms on the substrate.

The main disadvantage of the continuous MoS$_2$ films produced by the sulfurization approach is their nanocrystalline structure (with 20–30 nm grain-size) [44], typically resulting in poorer carrier mobility, if compared to the large and isolated monocrystalline MoS$_2$ flakes obtained by the CVD approach. However, the high uniformity and its good compatibility with the fabrication methods used in the semiconductor industry makes this approach appealing for some applications, e.g., MoS$_2$/semiconductor heterojunctions [52] or hydrogen evolution applications [53]. Hence, a detailed characterisation of structural/compositional, vibrational, optical, and electrical properties of MoS$_2$ films produced by Mo sulfurization remains highly desirable.

In this paper, few or multilayer MoS$_2$ on a SiO$_2$/Si substrate have been produced by sulfurization at 800 °C of very thin MoO$_3$ films, from ~2.8 nm to ~4.2 nm (i.e., the critical range for the transition from horizontally to vertically aligned layers). The compositional, morphological, structural, electrical, and optical emission properties of the grown films have been extensively investigated by the combination of several characterisation techniques with macro to nanoscale spatial resolution. This correlative analysis provides deep insight into the potentialities and limitations of this material system for applications.

2. Materials and Methods

The thin molybdenum-oxide films on SiO$_2$ (900 nm)/Si substrates were obtained by DC magnetron sputtering from a Mo-target (using a Quorum Q300-TD system), followed by natural oxidation in air. The sulfurization process, schematically illustrated in Figure 1, was carried out in a two-heating zones furnace (TSH12/38/500, Elite Thermal Systems Ltd., Market Harborough, UK), with the first zone (at a temperature of 150 °C) hosting a crucible with 300 mg sulphur (purity 99.9%, product 28260.234, VWR Chemicals, Radnor, PA, USA), and the second zone (at a temperature of 800 °C) hosting the MoO$_3$/SiO$_2$/Si sample. Starting from a base pressure of 4×10^{-6} bar, the Ar carrier gas (purity 5.0, Messer, Budapest, Hungary) with a flux of 100 sccm transported the S vapours from the first to the second zone. The duration of the sulfurization process was 60 min.

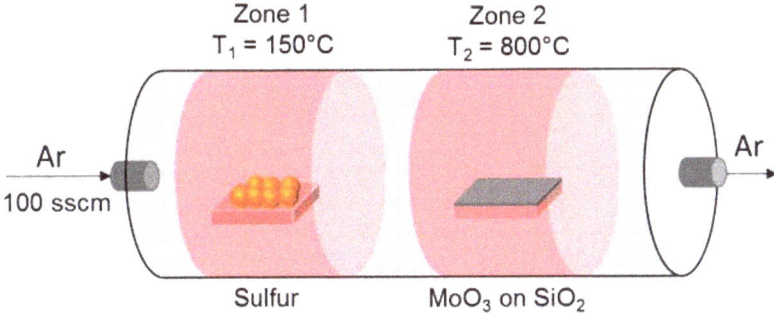

Figure 1. Schematic illustration of the sulfurization process of the thin MoO$_3$ films on the SiO$_2$/Si substrates.

Morphological analyses on the as-deposited MoO$_3$ films and after the sulfurization process were carried out by Tapping mode Atomic Force Microscopy using a DI3100 system by Bruker (Santa Barbara, CA, USA) with Nanoscope V electronics. The compositional properties of the as-deposited metal films and MoS$_2$ formation after the sulfurization process were evaluated by X-ray photoelectron spectroscopy (XPS) using Escalab Xi+ equipment by Thermo Fisher (Waltham, MA, USA), with a monochromatic Al Kα X-ray source (energy = 1486.6 eV). The spectra were collected at a take-off angle of 90° relative to the sample surface and pass energy of 20 eV. The instrument resolution was 0.45 eV (FWHM of the Ag 3d$_{5/2}$ peak). The spectra were aligned using C1s (285 eV) as reference.

High-resolution transmission electron microscopy (HR-TEM), high angle annular dark-field scanning transmission electron microscopy (HAADF-STEM), and energy dispersion spectroscopy (EDS) analyses of the MoS$_2$ thin films were carried out with an aberration-corrected Titan Themis 200 microscope by Thermo Fisher (Waltham, MA USA). To this aim, cross-sectioned samples were prepared by a focused ion beam (FIB). Raman spectroscopy and mapping of MoS$_2$ vibrational peaks were carried out by WiTec Alpha equipment by WiTec (Ulm, Germany), using laser excitation at 532 nm, 1.5 mW power, and 100× objective. Photoluminescence spectra (PL) were collected using a Horiba (Palaiseau, France) system with a laser source of 532 nm. To confirm the uniformity of the MoS$_2$ thin layer across the substrate, the Raman and PL analyses have been performed at different positions on the sample. Finally, nanoscale resolution current mapping of MoS$_2$ on SiO$_2$ was performed by conductive Atomic Force Microscopy (C-AFM) with a DI3100 system by Bruker (Santa Barbara, CA, USA), using Pt-coated Si tips with ~5 nm curvature radius.

3. Results and Discussion

Figure 2a shows a typical AFM morphology of as-deposited MoO$_3$ on the SiO$_2$/Si substrate using the lowest sputtering time (30 s). This analysis indicates a very low root mean square (RMS) surface roughness of 0.35 nm. Similar roughness values have been measured for MoO$_3$ film thicknesses deposited at higher sputtering times. The thickness of the as-deposited films was also evaluated by AFM step height measurements performed on intentionally scratched regions of the films. Figure 2b,c show the morphologies and corresponding line profiles for films deposited with two different sputtering times (30 s and 45 s), resulting in ~2.8 nm and ~4.2 nm thickness, respectively.

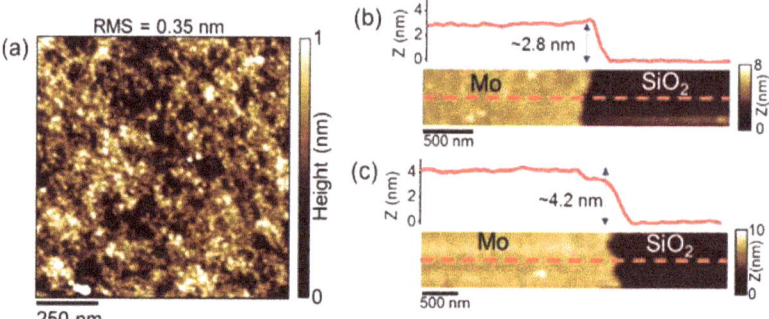

Figure 2. (a) Typical AFM morphology of as-deposited MoO$_3$ thin films on SiO$_2$, with the indication of the root mean square (RMS) roughness. (b,c) Determination of the thickness of films deposited with two different sputtering times by measurement of the step heights (~2.8 nm and ~4.2 nm) with respect to SiO$_2$ on scratched regions.

XPS compositional analyses performed on the thinnest deposited films revealed that they are predominantly composed of MoO$_3$, with a small (<1%) MoO$_2$ contribution. Recently, Vangelista et al. [44] also reported the complete oxidation (ascribed to air exposure after the deposition) of evaporated Mo films with similar thickness, used for subsequent MoS$_2$ growth by sulfurization. The same authors [44] explained the conversion of MoO$_3$ to MoS$_2$ upon exposure to sulphur according to the following chemical reaction:

$$2\ MoO_3(s) + 7\ S(g) \rightarrow 2\ MoS_2(s) + 3\ SO_2(g), \tag{1}$$

which is the result of two intermediate steps:

$$MoO_3 + (x/2)\ S \rightarrow MoO_{3-x} + (x/2)\ SO_2 \tag{2}$$

$$MoO_{3-x} + [(7-x)/2]\ S \rightarrow MoS_2 + [(3-x)/2]\ SO_2 \tag{3}$$

i.e., the S-induced reduction of the MoO_3 to a sub-stoichiometric oxide MoO_{3-x} (2), followed by its conversion to MoS_2 (3), with the formation of gaseous SO_2 as a by-product.

After the sulfurization process at 800 °C, XPS analyses were performed to evaluate the successful conversion of MoO_3 to MoS_2. Figure 3a reports an overview spectrum, allowing the quantification of the percentage of elemental concentrations on the sample surface. In particular, molybdenum and sulphur percentages of 3.26% and 6.82%, respectively, were evaluated (besides the large Si and O background), which were close to the stoichiometric [Mo]/[S] ratio for MoS_2. More detailed information on the Mo and S bonding was deduced from the $Mo3d_{3/2}$, $Mo3d_{5/2}$, and S2s core levels in Figure 3b, and the $S2p_{1/2}$ and $S2p_{3/2}$ core levels in Figure 3c. Two doublets were found in the Mo 3d spectrum, and both doublets were fitted with a peak separation of 3.1 eV [44,54,55]. In particular, the deconvolution of the Mo3d peaks shows the predominance of the Mo^{4+} component, associated with $2H-MoS_2$, accompanied by a smaller Mo^{6+} contribution, associated with the presence of residual MoO_3. The two $S2p_{1/2}$ and $S2p_{3/2}$ peaks [44,54,55] in Figure 3c confirm that sulphur is mainly in the form of sulphide, with a small S-O component.

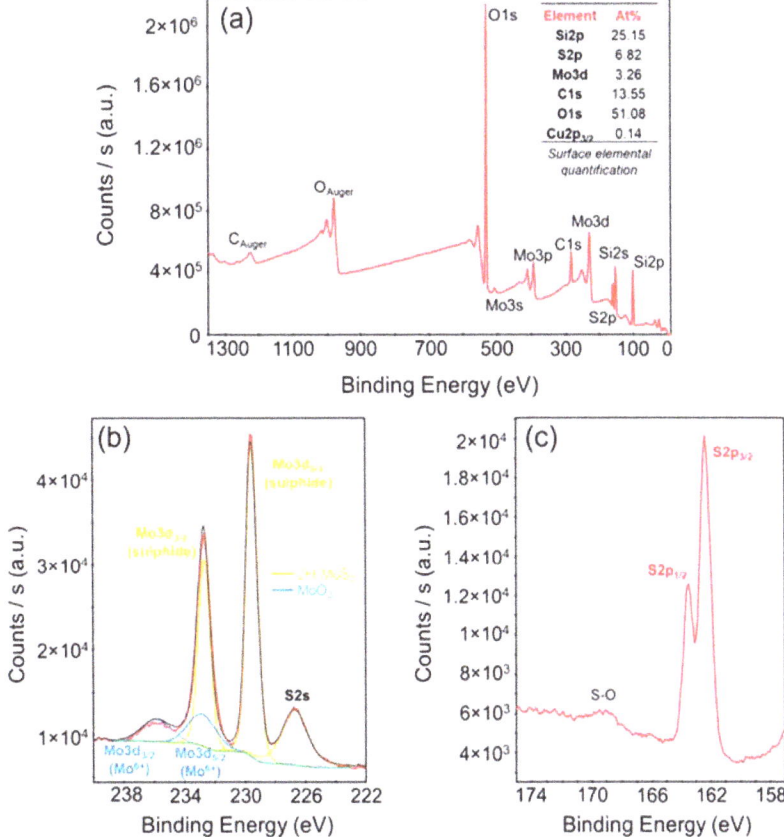

Figure 3. (a) Survey XPS spectrum of MoS_2 on SiO_2 produced by sulfurization of the 2.8 nm MoO_3 film, with the indication of the evaluated surface elemental composition. (b) XPS spectra of the Mo 3d and S 2s core levels, with the deconvolution of the Mo^{4+} contribution (related to MoS_2) and the Mo^{6+} contribution (related to residual MoO_3). (c) S 2p core levels spectra, indicating the predominance of the sulphide contribution, with a small S-O component.

The structural properties of the MoS$_2$ films were also investigated at nanoscale by transmission electron microscopy on cross-sectioned samples. Figure 4a,b show representative HR-TEM and HAADF-STEM analyses on the few-layers MoS$_2$ sample obtained by sulfurization of the ~2.8 nm MoO$_3$ film. The diffraction contrast in the HR-TEM image Figure 4a demonstrates the presence of two or three crystalline layers embedded between the amorphous SiO$_2$ substrate and amorphous carbon (a–c) protective film. These layers are predominantly oriented parallel to the substrate, with nanometric scale corrugations. Furthermore, an interlayer spacing of ~0.6 nm is directly evaluated from the HRTEM image of a 3L-MoS$_2$ reported in the insert of Figure 4a. The number of MoS$_2$ layers and their nearly parallel orientation with respect to the substrate is confirmed by the HAADF-STEM image in Figure 4b collected on the same sample. On the other hand, a more irregular configuration of the layers can be observed from the HRTEM (Figure 4c) and HAADF-STEM (Figure 4d) analyses performed on the MoS$_2$ multilayer produced by sulfurization of ~4.2 nm film. In fact, in the analysed specimen volume, horizontally oriented MoS$_2$ layers co-exist with layers standing up with respect to the SiO$_2$ surface. This observation is fully consistent with previous reports showing a transition from horizontal to vertically oriented growth for film thickness larger than 3 nm [47].

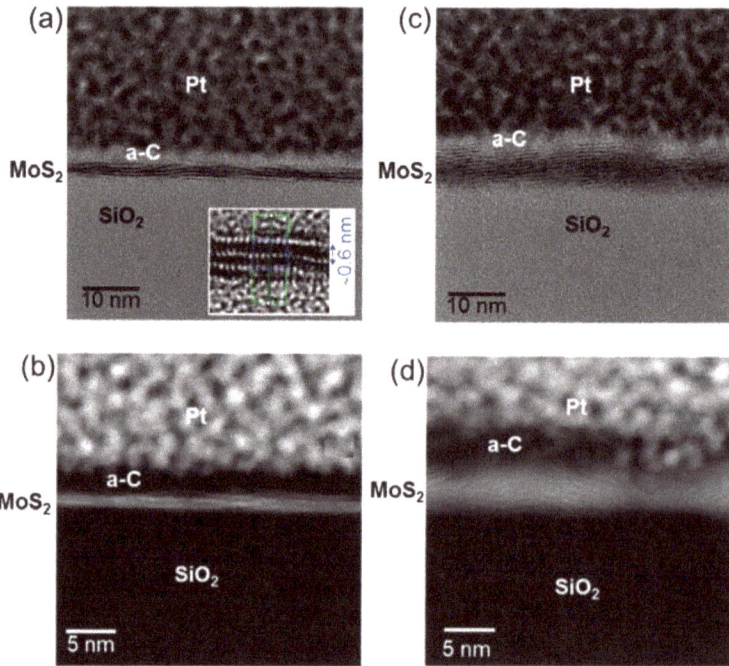

Figure 4. Cross sectional HR-TEM (**a**) and HAADF-STEM (**b**) images of few-layers MoS$_2$ obtained by sulfurization of the ~2.8 nm MoO$_3$ film on the SiO$_2$ substrate. MoS$_2$ is composed by nearly horizontally aligned 2–3 layers. The interlayer spacing in a 3-layers region is evaluated from the HR-TEM in the insert of panel (**a**). Cross sectional HR-TEM (**c**) and HAADF-STEM (**d**) of multilayers MoS$_2$ obtained by sulfurization of the ~4.2 nm MoO$_3$ film.

The layers number uniformity of the grown MoS$_2$ films was also investigated on micrometer scale areas and with high statistics by Raman spectroscopy. Figure 5 shows two typical Raman spectra of the few-layers (i.e., 2 L–3 L) MoS$_2$ (black line) and of the multilayer MoS$_2$ (red line) grown on SiO$_2$ by the sulfurization process. The two characteristic in-plane (E$_{2g}$) and out-of-plane (A$_{1g}$) vibrational modes of MoS$_2$ are clearly identified, and the typical redshift of the E$_{2g}$ peak and blue shift of the A$_{1g}$ with increasing the number of layers [19] is observed. In particular, the difference $\Delta\omega = \omega_{A_{1g}} - \omega_{E_{2g}}$ between the wavenumbers of these two main modes is commonly taken as a way to evaluate the number of MoS$_2$ layers, with larger $\Delta\omega$ values generally associated with a thicker MoS$_2$.

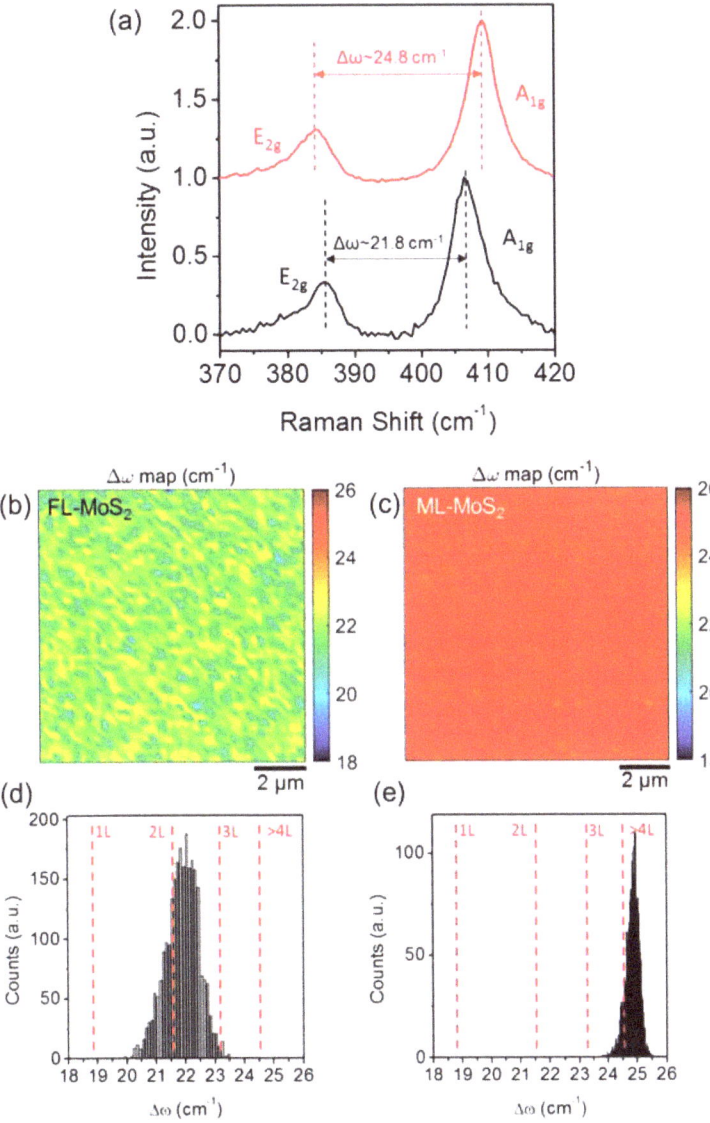

Figure 5. (a) Representative Raman spectra of the few-layers (FL) MoS$_2$ (black-line) and multilayer (ML) MoS$_2$ samples obtained by sulfurization of the 2.8 and 4.2 nm MoO$_3$ films on SiO$_2$. Colour maps of the A$_{1g}$-E$_{2g}$ wavenumber difference $\Delta\omega$ obtained from arrays of Raman spectra collected on 10 µm × 10 µm scan areas on the FL-MoS$_2$ (b) and on the ML-MoS$_2$ (c) samples. Histogram of $\Delta\omega$ values showing a distribution with a peak at $\omega \approx 21.8 \pm 0.6$ cm^{-1} for the FL-MoS$_2$ sample associated to 2 L–3 L MoS$_2$ (d) and $\omega \approx 24.8 \pm 0.4$ cm^{-1} for the ML-MoS$_2$ sample, corresponding to >4 L MoS$_2$ thickness (e).

The colour maps in Figure 5b,c illustrate the spatial distribution of the $\Delta\omega$ values obtained from arrays of 50 × 50 Raman spectra collected on 10 μm × 10 μm scan areas. Figure 5d,e show the histograms of the $\Delta\omega$ values reported in the two maps, with the indication of the corresponding number of MoS$_2$ layers according to the calibration reported in Ref. [19]. The two distributions are quite uniform and exhibit a $\omega \approx 21.8 \pm 0.6$ cm^{-1} for the few-layer MoS$_2$ sample and $\omega \approx 24.8 \pm 0.4$ cm^{-1} for the multilayer MoS$_2$ sample. These $\Delta\omega$ values are associated with a 2 L–3 L MoS$_2$ thickness for the first sample, in very good agreement with TEM analyses in Figure 4, and to >4 L MoS$_2$ for the second one.

In the following, we will concentrate our attention on the 2 L–3 L MoS$_2$ sample, since the horizontal configuration of the layers makes it more suitable for electronic applications, similarly to 2H-MoS$_2$ samples produced by CVD or by exfoliation from bulk molybdenite.

The doping type and the biaxial strain (ε) of the thin MoS$_2$ film were also evaluated from the Raman maps by a correlative plot of A$_{1g}$ versus E$_{2g}$ peaks positions, as recently discussed in Ref. [23]. Figure 6a shows as blue circles the ω_{A1g} and ω_{E2g} values extracted from all the Raman spectra in the array of Figure 5. The red line in Figure 6a represents the ideal ω_{A1g} vs. ω_{E2g} dependence (i.e., the strain line) for a purely strained 3L-MoS$_2$ film. This relation is obtained from the combination of the following two expressions:

$$\omega_{E_{2g}} = \omega^0_{E_{2g}} - 2\gamma_{E_{2g}}\omega^0_{E_{2g}}\varepsilon \quad (4)$$

$$\omega_{A_{1g}} = \omega^0_{A_{1g}} - 2\gamma_{A_{1g}}\omega^0_{A_{1g}}\varepsilon \quad (5)$$

Here, $\gamma_{E_{2g}} = 0.39$ and $\gamma_{A_{1g}} = 0.09$ are the Grüneisen parameters for the two vibrational modes of 3L-MoS$_2$, estimated from the literature values of the peaks shift rates as a function of strain percentage (-3 cm^{-1}/% and -0.7 cm^{-1}/% for the E$_{2g}$ and A$_{1g}$ peaks, respectively) [56]. $\omega^0_{E_{2g}}$ and $\omega^0_{A_{1g}}$ represent the E$_{2g}$ and A$_{1g}$ frequencies for an ideally unstrained and undoped 3L-MoS$_2$. Here, the literature values for a suspended 3L-MoS$_2$ membrane ($\omega^0_{E_{2g}} = 382.9$ cm^{-1} and $\omega^0_{A_{1g}} = 406.4$ cm^{-1}) [56], not affected by the interaction with the substrate, were taken as the best approximation for these ideal values. This reference point is reported as a red square in Figure 6a, while the two arrows with opposite directions along the strain line indicate the tensile (red-shift) and compressive strain (blue-shift), respectively. Furthermore, the black dashed lines serve as guides to estimate the strain values. The distribution of the experimental points (blue circles) in the plot of Figure 6a clearly indicates that the thin MoS$_2$ film on SiO$_2$ is compressively strained. Figure 6b shows the 2D map of the compressive strain, calculated from the map of ω_{E2g} values by applying Equation (4). Furthermore, the corresponding histogram of the ε values is reported in Figure 6c, from which an average strain value $\varepsilon \approx -0.78\% \pm 0.18\%$ can be deduced.

The strain line separates the n-type and p-type doping regions in the $\omega_{A1g} - \omega_{E2g}$ diagram in Figure 6a. Noteworthy, the experimental points in Figure 6a are partially located in the n-type region and partially in the p-type one. Unintentional n-type doping is typically reported for MoS$_2$ films produced by different synthesis methods (such as mechanical exfoliation or CVD) and it is commonly ascribed to native defects present in the material [57–60]. Here, the observed p-type doping in some regions of the MoS$_2$ film produced by sulfurization can be associated with the presence of residual MoO$_3$, as deduced by XPS. In fact, several studies demonstrated how intentionally introducing MoO$_3$ in pristine (n-type) MoS$_2$, e.g., by O$_2$ plasma treatments, results in p-type doping of the material [61,62].

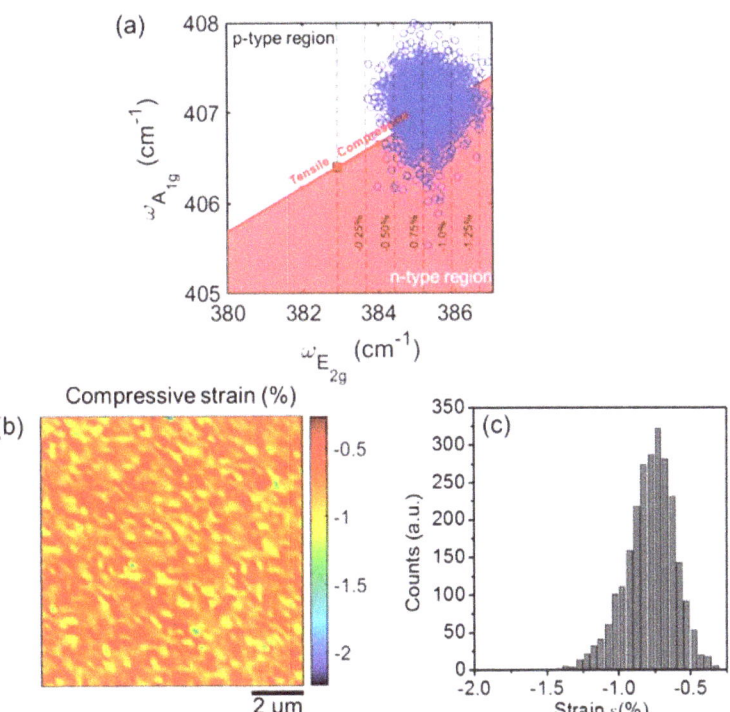

Figure 6. (a) Correlative plot of the ω_{A1g} and ω_{E2g} values (blue circles) extracted from all the Raman spectra in the array of Figure 5. The red line represents the ideal ω_{A1g} vs. ω_{E2g} dependence (i.e., the strain line) for a purely strained 3L-MoS$_2$ film. The red square corresponds to the frequencies $\omega_{E_{2g}^0}$ and $\omega_{A_{1g}^0}$ for an ideally unstrained and undoped 3L-MoS$_2$, while the two red arrows with opposite directions along the strain line indicate the tensile (red-shift) and compressive strain (blue-shift), respectively. (b) Map and (c) corresponding histogram of the compressive strain on a 10 μm × 10 μm area.

The MoS$_2$ thin layers produced by MoO$_3$ thin films sulfurization exhibit large resistivity values in the range of 10–100 Ω·cm [63]. This can be ascribed, in part, to the nanocrystalline structure of the films, i.e., the large density of grain boundaries, which are known to introduce resistive contributions in the current path [64]. On the other hand, the local changes in the compressive strain distribution, as well in the carrier density, deduced by Raman mapping is expected to have an effect on the electrical properties of the few-layers of MoS$_2$. To get direct information on the homogeneity of conductivity in this film, local current mapping has been carried out by C-AFM, as schematically depicted in Figure 7a. In this configuration, the current locally injected from the AFM metal tip flows in the MoS$_2$ film and is finally collected from the macroscopic front contact. Due to the nanoscale size of the tip contact, the dominant contributions to the measured resistance are represented by the local tip/MoS$_2$ contact resistance and the spreading resistance in the MoS$_2$ region underneath the tip. Figure 7b shows the contact-mode morphological image on the sample surface, from which an RMS roughness ≈ 0.5 nm slightly higher than the one of the as-deposited MoO$_3$ film (Figure 2a) was deduced. Figure 7c,d report the corresponding C-AFM current map and the histogram of the measured current values. The current map clearly shows submicrometer lateral variations of the conductivity, which are only partially correlated to the morphology, while the histogram shows a Gaussian distribution of these values, resembling the shape of the strain distribution in Figure 7d. From this comparison, we can speculate that these mesoscopic-scale inhomogeneities can be partially ascribed to the lateral changes in the strain and carrier density detected by Raman.

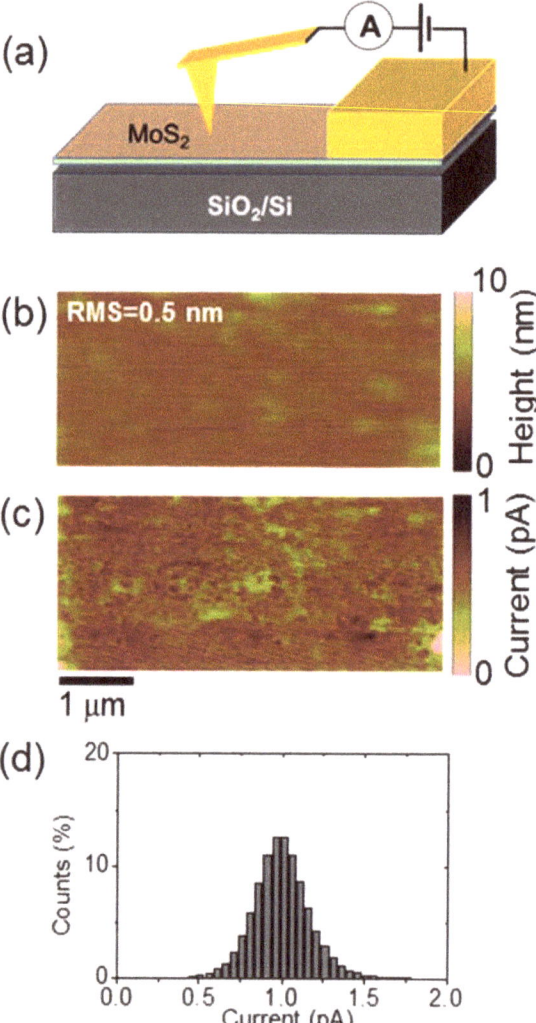

Figure 7. (a) Schematic of the C-AFM setup for local conductivity mapping of few-layers MoS$_2$ on SiO$_2$. (b) Morphology and (c) current map simultaneously measured with tip-to-sample bias of 5 V. (d) Histogram of current values from the C-AFM map.

In the last section of this paper, Raman and photoluminescence spectra acquired on the few-layers MoS$_2$ samples produced by sulfurization have been compared with reference spectra acquired on CVD-grown MoS$_2$ samples with a similar thickness.

Figure 8 shows a typical Raman spectrum of 3L-MoS$_2$ on SiO$_2$ produced by MoO$_3$ sulfurization, compared with a spectrum of a 3L-MoS$_2$ sample grown by CVD on SiO$_2$ [65], reported as reference. Some remarkable differences can be clearly observed between MoS$_2$ layers prepared using the two different approaches. In fact, besides a lower E_{2g}/A_{1g} intensity ratio, the two vibrational peaks exhibit a more pronounced asymmetric shape in the 3L-MoS$_2$ produced by sulfurization as compared to the CVD-grown one. The deconvolution analysis of the Raman spectra with four Gaussian contributions, associated with the main E_{2g} and A_{1g} modes and the disorder activated LO(M) and ZO(M) modes [66], is also presented in Figure 8. These LO(M) and ZO(M) components are very small in the Raman spectra of CVD 3L-MoS$_2$, whereas their weight is higher in the 3L-MoS$_2$ produced by sulfurization. In this latter case, they can be ascribed both to the nanocrystalline nature of the film, as well as to the presence of residual MoO$_3$, as deduced from the XPS analyses.

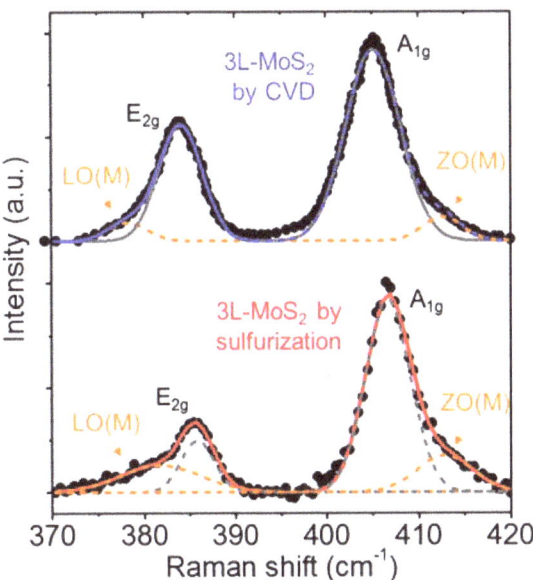

Figure 8. Raman spectrum for 3L-MoS$_2$ produced by sulfurization (red), compared with a reference spectrum for CVD grown 3L-MoS$_2$ (blue). Data for CVD 3L-MoS$_2$ were adapted with permission from [65], copyright Elsevier 2020.

Figure 9 shows the comparison between a PL spectrum measured on the 3L-MoS$_2$ produced by sulfurization with a reference spectrum for CVD grown 3L-MoS$_2$, taken from Ref. [65]. For both spectra, acquired using a 532 nm wavelength laser source, the main emission peak at an energy of 1.86 eV can be observed. However, significant differences in spectral features can be clearly identified from a detailed deconvolution analysis.

The PL spectrum of CVD MoS$_2$ can be fitted by three Gaussian peaks, associated with the two exciton contributions (A^0 at 1.86 ± 0.01 eV and B at 1.99 ± 0.01 eV, due to the spin-orbit splitting of the valence band) and the trionic contribution (X_T at 1.78 ± 0.01 eV) [65]. On the other hand, the deconvolution analysis of the spectrum for the sulfurization grown sample allowed us to identify a fourth component X_D at 1.75 ± 0.01 eV, besides the trion (X_T at 1.78 ± 0.01 eV) and exciton peaks (A^0 at 1.86 ± 0.01 eV and B at 1.95 ± 0.01 eV). Noteworthy, the presence of this X_D contribution is accompanied by a strong decrease in the spectral weight of the exciton peak B, as compared to the case of the CVD sample, as well as its FWHM reduction. The occurrence of a similar feature X_D, associated with point defects in the MoS$_2$ lattice, has been recently reported by Chow et al. [67] for the PL spectra of MoS$_2$ flakes subjected to soft Ar-plasma irradiation, and it was also accompanied by a decrease in the exciton peak B with respect to unirradiated flakes. Hence, the observed X_D contribution for our samples produced by sulfurization was ascribed to a higher density of point defects with respect to CVD grown samples.

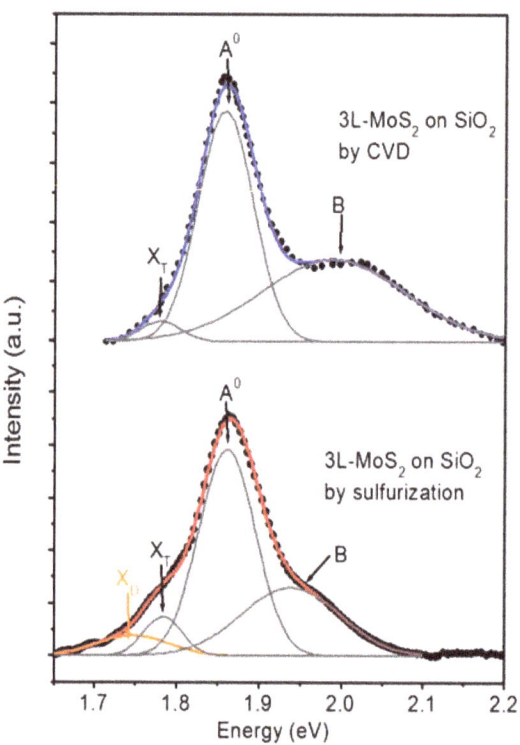

Figure 9. Photoluminescence (PL) spectra for 3L-MoS$_2$ produced by sulfurization, compared with a reference spectrum for CVD grown 3L-MoS$_2$. The deconvolution analysis indicated the presence of the excitonic contributions A^0, B, and of the trionic contribution X$_T$ (grey lines) for the CVD grown sample. In addition, the defect-related peak X$_D$ (orange line) is identified in the sulfurization grown sample. Data for CVD 3L-MoS$_2$ were adapted with permission from [65], copyright Elsevier 2020.

4. Conclusions

In conclusion, we reported a detailed analysis of the compositional, morphological, structural, electrical, and optical emission properties of few or multilayer MoS$_2$ on a SiO$_2$/Si substrate produced by sulfurization of very thin MoO$_3$ films at 800 °C. Both Raman mapping and TEM/STEM analyses showed the formation of 2–3 layers of MoS$_2$ nearly aligned with the SiO$_2$ surface after sulfurization of the thinnest MoO$_3$ film, whereas multilayers of MoS$_2$ (partially standing up) were observed for the thicker MoO$_3$ film. The strain distribution in the few-layer MoS$_2$ on SiO$_2$ was evaluated by the correlative plot of the characteristic A$_{1g}$-E$_{2g}$ Raman modes, showing the occurrence of a compressive strain $\varepsilon \approx -0.78 \pm 0.18\%$. Furthermore, the co-existence of submicrometer areas with n- and p-type doping is detected, with the p-type doping probably due to the presence of residual MoO$_3$, as revealed by XPS analyses. Nanoscale resolution current mapping by C-AFM showed conductivity inhomogeneities in the few-layer MoS$_2$, which are well correlated to the lateral changes in the strain detected by Raman. Finally, the characteristics spectroscopic signatures of the defects/disorder were identified by comparing Raman and PL spectra of sulfurization grown MoS$_2$ with reference analyses of CVD-grown single crystalline MoS$_2$.

The demonstrated MoS$_2$ growth method is quite versatile and can be extended to different substrates, besides SiO$_2$. In particular, the adoption of crystalline substrates (such as sapphire, GaN, and 4H-SiC) with the hexagonal basal plane and good lattice matching with MoS$_2$ is expected to enhance the domain size and electronic quality of the grown films. Furthermore, the homogeneous large area few-layer MoS$_2$ can be transferred to arbitrary substrates (including flexible ones) [68] and find applications in different fields of microelectronics, flexible electronics, and sensing.

Author Contributions: Conceptualization, F.G. and A.K.; methodology, A.K.; software, S.E.P.; formal analysis, S.E.P.; investigation, A.K., S.E.P., E.S., G.G., P.F., A.S., M.N., S.D.F., S.A., M.C. and B.P.; resources, S.D.F.; data curation, S.E.P.; writing—original draft preparation, S.E.P.; writing—review and editing, all authors; supervision, F.G., B.P. and F.M.G.; project administration, F.G.; funding acquisition, F.G., B.P. and F.R. All authors have read and agreed to the published version of the manuscript.

Funding: This work was funded, in part, by MUR in the framework of the FlagERA-JTC 2019 project ETMOS. E.S. acknowledges the PON project EleGaNTe (ARS01_01007) funded by MUR for financial support. B.P acknowledges funding from the national project TKP2021-NKTA-05. Furthermore, B.P. acknowledges VEKOP-2.3.3-15-2016-00002 of the European Structural and Investment Funds for providing the microscope facility. Part of the experiments was carried out using the facilities of the Italian Infrastructure Beyond Nano.

Institutional Review Board Statement: Not applicable.

Informed Consent Statement: Not applicable.

Data Availability Statement: The data that support the findings of this study are available from the corresponding author upon reasonable request.

Acknowledgments: We would like to acknowledge the Thermo Fisher Scientific Applications Laboratory, East Grinstead, UK, for providing XPS spectra on MoS_2 layers.

Conflicts of Interest: The authors declare no conflict of interest.

References

1. Manzeli, S.; Ovchinnikov, D.; Pasquier, D.; Yazyev, O.V.; Kis, A. 2D transition metal dichalcogenides. *Nat. Rev. Mater.* **2017**, *2*, 17033. [CrossRef]
2. Lopez-Sanchez, O.; Lembke, D.; Kayci, M.; Radenovic, A.; Kis, A. Ultrasensitive Photodetectors Based on Monolayer MoS_2. *Nat. Nanotechnol.* **2013**, *8*, 497–501. [CrossRef]
3. Yin, Z.; Li, H.; Li, H.; Jiang, L.; Shi, Y.; Sun, Y.; Lu, G.; Zhang, Q.; Chen, X.; Zhang, H. Single-Layer MoS_2 Phototransistors. *ACS Nano* **2012**, *6*, 74–80. [CrossRef] [PubMed]
4. Li, H.; Yin, Z.; He, Q.; Li, H.; Huang, X.; Lu, G.; Fam, D.W.H.; Tok, A.I.Y.; Zhang, Q.; Zhang, H. Fabrication of Single-and Multilayer MoS_2 Film-Based Field-Effect Transistors for Sensing NO at Room Temperature. *Small* **2012**, *8*, 63–67. [CrossRef] [PubMed]
5. Radisavljevic, B.; Whitwick, M.B.; Kis, A. Integrated Circuits and Logic Operations Based on Single-Layer MoS_2. *ACS Nano* **2011**, *5*, 9934–9938. [CrossRef] [PubMed]
6. Ayari, A.; Cobas, E.; Ogundadegbe, O.; Fuhrer, M.S. Realization and Electrical Characterization of Ultrathin Crystals of Layered Transition-Metal Dichalcogenides. *J. Appl. Phys.* **2007**, *101*, 014507. [CrossRef]
7. Luo, Y.K.; Xu, J.; Zhu, T.; Wu, G.; McCormick, E.J.; Zhan, W.; Neupane, M.R.; Kawakami, R.K. Opto-Valleytronic Spin Injection in Monolayer MoS_2/Few-Layer Graphene Hybrid Spin Valves. *Nano Lett.* **2017**, *17*, 3877–3883. [CrossRef]
8. Jiang, J.; Chen, Z.; Hu, Y.; Xiang, Y.; Zhang, L.; Wang, Y.; Wang, G.-C.; Shi, J. Flexo-photovoltaic effect in MoS_2. *Nat. Nanotechnol.* **2021**, *16*, 894–901. [CrossRef]
9. Hu, J.; Yu, L.; Deng, J.; Wang, Y.; Cheng, K.; Ma, C.; Zhang, Q.; Wen, W.; Yu, S.; Pan, Y.; et al. Sulfur vacancy-rich MoS_2 as a catalyst for the hydrogenation of CO_2 to methanol. *Nat. Catal.* **2021**, *4*, 242–250. [CrossRef]
10. Li, G.; Chen, Z.; Li, Y.; Zhang, D.; Yang, W.; Liu, Y.; Cao, L. Engineering Substrate Interaction To Improve Hydrogen Evolution Catalysis of Monolayer MoS_2 Films beyond Pt. *ACS Nano* **2020**, *14*, 1707–1714. [CrossRef]
11. Mak, K.F.; Lee, C.; Hone, J.; Shan, J.; Heinz, T.F. Atomically Thin MoS_2: A New Direct-Gap Semiconductor. *Phys. Rev. Lett.* **2010**, *105*, 136805. [CrossRef] [PubMed]
12. Kuc, A.; Zibouche, N.; Heine, T. Influence of Quantum Confinement on the Electronic Structure of the Transition Metal Sulfide TS_2. *Phys. Rev. B Condens. Matter Mater. Phys.* **2011**, *83*, 245213. [CrossRef]
13. Radisavljevic, B.; Radenovic, A.; Brivio, J.; Giacometti, V.; Kis, A. Single-Layer MoS_2 Transistors. *Nat. Nanotechnol.* **2011**, *6*, 147–150. [CrossRef] [PubMed]
14. Wu, W.; De, D.; Chang, S.C.; Wang, Y.; Peng, H.; Bao, J.; Pei, S.S. High mobility and high on/off ratio field-effect transistors based on chemical vapor deposited single-crystal MoS_2 grains. *Appl. Phys. Lett.* **2013**, *102*, 142106. [CrossRef]
15. Yoon, Y.; Ganapathi, K.; Salahuddin, S. How Good Can Monolayer MoS_2 Transistors Be? *Nano Lett.* **2011**, *11*, 3768–3773. [CrossRef] [PubMed]

16. Giannazzo, F.; Greco, G.; Roccaforte, F.; Sonde, S.S. Vertical Transistors Based on 2D Materials: Status and Prospects. *Crystals* **2018**, *8*, 70. [CrossRef]
17. Giannazzo, F. Engineering 2D heterojunctions with dielectrics. *Nat. Electron.* **2019**, *2*, 54. [CrossRef]
18. Novoselov, K.S.; Jiang, D.; Schedin, F.; Booth, T.J.; Khotkevich, V.V.; Morozov, S.V.; Geim, A.K. Two-dimensional atomic crystals. *Proc. Natl. Acad. Sci. USA* **2005**, *102*, 10451–10453. [CrossRef]
19. Lee, C.; Yan, H.; Brus, L.E.; Heinz, T.F.; Hone, J.; Ryu, S. Anomalous lattice vibrations of single-and few-layer MoS_2. *ACS Nano* **2010**, *4*, 2695–2700. [CrossRef]
20. Velický, M.; Donnelly, G.E.; Hendren, W.R.; McFarland, S.; Scullion, D.; DeBenedetti, W.J.I.; Correa, G.C.; Han, Y.; Wain, A.J.; Hines, M.A.; et al. Mechanism of Gold-Assisted Exfoliation of Centimeter-Sized Transition-Metal Dichalcogenide Monolayers. *ACS Nano* **2018**, *12*, 10463–10472. [CrossRef]
21. Desai, S.B.; Madhvapathy, S.R.; Amani, M.; Kiriya, D.; Hettick, M.; Tosun, M.; Zhou, Y.; Dubey, M.; Ager, J.W., III; Chrzan, D.; et al. Gold-Mediated Exfoliation of Ultralarge Optoelectronically-Perfect Monolayers. *Adv. Mater.* **2016**, *28*, 4053–4058. [CrossRef]
22. Magda, G.Z.; Pető, J.; Dobrik, G.; Hwang, C.; Biró, L.P.; Tapasztó, L. Exfoliation of Large-Area Transition Metal Chalcogenide Single Layers. *Sci. Rep.* **2015**, *5*, 14714. [CrossRef]
23. Panasci, S.E.; Schilirò, E.; Migliore, F.; Cannas, M.; Gelardi, F.M.; Roccaforte, F.; Giannazzo, F.; Agnello, S. Substrate impact on the thickness dependence of vibrational and optical properties of large area MoS_2 produced by gold-assisted exfoliation. *Appl. Phys. Lett.* **2021**, *119*, 093103. [CrossRef]
24. Panasci, S.E.; Schilirò, E.; Greco, G.; Cannas, M.; Gelardi, F.M.; Agnello, S.; Roccaforte, F.; Giannazzo, F. Strain, Doping, and Electronic Transport of Large Area Monolayer MoS_2 Exfoliated on Gold and Transferred to an Insulating Substrate. *ACS Appl. Mat. Interf.* **2021**, *13*, 31248–31259. [CrossRef] [PubMed]
25. Coleman, J.N.; Lotya, M.; O'Neill, A.; Bergin, S.D.; King, P.J.; Khan, U.; Young, K.; Gaucher, A.; De, S.; Smith, R.J.; et al. Two-dimensional nanosheets produced by liquid exfoliation of layered materials. *Science* **2011**, *331*, 568–571. [CrossRef] [PubMed]
26. Lee, Y.H.; Zhang, X.-Q.; Zhang, W.; Chang, M.-T.; Lin, C.-T.; Chang, K.-D.; Yu, Y.-C.; Wang, J.T.-W.; Chang, C.-S.; Li, L.-J.; et al. Synthesis of Large-Area MoS_2 Atomic Layers with Chemical Vapor Deposition. *Adv. Mater.* **2012**, *24*, 2320–2325. [CrossRef]
27. Zhan, Y.; Liu, Z.; Najmaei, S.; Ajayan, P.M.; Lou, J. Large-Area Vapor-Phase Growth and Characterization of MoS_2 Atomic Layers on a SiO_2 Substrate. *Small* **2012**, *8*, 966–971. [CrossRef]
28. Ho, Y.-T.; Ma, C.-H.; Luong, T.-T.; Wei, L.-L.; Yen, T.-C.; Hsu, W.-T.; Chang, W.-H.; Chu, Y.-C.; Tu, Y.-Y.; Pande, K.P.; et al. Layered MoS_2 Grown on c-Sapphire by Pulsed Laser Deposition. *Phys. Status Solidi RRL* **2015**, *9*, 187–191. [CrossRef]
29. Fu, D.; Zhao, X.; Zhang, Y.-Y.; Li, L.; Xu, H.; Jang, A.-R.; Yoon, S.I.; Song, P.; Poh, S.M.; Ren, T.; et al. Molecular Beam Epitaxy of Highly Crystalline Monolayer Molybdenum Disulfide on Hexagonal Boron Nitride. *J. Am. Chem. Soc.* **2017**, *139*, 9392–9400. [CrossRef]
30. Valdivia, A.; Tweet, D.J.; Conley, J.F., Jr. Atomic layer deposition of two dimensional MoS_2 on 150 mm substrates. *J. Vac. Sci. Technol.* **2016**, *34*, 21515. [CrossRef]
31. Najmaei, S.; Liu, Z.; Zhou, W.; Zou, X.; Shi, G.; Lei, S.; Yakobson, B.I.; Idrobo, J.-C.; Ajayan, P.M.; Lou, J. Vapour phase growth and grain boundary structure of molybdenum disulphide atomic layers. *Nat. Mater.* **2013**, *12*, 754–759. [CrossRef] [PubMed]
32. Liu, H.F.; Wong, S.L.; Chi, D.Z. CVD growth of MoS_2-based two-dimensional materials. *Chem. Vap. Depos.* **2015**, *21*, 241–259. [CrossRef]
33. Jeon, J.; Jang, S.K.; Jeon, S.M.; Yoo, G.; Jang, Y.H.; Park, J.H.; Lee, S. Layer-controlled CVD growth of large-area two-dimensional MoS_2 films. *Nanoscale* **2015**, *7*, 1688–1695. [CrossRef] [PubMed]
34. Chen, J.; Tang, W.; Tian, B.; Liu, B.; Zhao, X.; Liu, Y.; Ren, T.; Liu, W.; Geng, D.; Jeong, H.Y.; et al. Chemical Vapor Deposition of High-Quality Large-Sized MoS_2 Crystals on Silicon Dioxide Substrates. *Adv. Sci.* **2016**, *3*, 1600033. [CrossRef] [PubMed]
35. Zhang, Z.; Chen, P.; Duan, X.; Zang, K.; Luo, J.; Duan, X. Robust epitaxial growth of two-dimensional heterostructures, multiheterostructures, and superlattices. *Science* **2017**, *357*, 788–792. [CrossRef]
36. Liu, B.; Fathi, M.; Chen, L.; Abbas, A.; Ma, Y.; Zhou, C. Chemical vapor deposition growth of monolayer WSe_2 with tunable device characteristics and growth mechanism study. *ACS Nano* **2015**, *9*, 6119–6127. [CrossRef]
37. Tang, L.; Tan, J.; Nong, H.; Liu, B.; Cheng, H.M. Chemical Vapor Deposition Growth of Two-Dimensional Compound Materials: Controllability, Material Quality, and Growth Mechanism. *Acc. Mater. Res.* **2020**, *2*, 36–47. [CrossRef]
38. Wang, S.; Rong, Y.; Fan, Y.; Pacios, M.; Bhaskaran, H.; He, K.; Warner, J.H. Shape evolution of monolayer MoS_2 crystals grown by chemical vapor deposition. *Chem. Mater.* **2014**, *26*, 6371–6379. [CrossRef]
39. Yang, S.Y.; Shim, G.W.; Seo, S.B.; Choi, S.Y. Effective shape-controlled growth of monolayer MoS_2 flakes by powder-based chemical vapor deposition. *Nano Res.* **2017**, *10*, 255–262. [CrossRef]
40. Wu, C.R.; Chang, X.R.; Wu, C.H.; Lin, S.Y. The growth mechanism of transition metal dichalcogenides by using sulfurization of pre-deposited transition metals and the 2D crystal hetero-structure establishment. *Sci. Rep.* **2017**, *7*, 42146. [CrossRef]
41. Li, D.; Xiao, Z.; Mu, S.; Wang, F.; Liu, Y.; Song, J.; Huang, X.; Jiang, L.; Xiao, J.; Liu, L.; et al. A facile space-confined solid-phase sulfurization strategy for growth of high-quality ultrathin molybdenum disulfide single crystals. *Nano Lett.* **2018**, *18*, 2021–2032. [CrossRef] [PubMed]
42. Taheri, P.; Wang, J.; Xing, H.; Destino, J.F.; Arik, M.M.; Zhao, C.; Kang, K.; Blizzard, B.; Zhang, L.; Zhao, P. Growth mechanism of largescale MoS_2 monolayer by sulfurization of MoO_3 film. *Mater. Res. Expr.* **2016**, *3*, 075009. [CrossRef]

43. Hutar, P.; Spankova, M.; Sojkova, M.; Dobrocka, E.; Vegso, K.; Hagara, J.; Halahovets, Y.; Majkova, E.; Siffalovic, P.; Hulman, M. Highly crystalline MoS$_2$ thin films fabricated by sulfurization. *Phys. Status Solidi (B)* **2019**, *256*, 1900342. [CrossRef]
44. Vangelista, S.; Cinquanta, E.; Martella, C.; Alia, M.; Longo, M.; Lamperti, A.; Mantovan, R.; Basso Basset, F.; Pezzoli, F.; Molle, A. Towards a uniform and large-scale deposition of MoS$_2$ nanosheets via sulfurization of ultra-thin Mo based solid films. *Nanotechnology* **2016**, *27*, 175703. [CrossRef]
45. Kong, D.; Wang, H.; Cha, J.J.; Pasta, M.; Koski, K.J.; Yao, J.; Cui, Y. Synthesis of MoS$_2$ and MoSe$_2$ Films with Vertically Aligned Layers. *Nano Lett.* **2013**, *13*, 1341–1347. [CrossRef] [PubMed]
46. Cho, S.-Y.; Kim, S.J.; Lee, Y.; Kim, J.-S.; Jung, W.-B.; Yoo, H.-W.; Kim, J.; Jung, H.-T. Highly Enhanced Gas Adsorption Properties in Vertically Aligned MoS$_2$ Layers. *ACS Nano* **2015**, *9*, 9314–9321. [CrossRef]
47. Jung, Y.; Shen, J.; Liu, Y.; Woods, J.M.; Sun, Y.; Cha, J.J. Metal Seed Layer Thickness-Induced Transition from Vertical to Horizontal Growth of MoS$_2$ and WS$_2$. *Nano Lett.* **2014**, *14*, 6842–6849. [CrossRef]
48. Stern, C.; Grinvald, S.; Kirshner, M.; Sinai, O.; Oksman, M.; Alon, H.; Meiron, O.E.; Bar-Sadan, M.; Houben, L.; Naveh, D. Growth Mechanisms and Electronic Properties of Vertically Aligned MoS$_2$. *Sci. Rep.* **2018**, *8*, 16480. [CrossRef]
49. Shang, S.-L.; Lindwall, G.; Wang, Y.; Redwing, J.M.; Anderson, T.; Liu, Z.-K. Lateral Versus Vertical Growth of Two-Dimensional Layered Transition-Metal Dichalcogenides: Thermodynamic Insight into MoS$_2$. *Nano Lett.* **2016**, *16*, 5742–5750. [CrossRef]
50. Sojková, M.; Vegso, K.; Mrkyvkova, N.; Hagara, J.; Hutár, P.; Rosová, A.; Čaplovičová, M.; Ludacka, V.; Majková, E.; Siffalovic, P.; et al. Tuning the orientation of few-layer MoS$_2$ films using one-zone sulfurization. *RSC Adv.* **2019**, *9*, 29645–29651. [CrossRef]
51. Shahzad, R.; Kim, T.; Kang, S.W. Effects of temperature and pressure on sulfurization of molybdenum nano-sheets for MoS$_2$ synthesis. *Thin Solid Film.* **2017**, *641*, 79–86. [CrossRef]
52. Lee II, E.W.; Ma, L.; Nath, D.N.; Lee, C.H.; Arehart, A.; Wu, Y.; Rajan, S. Growth and electrical characterization of two-dimensional layered MoS$_2$/SiC heterojunctions. *Appl. Phys. Lett.* **2014**, *105*, 203504. [CrossRef]
53. Wang, H.; Zhang, Q.; Yao, H.; Liang, Z.; Lee, H.-W.; Hsu, P.-C.; Zheng, G.; Cui, Y. High electrochemical selectivity of edge versus terrace sites in two-dimensional layered MoS$_2$ materials. *Nano Lett.* **2014**, *14*, 7138–7144. [CrossRef] [PubMed]
54. Hadouda, H.; Pouzet, J.; Bernede, J.C.; Barreau, A. MoS$_2$ thin film synthesis by soft sulfurization of a molybdenum layer. *Mater. Chem. Phys.* **1995**, *42*, 291–297. [CrossRef]
55. Naujokaitis, A.; Gaigalas, P.; Bittencourt, C.; Mickevičius, S.; Jagminas, A. 1T/2H MoS$_2$/MoO$_3$ hybrid assembles with glycine as highly efficient and stable electrocatalyst for water splitting. *Int. J. Hydrog. Energy* **2019**, *44*, 24237–24245. [CrossRef]
56. Lloyd, D.; Liu, X.; Christopher, J.S.; Cantley, L.; Wadehra, A.; Kim, B.L.; Goldberg, B.B.; Swan, A.K.; Bunch, J.S. Band Gap Engineering with Ultralarge Biaxial Strains in Suspended Monolayer MoS$_2$. *Nano Lett.* **2016**, *16*, 5836–5841. [CrossRef] [PubMed]
57. Bampoulis, P.; van Bremen, R.; Yao, Q.; Poelsema, B.; Zandvliet, H.J.W.; Sotthewes, K. Defect Dominated Charge Transport and Fermi Level Pinning in MoS$_2$/Metal Contacts. *ACS Appl. Mater. Interfaces* **2017**, *9*, 19278–19286. [CrossRef]
58. Sotthewes, K.; van Bremen, R.; Dollekamp, E.; Boulogne, T.; Nowakowski, K.; Kas, D.; Zandvliet Harold, J.W.; Bampoulis, P. Universal Fermi-Level Pinning in Transition-Metal Dichalcogenides. *J. Phys. Chem. C* **2019**, *123*, 5411. [CrossRef] [PubMed]
59. Giannazzo, F.; Schilirò, E.; Greco, G.; Roccaforte, F. Conductive Atomic Force Microscopy of Semiconducting Transition Metal Dichalcogenides and Heterostructures. *Nanomaterials* **2020**, *10*, 803. [CrossRef] [PubMed]
60. Giannazzo, F.; Fisichella, G.; Piazza, A.; Agnello, S.; Roccaforte, F. Nanoscale Inhomogeneity of the Schottky Barrier and Resistivity in MoS$_2$ Multilayers. *Phys. Rev. B* **2015**, *92*, 081307. [CrossRef]
61. Zhu, H.; Qin, X.; Cheng, L.; Azcatl, A.; Kim, J.; Wallace, R.M. Remote Plasma Oxidation and Atomic Layer Etching of MoS$_2$. *ACS Appl. Mater. Interfaces* **2016**, *8*, 19119–19126. [CrossRef] [PubMed]
62. Giannazzo, F.; Fisichella, G.; Greco, G.; Di Franco, S.; Deretzis, I.; La Magna, A.; Bongiorno, C.; Nicotra, G.; Spinella, C.; Scopelliti, M.; et al. Ambipolar MoS$_2$ Transistors by Nanoscale Tailoring of Schottky Barrier Using Oxygen Plasma Functionalization. *ACS Appl. Mater. Interfaces* **2017**, *9*, 23164–23174. [CrossRef]
63. Hamada, T.; Tomiya, S.; Tatsumi, T.; Hamada, M.; Horiguchi, T.; Kakushima, K.; Tsutsui, K.; Wakabayashi, H. Sheet Resistance Reduction of MoS$_2$ Film Using Sputtering and Chlorine Plasma Treatment Followed by Sulfur Vapor Annealing. *IEEE J. Electron Devices Soc.* **2021**, *9*, 278–285. [CrossRef]
64. Giannazzo, F.; Bosi, M.; Fabbri, F.; Schilirò, E.; Greco, G.; Roccaforte, F. Direct Probing of Grain Boundary Resistance in Chemical Vapor Deposition-Grown Monolayer MoS$_2$ by Conductive Atomic Force Microscopy. *Phys. Status Solidi RRL* **2020**, *14*, 1900393. [CrossRef]
65. Golovynskyi, S.; Irfan, I.; Bosi, M.; Seravalli, L.; Datsenko, O.I.; Golovynska, I.; Li, B.; Lin, D.; Qu, J. Exciton and trion in few-layer MoS$_2$: Thickness- and temperature-dependent photoluminescence. *Appl. Surf. Sci.* **2020**, *515*, 146033. [CrossRef]
66. Mignuzzi, S.; Pollard, A.J.; Bonini, N.; Brennan, B.; Gilmore, I.S.; Pimenta, M.A.; Richards, D.; Roy, D. Effect of disorder on Raman scattering of single-layer MoS$_2$. *Phys. Rev. B* **2015**, *91*, 195411. [CrossRef]
67. Chow, P.K.; Jacobs-Gedrim, R.B.; Gao, J.; Lu, T.-M.; Yu, B.; Terrones, H.; Koratkar, N. Defect-Induced Photoluminescence in Monolayer Semiconducting Transition Metal Dichalcogenides. *ACS Nano* **2015**, *9*, 1520–1527. [CrossRef]
68. Watson, A.J.; Lu, W.; Guimaraes, M.H.D.; Stöhr, M. Transfer of large-scale two-dimensional semiconductors: Challenges and developments. *2D Mater.* **2021**, *8*, 032001. [CrossRef]

Article

Highly Homogeneous Current Transport in Ultra-Thin Aluminum Nitride (AlN) Epitaxial Films on Gallium Nitride (GaN) Deposited by Plasma Enhanced Atomic Layer Deposition

Emanuela Schilirò [1], Filippo Giannazzo [1,*], Salvatore Di Franco [1], Giuseppe Greco [1], Patrick Fiorenza [1], Fabrizio Roccaforte [1], Paweł Prystawko [2,3], Piotr Kruszewski [2,3], Mike Leszczynski [2,3], Ildiko Cora [4], Béla Pécz [4], Zsolt Fogarassy [4] and Raffaella Lo Nigro [1,*]

[1] CNR-IMM, Strada VIII, 5, 95121 Catania, Italy; emanuela.schiliro@imm.cnr.it (E.S.); salvatore.difranco@imm.cnr.it (S.D.F.); giuseppe.greco@imm.cnr.it (G.G.); patrick.fiorenza@imm.cnr.it (P.F.); fabrizio.roccaforte@imm.cnr.it (F.R.)
[2] Top-GaN Ltd., Sokolowska 29/37, 01-142 Warsaw, Poland; pprysta@unipress.waw.pl (P.P.); kruszew@unipress.waw.pl (P.K.); mike@unipress.waw.pl (M.L.)
[3] Institute of High Pressure Physics, Polish Academy of Sciences, Sokolowska 29/37, 01-142 Warsaw, Poland
[4] Centre for Energy Research, Institute for Technical Physics and Materials Science Research, Konkoly-Thege, 29-33, 1121 Budapest, Hungary; cora.ildiko@energia.mta.hu (I.C.); pecz.bela@energia.mta.hu (B.P.); fogarassy.zsolt@energia.mta.hu (Z.F.)
* Correspondence: filippo.giannazzo@imm.cnr.it (F.G.); raffaella.lonigro@imm.cnr.it (R.L.N.)

Abstract: This paper reports an investigation of the structural, chemical and electrical properties of ultra-thin (5 nm) aluminum nitride (AlN) films grown by plasma enhanced atomic layer deposition (PE-ALD) on gallium nitride (GaN). A uniform and conformal coverage of the GaN substrate was demonstrated by morphological analyses of as-deposited AlN films. Transmission electron microscopy (TEM) and energy dispersive spectroscopy (EDS) analyses showed a sharp epitaxial interface with GaN for the first AlN atomic layers, while a deviation from the perfect wurtzite stacking and oxygen contamination were detected in the upper part of the film. This epitaxial interface resulted in the formation of a two-dimensional electron gas (2DEG) with a sheet charge density $n_s \approx 1.45 \times 10^{12}$ cm^{-2}, revealed by Hg-probe capacitance–voltage (C–V) analyses. Nanoscale resolution current mapping and current–voltage (I–V) measurements by conductive atomic force microscopy (C-AFM) showed a highly homogeneous current transport through the 5 nm AlN barrier, while a uniform flat-band voltage ($V_{FB} \approx 0.3$ V) for the AlN/GaN heterostructure was demonstrated by scanning capacitance microscopy (SCM). Electron transport through the AlN film was shown to follow the Fowler–Nordheim (FN) tunneling mechanism with an average barrier height of $<\Phi_B> = 2.08$ eV, in good agreement with the expected AlN/GaN conduction band offset.

Keywords: AlN; GaN; atomic layer deposition

1. Introduction

Due to its large and direct bandgap (6.2 eV), good thermal stability and piezoelectric properties, aluminum nitride (AlN) has been the object of significant attention for optoelectronic applications, such as ultraviolet light emitting diodes, photodetectors and sensor systems [1–3]. In particular, owing to the epitaxial interface with GaN and the relatively high dielectric permittivity ($\kappa \approx 8$), AlN ultra-thin films have been considered as gate dielectrics in AlGaN/GaN metal insulator semiconductor–high electron mobility transistors (MIS-HEMTs) [4] and/or as passivation layers for AlGaN/GaN heterostructures, as an alternative to the conventional silicon nitride (SiN$_X$) [5–7]. The inherent lattice mismatch, of about 2.4%, between the AlN and GaN crystal structures is responsible for a tensile strain in AlN films grown on GaN. The piezoelectric polarization associated with such tensile strain, combined with the spontaneous polarization of the AlN and GaN materials, results

in the formation of a two-dimensional electron gas (2DEG) [8] at their interface, which can be exploited for the fabrication of AlN/GaN HEMTs suitable for RF applications [9–12]. Furthermore, high crystalline quality ultra-thin AlN layers on GaN have been recently employed as tunneling barriers of vertical hot electron transistors (HETs) with a graphene base, currently regarded as promising candidates for future ultra-high-frequency (THz) applications [13–15].

AlN thin films on GaN are typically deposited by molecular beam epitaxy (MBE) or metal organic chemical vapor deposition (MOCVD) at relatively high temperatures (>700 °C), required to obtain a high quality epitaxial interface [10,16], and a 2DEG sheet density in the order of 10^{13} cm^{-2}. However, tensile-strained AlN layers with a thickness above a critical value of ~7 nm are typically subjected to relaxation or cracking phenomena during the cooling process from deposition to room temperature, due to the large thermal expansion coefficient mismatch with GaN [17,18]. More generally, such high growth temperatures can represent a serious concern in terms of process integration of AlN gate dielectrics or passivation layers in the fabrication flow of AlGaN/GaN HEMTs. In this context, the Atomic Layer Deposition (ALD) technique has been recently considered as an alternative method for the growth of thin AlN films on GaN [5,19,20] due to its unique ability to provide uniform and conformal coverage with nanometric control of the thickness, and the low process temperature in the range of 100–400 °C. Typically, trimethylaluminum (TMA) and ammonia (NH$_3$) are employed as the aluminum precursor and co-reactant, respectively, and the plasma-enhanced ALD (PE-ALD) mode is used to improve the NH$_3$ reactivity by plasma ignition in order to obtain AlN layers with suitable structural quality. PE-ALD grown AlN films on GaN typically exhibit a good epitaxial quality, giving rise to the formation of an interfacial 2DEG. However, the measured sheet electron density values are typically lower than in MBE-grown AlN with equivalent thickness and were found to depend on the deposition conditions [19] as well as on the deposited AlN thickness [21]. Moreover, significant oxygen incorporation is commonly observed in ALD grown AlN films, with the highest concentration at the film surface, probably due to exposure to the atmosphere after the deposition process [22–24]. The oxygen interdiffusion through the AlN layer occurs for few nanometers, but in the ultrathin layers the oxygen incorporation can reach also the interface region. In spite of the non-ideal quality of PE-ALD grown AlN, AlN/GaN transistors exploiting the interfacial 2DEG have been demonstrated using low-temperature (300 °C) PE-ALD on semi-insulating GaN [25]. Furthermore, AlN films deposited with such a low thermal budget proved to be effective passivation layers for AlGaN/GaN HETMs, leading to significant current collapse suppression and dynamic ON-resistance reduction without the use of a field plate [5,26].

In view of the above-discussed device applications, micro and nanoscale correlative studies of the structural, chemical and electrical properties of ALD grown ultra-thin AlN films on GaN would be highly desirable in order to assess their insulating properties. In particular, spatially resolved information on the lateral uniformity of current transport across the AlN thin films are currently missing and can be crucial to evaluate their suitability as tunneling barriers for vertical diodes or transistors.

In our work, the structural/compositional and electrical properties of 5 nm AlN films deposited by PE-ALD on GaN-on-sapphire substrates were investigated in detail by high resolution characterization techniques, i.e., transmission electron microscopy (TEM) combined with energy dispersive spectroscopy (EDS) and by conductive-atomic force microscopy (C-AFM). Chemically, the AlN layer is characterized by oxygen contamination, whose amount decreases moving from film surface to film/substrate interface. However, despite this contamination, the high degree of epitaxy at the AlN/GaN interface ensures the formation of a two-dimensional electron gas (2DEG), with a sheet charge density $n_s \approx 1.45 \times 10^{12}$ cm^{-2}. A uniform vertical current transport by electron injection through the AlN barrier was demonstrated by C-AFM current mapping. Furthermore, local current–voltage (I–V) measurements showed that the current transport follows the

Fowler–Nordheim (FN) tunneling mechanism, with an average AlN/GaN barrier height of $<\Phi_B> = 2.08$ eV.

2. Materials and Methods

MOCVD n-type (~10^{17} cm^{-3}) GaN grown on sapphire was used as substrate for the AlN deposition, which was carried out in a PE-ALD LL SENTECH reactor (Sentech, Instruments GmbH, Berlin, Germany) using trimethylaluminum (TMA) as the Al precursor (Air liquide, Catania, Italy) and NH$_3$-plasma as co-reactant. A capacitively coupled plasma (CCP) source working through a 13.56 MHz RF-generator with a power of 200 W was used to generate the NH$_3$-plasma reaction gas. Each ALD cycle consisted of 30 ms and 15 ms pulse times of TMA and NH$_3$-plasma, respectively, alternated with a purging pulse of N$_2$ to remove unreacted precursors and clean the deposition chamber. The deposition processes were performed at a temperature of 300 °C and a pressure of 20 Pa. The cycle number (60 deposition cycles) during the ALD process was established in order to achieve the desired thickness of 5 nm. Preliminary morphological analyses of the as-deposited AlN layers were carried out by tapping mode Atomic force microscopy (AFM), using a D3100 microscope (Bruker, San Francisco, CA, United States) with a Nanoscope V controller. Capacitance–voltage (C–V_g) measurements on AlN film on GaN were performed using a mercury (Hg)-probe system. This method is highly beneficial because it provides a straightforward evaluation of the electrical behavior without any step of processing for the fabrication of capacitors. The capacitance was evaluated by measurements acquired between two front contacts, the smallest one consisting of a liquid Hg droplet with a controlled volume, and the other one consisting of a metal ring with a much larger area.

Cross-sectioned samples were prepared by focused ion beam (FIB) (SCIOS2 SEM+FIB dual beam manufactured by ThermoFisher, Brno, Czech Republic) and high resolution structural/chemical characterization by transmission electron microscopy (TEM), scanning transmission electron microscopy (STEM) and energy dispersion spectroscopy (EDS) performed with an aberration-corrected Titan Themis 200 microscope (ThermoFisher, Eindhoven, Netherlands).

Finally, the current transport across the 5 nm AlN layer on GaN was investigated at the nanoscale by performing conductive-atomic force microscopy (C-AFM) current mapping and local current–voltage (I–V_{tip}) characterizations with diamond-coated Si tips, using DI 3100 AFM equipment (Bruker, San Francisco, CA, USA) with Nanoscope V electronics. Furthermore, local dC/dV vs. V_{tip} characteristics were collected by the scanning capacitance microscopy (SCM) module, using same diamond-coated Si tips, in order to evaluate the uniformity of the flatband voltage (V_{FB}) for the tip/AlN/GaN heterostructure.

3. Results

Two representative AFM morphological images of the virgin GaN-on-sapphire substrate (a) and after the PE-ALD of AlN (b) are shown in Figure 1. The atomic terraces of the GaN surface remained clearly visible after deposition of the ultrathin (5 nm) AlN film, confirming the uniform and conformal coverage by the ALD process. The increased root mean square (RMS) roughness, from 0.28 nm of the bare GaN to 0.54 nm of the AlN coated surface, is due to the morphology of the deposited film.

A detailed structural and chemical investigation of the AlN film and its interface with GaN was carried out by high angle annular dark field (HAADF) STEM measurements combined with EDS, and by high-resolution TEM. Figure 2a reports a cross-sectional HAADF image, showing a very sharp atomic number Z-contrast between the AlN thin film and the GaN substrate. The Pt layer on top of AlN was used as protection during FIB sample preparation. The Z contrast allowed us to clearly visualize the interface between the AlN film and GaN and to precisely evaluate the film thickness, which coincided with the expected thickness of 5 nm. Furthermore, Figure 2b–f report the corresponding EDS chemical maps of Ga, N, Al, O and Pt, shown with different elemental combinations, from which the distribution of the different species in the analyzed stack could be clearly deduced. In particular, the presence of unintentional oxygen contamination within the deposited film was observed, similarly to what was reported in other papers on PE-ALD grown AlN layers [22,27]. In order to provide quantitative compositional information, the scan lines of the percent atomic concentrations for the Ga, Al, N and O elements in the stack are shown in Figure 2g. The interface between the GaN substrate and the deposited Al (O) N film, taken as the crossing point between the Ga and Al profiles, was indicated by the vertical dashed line at z = 0. A gradient in the oxygen concentration was clearly observed, with a decrease from ~70% at the film surface to ~15% at the interface with GaN. It should be noted that the evaluated oxygen percentage can be affected by artifacts, e.g., the natural oxidation of the cross-sectioned surface of the TEM lamella, which can justify the 10% oxygen content measured in the GaN region. The observed oxygen concentration gradient in the deposited Al (O) N film provides some indication of the possible sources of the oxygen contamination. In fact, oxygen incorporation during the PEALD growth, due to the presence of oxygen-based species activated by the plasma, would result in a uniform concentration within the deposited films. On the other hand, the decreasing oxygen concentration from the film surface to the interface with GaN is more consistent with oxygen incorporation occurring after the AlN layer growth by diffusion from the surface. This may happen either in the cooling step of the ALD process, in the presence or oxygen gas residuals in the chamber or, most probably, by exposure to the air atmosphere. In this respect, it can be important to evaluate the time-scale in which the oxidation occurs. The TEM-based chemical characterizations reported above are typically performed within one week from the sample deposition. Furthermore, analyses performed after longer times (approximately one month) exhibit the same qualitative behavior, suggesting that the samples do not undergo long time aging effects. As discussed later on in this paper, non-destructive electrical measurements (capacitance–voltage and C-AFM current maps) were also performed on the as-deposited samples, as well as after some days from the deposition. No significant variations of the electrical parameters (2DEG carrier density, homogeneity of injected current) were detected, suggesting that the oxidation occurred in the early stages, i.e., within one hour, from the exposure to the air.

In order to evaluate the lattice structure in the interface region between the deposited AlN film and the GaN substrate, a high-resolution TEM image is reported in Figure 3, showing an atomically abrupt AlN/GaN interface, with a perfectly epitaxial alignment in the first AlN atomic layers. The AlN film exhibited the hexagonal stacking of the wurtzite structure characteristic of GaN material in the interfacial region, whereas a deviation from this stacking order could be observed at a distance of ~1 nm from the interface. The measured values of the (0002) plane distances were 0.2573 nm for GaN and 0.2472 nm for AlN. The X-ray reference standards for the two crystals were 0.259 nm for GaN (0002) plane distances (JCPDS card 02-1078) and 0.249 nm for the AlN (0002) plane distances (JCPDS card 25-1133). Hence, the determined values are in good agreement with the references.

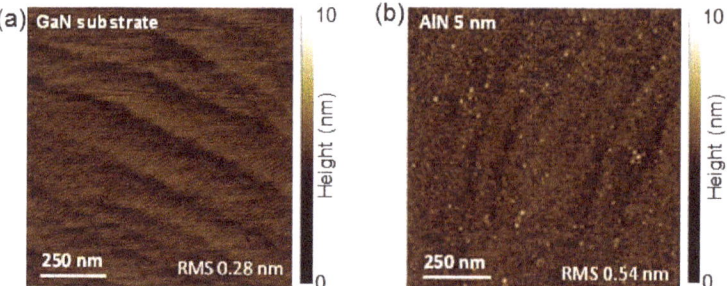

Figure 1. Morphological images of the virgin GaN substrate (**a**) and after PE-ALD of 5 nm thick AlN film (**b**).

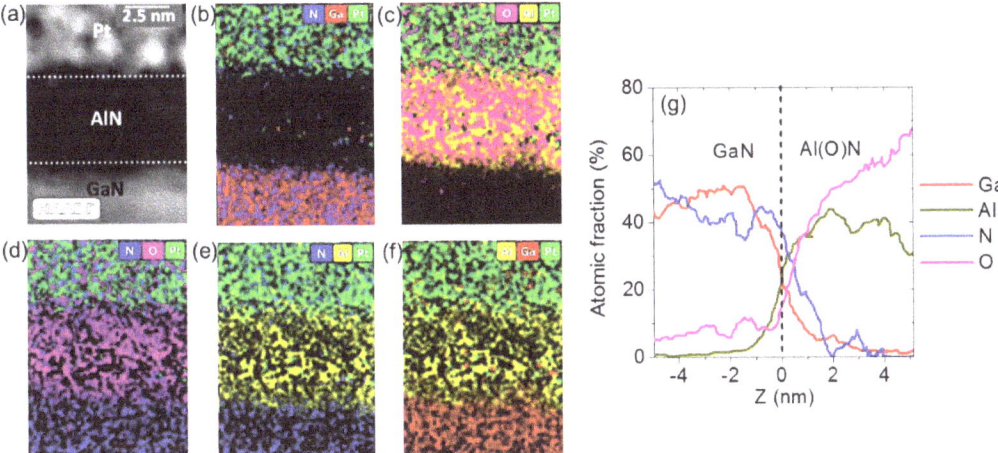

Figure 2. (a) Cross-sectional HAADF-STEM image of the 5 nm AlN film on GaN. (b–f) Corresponding EDS chemical maps of Ga, N, Al, O and Pt, shown with different elemental combinations, from which the distribution of the different species in the analyzed stack can be clearly deduced. (g) EDS scan lines of the percent atomic concentrations for the Ga, N, Al and O species.

Figure 3. High resolution TEM image of the AlN/GaN interface region.

Noteworthily, in spite of the very large oxygen content in the surface region of this 5 nm thick film, the epitaxial arrangement of AlN with GaN was preserved in the near interface region, guaranteeing the generation of a 2DEG, as confirmed by Hg-probe capacitance–voltage (C–V_g) measurements. In particular, Figure 4a shows a typical C–V_g curve measured at 100 kHz frequency. The 2DEG sheet carrier density n_s as a function of V_g (see Figure 4b) was calculated by integration of the C–V_g and subtracting the contribution associated with the GaN substrate doping. The relatively low values of $n_s(0) = 1.45 \times 10^{12}$ cm^{-2} and of the 2DEG pinch-off voltage ($V_{po} = -1.8$ V) can be explained by the small thickness (~1 nm) of epitaxial AlN as compared to the total of deposited thickness (5 nm), as deduced from TEM analyses.

Then, the vertical current transport across the ultra-thin AlN barrier layer on GaN was investigated at the nanoscale by C-AFM. Figure 5a,b show the typical morphological image and the corresponding current map collected by scanning the diamond tip on the sample surface, while applying a bias $V_{tip} = 5$ V with respect to a large area electrode deposited on top of AlN, as schematically illustrated in the inset of Figure 5c. Quite uniform electron injection from the interfacial 2DEG through the thin AlN layer could be deduced from this map. To gain further insight in the current transport mechanism through the AlN film, local current–voltage (I–V_{tip}) measurements were performed by displacing the tip on an array of 5 × 5 positions. The collected I–V_{tip} curves exhibited a rectifying behavior, with a very low current level under reverse (negative) polarization of the tip, and an exponential increase of the current for positive bias values $V_{tip} > 3$ V.

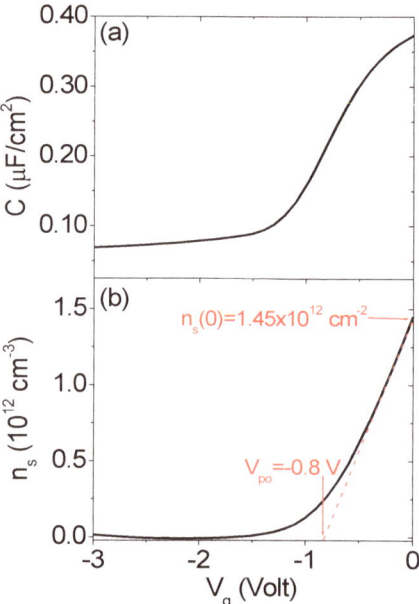

Figure 4. (a) Capacitance–voltage (C–V_g) curves measured by the Hg–probe setup on the AlN/GaN heterostructure. (b) 2DEG sheet carrier density n_s (cm^{-2}) as a function of V_g obtained by integration of the C–V_g curve and subtraction of the GaN doping contribution. The carrier density at $V_g = 0$ and the 2DEG pinch-off bias (V_{po}) are indicated.

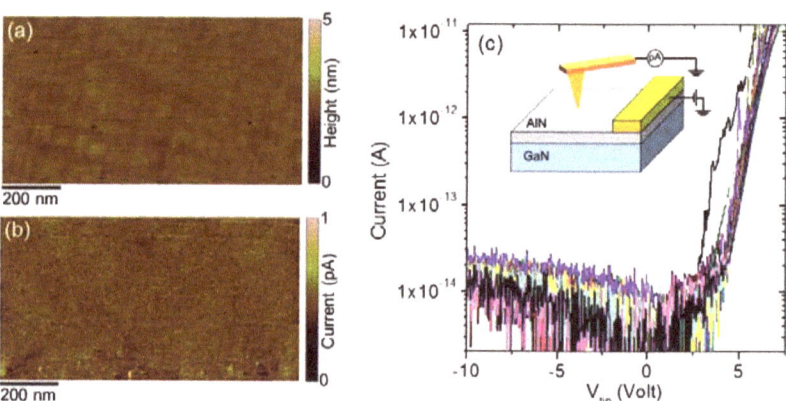

Figure 5. (a) Morphology and (b) vertical current map on 5 nm AlN film on GaN measured by C-AFM at a tip bias $V_{tip} = 5$ V. (c) Local I–V curves measured on an array of 5 × 5 positions of the diamond-tip on the AlN surface. The experimental configuration for C-AFM measurements is schematically illustrated in the insert of panel (c).

As a complementary analysis to C-AFM current mapping, Figure 6 reports a set of dC/dV vs. V_{tip} characteristics measured on an array of 5 × 5 positions of the diamond tip on the AlN surface, using the SCM setup (as schematically depicted in the inset of the same figure) [28]. The nanoscale differential capacitance for the AlN/GaN heterostructure depends on the local AlN barrier thickness and dielectric constant, as well as on the GaN doping and interfacial 2DEG density. Furthermore, the peak voltage in the curves corresponds to the local flatband voltage (V_{FB}) of the diamond tip/AlN/GaN metal/insulator/semiconductor system, which is related both to the tip/semiconductor workfunction difference and to charges in the AlN Film. The fact that the local dC/dV curves measured at different surface positions all overlapped each other demonstrates a high lateral uniformity of the dielectric properties of the AlN film, as well as of the carrier density at the interface with GaN. In particular, the determination of the local flatband voltage value (V_{FB} = 0.3 V) is important to gain deeper insight in the current transport mechanism through the AlN layer, starting from the local I–V_{tip} characteristics in Figure 5c.

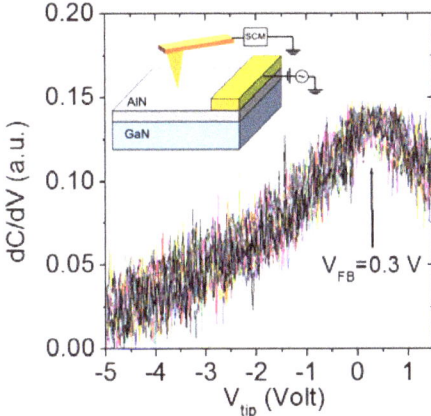

Figure 6. Local dC/dV–V_{tip} curves measured on an array of 5 × 5 positions of the diamond-tip on the AlN surface. The flatband voltage V_{FB} = 0.3V for the diamond tip/AlN/GaN heterostructure is indicated. The experimental configuration for SCM measurements is schematically illustrated in the inset.

The exponential dependence of the current in these characteristics was modelled by the Fowler–Nordheim (FN) tunneling mechanism, typically employed to describe electronic transport across thin insulating films [29]. According to the FN equation, the current tunneling through the triangular barrier can be expressed as:

$$I = \frac{q^3 m E^2}{8\pi h \Phi_B m_{ox}} exp\left[-\frac{8\pi \sqrt{2 m_{ox} \Phi_B^3}}{3qh} \frac{1}{E}\right] \quad (1)$$

where E = ($V_{tip} - V_{FB}$)/d is the local electric field applied by the tip (d = 5 nm being the barrier layer thickness), Φ_B is the energy barrier at the AlN/GaN interface, q is the electron charge, h is the Boltzmann constant and m_{ox} is the effective tunneling mass of the thin barrier layer. Since the deposited Al (O) N layer featured a large oxygen concentration gradient (from ~70% at the surface to ~15% at the interface with GaN), the tunneling effective mass should be an intermediate value between the AlN and Al_2O_3 ones. However, quite similar effective mass values ($m_{ox} \approx 0.4\ m_0$, m_0 being the free electron mass) were reported in the literature for Al_2O_3 [30] and AlN [31]. Hence, the $m_{ox} \approx 0.4\ m_0$ value was considered in Equation (1).

Figure 7a shows the FN plot (i.e., ln (I/E^2) as a function of 1/E) for one of the forward I–V curves in Figure 5c. At high electric field values, the linear fit of this curve exhibited a correlation factor R very close to unity, indicating excellent agreement of the data with the FN model. A barrier height Φ_B = 2.01 eV was extracted from the slope of the fit. Furthermore, Figure 7b shows the histogram of Φ_B values obtained by performing the same fitting procedure on each of the I–V curves in Figure 5c. An average barrier height <Φ_B> = 2.08 eV with a standard deviation of ±0.19 eV was evaluated from this distribution. Noteworthly, these values were in reasonable agreement with the calculated ones for the AlN/GaN conduction band offset ΔE_C (from 2.1 to 2.7 eV) [32,33]. This result indicates that in spite of oxygen incorporation in the PE-ALD grown thin film, the current injection behavior is ultimately determined by the high quality epitaxial interface between AlN and GaN.

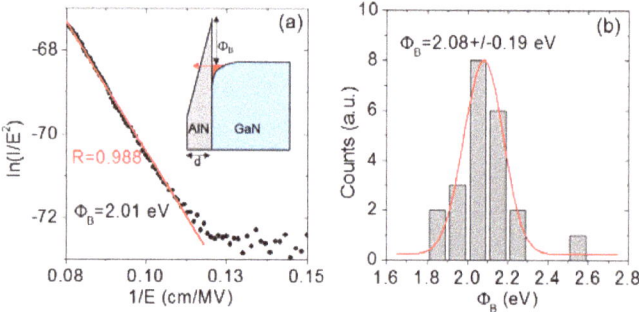

Figure 7. (a) Fowler–Nordheim plot of a forward bias I–V curve measured on AlN (5nm)/GaN and results of the linear fit. The schematic band-diagram of the heterostructure under forward polarization is reported in the insert. (b) Histogram of the barrier height values obtained by fitting of the I–V curves acquired at different surface positions.

4. Conclusions

In conclusion, ultra-thin (5 nm) AlN films with uniform and conformal morphology to the GaN substrate were grown by PE-ALD at a temperature of 300 °C. Structural investigation by high-resolution TEM demonstrated an atomically abrupt interface between GaN and AlN, with a perfect epitaxial alignment of the first atomic layers. However, a deviation from the wurtzite stacking was observed at a distance of ~1 nm from the interface. Chemical analysis by EDS profile demonstrated oxygen contamination of the AlN layer. This contamination, attributable to the atmosphere exposure after the ALD process, is mainly observed on the surface region, whereas it reduces to a rather low value (~10–15%) at the interface. The epitaxial interface results in the formation of a 2DEG with a sheet carrier density of 1.45×10^{12} cm^{-2}. The current map by C-AFM demonstrated a uniform vertical current transport by the electron injection from the interfacial 2DEG through the AlN barrier layer. The current transport was identified with the Fowler–Nordheim (FN) tunneling mechanism, and an average barrier height value of <Φ_B> = 2.08 eV was estimated, in good agreement with the expected AlN/GaN conduction band offset.

This work is useful for future application of AlN thin films by ALD as a tunneling barrier for GaN-based vertical devices. The incorporation of oxygen inside the AlN layer is certainly a crucial aspect for the possible effects on the structural and electrical properties of the AlN films. For this reason, it needs to be controlled to improve the AlN stability, for example by optimization of the ALD process, the cooling step and/or the post-deposition treatment. However, the ALD process, despite the low deposition temperature, guarantees an optimal epitaxy, mainly in the first atomic layers, which is appropriate for the 2DEG formation and highly uniform current injection.

Author Contributions: Conceptualization, R.L.N. and F.G.; methodology, F.G., P.F. and G.G.; formal analysis, F.G., P.F. and E.S.; investigation, E.S., P.P., P.K., I.C. and Z.F.; resources, S.D.F.; data curation, E.S.; writing—original draft preparation, E.S.; writing—review and editing, R.L.N. and F.G.; supervision, R.L.N. and F.G.; project administration, F.R. and F.G; funding acquisition, F.R., F.G., B.P. and M.L. All authors have read and agreed to the published version of the manuscript.

Funding: This project has been funded, in part, by MUR in the framework of the PON project EleGaNTe (ARS01_01007) and of the FlagERA-JTC 2019 project "ETMOS" and in part was partially supported by the Polish National Center for Research and Development through Project No. WPC/20/DefeGaN/2019. The CNR-HAS 2019–2022 bilateral project GHOST II and CNR-PAS 2017–2019 bilateral project ETNA II are acknowledged for travelling support. B. Pecz thanks the support of VEKOP-2.3.3-15-2016-00002 of the European Structural and Investment Funds. Part of the experiments have been carried out using the facilities of the Italian Infrastructure Beyond Nano.

Data Availability Statement: The data that support the findings of this study are available from the corresponding author upon reasonable request.

Conflicts of Interest: The authors declare no conflict of interest.

References

1. Taniyasu, Y.; Kasu, M.; Makimoto, T. An aluminium nitride light-emitting diode with a wavelength of 210 nanometres. *Nature* **2006**, *441*, 325. [CrossRef]
2. Pantha, B.N.; Dahal, R.; Nakarmi, M.L.; Nepal, N.; Li, J.; Lin, J.Y.; Jiang, H.X.; Paduano, Q.S.; Weyburne, D. Correlation between optoelectronic and structural properties and epilayer thickness of AlN. *Appl. Phys. Lett.* **2007**, *90*, 241101. [CrossRef]
3. Serina, F.; Ng, K.Y.S.; Huang, C.; Auner, G.W.; Rimai, L.; Naik, R. Pd/AlN/SiC thin-film devices for selective hydrogen sensing. *Appl. Phys. Lett.* **2001**, *79*, 3350–3352.
4. Greco, G.; Fiorenza, P.; Iucolano, F.; Severino, A.; Giannazzo, F.; Roccaforte, F. Conduction Mechanisms at Interface of AlN/SiN Dielectric Stacks with AlGaN/GaN Heterostructures for Normally-off High Electron Mobility Transistors: Correlating Device Behavior with Nanoscale Interfaces Properties. *ACS Appl. Mater. Interfaces* **2017**, *9*, 35383–35390. [CrossRef]
5. Huang, S.; Jiang, Q.; Yang, S.; Zhou, C.; Chen, K.J. Effective Passivation of AlGaN/GaN HEMTs by ALD-Grown AlN Thin Film. *IEEE Electron. Device Lett.* **2012**, *33*, 516–518. [CrossRef]
6. Zhao, S.X.; Liu, X.-Y.; Zhang, L.-Q.; Huang, H.-F.; Shi, J.-S.; Wang, P.-F. Impacts of thermal atomic layer-deposited AlN passivation layer on GaN-on-Si high electron mobility transistors. *Nanoscale Res. Lett.* **2016**, *11*, 137. [CrossRef]
7. Hsieh, T.-E.; Chang, E.Y.; Song, Y.-Z.; Lin, Y.-C.; Wang, H.-C.; Liu, S.-C.; Salahuddin, S.; Hu, C.C. Gate recessed quasi-normally off Al$_2$O$_3$/AlGaN/GaN MIS-HEMT with low threshold voltage hysteresis using PEALD AlN interfacial passivation layer. *IEEE Electron. Device Lett.* **2014**, *35*, 732–734.
8. Jeganathan, K.; Ide, T.; Shimizu, M.; Okumura, H. Strain relaxation correlated with the transport properties of AlN/GaN heterostructure grown by plasma-assisted molecular-beam epitaxy. *J. Appl. Phys.* **2003**, *93*, 4. [CrossRef]
9. Bernardini, F.; Fiorentini, V. Macroscopic polarization and band offsets at nitride heterojunctions. *Phys. Rev. B* **1998**, *57*, 16. [CrossRef]
10. Smorchkova, I.P.; Keller, S.; Heikman, S.; Elsass, C.R.; Heying, B.; Fini, P.; Speck, J.S.; Mishra, U.K. Tow-dimension electron-gas AlN/GaN heterostructures with estremely thin AlN barriers. *Appl. Phys. Lett.* **2000**, *77*, 24. [CrossRef]
11. Jeganathan, K.; Ide, T.; Shen, S.X.Q.; Shimizu, M.; Okumura, H. 2-DEG characteristics of AlN/GaN heterointerface on sapphire substrate grown by plasma –assisted MBE. *Phys. Stat. Sol.(b)* **2001**, *228*, 613–616. [CrossRef]
12. Gao, Z.; Meneghini, M.; Harrouche, K.; Kabouche, R.; Chiocchetta, F.; Okada, E.; Rampazzo, F.; De Santi, C.; Medjdoub, F.; Meneghesso, G.; et al. Short Term Reliability and Robustness of ultra-thin barrier, 110 nm-gate AlN/GaN HEMTs. In *Proceedings of the IEEE International Symposium on the Physical and Failure Analysis of Integrated Circuits (IPFA)*, Singapore, 20–23 July 2020; pp. 1–6.
13. Giannazzo, F.; Greco, G.; Schilirò, E.; Lo Nigro, R.; Deretzis, I.; La Magna, A.; Roccaforte, F.; Iucolano, F.; Ravesi, S.; Frayssinet, E.; et al. High performance Graphene/AlGaN/GaN Schottky junctions for hot electron transistors. *ACS Appl. Electron. Mater.* **2019**, *1*, 2342–2354. [CrossRef]
14. Zubair, A.; Nourbakhsh, A.; Hong, J.-Y.; Qi, M.; Song, Y.; Jena, D.; Kong, J.; Dresselhaus, M.; Palacios, T. Hot electron transistor with van der Waals Base-collectror heterojunction and High-performance GaN emitter. *Nano Lett.* **2017**, *17*, 3089–3096. [CrossRef]
15. Prystawko, P.; Giannazzo, F.; Krysko, M.; Smalc-Koziorowska, J.; Schilirò, E.; Greco, G.; Roccaforte, F.; Leszczynski, M. Growth and characterization of thin Al-rich AlGaN on bulk GaN as an emitter-base barrier for hot electron transistor. *Mate. Sci. Semicond. Process* **2019**, *93*, 153–157. [CrossRef]
16. Natali, F.; Byrne, D.; Dussaigne, A.; Grandjean, N.; Massies, J.; Damilano, B. High-Al-content crack-free AlGaN/GaN Bragg mrrors grown by molecular-beam epitaxy. *Appl. Phys. Lett.* **2003**, *82*, 499. [CrossRef]
17. Figge, S.; Kroncke, H.; Hommel, D. Temperature dependence of the thermal expansion of AlN. *Appl. Phys. Lett.* **2009**, *94*, 101915. [CrossRef]
18. Faria, F.A.; Nomoto, K.; Hu, Z.; Rouvimov, S.; Xing, H.; Jena, D. Low temperature AlN growth by MBE and its applications in HEMTs. *J. Cryst. Growth* **2015**, *425*, 133–137. [CrossRef]
19. Shih, H.-Y.; Lee, W.-H.; Kao, W.-C.; Chuang, Y.-C.; Lin, R.-M.; Lin, H.-C.; Shiojiri, M.; Chen, M.-J. Low-temperature atomic layer epitaxy of AlN ultrathin films by layer-by-layer, in-situ atomic layer annealing. *Sci. Rep.* **2017**, *7*, 39717. [CrossRef] [PubMed]

20. Schilirò, E.; Giannazzo, F.; Bongiorno, C.; Di Franco, S.; Greco, G.; Roccaforte, F.; Prystawko, P.; Kruszewski, P.; Leszczyński, M.; Krysko, M.; et al. Structural and electrical properties of AlN thin films on GaN substrates grown by plasma enhanced-Atomic Layer Deposition. *Mater. Sci. Semicond. Process* **2019**, *97*, 35–39. [CrossRef]
21. Voon, K.J.; Bothe, K.M.; Motamedi, P.; Cadien, K.C.; Barlage, D.W. Polarization charge properties of low-temperature atomic layer deposition of AlN on GaN. *J. Phys. D Appl. Phys.* **2014**, *47*, 345104. [CrossRef]
22. Van Bui, H.; Wiggers, F.B.; Gupta, A.; Nguyen, M.D.; Aarnink, A.A.I.; de Jong, M.P.; Kovalgin, A.Y. Initial growth, refractive index, and crystallinity of thermal and plasma enhanced atomic layer deposition AlN films. *J. Vac. Sci. Technol. A* **2015**, *33*, 01A111. [CrossRef]
23. Korbutowicz, R.; Zakrzewski, A.; Rac-Rumijowska, O.; Stafiniak, A.; Vincze, A. Oxidation rates of aluminium nitride thin films: Effect of composition of the atmosphere. *J. Mater. Sci. Mater. Electron.* **2017**, *28*, 13937. [CrossRef]
24. Chen, Y.; Hou, X.; Fang, Z.; Wang, E.; Chen, J.; Bei, G. Adsorption and Reaction of Water on the AlN(0001) Surface from First Principles. *J. Phys. Chem. C* **2019**, *123*, 5460. [CrossRef]
25. Liu, C.; Liu, S.; Huang, S.; Chen, K.J. Plasma-Enhanced Atomic Layer Deposition of AlN Epitaxial Thin Film for AlN/GaN Heterostructure TFTs. *IEEE Electron. Device Lett.* **2013**, *34*, 1106. [CrossRef]
26. Chen, K.J.; Huang, S. AlN passivation by plasma-enhanced atomic layer deposition for GaN-based power switches and power amplifiers. *Semicond. Sci. Technol.* **2013**, *28*, 074015. [CrossRef]
27. Miao, M.; Cadien, K. AlN PEALD with TMA and forming gas: Study of plasma reaction mechanisms. *RSC Adv.* **2021**, *11*, 12235. [CrossRef]
28. Fiorenza, P.; Di Franco, S.; Giannazzo, F.; Roccaforte, F. Nanoscale probing of the lateral homogeneity of donors concentration in nitridated SiO$_2$/4H–SiC interfaces. *Nanotechnology* **2016**, *27*, 315701. [CrossRef] [PubMed]
29. Fiorenza, P.; Lo Nigro, R.; Raineri, V.; Salinas, D. Conductive Atomic Force Microscopy Studies on the Reliability of Thermally Oxidized SiO$_2$/4H-SiC. *Mater. Sci. Forum* **2007**, *556*, 501–504. [CrossRef]
30. Perevalov, T.V.; Shaposhnikov, A.V.; Gritsenko, V.A.; Wong, H.; Han, J.H.; Kim, C.W. Electronic structure of α-Al$_2$O$_3$: Ab initio simulations and comparison with experiment. *JETP Lett.* **2007**, *85*, 165–168. [CrossRef]
31. Borga, M.; De Santi, C.; Stoffels, S.; Bakeroot, B.; Li, X.; Zhao, M.; Van Hove, M.; Decoutere, S.; Meneghesso, G.; Meneghini, M.; et al. Modeling of the Vertical Leakage Current in AlN/Si Heterojunctions for GaN Power Applications. *IEEE Trans. Electron. Devices* **2020**, *67*, 595–599. [CrossRef]
32. Rizzi, A.; Lantier, R.; Monti, F.; Lüth, H.; Della Sala, F.; Di Carlo, A.; Lugli, P. AlN and GaN epitaxial heterojunctions on 6H–SiC(0001): Valence band offsets and polarization fields. *J. Vac. Sci. Technol. B* **1999**, *17*, 1674. [CrossRef]
33. Roccaforte, F.; Fiorenza, P.; Lo Nigro, R.; Giannazzo, F.; Greco, G. Physics and technology of gallium nitride materials for power electronics. *Riv. Nuovo Cim.* **2018**, *41*, 625–681.

Structural Characteristics of the Si Whiskers Grown by Ni-Metal-Induced-Lateral-Crystallization

Béla Pécz [1,*], Nikolaos Vouroutzis [2], György Zoltán Radnóczi [1], Nikolaos Frangis [2] and John Stoemenos [2]

1. Centre for Energy Research, Institute for Technical Physics and Materials Science, EK MFA, Konkoly-Thege Miklós út 29-33, 1121 Budapest, Hungary; gy.radn@mfa.kfki.hu
2. Department of Physics, Aristotle University of Thessaloniki, 54124 Thessaloniki, Greece; nikosv@auth.gr (N.V.); frangis@auth.gr (N.F.); stoimeno@auth.gr (J.S.)
* Correspondence: pecz.bela@ek-cer.hu

Abstract: Si whiskers grown by Ni-Metal-Induced-Lateral-Crystallization (Ni-MILC) were grown at 413 °C, intentionally below the threshold for Solid State Crystallization, which is 420 °C. These whiskers have significant common characteristics with whiskers grown by the Vapor Liquid Solid (VLS) method. The crystalline quality of the whiskers in both methods is the same. However, in VLS, a crystalline substrate is required, in contrast to the amorphous one in Ni-MILC for the growth of single crystalline whiskers. Moreover, whiskers grown by VLS have a polygonal cross-section with their diameter determined by the diameter of the hemispherical metallic catalysts. On the other hand, in the Ni-MILC, the cross-section of the whiskers depends on the size of the $NiSi_2$ grain from which they are emanated. This was confirmed by observing the crossing whiskers and the rotational Moiré patterns in the crossing area. The structure of disturbed short and thin nonlinear branches on the side-walls of the whiskers was studied. In the whiskers grown by the VLS method, significant contamination occurs by the metallic catalyst degrading the electrical characteristics of the whisker. Such Si whiskers are not compatible with the current CMOS process. Whiskers grown by Ni-MILC at 413 °C are also contaminated by Ni. However, the excess Ni is in the form of tetrahedral $NiSi_2$ inclusions which are coherent with the Si matrix due to the very low misfit of 0.4% between them. These whiskers are compatible with current CMOS process and Thin Film Transistors (TFTs).

Keywords: crystallization of silicon; transmission electron microscopy; Moiré fringes

1. Introduction

Polycrystalline silicon (poly-Si) films are used in a wide range of applications, such as large-area electronics, including Thin-Film Transistors (TFTs), solar cells and sensors. Solid-Phase-Crystallization (SPC) is one of the simplest methods to crystallize amorphous silicon (a-Si) films, though it requires temperatures above 600 °C [1,2]. In most applications, the substrate is low-cost soft glass which requires lower process temperatures. The crystallization temperature of a-Si can be lowered by the Ni-Metal-Induced-Lateral-Crystallization (Ni-MILC). For the MILC, the preferred metal up to this date has been nickel (Ni) due to its low residual metal contamination in the poly-Si region [3]. In this case, the a-Si crystallized temperatures can be as low as 413 °C under the presence of nickel-disilicide, $NiSi_2$. The crystallization temperature of a-Si lowers under the presence of $NiSi_2$ because Ni atoms from the $NiSi_2$/a-Si interlayer diffuse into a-Si, reducing the strength of the covalent bonds at the interface caused by their interaction with the free electrons from the metallic phase [4].

At the relatively low temperature of 413 °C, whiskers are only grown by Ni-MILC, which makes them worth comparing to those ones grown by the standard VLS method, [5,6]. In the VLS process, the seed for the growth of the Si whisker is a droplet of liquid metal-Si alloy, in most cases this is Au-Si alloy on a (111) Si substrate. The liquid droplet is a preferred site for the Si deposition from the vapor phase; hence, the droplet becomes supersaturated with Si. Subsequently, the excess Si precipitates on the leading face of the Si whisker at the backside of the droplet, resulting in the growth of the Si whisker [5]. In both methods, long single crystalline whiskers are formed. In the VLS case, the isolated whiskers are perpendicular to the substrate, in the MILC case, they are parallel to the substrate and surrounded by a-Si.

In the case of Ni-MILC, the seeds are $NiSi_2$ crystallites which are formed after the reaction of Ni with the a-Si film at temperatures as low as 250 °C [7]. The $NiSi_2$ is cubic, having the CaF_2 structure and lattice mismatch with crystalline Si of only 0.4%. During annealing, nickel atoms from the $NiSi_2$ seeds diffuse into a-Si, forming new layers of $NiSi_2$ and leaving behind vacancies, accumulated at the backside of the $NiSi_2$ grain. Subsequently, a diamond type rearrangement of the Si bonds occurs, resulting in an epitaxial Si layer at the backside of the $NiSi_2$ module. This continuous process forms Si whiskers, as described in detail in Refs. [8,9]. In this study, we will show that whiskers grown in a-Si by Ni-MILC at 413 °C are similar to those grown by the VLS process. It is worth noticing that the residual Ni contamination of the Si whiskers grown by Ni-MILC is significantly lower in respect to those grown by VLS, where the metal impurity is gold, which is detrimental for electrical properties [10].

We want to note that at high temperature (typically 600 °C), MILC process, also Solid State Crystallization (SPC), happens in a significant way. Namely, the Si whiskers act as seeds facilitating the SPC crystallization around the whiskers (this will be shown later). As this second growth (SPC) process around the whiskers occurs spontaneously, large, highly defected crystallites are formed. The process is described widely in the literature, while the extremely low-temperature case where SPC is completely avoided is worth studying as well.

In order to study the influence of the SPC in the Ni-MILC process, annealing was performed at 600, 555, 490, 454, 420 and 413 °C. In each case, the contribution of the SPC was estimated by Transmission Electron Microscopy (TEM) observation of the mosaic structure development around the whiskers. It was shown that even at 454 °C, the influence of the SPC was noticeable; below 420 °C, no influence of the SPC was observed. These results are included in our previous papers, Refs. [7,11,12]. This should be considered as the threshold of the SPC in Ni-MILC. In the present work, we have studied the structural characteristics of whiskers grown below this threshold, namely at 413 °C, which corresponds to the lowest temperature annealing we have performed. In this manner, we could study the formation of Si nanowires, which is the characteristic of Ni-MILC process, and compare the results to vertical Si nanowires grown on single crystalline silicon by the Au-VLS method.

2. Materials and Methods

The specimen preparation for the Ni-MILC experiment at 413 °C was already presented in detail in Refs. [11,12]. A brief presentation of the procedure is shown schematically in Figure 1. The specimens were annealed at 250 °C for 10 min in nitrogen atmosphere for the formation of $NiSi_2$ pads, as shown in Figure 1f. The nonreacted Ni was etched by HNO_3, (Sigma Aldrich, Athens, Greece) Figure 1g. The thickness of the deposited Ni film was chosen to give stoichiometric $NiSi_2$ to all the depth of the a-Si film. In this way, a pattern of $NiSi_2$ pads was formed. Annealing was performed for the realization of the Ni-MILC process. For this purpose, samples with dimensions of 15 mm × 6 mm were placed in quartz ampoules which were sealed in vacuum {8 × 10^{-2} (Pa)} and annealed at 413 °C for 11 Ds (days), and for 32 Ds. Annealing was performed in an oven equipped with a temperature controller; moreover, a thermocouple was also used to check the actual temperature of the specimens. The accuracy of the temperature measurement is ±1 °C. Conventional MILC specimens were annealed at 520 °C for 1 h in nitrogen atmosphere for reference purposes. Specimens for Plane View TEM (PVTEM) observations were prepared by etching the capping protection SiO_2 layer, the SiO_2 buffer layer and the glass substrate using HF (Sigma Aldrich, Athens, Greece) and subsequently lifting off the Si film on gold micro-grids. For the structural characterization, a 2010 JEM microscope (JEOL Corp. Tokyo,

Japan) as well as a Thermo Fisher THEMIS 200 image corrected microscope (Eindhoven, The Netherlands) was used.

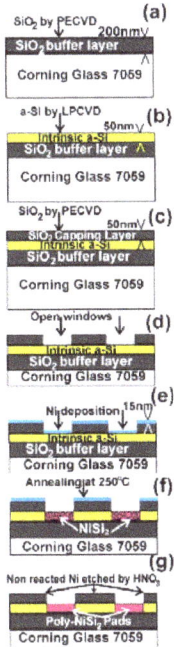

Figure 1. Schematic representation of the specimen preparation for the Ni-MILC experiment at 413 °C. (**a**) Deposition of 200 nm thick SiO_2 buffer layer on glass substrate by PECVD. (**b**) Deposition of 50 nm a-Si by LPCVD. (**c**) Deposition of a 50 nm thick SiO_2 capping layer by PECVD. (**d**) Open windows in the SiO_2 capping layer for the pad formation. (**e**) Deposition of 15 nm thick nickel. (**f**) Annealing at 250 °C for 10 min in order to form polycrystalline $NiSi_2$ in the area of the windows. (**g**) The nonreacted Ni is etched by HNO_3.

3. Results and Discussion

A Si whisker grown by Ni-MILC at 413 °C is not affected by Solid Phase Crystallization (SPC) [7,11]. In contrast, the same process in the range of temperatures 500–600 °C is strongly affected by SPC, creating a high density of defects. Therefore, the absence of SPC at Ni-MILC at 413 °C results in better quality Si whiskers comparable to those grown by the VLS method.

At first glance, the contribution of SPC in Ni-MILC should be insignificant because the incubation period for random nucleation at 600 °C is more than 10 h [2]. However, the incubation period for a-Si crystallization in Ni-MILC is zero, as was shown by an in situ TEM experiment, Radnoczi et al. [7]. Therefore, SPC is significant in Ni-MILC because the pre-existing whiskers act as seeds for crystallization unless the annealing temperature is sufficiently low to prevent the crystallization.

The contribution of the SPC at 520 °C is shown in the TEM micrographs in Figure 2a,b. Figure 2a shows the formation of Si whiskers in the areas denoted by the letters D and F after annealing for 2 min. The same areas are shown in Figure 2b 6 min later. Now, the whiskers are surrounded by misoriented Si grains due to SPC using the whiskers as seeds. The significance of SPC in Ni-MILC above 500 °C is shown in the high magnification micrograph in Figure 2c where the whiskers are surrounded by slightly misoriented grains, resulting in a mosaic structure. Overlapping grains give a Moiré pattern of rotational type [13], which is denoted by the letter M in Figure 2c. More details on the SPC involvement in Ni-MILC above 500 °C are shown by M. Miyasaka et al. [14], also by Radnoczi, G.Z. et al. [7].

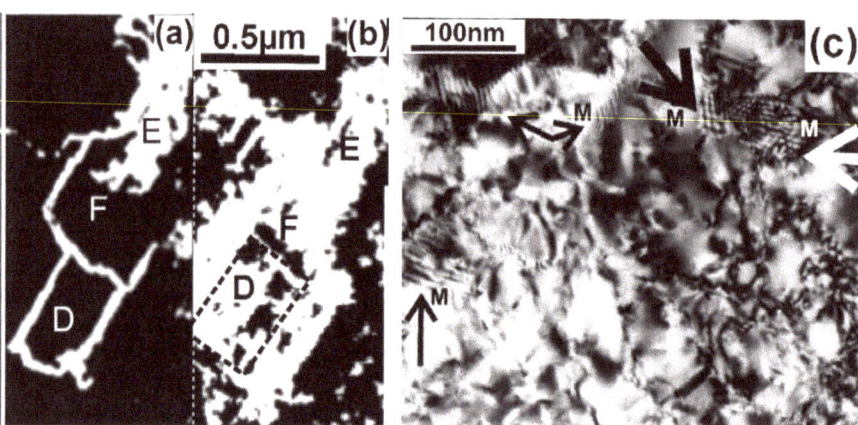

Figure 2. TEM micrographs from in situ Ni-MILC at 520 °C where SPC is significant. (**a**) In the areas D and F, Si whiskers are evident, frequently changing direction, forming a loop in area D. (**b**) The same area 2 min later, the areas D and F are covered by slightly misoriented grains due to SPC. (**c**) Slightly misoriented overlapping grains due to the SPC process give Moiré patterns of rotational type shown by arrows.

3.1. Tweed-Like Structure in Ni-MILC at 413 °C

The SPC process can be completely inhibited by lowering the annealing temperature to 413 °C, resulting in pure Ni-MILC. The films consist of a mixture of whiskers growing fast along the [111] crystallographic direction and whiskers grown slowly, having random crystallographic orientations, other than the [111] [5]. The overall view of such a film is shown at the low magnification micrographs in Figure 3a. The NiSi$_2$ pad, denoted by the letter P, is surrounded by a net of fast [111] type and slow type whiskers, resulting in a tweed-like structure; this is shown in the high magnification macrograph in Figure 3b, where three parallel fast [111] whiskers, A, B, C, are intersected by the slow [112] whisker E. At the edges of the tweed-like film, bands of long parallel [111] type whiskers are observed as shown in Figure 3a. This is the result of the natural crystal filtering due to growth-velocity competition which is observed when grains meet other grains that have already been crystallized [13,14]. The observed long whiskers must be exactly parallel to the substrate; otherwise, they touch the surface or the bottom of the film and stop. Whiskers as long as 9 µm were observed, as shown in Figure 3a. The crystal filtering effect was also observed in the Ni-MILC at 550 °C, where SPC is also involved, by artificial preferred filtration through a narrow neck in the a-Si which was formed artificially by lithography, creating a SiO$_2$ barrier in the a-Si, before the onset of Ni-MILC [15,16].

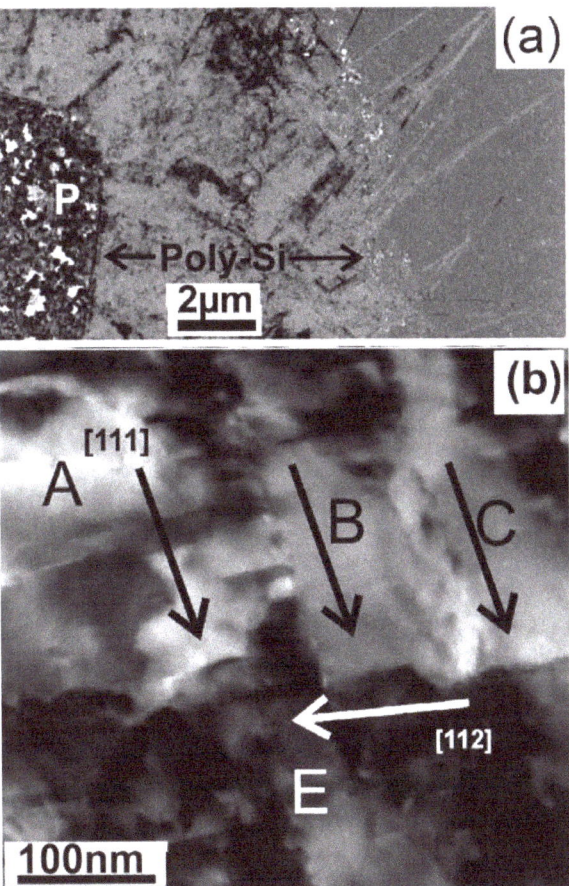

Figure 3. TEM micrographs from Ni-MILC at 413 °C where SPC is completely suppressed. (**a**) Overall view of the structure around the pad denoted by the letter P. A continuous poly-Si film consisting of a mixture of fast and slow whiskers resulting in a tweed-like structure is extended up to 8 µ. Then, long fast [111] type whiskers emanate due to growth–death competition mechanism. (**b**) The tweed-like structure shown at higher magnification.

3.2. Crossover of the Whiskers in Ni-MILC at 413 °C

In some cases, the whiskers can cross each other, as shown in Figure 4a, denoted by the letters A, B and C. Very often, Moiré patterns are formed in the crossing area, revealing overlapping of the whiskers in this area. This is evident in the areas A and B, as shown in the higher magnification micrograph of Figure 4b.

The formation of Moiré patterns in two crossing whiskers was systematically studied as shown in Figure 5a; the crossing whiskers are denoted by the letters A and B. The diffraction pattern in the inset of Figure 5a was taken from the crossing area and corresponds to the (112) zone, revealing that the whisker A grows along the [$\overline{1}$11] direction; in other words, it is a fast type whisker. The reflection $2\overline{2}0$ is common for both whiskers and is split, making a small angle of about 3.5°. These double spots create the Moiré patterns in the crossing area. The Moiré patterns are extended perpendicular to the $g_{2\overline{2}0}$ reflection, namely along the [$\overline{1}$11] direction. Therefore, the Moiré patterns are of the rotation type [13], having a periodicity of 2.7 nm. The direction of growth of the whisker B is the [$\overline{1}$12]. This was deduced considering the angle which it forms with whisker A and with the common direction [110]. These are 62° and 30°, respectively; only the [112] direction forms such angles with the [111] and [110] directions. Therefore, the whisker B is a slow type whisker.

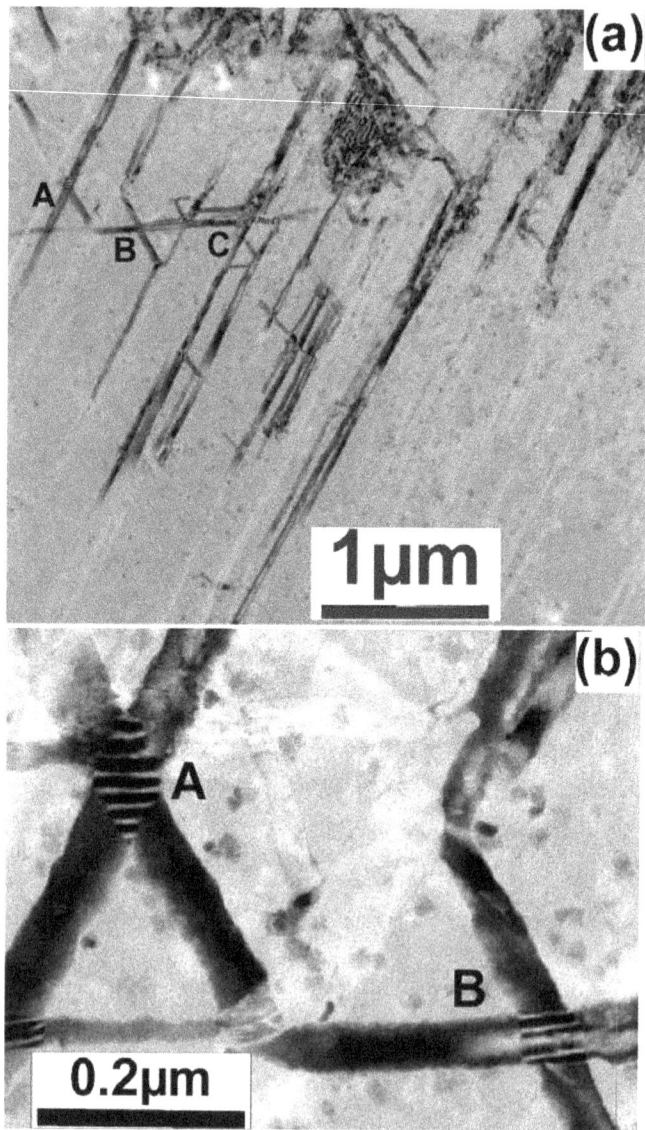

Figure 4. TEM micrographs. (**a**) Overall view of crossing whiskers; in some cases, the same whisker crosses several whiskers having different orientations denoted by the letters A, B and C. (**b**) The crossing areas A and B at higher magnification reveal the formation of Moiré fringes.

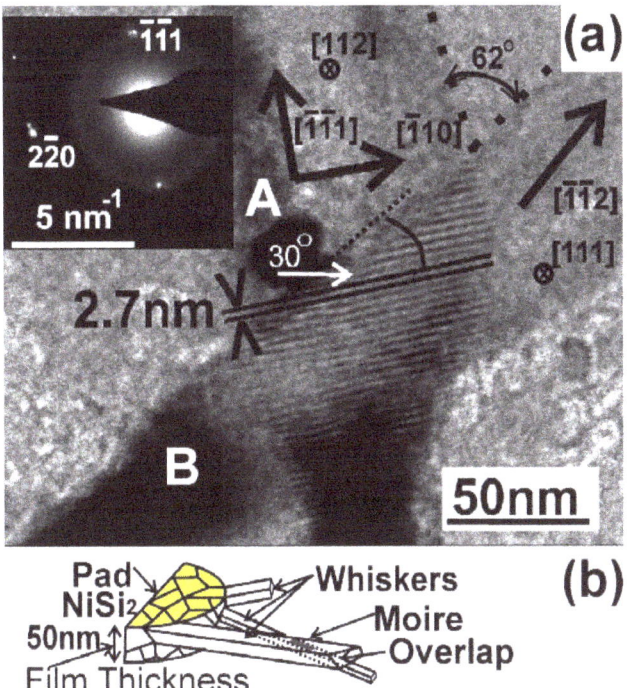

Figure 5. (**a**) High magnification TEM micrograph from the crossing area of two whiskers A and B in the inset is the corresponding diffraction pattern. The two whiskers have common reflection of 220, which is split; the Moiré fringes are perpendicular to this reflection, revealing that they are of the rotational type. (**b**) Schematic representation in 3D of two overlapping whiskers emanating from the NiSi$_2$ pad. The total thickness of the overlapping whiskers A and B must not exceed the thickness of the film.

A more accurate estimation of the misorientation of the two whiskers can be deduced by applying the equation

$$\theta = d/D \qquad (1)$$

where D is the periodicity of the Moiré patterns, d the spacing of the lattice planes of the operating diffraction, in our case d_{220} = 0.192 nm and θ the angle of the misorientation in rad. For D = 2.7 nm, we have θ = 0.071 rad = 4.07°; this is the exact angle between the split 220 spots. The overlap of the two whiskers A and B is shown schematically in 3D in Figure 5b. The total thickness of the overlapping whiskers A and B must not exceed the thickness of the film, which is 50 nm.

According to Equation (1), when the overlapping whiskers form a relatively large misorientation angle θ, the periodicity of the rotational Moiré patterns is small, requiring high-resolution TEM to be revealed; this is shown in the high-resolution TEM micrograph in Figure 6. In this case, two fast [111] type whiskers A and B partially overlap, creating rotational Moiré patterns with periodicity D_{111} = 1.38 nm, as shown in Figure 6. The misorientation angle θ was calculated from Equation (1) with common reflection 111, (d_{111} = 0.3138 nm), resulting in θ = 13.035°. Since the whiskers A and B have the (110) zone axis, they also have the reflections 22$\bar{0}$ and 002 in common; therefore, rotation type Moiré should also be observed from these reflections. It is worth noticing that the 200 reflection is forbidden in the diamond structure; however, it appears, especially in the section (110) due to double reflection of the $\bar{1}$11 and 11$\bar{1}$ spots; that is why it is denoted with a star (*). However, the Moiré patterns are intense only for reflections which are close to the "two beam" case, fading fast outside of it. This is the case in Figure 6, where only one set of Moiré patterns is observed.

Figure 6. High-resolution TEM micrograph from two partially overlapping [111] type whiskers A and B; the overlapping area is denoted by the letter C. The observed rotational Moiré pattern has a periodicity of D_{111} = 1.38 nm.

Another example of two partially overlapping parallel whiskers, A and B, is shown in Figure 7. The related diffraction pattern in the inset of Figure 7 confirms that the parallel whiskers A and B are of the slow type, grown along the [$\bar{1}$10] direction with their (110) planes perpendicular to the electron beam. The periodicity of the Moiré pattern is 11 nm, also running parallel to this direction, revealing that they are created from the strong 002 reflection which is perpendicular to the [$\bar{1}$10] direction. According to Equation (1), the angle of rotation θ for the reflection 002 is only 1.4°, too small to be distinguished in the diffraction pattern.

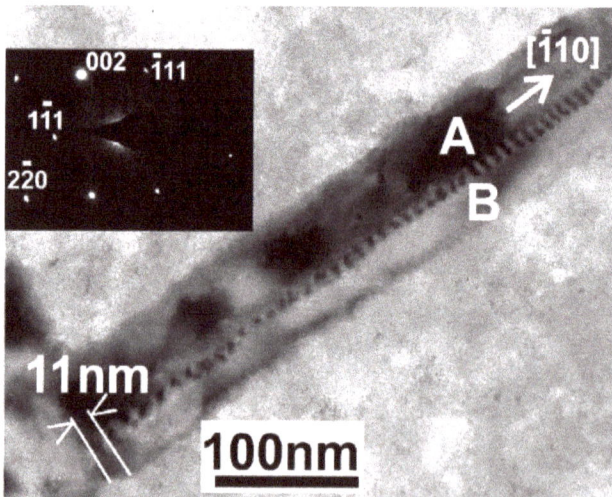

Figure 7. TEM micrograph of two partially overlapping parallel whiskers A and B. The related diffraction pattern in the inset reveals that the parallel whiskers A and B are in the (110) section, grown along the [$\bar{1}$10] direction, and therefore are of the slow type.

The cross-section of the whiskers grown by VLS are symmetric polygonal, growing from a single crystalline Si substrate [5]. In contrast, in the Ni-MILC, the Si whiskers grow from NiSi$_2$ grains which have different size, shape and orientation. This explains why two whiskers having width of about 50 nm, as shown in Figure 5a, can overlap in a 50 nm thick film. Obviously, the cross-section of the whiskers in Ni-MILC is not symmetric polygonal, as shown schematically in the 3D Figure 5b. This is a significant dissimilarity in the two processes.

The Moiré patterns are very sensitive to any lattice misorientation. The exclusion of the SPC process results in homogeneous Moiré patterns in the overlapping whiskers.

If the overlapping whiskers are also affected by the SPC process causing random small misorientations (Ni-MILC temperature above 500 °C), then the overlapping area would be divided into smaller areas, exhibiting rotational Moiré patterns of different periodicity and orientation due to the misoriented grains as shown in Figure 2c.

3.3. Width of the Whiskers

Whiskers grown by VLS have polygonal cross-section with a diameter determined by the diameter D of the hemispherical metallic catalysts according to the equation:

$$D = 4V_L \sigma_{LV}/RT \ln(s) \qquad (2)$$

where V_L is the molar volume of the metallic droplet, σ_{LV} the liquid-vapor surface energy and s the degree of supersaturation of the vapor [10]. Nevertheless, Oswald ripening mechanism leads to the formation of larger droplets of metal catalyst. On the other hand, in the Ni-MILC case the cross-section of the whiskers depends on the size of the NiSi$_2$ grain from which they are emanated. Thus, the mean size of the grains in the NiSi$_2$ pads grown at 250 °C is 60 nm, but most of them are below 50 nm in the perpendicular direction as schematically shown in Figure 5b. The cross-section of the Si whiskers is fitted to the facet of NiSi$_2$ grain from which they are emanated. Therefore, the whiskers are not symmetrical, as already schematically described in Figure 5b.

3.4. Saw-Tooth Faceting of the Side-Walls of the Whiskers

In the fast <111> whiskers grown by Ni-MILC, saw-tooth faceting of the side-walls is frequently observed, with the longest segments of the tooth to be the (111) planes, as shown in Figure 8. Similar structures were observed in whiskers grown by VLS [5]. Saw-tooth faceting occurs when the side-walls are not stable; namely, they do not belong to the equilibrium crystal shape. In this case, the surface breaks into stable saw-tooth facets [17].

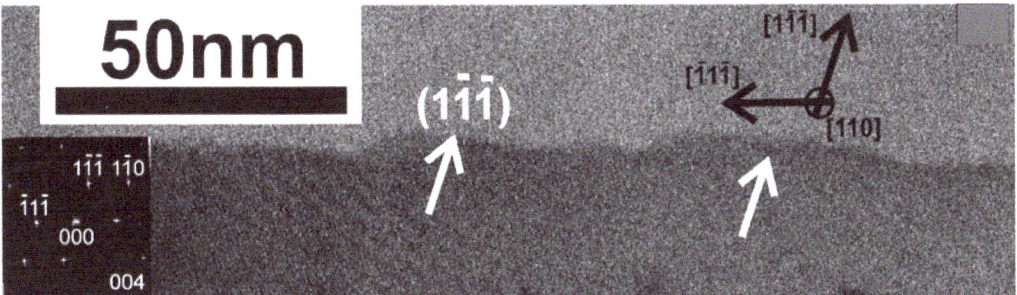

Figure 8. Cross-section TEM micrograph from fast [111] whiskers viewed in (110) section. A saw-tooth faceting of the side-walls is evident, with the longest segments of the tooth being the (111) planes.

3.5. Straight Whiskers in Ni-MILC at 413 °C

In Ni-MILC above 520 °C, the fast [111] type whiskers prevail, changing their course frequently to other equivalent <111> directions, facilitating in this way the crystallization [13], as shown in the TEM micrograph in Figure 2a,b. In contrast, the whiskers in Ni-MILC at 413 °C are, in general, straight, rarely changing their course as shown in Figures 3a and 4a. It is speculated that the reason for this difference is the extra dangling bonds which are required when a [111] whisker changes its course to another equivalent direction, say the [1$\bar{1}$1] as schematically shown in Figure 9. The whisker A is a fast [111] one growing linearly to a length L; the whisker B is also fast, having the same length, which during the growth was switched to another equivalent [1$\bar{1}$1] direction. For the switching, an extra part is required, denoted by red in Figure 9. Therefore, extra dangling bonds are created for the same length, making this change unfavorable from the energetic point of view, especially at lower temperatures. The switching to the [1$\bar{1}$1] direction is also shown in the schematic atomic representation viewed in the ($\bar{1}$10) section in Figure 9. The extra dangling bonds included in the red area are evident. It is worth noticing that the Ni-MILC at 413 °C is a very slow process permitting the atoms to find the lowest energy position minimizing the dangling bonds and resulting in straight whiskers as in VLS. This is not the case in the conventional Ni-MILC above 520 °C where significant SPC occurs. In this case, the <111> whiskers change their course frequently to another equivalent <111> direction, facilitating, in this way, the crystallization of the intermediate amorphous space by SPC growth as it is shown in Figure 2; see also M. Miyasaka et al. [14]. This is a consequence of the minimum action principle, namely the system takes the lower energy state in the minimum time.

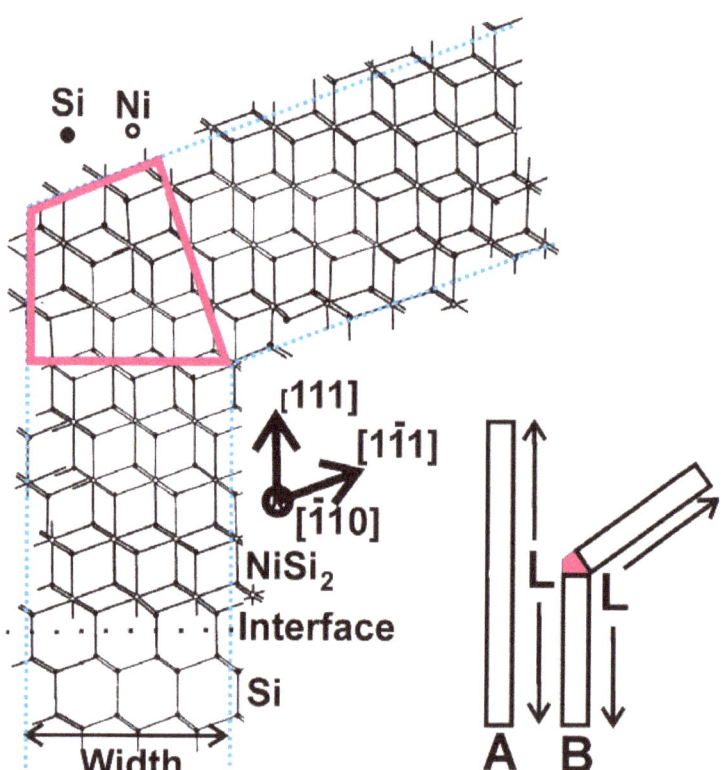

Figure 9. Schematic representation of a fast [111] whisker denoted by the letter A which grows linearly having a length L. Compare this whisker with the whisker B having the same total length L. During the growth, the whisker B switches to the equivalent [1$\bar{1}$1] direction. Although the two whiskers have the same length, an extra part denoted by red is required for the switching, including the formation of extra dangling bonds. This is also shown schematically in atomic scale in the section ($\bar{1}$10).

3.6. Disturbed Ni-MILC at 413 °C

In some cases, the Ni-MILC at 413 °C is disturbed so that short and thin nonlinear branches appear at the side-walls of the whisker as shown in the whiskers A and B in the DF-PVTEM micrograph in Figure 10a. It is speculated that the disturbance of the crystallization is due to contamination. Similarly, side-wall branches were observed due to contamination in nanowires grown by VLS [5]. In Figure 10a, in the area A, the formation of these branches is followed by splitting of the original whisker into two thinner ones, which are parallel to the original. In the region B, the crystallization stops after the formation of the side-wall branches. These branches are microcrystalline, consisting of grains having a mean size of 7 nm as shown in Figure 10b. In the grain denoted by the letter T in Figure 10b, a pattern with periodicity of three times the d_{111} spacing of the Si lattice, $D = 3d_{111} = 0.95$ nm, was observed along the direction [1$\underline{1}$1]. This is confirmed by the extra spots in the Fast Fourier Transform (FFT) shown in the inset, in the bottom of Figure 10b. This is not a superlattice structure in Si; they are simply Moiré patterns which are formed by double diffraction of the electron beam in the Si matrix and an overlapping (111) type twin, i.e., a Σ3 type twin, viewed in the (110) section.

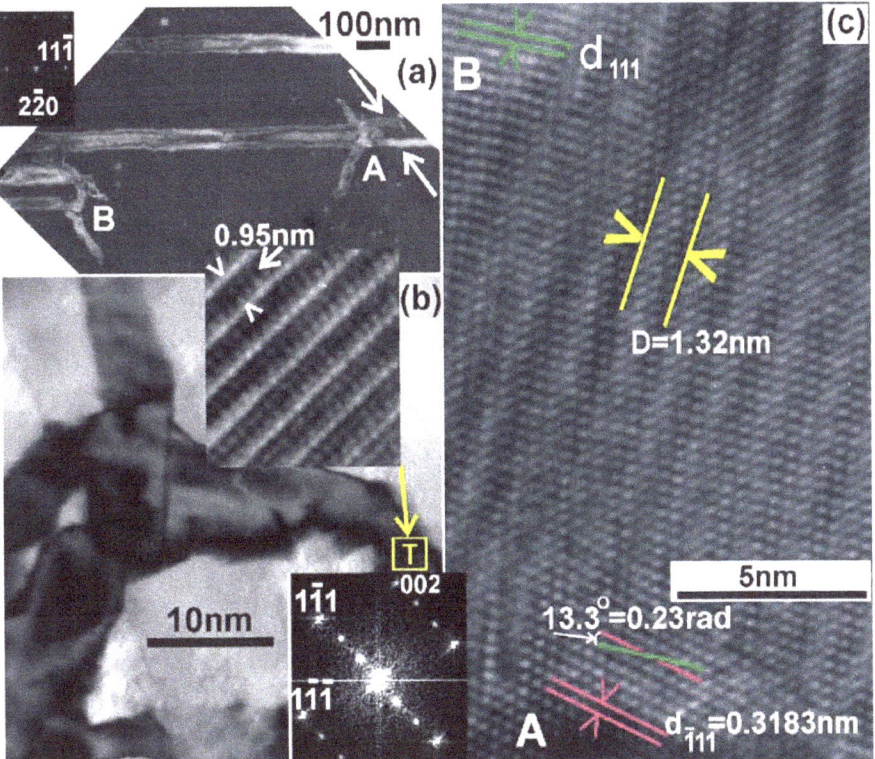

Figure 10. (a) DF-PVTEM micrograph showing disturbed nonlinear branches at the side-walls of the whiskers A and B. In the whisker A after the formation of the disturbed branches, the whisker was split into two parallel ones. In the case of whisker B, the growth was stopped. Both the whiskers were fast [111] types viewed in the (220) section. (b) The nonlinear branches consist of highly defected grains. In the area denoted by the letter T, Moiré pattern is observed with periodicity $D_{111} = 3d_{111}$; these are formed by double diffraction of the electron beam in the matrix and an overlapping (111) twin; when viewed in the (110) section, this is confirmed by the Fast Fourier Transform shown in the inset. (c) Two overlapping grains, slightly misoriented A and B, are viewed in the (110) section, having the common (111) reflection in strong contrast. Moiré pattern of rotation type is observed, having periodicity of $D_{111} = 1.38$ nm, which corresponds to a misorientation of 1.34°.

Very often, grains with different orientations overlap, giving Moiré pattern as shown in Figure 10c. The grain A viewed in the exact (110) section overlaps with the grain B which gives strong contrast from the (111) lattice planes which are rotated 13.3° (0.23 rad) in respect to the grain A, as shown in Figure 10c. Moiré pattern of the rotation type is formed in the overlapping area with periodicity $D = d/\theta = 0.3183$ nm/0.23 = 1.38 nm. This was confirmed by measuring the periodicity of the Moiré patterns D in Figure 10c, which was found to be D = 1.32 nm. It is evident that these short and thin, highly defected whiskers were grown by the SPC process.

3.7. Impurities in the Si Whiskers

In the VLS method, many metals are used as catalysts for the growth of Si whiskers; from these, the most successful is gold. However, due to the contact between the liquid Au alloy and the whisker at a high temperature, the Si is inevitably contaminated by gold. This contamination increases the impurity level in the Si, degrading the electrical characteristics of the whisker [18]. Although there is a detailed paper on gold detection in Si nanowires [19], which says that incorporated gold does not influence in a significant way the carrier mobility in Si wires, when the surface density is low, the authors also mention that there are still challenging tasks in that technology. We also note that the gold concentration in the nanowires grown by the VLS method is significantly higher than the solubility limit of gold in the bulk Si, which is not very promising. Reference [19] points out that low surface density is essential; however, in Si, the lowest surface densities are found on (001) which is actually used in all CMOS technology because of the orientation of the wafers. In the case of the VLS grown nanowires, however, the side-walls are different and in some, saw-tooth faceting is observed in the (112) type side-walls of nanowires grown along the [111] direction by the VLS process [17]. Therefore, such Si whiskers are generally still not compatible with the current CMOS process [12]. Of course, the Ni-VLS process can be carried out as well and may give superior silicon wires with (111) orientation [20]; however, this requires a very high temperature of 1100 °C.

The whiskers grown by Ni-MILC are also contaminated by Ni metal as SIMS measurements in Si films grown at 575 °C reveal. Although the solubility limit of Ni in Si is very low (10^{13} atoms/cm^3) at this temperature [21], a Ni concentration of 4×10^{19} atoms/cm^3 or 0.08 at % Ni was measured. However, we have shown recently that the excess Ni in the Si whiskers is in the form of tetrahedral NiSi$_2$ inclusions bounded by {111} coherent interfaces with the Si matrix [11]. The size of the inclusions ranges from a few atoms to 20 nm. The tetrahedral inclusions are formed by trapping NiSi$_2$ clusters at the Si/NiSi$_2$ interface during the whisker growth. The easy precipitation of NiSi$_2$ in Si is attributed to the very low misfit, which is 0.4%. Due to the small misfit of the NiSi$_2$ with the Si lattice and the small size of the tetrahedral inclusions, they cannot create misfit dislocations in their interfaces with the Si matrix. However, they do create some strain which gives a weak contrast in TEM. The high-resolution TEM micrograph in Figure 11 shows a V shape tetrahedral NiSi$_2$ inclusion viewed in the (110) section. The NiSi$_2$ inclusions are clearly visible in Z contrast; see Vouroutzis, N. et al. [11]. For the Si whisker grown by Ni-MILC at 413 °C, the average concentration of Ni is lower, 1.76×10^{19} Ni atoms/cm^3 or in percentage 0.035 at %. The lower value of Ni concentration is attributed to the lowering of processing temperature. It is worth noticing that the amount of nickel inside the crystallized region depends on the annealing temperature, not on the annealing time [22]. It was shown that Si-whiskers grown by Ni-MILC are compatible with the CMOS processes and Thin Film Transistors were fabricated exhibiting very good performance [23]. The transistors presented in that publication were fabricated on polycrystalline Si after Ni-MILC above 540 °C where SPC is already also involved. Our nanowires were grown by Ni-MILC at 413 °C; where SPC is completely avoided is of the quality of the nanowires grown by VLS. Therefore, we believe that our material is useful from the technological point of view.

Nevertheless, the NiSi$_2$ inclusions in the Si whiskers trap other metallic impurities there; this is a pathway for engineering impurities in Si [24].

In the Ni-MILC at 413 °C (i.e., the present experiments), the Ni concentration is 50% lower than at 575 °C, so we may expect additional improvement of the device behavior. This reduction of the Ni concentration is attributed to the lower process temperature. The exact influence of the NiSi$_2$ inclusions on the electrical behavior of the nanowires is not known and further electrical characterization is required in order to reveal their influence on the device performance.

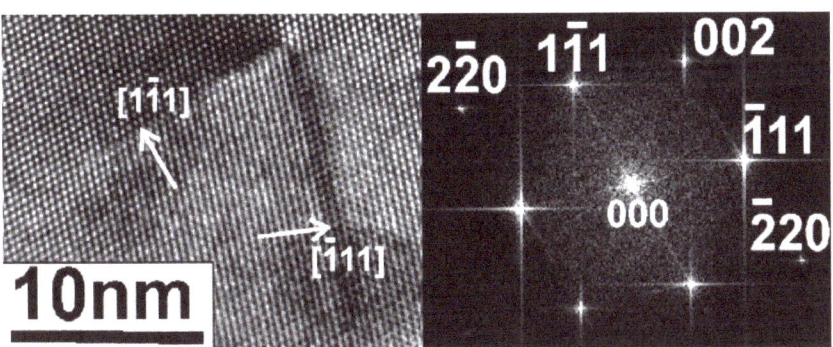

Figure 11. High-resolution TEM micrograph reveals a tetrahedral NiSi$_2$ inclusion viewed in the (110) section as showing the related FFT in the lower left corner. The same defect is shown at low magnification in the upper right corner.

4. Conclusions

The VLS mechanism as well as Ni-MILC at 413 °C is a 1D crystal growth mechanism that is assisted by a metal catalyst. It results in the creation of whiskers and rods. The structural characteristics of the Si whiskers grown by Ni-MILC at temperature 413 °C were compared to those grown by the VLS method. The similarities are attributed to the suppression of the SPC at the side-bands of the whiskers in both methods. The whiskers are single crystalline, but those grown by the VLS require a single crystalline substrate and are grown perpendicular to it. In the case of Ni-MILC, the whiskers are grown parallel to an amorphous substrate; they emanate from the crystallographic facet of the NiSi$_2$ grains. However, only whiskers which are parallel to the substrate can survive; from these, the prevalent ones are those which are grown fast due to the growth death competition mechanism [16]; these are the fast [111] whiskers.

The use of Au as the catalyst in VLS increases the impurity level in the bandgap of the Si whiskers, making them incompatible with the CMOS process. The Ni-MILC at 413 °C is a low-temperature process resulting in low Ni metal contamination level; in addition to the Ni forms, NiSi$_2$ coherent inclusions in the Si whiskers act as traps for other metallic impurities, permitting the CMOS technology to be compatible with the Ni-MILC process. Moreover, the Si single crystalline whiskers grown by the low-temperature Ni-MILC technique can gain other applications in the nanomaterial subject. All the characteristics of the whiskers grown by VLS and Ni-MILC at 413 °C are summarized in Table 1.

Table 1. Comparison of the Si whiskers grown by the VLS and the Ni-MILC at 413 °C methods.

Characteristics	VLS Method	Ni-MILC Method at 413 °C
Direction of growth	Perpendicular to the substrate	Parallel to the substrate
SPC growth	Suppressed	Suppressed
Temperature of the process	High	Low
Substrate	Single crystalline	Amorphous
Crystalline whiskers	This of substrate orientation	Fast [111]
Width of the whiskers	Polygonal with diameter of the hemispherical metallic catalysts	Depends on the size of the starting NiSi$_2$ grain
Electrical characteristics	Not compatible with CMOS process due to metallic contamination	Compatible with CMOS process in spite of Ni contamination

Author Contributions: J.S. and B.P. designed the experiments and wrote the text of the paper. Furthermore J.S. prepared Figures. N.V. made all of the electron diffraction study, while G.Z.R. and N.F. carried out the high resolution microscopy. All authors discussed the results and commented on the manuscript. All authors have read and agreed to the published version of the manuscript.

Funding: Research infrastructure was provided by VEKOP-2.3.3-15-2016-00002 project.

Data Availability Statement: Authors provide experimental data for any reasonable request.

Conflicts of Interest: There is no conflict of interest.

References

1. Puglisi, R.A.; Tanabe, H.; Chen, C.M.; Atwater, H.A. Large-grained polycrystalline Si films obtained by selective nucleation and solid phase epitaxy. *Mater. Sci. Eng. B* **2000**, *73*, 212. [CrossRef]
2. Qin, M.; Poon, M.C.; Fan, L.J.; Chan, M.; Yuen, C.Y.; Chan, W.Y. Study of grain growth of polysilicon formed by nickel-induced-lateral-crystallyzation of amorphous silicon and subsequent high temperature annealing. *Thin Solid Film.* **2002**, *406*, 17. [CrossRef]
3. Mohiddon, M.A.; Krishna, M.G.; Dalba, G.; Rocca, F. Transmission electron microscopy study of Ni–Si nanocomposite films. *Mater. Sci. Eng. B* **2012**, *177*, 1108. [CrossRef]
4. Anderson, C.; Kortshagen, U. Seeding Solid Phase Crystallization of Amorphous Silicon Films with Embedded Nanocrystals. *MRS Online Proc.* **2008**, *1066*, A06–A14. [CrossRef]
5. Wagner, R.S.; Doherty, C.J. Controlled Vapor-Liquid-Solid Growth of Silicon Crystals. *J. Electrochem. Soc.* **1966**, *113*, 1300. [CrossRef]
6. Givargizov, E.I. Fundamental aspects of VLS growth. *J. Cryst. Growth* **1975**, *31*, 20. [CrossRef]
7. Radnóczi, G.Z.; Dodony, E.; Battistig, G.; Vouroutzis, N.; Kavouras, P.; Stoemenos, J.; Frangis, N.; Kovács, A.; Pécz, B. Structural characterization of nanostructures grown by Ni metal induced lateral crystallization of amorphous-Si. *J. Appl. Phys.* **2016**, *119*, 065303. [CrossRef]
8. Hayzelden, C.; Batstone, J.L. Silicide formation and silicide-mediated crystallization of nickel-implanted amorphous silicon thin films. *J. Appl. Phys.* **1993**, *73*, 8279. [CrossRef]
9. Su, C.J.; Huang, Y.F.; Lin, H.C.; Huang, T.Y. Characterizations of polycrystalline silicon nanowire thin-film transistors enhanced by metal-induced lateral crystallization. *Solid State Electron.* **2012**, *77*, 20. [CrossRef]
10. Choi, H.J. Vapor–Liquid–Solid Growth of Semiconductor Nanowires. In *Semiconductor Nanostructures for Optoelectronic Devices*; NanoScience and Technology Series; Gyu-Chul, Y., Ed.; Springer: Berlin/Heidelberg, Germany, 2012; Chapter 1; pp. 1–36.
11. Radnóczi, G.Z.; Knez, D.; Hofer, F.; Frangis, N.; Vouroutzis, N.; Stoemenos, J.; Pécz, B. Inclusions in Si whiskers grown by Ni metal induced lateral crystallization. *J. Appl. Phys.* **2017**, *121*, 145301. [CrossRef]
12. Vouroutzis, N.; Stoemenos, J.; Frangis, N.; Radnóczi, G.Z.; Knez, D.; Hofer, F.; Pécz, B. Structural characterization of poly-Si Films crystallized by Ni Metal Induced Lateral Crystallization. *Sci. Rep.* **2019**, *9*, 2844. [CrossRef]
13. Hirsch, P.B.; Howie, A.; Nicholson, R.B.; Pashley, D.W. *Electron Microscopy of Thin Crystals*; Butterworths/Heinemann: London, UK, 1965.
14. Miyasaka, M.; Makihira, K.; Asano, T.; Polychroniadis, E.; Stoemenos, J. In situ observation of nickel metal-induced lateral crystallization of amorphous silicon thin films. *Appl. Phys. Lett.* **2002**, *80*, 944. [CrossRef]
15. Haji, L.; Joubert, P.; Stoemenos, J.; Economou, N.A. Mode of growth and microstructure of polycrystalline silicon obtained by solid-phase crystallization of an amorphous silicon film. *J. Appl. Phys.* **1994**, *75*, 3944. [CrossRef]
16. Kim, M.S.; Lee, J.S.; Kim, Y.S.; Joo, S.K. The Effects of Crystal Filtering on Growth of Silicon Grains in Metal-Induced Lateral Crystallization. *Electrochem. Solid State Lett.* **2006**, *9*, G56. [CrossRef]
17. Ross, F.M.; Tersoff, J.; Reuter, M.C. Sawtooth Faceting in Silicon Nanowires. *Phys. Rev. Lett.* **2005**, *95*, 146104. [CrossRef]
18. Adhikari, H.; Marshall, A.F.; Goldthorpe, I.A.; Chidsey, C.E.D.; McIntyre, P.C. Metastability of Au−Ge Liquid Nanocatalysts: Ge Vapor–Liquid–Solid Nanowire Growth Far below the Bulk Eutectic Temperature. *ACS Nano.* **2007**, *1*, 415. [CrossRef] [PubMed]
19. Allen, J.E.; Hemesath, E.R.; Perea, D.E.; Lensch-Falk, J.L.; Li, Z.Y.; Yin, F.; Gass, M.H.; Wang, P.; Bleloch, A.L.; Palmer, R.E.; et al. High resolution detection of Au catalyst atoms in Si nanowires. *Nat. Nanotechnol.* **2008**, *3*, 168. [CrossRef]
20. Li, F.J.; Yuehua, H.; Shu, W.; Sam, Z. Structure-sensitive principle in silicon nanowire growth. *Thin Solid Film.* **2020**, *697*, 137814. [CrossRef]
21. Weber, E.R. Transition metals in silicon. *Appl. Phys. A* **1983**, *30*, 1–22. [CrossRef]
22. Cheng, C.F.; Poon, V.M.C.; Kok, W.; Chan, M. Modeling of grain growth mechanism by nickel silicide reactive grain boundary effect in metal-induced-lateral-crystallization. *IEEE Trans. Electron Devices* **2003**, *50*, 1467. [CrossRef]
23. Lee, S.W.; Joo, S.K. Low temperature poly-Si thin-film transistor fabrication by metal-induced lateral crystallization. *IEEE Electron Device Lett.* **1996**, *17*, 160.
24. Fenning, D.P.; Newman, B.K.; Bertoni, M.I.; Hudelson, S.; Bernardis, S.; Marcus, M.A.; Fakra, S.C.; Buonassisi, T. Local melting in silicon driven by retrograde solubility. *Acta Mater.* **2013**, *61*, 4320. [CrossRef]

Article

High-Resolution Two-Dimensional Imaging of the 4H-SiC MOSFET Channel by Scanning Capacitance Microscopy

Patrick Fiorenza [1,*], Mario S. Alessandrino [2], Beatrice Carbone [2], Alfio Russo [2], Fabrizio Roccaforte [1] and Filippo Giannazzo [1]

1. Consiglio Nazionale delle Ricerche—Istituto per la Microelettronica e Microsistemi (CNR-IMM), Strada VIII 5, 95121 Catania, Italy; fabrizio.roccaforte@imm.cnr.it (F.R.); filippo.giannazzo@imm.cnr.it (F.G.)
2. STMicroelectronics, Stradale Primosole 50, 95121 Catania, Italy; santi.alessandrino@st.com (M.S.A.); beatrice.carbone@st.com (B.C.); alfio-lip.russo@st.com (A.R.)
* Correspondence: patrick.fiorenza@imm.cnr.it

Abstract: In this paper, a two-dimensional (2D) planar scanning capacitance microscopy (SCM) method is used to visualize with a high spatial resolution the channel region of large-area 4H-SiC power MOSFETs and estimate the homogeneity of the channel length over the whole device perimeter. The method enabled visualizing the fluctuations of the channel geometry occurring under different processing conditions. Moreover, the impact of the ion implantation parameters on the channel could be elucidated.

Keywords: scanning probe microscopy; scanning capacitance microscopy; 4H-SiC; power-MOSFET

1. Introduction

Silicon-carbide (4H-SiC) metal-oxide-semiconductor field-effect transistors (MOSFETs) are raising the interest of the scientific community, owing to their applications and excellent performances in power electronics [1]. In the fabrication of vertical 4H-SiC MOSFETs, ion implantation is used to introduce dopant species (phosphorous for n-type and aluminum for p-type) in selective regions of the material, followed by high-temperature annealing for the electrical activation [2,3]. Hence, to accurately predict the device performance, both the active doping concentration and the geometry (e.g., size of the implanted region, junction depths, etc.) of the implanted MOSFET regions must be monitored at the nanoscale. In fact, while the diffusion coefficients in SiC are extremely low, the two-dimensional lateral spread of implanted atoms can affect the dopant distribution and, hence, the device behavior [4]. Hence, to accurately predict the MOSFET performance, both the active doping concentration and the geometry of the implanted regions (e.g., size, junction depths, etc.) must be monitored at the nanoscale. In fact, while the implantation doping in SiC is precisely localized after post-implantation annealing due to the extremely low diffusivity of the dopant species, the two-dimensional lateral spread of implanted atoms [4] and channeling effect in the hexagonal 4H-SiC lattice [5] can affect the dopant distribution.

In 4H-SiC power MOSFETs, the inversion channel length (in the order of few hundreds of nanometers) and the JFET (junction field-effect transistor) doping critically influence the threshold-voltage (V_{th}), on-resistance (R_{ON}), leakage current during the forward blocking mode, and gate-oxide-related ruggedness. Clearly, for high-current-level applications, 4H-SiC power MOSFETs are designed with large active areas (>10 mm^2) and long perimeter (in the order of thousands of mm). Hence, the inversion of channel length and the JFET size must be extremely uniform along all the device perimeters to ensure the performance reproducibility. Thus, two-dimensional (2D) electrical imaging techniques combining high resolution (tens of nanometers) and the ability to probe large areas are needed to obtain statistically relevant information on the whole device periphery and, eventually, monitor anomalies of the electrical behavior.

In 4H-SiC MOSFET, the channel length is the distance of the p-type body from the n$^+$-source junctions under the gate insulator [6,7]. These junctions' positions depend on the doping of the n-type drift layer and on the electrical activation of aluminum and phosphorous implants employed for the formation of the body and source, respectively. Moreover, other factors can affect the device characteristics, e.g., the off-cut angle of the 4H-SiC crystals along the (11–20) direction, the shape of the hard masks used for selective ion implantation doping, etc. As an example, the lateral straggling of implanted Al in 4H-SiC has been observed to depend on the crystallographic orientation [8] and can result in asymmetric p-type doping profiles. Furthermore, for the degenerate phosphorous-implanted 4H-SiC, an electrical activation of n-type dopant in the order of 80% has been evaluated after annealing at typical temperatures of 1675 °C [9], whereas ~39% activation has been reported for high concentration Al implants (required for ohmic contact formation on the p-type body) under the same annealing conditions [10]. Clearly, the incomplete dopant activation in 4H-SiC introduces a degree of uncertainness for the device design. Finally, the fabrication steps may introduce topographic features and misalignments that can result in a non-uniform channel length over large distances. The electrical properties of p-type implanted layers after post-implantation annealing can be estimated by Hall measurements [10,11], which give an average behavior of "box-like" profiles. However, as the MOSFET body region is created by specific implants at different energies and doses, the knowledge of the active p-type dopant concentration depth profile is required, which cannot be easily assessed by averaged techniques. For this purpose, depth-resolved characterizations methods, such as SCM, can be applied to study the MOSFET body region [12], but they require specific epitaxial samples in order to calibrate the doping level.

Usually, scanning electron microscopy (SEM) analyses on cross-sectioned samples are routinely used to obtain information on the extension of the n$^+$- and p$^-$-implanted regions in 4H-SiC power devices, by exploiting the sensitivity of secondary electrons' contrast to potential variations in this wide-bandgap semiconductor [13]. However, this technique suffers from a certain degree of uncertainty in the determination of the electrical junction position, as it is sensitive only to high concentrations.

In recent years, two-dimensional (2D) carrier profiling techniques based on atomic force microscopy, such as scanning capacitance microscopy (SCM) and scanning spreading resistance microscopy (SSRM), have been also explored to evaluate the electrically active profiles in ion-implanted 4H-SiC [14]. In particular, the SCM technique, based on local differential capacitance (dC/dV) measurements with a sliding metal tip, is very powerful for the delineation of the electrical junction position in semiconductor devices, by exploiting the sensitivity to the doping type of the dC/dV phase signal [15].

Usually, SCM is used for the semiconductor carrier profile and for the determination of the p–n junctions [16,17]. However, the cross-sectional methodologies (TEM, SEM, etc.) suffer from a lack of statistical relevance due to the fact that the information comes from a limited volume fraction of the device (~1 µm in depth) cross-section.

SCM analyses are often performed on cross-sections of 4H-SiC MOSFETs to evaluate the channel length [18]. However, cross-sectional analyses provide information only on a specific region of a device. On the other hand, 2D planar measurements are more adequate for monitoring the variations of the channel length along the device perimeter.

In this paper, 2D scanning capacitance microscopy (SCM) in planar mode is used to monitor the channel length in 4H-SiC power MOSFETs with a high statistical relevance over areas in the order of 10^{-2} mm^2. In particular, the method enabled the visualization of the fluctuations of the channel geometry occurring under different devices' processing conditions. It is important to emphasize that in this planar configuration, standard SEM methods are not able to provide reliable information on the 4H-SiC power MOSFETs' channel length. Moreover, the impact of the ion implantation parameters on the channel is discussed, pointing out the need for their fine tuning to optimize the trade-off between the total series resistance (R_{on}) and threshold voltage (V_{th}).

2. Materials and Methods

Vertical power MOSFETs were fabricated on 4°-off-axis n-type (0001) 4H-SiC epitaxial layers (between 9×10^{15} and 2×10^{16} cm^{-3}), P-implanted source region ($N_D \sim 10^{20}$ cm^{-3}) and an Al-implanted body region ($N_A \sim 10^{17}$ cm^{-3}) [19]. The fabrication starts from zero-micropipe production-grade n^{++} substrates followed by CVD epitaxy process. After the growth of the epitaxial layer, the p-type body of the MOSFET is fabricated by ion implantation of aluminum. After a standard RCA cleaning, the gate oxide was a 40 nm thick deposited SiO$_2$ layer [20]. Oxide layers have been deposited at a temperature higher than 700 °C by means of a low-pressure chemical vapor deposition (LPCVD) furnace using dichlorosilane (DCS) and nitrous oxide (NO) as silicon and oxygen precursors, respectively [21]. Nickel silicide is used to form ohmic contacts on the source body and drain. Polysilicon is used as a metal gate, and polyamide is used as surface passivation [22].

Some parameters of 4H-SiC MOSFETs concerning the doping of the epitaxial layer and the implantation of both the p-type body and the source region were varied, as reported in Table 1. In particular, a specific concentration is used as a reference for samples A and B. Devices C and D possess an increased body-doping concentration and a reduced epilayer-doping concentration, respectively. The device E possess both changed parameters (Table 1).

Table 1. Sample description: two reference samples A and B are compared with a p-type implanted dose variation in C, epitaxial layer doping variation in D, and their combination in E.

Sample	Definition
A	Reference
B	Reference
C	+ Body dose
D	− Epi doping
E	− Epi doping + Body dose

The power MOSFETs were tested by current–voltage (I–V) measurements, carried out using an Agilent B1505A parameter analyzer. After this macroscopic (i.e., device level) electrical characterization for the determination of the key electrical parameters (R_{on}, V_{th}), the devices were completely delayered from the passivation, metal, and gate oxide layers to expose the 4H-SiC bare surface. The delayering is obtained by dipping the device out of the package into an HF/H$_2$O (40–60%) acid solution for 20 min [23]. Afterward, the delayered devices were subjected to an immersion in H$_2$O$_2$ at 40 vol. for 20 min [15]. This treatment also results in the formation of a native oxide on the SiC surface, which is necessary for the nanoscale resolution capacitance mapping by SCM [15]. These analyses were carried out using a DI3100 AFM with a Nanoscope V controller. Doped diamond-coated Si tips were employed to ensure electrical stability during large area scans on the structured 4H-SiC surface.

3. Results and Discussion

Figure 1a shows the basic structure of the planar power MOSFET in a cross-section where the channel regions are delimitated between the JFET and the source in the body-region ion implantation edges. On the other hand, Figure 1b shows the top view of the power MOSFET where the channel geometry is indicated, and, in particular, its length (L) is in the order of 200 nm and its width (W) is in the order of several millimeters.

As previously discussed, the common procedure to monitor the channel shape and length is in the cross-section by the device cleavage. Figure 2 shows the cross-sectional SCM image of a typical elementary cell of a 4H-SiC power MOSFET. In particular, the SCM image (Figure 2) also gives information on the space charge region (SCR). In particular, using the SCM, the SCR and the p-type doped body region results were distinguishable compared to the n-type JFET/drift region and to the source region. The channel can be recognized in the region near the surface delimited between the two n-type regions, and its shape can be influenced by several processing parameters.

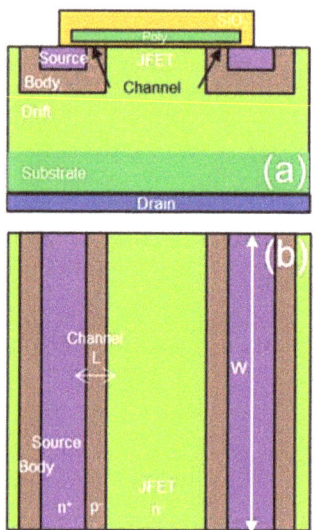

Figure 1. 4H-SiC MOSFET schematic cross-section (**a**) and schematic top view (**b**).

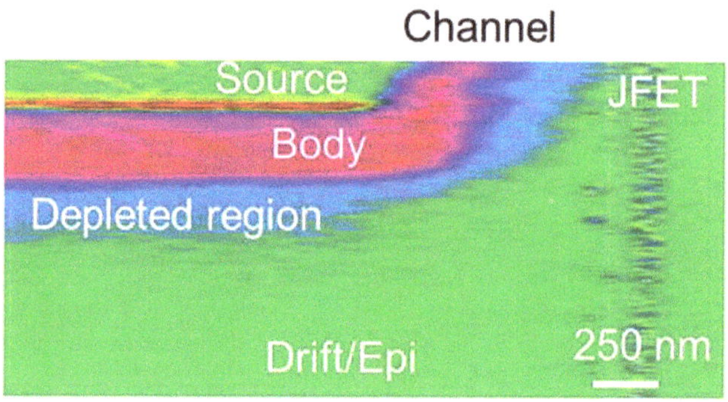

Figure 2. Cross section SCM image of the elementary MOSFET cell.

In the proposed method, the information on the channel length is collected from the top of the device, thus enabling the visualization of the entire device perimeter, which is not possible by standard cross-section approach. Figure 3a shows the 3D schematic structure of the elementary cell of the MOSFET after the gate stack delayering. As can be noticed, the SCM tip can scan the different regions of the device, collecting information both on the channel length L and width W, important parameters to understand the physics of large area power MOSFETs. In order to better understand how important this aspect is, it is possible to consider how for a given technology design, the resulting electrical properties of the MOSFETs suffer from some degree of uncertainness on the L and W definition.

Figure 3b shows the AFM morphology map collected in contact mode onto the bare 4H-SiC semiconductor surface, exposing both the n- and p-type regions of the vertical MOSFET.

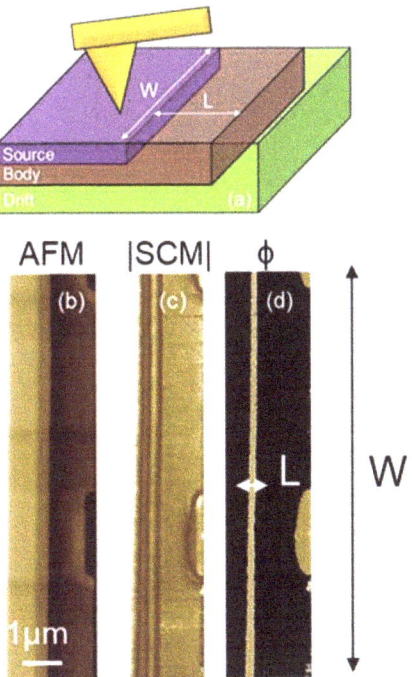

Figure 3. (a) Schematic description of the in-plan 2D SCM measurements on the MOSFET channel along W and across the L directions. (b) AFM morphology, (c) SCM amplitude, and (d) SCM phase (ϕ) of the reference sample.

The in-plan top-view capacitance mapping [24] was performed while the semiconductor surface is scanned with the metal tip and a modulating bias with amplitude V at 100 kHz frequency is applied to the sample, and the capacitance variation ΔC in response to this modulation is recorded with the SCM sensor. Besides the |SCM| signal amplitude |ΔC|, which is related to the net active dopants concentration (N_A-N_D) in the semiconductor underneath the tip (Figure 3c), also the phase signal is recorded, which is very sensitive to the type of majority carriers in the region underneath the tip [25].

Figure 3b–d show, respectively, the morphology (AFM), SCM amplitude, and phase signal (ϕ) of a reference device. As can be seen in Figure 3d, the channel length is measurable and uniform (i.e., with a constant size) along the W direction in the un-optimized device. This information is undetectable using standard techniques.

The determination of the experimental and theoretical accuracy in delineating the electrical junction in p–n samples by SCM is still a challenging problem. This is due to the artifacts introduced by the sample cross-section preparation [26] such as morphological features (scratches) and surface contaminations that may introduce surface states, deteriorating the probed electrical signal. Furthermore, at a p–n junction, there exists a built-in depletion region where the net carrier concentration decreases from the bulk levels to zero on each side of the junction. In the p–n junctions, the measured SCM phase ϕ is positive for p-type material and negative for the n-type semiconductor. The apparent junction location (ϕ = 0°) can be moved throughout the depletion region in the vicinity of a p–n junction by SCM tip AC bias [27], as schematically depicted in Figure 4a. Hence, the SCM measurement may affect the estimation of the channel length increasing the depletion region under the tip. In order to overcome this problem, it is important to fix some experimental conditions. In order to avoid the perturbation of the depletion region in correspondence with the p–n junction, the DC bias is kept equal to zero. Hence, the best SCM setup is obtained by varying the AC bias amplitude. It has to be emphasized that the AC bias may also affect the depletion region in correspondence with the p–n junction. Then, it must be kept as small as possible, minimizing the noise/signal ratio. In this context, the chosen criterion is to keep a noise/signal ratio, minimizing the root mean square (RMS) of the SCM ϕ map. Figure 4b shows that the SCM RMS value decreases, increasing the AC tip bias. On the other hand, Figure 4b also shows how a given channel length is overestimated increasing the AC tip bias. Hence, the AC tip bias of choice is the value that lies at the minimum of the two lines depicted in Figure 4b (i.e., AC bias at 2 V).

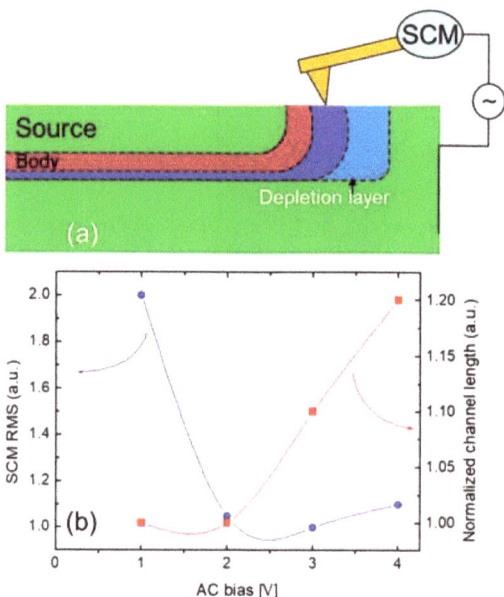

Figure 4. (a) Schematic description of the SCM tip influencing the depletion region at the p–n junction. (b) SCM RMS and normalized channel length vs. SCM tip AC bias.

After illustrating the in-plane SCM measurement configuration and the optimal bias conditions to evaluate the channel length, some applications of this method to different MOSFET devices will be illustrated.

Figure 5 is used to describe the procedure to extract the V_{th} value on the reference sample (A and B) and the characteristic MOSFETs curves used to measure the R_{ON} at a V_G = +15 V and at I_D value of 10 A. Hence, the typical values are R_{ON} = 23 mΩ (at a V_G = +15 V and I_D = 10 A), and the Vth (I_D = 250 µA) is about 2.7 V for the reference sample.

Figure 6 shows the empirical correlation between the resistance of a group of devices, expressed in terms of the MOSFET on-state resistance (R_{On}) at a given current value (i.e., 10 A), as a function of the threshold voltage (V_{th}) defined as the gate bias needed to turn on the MOSFET achieving a given current value (i.e., 250 µA). In order to better visualize the parameters under investigation, both the R_{On} and the V_{th} are normalized to the values obtained on sample A. Noteworthily, the experimental data are linearly correlated, i.e., the on-resistance increases with increasing the threshold voltage, in good agreement with the results presented by Noguchi et al. [28].

Figure 7a shows the SCM ϕ profile averaging 10 µm along the W width of the MOSFET channels under investigation. As can be seen, different channel lengths are measured on the devices under investigation. The channel lengths were measured, assuming as minimum the distance between the upper part of the positive SCM ϕ profile and as maximum the distance when the SCM ϕ crosses zero. From the interpolation between the experimental points and the crossing of SCM φ zero value, it can be argued that the spatial resolution is about 25 nm. The measured channel lengths are depicted as a function of the macroscopic parameters $R_{On}^{Normalized}$ and the $V_{th}^{Normalized}$ in Figure 7b,c, respectively. As can be noticed, a variation of the channel length smaller than 5% can produce appreciable variation of both R_{On} and V_{th}, as in samples A and B, which are identical.

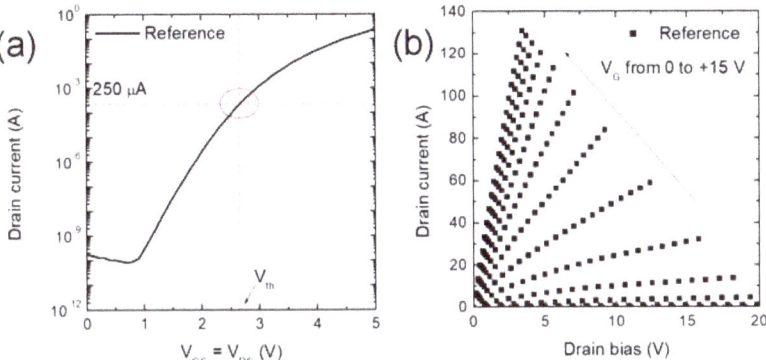

Figure 5. Experimental electrical measurements carried out on a reference MOSFET. The trans-characteristic I_D-V_{GS} is shown to demonstrate how the V_{th} value is defined at fixed current value (**a**). (**b**) The output characteristics I_D-V_D reported for V_G values up to +15 V are used to determine the R_{ON} value at 10 A.

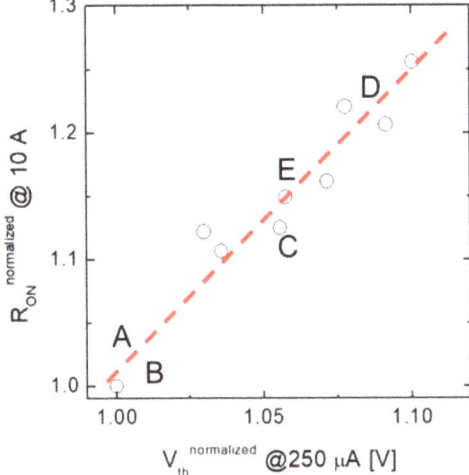

Figure 6. Empirical correlation between the on-resistance of a group of devices, R_{On} at 10 A vs. Vth (measured at 250 μA). Data are normalized to the values of sample A.

It can be concluded that the variation of the doping in the sample under investigation produced a variation in both the metallurgic position (i.e., the location where $N_A = N_D$) and the space charge region (SCR) at the n⁺–p–n⁻ source–body–JFET junctions, as schematically represented in Figure 8a. Furthermore, the increase of the p-type body implantation dose in sample C produces an increased distance between the n⁺–p and p–n⁻ junctions, resulting in a wider channel (Figure 8b). In particular, for a fixed n⁻ epitaxial concentration in the JFET region, the p–n⁻ junction with the body is moved toward the n⁻ region once the p-type dose is increased (Figure 8b). By contrast, the n⁺–p junction between the source and the body is moved toward the source. On the other hand, the reduction of the n⁻ epitaxial layer concentration in sample D shifted the p–n⁻ junction toward the JFET and increased the SCR width between the body and the JFET (Figure 8c). Thus, the channel length of sample D is larger than A and B but smaller than C (Figure 8c). Finally, the combination of the increase of the body dose and a reduction of the epi-layer doping produced an intermediate channel length for sample E, as schematically depicted in Figure 8d.

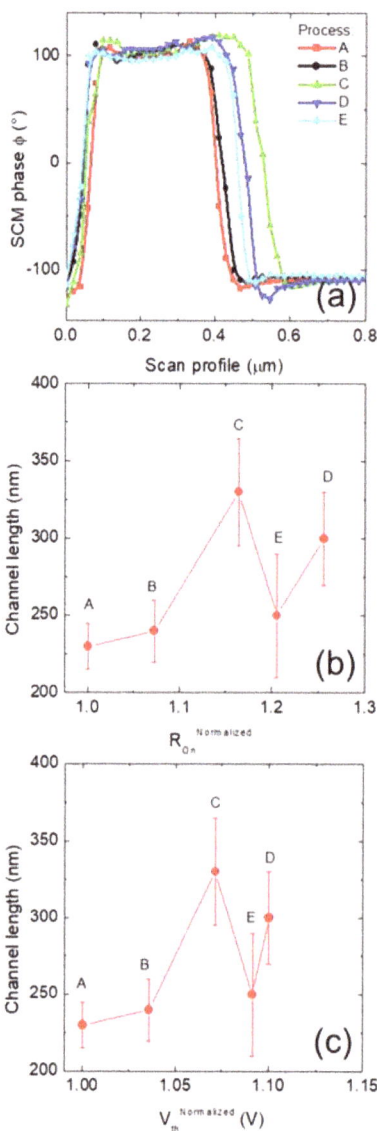

Figure 7. (a) SCM phase ϕ vs. scan profile averaged over 10 μm. Channel lengths vs. R_{On} (b) and vs. V_{th} (c).

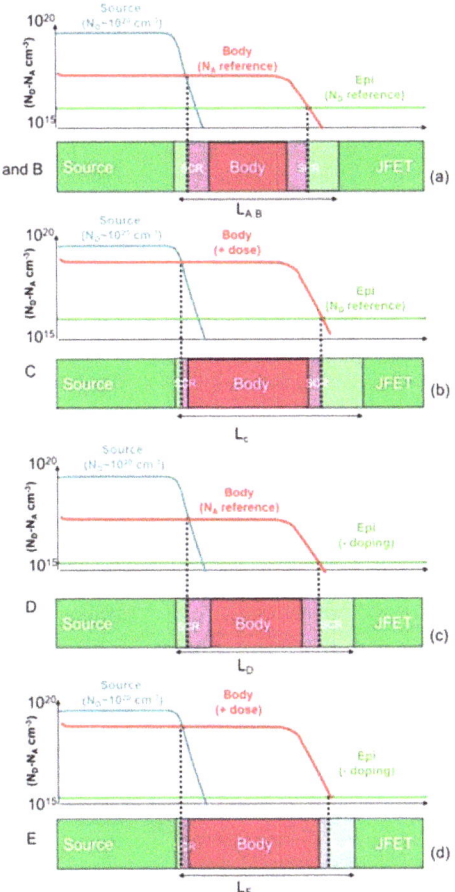

Figure 8. Schematic representation of the channel fabricated on the n⁺–p–n⁻ junction in the investigated samples. (**a**) Schematic representation of the reference samples (A and B), where the metallurgic junctions are represented by dashed lines when $N_A = N_D$, generating the space charge regions (SCR) in the n- and p-type semiconductor according to the doping levels in the different samples. In particular, the increase of the body dose (**b**) or a reduction of the epi-layer doping (**c**) produced an increase of the channel lengths for MOSFET C and D, respectively. On the other hand, the combination of the increase of the body dose and a reduction of the epi-layer doping produced an intermediate channel length for sample E (**d**).

In order to highlight the relevance of the proposed characterization technique, it is possible to consider how for a given technology design, the resulting electrical properties of the MOSFETs suffer from some degree of uncertainness of the L and W definition. In particular, an un-optimized lithographic process may induce large deviation from the ideal case. Figure 9a,b show respectively the morphology (AFM) and the SCM phase signal (ϕ) of an un-optimized device. As can be seen in Figure 9b, the channel length is not uniform along the W direction in the un-optimized device. This information is undetectable using standard cross-section techniques. In this specific case, the un-optimized device presented an anomalous R_{On} value for the designed V_{th} requirements, corresponding to a large on-resistance and sub-threshold leakage current.

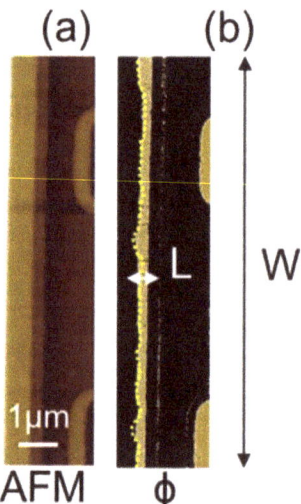

Figure 9. (a) AFM morphology and (b) SCM phase (ϕ) collected on a selected device that showed anomalous behavior compared with the desired design.

4. Conclusions

In conclusion, a powerful 2D imaging method to visualize the channel in large perimeter 4H-SiC MOSFETs channel is presented using the SCM phase ϕ signal. The large areal statistical information (up to 10^{-2} mm^2) can be used to validate the device processing and to obtain information on the device physics on semiconductors where the doping activation suffers from a certain degree of uncertainness. An appropriate sample choice is used to demonstrate the movement of the channel in the 3D MOSFET structure and to understand the electrical characteristics at the macroscopic scale.

Author Contributions: Conceptualization, P.F. and M.S.A.; methodology, B.C.; A.R. data curation, data supervision; F.G.; writing—original draft preparation, P.F.; writing—review, editing and funding acquisition, F.R. All authors have read and agreed to the published version of the manuscript.

Funding: This work was carried out in the framework of the ECSEL JU project REACTION (first and euRopEAn siC eigTh Inches pilOt liNe), grant agreement no. 783158.

Data Availability Statement: The data that support the findings of this study are available from the corresponding author upon reasonable request.

Acknowledgments: Enzo Fontana is acknowledged for the technical support with the MOSFETs' electrical characterization.

Conflicts of Interest: The authors declare no conflict of interest.

References

1. Kimoto, T.; Cooper, J. *Fundamentals of Silicon Carbide Technology: Growth, Characterization, Devices and Applications*; John Wiley & Sons: Singapore, 2014.
2. Capano, M.A.; Cooper, J.A., Jr.; Melloch, M.R.; Saxler, A.; Mitchel, W.C. Ionization energies and electron mobilities in phosphorus- and nitrogen-implanted 4H-silicon carbide. *J. Appl. Phys.* **2000**, *87*, 8773. [CrossRef]
3. Laube, M.; Schmid, F.; Pensl, G.; Wagner, G.; Linnarsson, M.; Maier, M. Electrical activation of high concentrations of N+ and P+ ions implanted into 4H-SiC. *J. Appl. Phys.* **2002**, *92*, 549. [CrossRef]
4. Jin, Q.; Nakajima, M.; Kaneko, M.; Kimoto, T. Lateral spreads of ion-implanted Al and P atoms in silicon carbide. *Jpn. J. Appl. Phys.* **2021**, *60*, 051001. [CrossRef]
5. Pichler, P.; Sledziewski, T.; Häublein, V.; Bauer, A.; Erlbacher, T. Channeling in 4H-SiC from an Application Point of View. *Mater. Sci. Forum* **2019**, *963*, 386–389. [CrossRef]

6. Baliga, B.J. *Silicon Carbide Power Devices*; World Scientific Co. Pte. Ltd.: Singapore, 2005.
7. Fiorenza, P.; Giannazzo, F.; Roccaforte, F. Characterization of SiO$_2$/4H-SiC Interfaces in 4H-SiC MOSFETs: A Review. *Energies* **2019**, *12*, 2310. [CrossRef]
8. Müting, J.; Bobal, V.; Neset Sky, T.; Vines, L.; Grossner, U. Lateral straggling of implanted aluminum in 4H-SiC. *Appl. Phys. Lett.* **2020**, *116*, 012101. [CrossRef]
9. Spera, M.; Greco, G.; Severino, A.; Vivona, M.; Fiorenza, P.; Giannazzo, F.; Roccaforte, F. Active dopant profiling and Ohmic contacts behavior in degenerate n-type implanted silicon carbide. *Appl. Phys. Lett.* **2020**, *117*, 013502. [CrossRef]
10. Spera, M.; Corso, D.; di Franco, S.; Greco, G.; Severino, A.; Fiorenza, P.; Giannazzo, F.; Roccaforte, F. Effect of high temperature annealing (T > 1650 °C) on the morphological and electrical properties of p-type implanted 4H-SiC layers. *Mater. Sci. Semicond. Proc.* **2019**, *93*, 274–279. [CrossRef]
11. Rambach, M.; Bauer, A.J.; Ryssel, H. Electrical and topographical characterization of aluminum implanted layers in 4H silicon carbide. *Phys. Stat. Sol. B* **2008**, *245*, 1315–1326. [CrossRef]
12. Giannazzo, F.; Roccaforte, F.; Raineri, V. Acceptor, compensation, and mobility profiles in multiple Al implanted 4H-SiC. *Appl. Phys. Lett.* **2007**, *91*, 202104. [CrossRef]
13. Buzzo, M.; Ciappa, M.; Stangoni, M.; Fichtner, W. Two-dimensional Dopant Profiling and Imaging of 4H Silicon Carbide Devices by Secondary Electron Potential Contrast. *Microelectron. Reliab.* **2005**, *45*, 1499–1504. [CrossRef]
14. Fiorenza, P.; Giannazzo, F.; Swanson, L.K.; Frazzetto, A.; Lorenti, S.; Alessandrino, M.S.; Roccaforte, F. A look underneath the SiO$_2$/4H-SiC interface after N$_2$O thermal treatments. *Beilstein J. Nanotechnol.* **2013**, *4*, 249. [CrossRef]
15. Giannazzo, F.; Calcagno, L.; Raineri, V.; Ciampolini, L.; Ciappa, M.; Napolitani, E. Quantitative carrier profiling in ion-implanted 6H–SiC. *Appl. Phys. Lett.* **2001**, *79*, 1211. [CrossRef]
16. Zavyalov, V.V.; McMurray, J.S.; Williams, C.C. Scanning capacitance microscope methodology for quantitative analysis of p-n junctions. *J. Appl. Phys.* **1999**, *85*, 7774. [CrossRef]
17. De Wolf, P.; Stephenson, R.; Trenkler, T.; Clarysse, T.; Hantschel, T.; Vandervorst, W. Status and review of two-dimensional carrier and dopant profiling using scanning probe microscopy. *J. Vac. Sci. Tech. B* **2000**, *18*, 361. [CrossRef]
18. Giannazzo, F.; Fiorenza, P.; Saggio, M.; Roccaforte, F. Nanoscale characterization of SiC interfaces and devices. *Mater. Sci. Forum* **2014**, *778–780*, 407–413. [CrossRef]
19. Giannazzo, A.F.F.; Fiorenza, P.; Raineri, V.; Roccaforte, F. Limiting mechanism of inversion channel mobility in Al-implanted lateral 4H-SiC metal-oxide semiconductor field-effect transistors. *Appl. Phys. Lett.* **2011**, *99*, 072117.
20. Fiorenza, P.; Bongiorno, C.; Giannazzo, F.; Alessandrino, M.S.; Messina, A.; Saggio, M.; Roccaforte, F. Interfacial electrical and chemical properties of deposited SiO$_2$ layers in lateral implanted 4H-SiC MOSFETs subjected to different nitridations. *Appl. Phys. Sci.* **2021**, *557*, 149752.
21. Severino, A.; Piluso, N.; di Stefano, M.A.; Cordiano, F.; Camalleri, M.; Arena, G. Study of the Post-Oxidation-Annealing (POA) Process on Deposited High-Temperature Oxide (HTO) Layers as Gate Dielectric in SiC MOSFET. *Mater. Sci. Forum* **2019**, *963*, 456–459. [CrossRef]
22. Fiorenza, P.; la Magna, A.; Vivona, M.; Roccaforte, F. Near interface traps in SiO$_2$/4H-SiC metal-oxide-semiconductor field effect transistors monitored by temperature dependent gate current transient measurements. *Appl. Phys. Lett.* **2016**, *109*, 012102. [CrossRef]
23. Fiorenza, P.; Alessandrino, M.S.; Carbone, B.; di Martino, C.; Russo, A.; Saggio, M.; Venuto, C.; Zanetti, E.; Giannazzo, F.; Roccaforte, F. Understanding the role of threading dislocations on 4H-SiC MOSFET breakdown under high temperature reverse bias stress. *Nanotechnology* **2020**, *31*, 125203. [CrossRef]
24. Fiorenza, P.; Lo Nigro, R.; Raineri, V.; Toro, R.G.; Catalano, M.R. Nanoscale imaging of permittivity in giant-κ CaCu$_3$Ti$_4$O$_{12}$ grains. *J. Appl. Phys.* **2007**, *102*, 116103. [CrossRef]
25. Giannazzo, F.; Goghero, D.; Raineri, V. Experimental aspects and modeling for quantitative measurements in scanning capacitance microscopy. *J. Vac. Sci. Technol. B* **2004**, *22*, 2391. [CrossRef]
26. Stangoni, M.; Ciappa, M.; Fichtner, W. Accuracy of scanning capacitance microscopy for the delineation of electrical junctions. *J. Vac. Sci. Tech. B* **2004**, *22*, 406. [CrossRef]
27. Kopanski, J.J.; Marchiando, J.F.; Rennex, B.G. Carrier concentration dependence of the scanning capacitance microscopy signal in the vicinity of p–n junctions. *J. Vac. Sci. Tech. B* **2000**, *18*, 409. [CrossRef]
28. Noguchi, M.; Iwamatsu, T.; Amishiro, H.; Watanabe, H.; Miura, K.K.N. Channel engineering of 4H-SiC MOSFETs using sulphur as a deep level donor. In Proceedings of the 2018 IEEE International Electron Devices Meeting (IEDM), San Francisco, CA, USA, 1–5 December 2018; pp. 8.3.1–8.3.4.

Article

Effect of Back-Gate Voltage on the High-Frequency Performance of Dual-Gate MoS$_2$ Transistors

Qingguo Gao [1,2], Chongfu Zhang [1,2,*], Ping Liu [1], Yunfeng Hu [1], Kaiqiang Yang [1], Zichuan Yi [1], Liming Liu [1], Xinjian Pan [1], Zhi Zhang [1], Jianjun Yang [1] and Feng Chi [1]

1 School of Electronic Information, University of Electronic Science and Technology of China Zhongshan Institute, Zhongshan 528402, China; gqgemw@163.com (Q.G.); liuping49@126.com (P.L.); shanhuyf@163.com (Y.H.); 201811022515@std.uestc.edu.cn (K.Y.); yizichuan@zsc.edu.cn (Z.Y.); limingliu@uestc.edu.cn (L.L.); xinjpan@163.com (X.P.); zz001@zsc.edu.cn (Z.Z.); sdyman@uestc.edu.cn (J.Y.); chifeng@semi.ac.cn (F.C.)
2 School of Information and Communication Engineering, University of Electronic Science and Technology of China, Chengdu 611731, China
* Correspondence: cfzhang@uestc.edu.cn

Citation: Gao, Q.; Zhang, C.; Liu, P.; Hu, Y.; Yang, K.; Yi, Z.; Liu, L.; Pan, X.; Zhang, Z.; Yang, J.; et al. Effect of Back-Gate Voltage on the High-Frequency Performance of Dual-Gate MoS$_2$ Transistors. *Nanomaterials* **2021**, *11*, 1594. https://doi.org/10.3390/nano11061594

Academic Editors: Patrick Fiorenza, Raffaella Lo Nigro, Béla Pécz and Jens Eriksson

Received: 30 May 2021
Accepted: 15 June 2021
Published: 17 June 2021

Publisher's Note: MDPI stays neutral with regard to jurisdictional claims in published maps and institutional affiliations.

Copyright: © 2021 by the authors. Licensee MDPI, Basel, Switzerland. This article is an open access article distributed under the terms and conditions of the Creative Commons Attribution (CC BY) license (https://creativecommons.org/licenses/by/4.0/).

Abstract: As an atomically thin semiconductor, 2D molybdenum disulfide (MoS$_2$) has demonstrated great potential in realizing next-generation logic circuits, radio-frequency (RF) devices and flexible electronics. Although various methods have been performed to improve the high-frequency characteristics of MoS$_2$ RF transistors, the impact of the back-gate bias on dual-gate MoS$_2$ RF transistors is still unexplored. In this work, we study the effect of back-gate control on the static and RF performance metrics of MoS$_2$ high-frequency transistors. By using high-quality chemical vapor deposited bilayer MoS$_2$ as channel material, high-performance top-gate transistors with on/off ratio of 10^7 and on-current up to 179 µA/µm at room temperature were realized. With the back-gate modulation, the source and drain contact resistances decrease to 1.99 kΩ·µm at V_{bg} = 3 V, and the corresponding on-current increases to 278 µA/µm. Furthermore, both cut-off frequency and maximum oscillation frequency improves as the back-gate voltage increases to 3 V. In addition, a maximum intrinsic f_{max} of 29.7 GHz was achieved, which is as high as 2.1 times the f_{max} without the back-gate bias. This work provides significant insights into the influence of back-gate voltage on MoS$_2$ RF transistors and presents the potential of dual-gate MoS$_2$ RF transistors for future high-frequency applications.

Keywords: MoS$_2$; radio-frequency transistors; contact resistance; dual-gate

1. Introduction

Since the first exfoliation of atomically thin graphene [1], two dimensional (2D) materials have demonstrated a wide range of remarkable properties for applications in future ubiquitous electronics [2,3]. Compared to bulk materials, their atomic-scale thickness provides a greater degree of electrostatic control, demonstrating the possibility of ultra-short channel devices with low power consumption [4]. As the most widely studied 2D material, graphene has shown great potential for device applications including high-frequency electronics, flexible electronics, spintronics, nanoelectromechanical systems, and energy storage due to its unique physical properties [5–12]. However, graphene does not have a band gap to limit its application in digital logic devices, and it also limits the maximum oscillation frequency of graphene radio-frequency (RF) transistors. Although band gap can be opened in graphene by artificial nanostructuring, chemical functionalization, etc., those processes add extra complexities with respect to practical applications [13]. Alternatively, another class of 2D material, called transition metal dichalcogenides (TMDCs) (MoS$_2$, WS$_2$, MoSe$_2$, and WSe$_2$), not only exhibits many graphene-like properties, such as mechanical flexibility, electrical properties, chemical stability, and the absence of dangling bonds, but also possesses a substantial band gap. TMDCs benefit from a rich pool of elements, and thus they can significantly adjust their electrical properties from metal to semiconductor by forming different compounds. A distinct feature of TMDC semiconductors is that the corresponding energy band structure changes from an indirect band gap to a direct band gap when the material thickness decreases from bulk material to monolayer. They show a wide range of bandgap modulation capability because of rich choices of chemical components, which enables the electronic application of various kinds. As the most studied TMDC material, MoS_2 has a non-zero band gap structure similar to bulk silicon, making it an ideal choice for making next-generation electronic and optoelectronic applications [4,14–20].

With technological advancements, the high-frequency performance of MoS_2 devices has attracted tremendous attention [16,18,21–24]. The high-frequency performance of MoS_2 RF transistors has been improved through optimizing structure such as self-aligned gate, embedded gate and edge-contacted, etc. [24–26]. In 2014, exfoliated MoS_2 RF transistors with self-aligned gate demonstrated intrinsic cut-off frequency f_T of 42 GHz and maximum oscillation frequency f_{max} of 50 GHz were reported [25]. In 2015, Krasnozhon et al. introduced edge-contacted in exfoliated trilayer MoS_2 RF transistors, obtaining a high extrinsic f_T of 6 GHz and intrinsic f_T of 25 GHz [26]. In 2017, with an optimized embedded gate structure, chemical vapor deposition (CVD) monolayer MoS_2 transistors with extrinsic f_T of 3.3 GHz and f_{max} of 9.8 GHz were fabricated [24]. In 2018, based on high-quality CVD bilayer MoS_2, high-frequency MoS_2 transistors with extrinsic maximum oscillation frequency of 23 GHz were demonstrated [16]. Gigahertz frequency mixer and amplifier based on MoS_2 high-frequency transistors were also constructed for potential RF circuit applications [16,27]. Those works demonstrated the potential of 2D MoS_2 for future novel high-frequency electronics. Although the high-frequency performance of MoS_2 RF transistors has made exciting advances, its cutoff frequency and maximum oscillation frequency are still lower than those of modern Si transistors, and the high-frequency performance of dual-gate MoS_2 transistors has not yet been reported.

In this dual-gate structure, the source and drain contact resistances can be modulated via the back-gate voltage, and the influence of the contact resistance on the direct-current (DC) and high-frequency performance of the device can be clearly resolved [28]. Bolshakov et al. presented a near-ideal subthreshold swing of ~60 mV/dec and a high field effect mobility of 100 cm^2/Vs based on dual-gate MoS_2 transistors with sub−10 nm top-gate dielectrics [29]. Lee et al. modulated the contact resistance and threshold voltage of dual-gate MoS_2 transistors with h-BN as gate dielectric through back-gate electrostatic doping [30]. Li et al. demonstrated a high photoresponsivity of 2.04×10^5 AW^{-1} with dual-gate MoS_2 phototransistors [31]. The dual-gate structure could also be used to investigate the effect of different dielectric interface on the device performance [32]. In addition, based on the dual-gate structure, graphene RF transistors with improved high-frequency performance by reducing the contact resistance using electrostatic doping have been demonstrated [33,34]. Thus, the influence of back-gate voltage on the high-frequency performance of MoS_2 RF transistors needs further investigation, which is of great significance for further improving the RF performance of MoS_2 transistors.

In this study, we fabricated dual-gate MoS_2 RF transistors with a top-gate length of 190 nm based on the CVD grown bilayer MoS_2. The static and high-frequency characteristics of dual-gate devices were systematically investigated. The contact resistances of the fabricated dual-gate devices under different back-gate voltages were extracted. A clear modulation of contact resistance R_c under the electrostatic doping of back-gate was demonstrated. Both DC and RF performance were improved under the electrostatic doping of back-gate. The electrical measurement of our dual-gate high-frequency MoS_2 transistors at V_{bg} = 3 V demonstrated a large current density of 278 µA/µm, a high intrinsic cut-off frequency of 19 GHz and maximum oscillation frequency of 29.7 GHz.

2. Materials and Methods

Chemical-vapor-deposited bilayer MoS_2 was used as the channel material in the dual-gate MoS_2 RF transistors as it has higher carrier mobility, lower contact resistance and improved low-frequency noise when compared with CVD monolayer MoS$_2$ [16,27,35]. Additionally, the CVD method is one of the most promising methods for synthesizing large areas and high-quality MoS$_2$. The CVD bilayer MoS$_2$ films were grown on soda-lime-silica glass substrates with 1.4 g sulfur and 1.5 mg MoO$_3$ as the precursors at atmospheric pressure. The details about the CVD bilayer growth process, material imaging and crystal structure characterization have been reported in our previous works [16,27]. After the CVD growth process, bilayer MoS$_2$ films were transferred onto highly resistive Si substrates with atomic-layer-deposited (ALD) 20-nm HfLaO. Here, high-resistance Si was used as the back-gate electrode and ALD HfLaO as the back-gate dielectric. As reported in previous work [16,36,37], HfLaO with high dielectric constant could provide improved interface quality and better electrostatic control with the MoS$_2$ channel, which is helpful for improving the DC and RF performance of the MoS$_2$ transistors. Figure 1 illustrates the fabrication process of dual-gate MoS$_2$ transistors. The fabrication of the MoS$_2$ devices typically starts after the MoS$_2$ films are transferred on top of the HfLaO/Si substrates. Figure 2a presents the MoS$_2$ films on HfLaO/Si substrates after being transferred. Then, as shown in Figure 1b, 20/60 nm Ni/Au metal stacks were deposited by electron beam evaporation (EBE) as the source and drain contact electrodes of MoS$_2$ dual-gate transistors. In this process, the samples were loaded into the E-beam evaporator (ALPHA-PLUSCO.Ltd., Ebeam-500S Pohang, Korea), and it was waited until the system reaches the pressure lower than 9×10^{-6} torr to start the deposition. The deposition rate of 20 nm Ni and 60 nm Au was used as 1 Å/s for both materials. The electrical isolation between different transistors was achieved by performing O$_2$ plasma etching for 30 s under an RF power of 50 W with a mixed gas flow of 20 sccm O$_2$ and 80 sccm Ar.

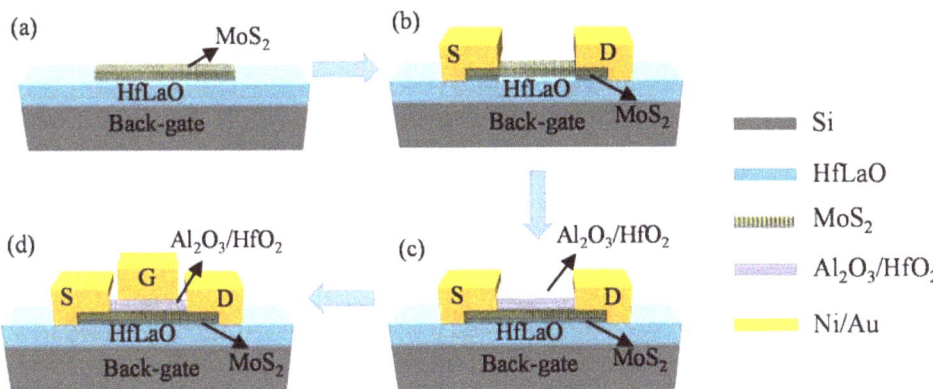

Figure 1. Process for fabricating the dual-gate MoS$_2$ field-effect transistors. (**a**) Bilayer MoS$_2$ is first transferred on HfLaO/Si substrates. (**b**) Source and drain contact metal deposition. (**c**) Top-gate dielectrics of Al$_2$O$_3$/HfO$_2$ deposition. (**d**) Top-gate metal pattern and deposition. S: source, D: drain, G: gate.

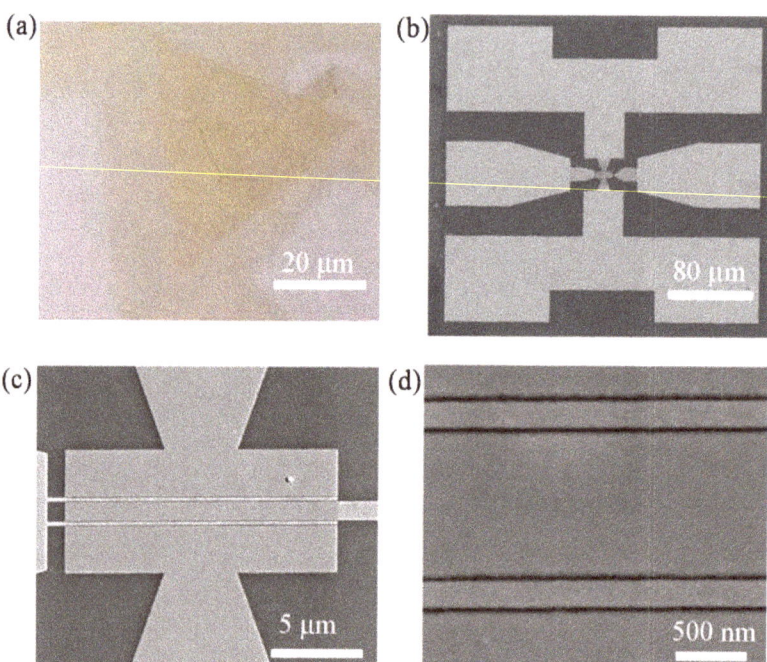

Figure 2. (a) The transferred bilayer MoS$_2$ on HfLaO/Si substrates. (b–d) SEM images of the 190 nm MoS$_2$ RF transistor with two-fingers structure showing excellent alignment.

The top gate dielectric of the transistors is an important medium for static control of the channel through the top gate electrode, and it has a very important influence on the static and high-frequency performance of the device. The top-gate dielectric is similar to the substrate dielectric, which will scatter the MoS$_2$ channel carriers, and the dielectric defects will also capture and release channel electrons. Because of the lack of dangling bonds on the surface of 2D materials, growing high-quality dielectrics on top of MoS$_2$ has always been a challenging process [38,39], due to the adsorption of the ALD precursors on a 2D MoS$_2$ surface often being more difficult than on conventional semiconductors with a 3D lattice, where plenty of dangling bonds are able help the adsorption during the ALD process. In this work, a two-step seed and growth processes were used in the formation of high-k top-gate dielectrics. First, a 2-nm Al layer was deposited on the MoS$_2$ surface by EBE and then naturally oxidized in the air to form a 6-nm Al$_2$O$_3$ layer. Then, 11 nm of HfO$_2$ was deposited by ALD using O$_3$ as the O source and tetrakis-ethylmethylaminohafnium (TEMAHf) as the Hf source. Finally, the top-gate metal was formed with 20 nm Ni/60 nm Au metal stack by EBE. In the above fabrication process, the patterns of the source, drain and gate electrodes were written using electron beam lithography. In this process, poly(methylmethacrylate) (PMMA) 950 A4 was spin-coated on the substrates at 3000 rpm for 60 s and baked at 180 °C for 180 s. The electron beam was set to a 3 nA current with an exposure dose of 800 µC/cm^2. Then, the pattern was developed in a 3:1 ratio of isopropyl alcohol (IPA) to methyl isobutyl ketone (MIBK) for 50 s, rinsed with IPA for 60 s, and dried with nitrogen gas. After the EBE deposition of electrodes, lift-off was performed in a beaker of acetone heated to 50 °C for 30 min. Then, the sample was rinsed with IPA and dried with a nitrogen flow. Figure 2b–d display the top scanning electron microscope (SEM) views of the dual-gate MoS$_2$ RF transistors with 190 nm top-gate length. The width of the two-fingers top-gate is 30 µm.

3. Results and Discussion

3.1. DC Characterization

Figure 3a,c show the transfer characteristics of the dual-gate MoS$_2$ transistor from both the back and top-gate configuration. High on/off ratios greater than 10^7 were achieved for both the back and top-gate modulation. Compared to graphene transistors, this superior on/off ratio is due to the larger band gap [40]. Figure 3b,d show the output characteristics under varied back and top-gate voltages. The gate voltages were varied from −3 V to 3 V with a 0.5 V step. Maximum on-current densities were observed at V_{ds} = 4 V are 277 µA/µm and 179 µA/µm for back-gate and top-gate modulation, respectively. The achieved maximum on-current density from back-gate is about 1.6 times the magnitude of that from the top-gate. This comes from the different configuration of back-gate and top-gate devices. As shown in Figure 1d, it can be seen that the highly resistive Si substrate has global control over the entire bilayer MoS$_2$ film. Since the channel carriers in the bilayer MoS$_2$ films accumulate with increasing back-gate voltage, it can be assumed that the bilayer MoS$_2$ is electrically doped under the effect of the back-gate voltage, which further leads to a reduction in the contact resistance between the source/drain (Ni/Au) and the bilayer MoS$_2$ film. In the case of top-gate configuration, the gate can only modulate the MoS$_2$ films underneath the gate metal [28,33,34]. In addition to the different gate structures, the different top and bottom dielectric layer may also play a critical role in determining the difference of DC measurement [19,32,41] and which need further investigation. In addition, a field-effect mobility of 15.8 cm^2/Vs was obtained from back-gate measurement by using the relation $\mu_{FE} = \frac{g_m L}{W C_{ox} V_{ds}}$, where the back-gate capacitance C_{ox} is 0.8 µF/cm^2.

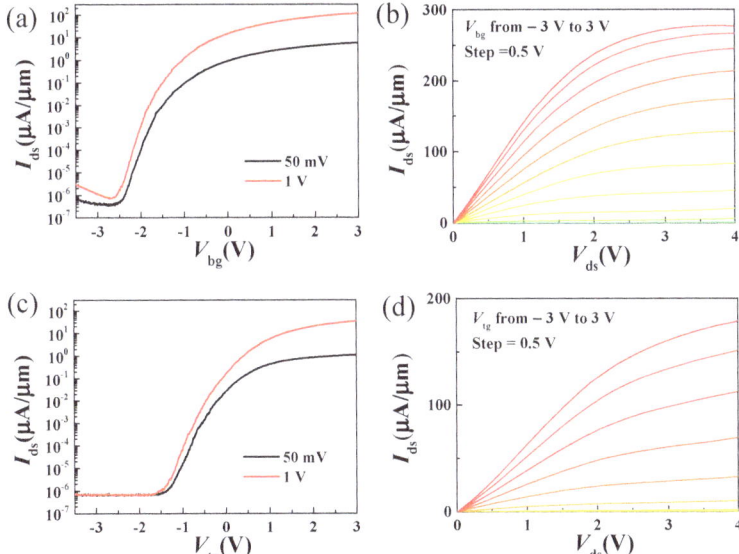

Figure 3. (a,b) Transfer and output characteristics of the MoS$_2$ dual-gate transistors from the back-gate controls. (c,d) Transfer and output characteristics of the MoS$_2$ dual-gate transistors from the top-gate controls.

Figure 4a shows the transfer curves of a dual-gate MoS$_2$ transistor with sweeping top-gate voltage at varied back-gate voltages. With the back-gate voltage increasing from 0 V to 3 V, the on-current density increases from 166 to 278 µA/µm, and the threshold voltage V_{th} negatively shifts from 1.1 to 0.1 V. To estimate contact resistances of dual-gate MoS$_2$ transistors under different back-gate voltages, an interpolation method reported in previous work was adopted [35,42]. In this interpolation method, contact resistances at different V_{bg}

were extracted by extrapolating the drain-to-source resistance vs. $1/(V_{tg} - V_{th})$, which contains the contribution from metal/MoS$_2$ contact and the regions between top-gate and source/drain electrodes. The dependence of the contact resistances versus V_{bg} is shown in Figure 4b. The extracted contact resistance is 5.5 k$\Omega \cdot \mu$m at V_{bg} = 0 V, and decreases to 1.99 k$\Omega \cdot \mu$m at V_{bg} = 3 V. The reduced R_c and increased on-current at larger V_{bg} can be attributed to the increased electrostatic doping carriers of bilayer MoS$_2$ in both the MoS$_2$/metal contact region and channel region [28,31,33,34].

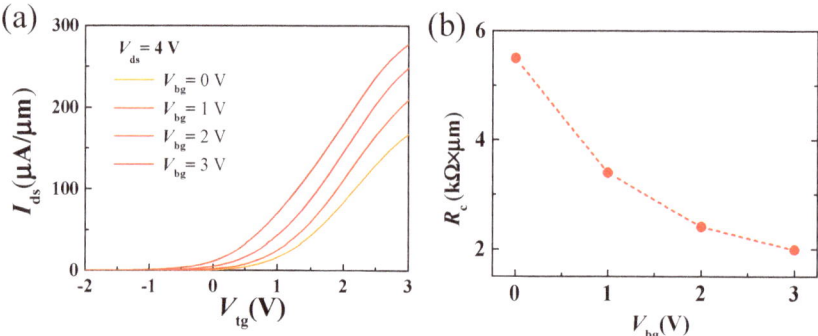

Figure 4. (a) Transfer properties of the dual-gate MoS$_2$ transistors obtained by sweeping the top-gate voltage with varying back-gate biases at V_{ds} = 4 V. (b) Extracted contact resistance as a function of back-gate voltage.

3.2. RF Characterization

The high-frequency performance of dual-gate MoS$_2$ transistors can be evaluated by the cutoff frequency (f_T) and the maximum frequency of oscillation (f_{max}), which can be obtained from the measured S-parameters [43,44]. The cutoff frequency is where the short-circuit current gain $|h_{21}|$ equals unity. The short-circuit current gain $|h_{21}|$ can be defined as:

$$h_{21} = \frac{-2S_{21}}{(1 - S_{11})(1 + S_{22}) + S_{12}S_{21}}. \tag{1}$$

Similarly, the maximum frequency of oscillation was found when the unilateral power gain U was unity, where the U can be defined as:

$$U = \frac{\left|\frac{S_{21}}{S_{12}} - 1\right|^2}{2K\left|\frac{S_{21}}{S_{12}}\right| - 2\text{Re}\left(\frac{S_{21}}{S_{12}}\right)}, \tag{2}$$

where K is the stability factor and $K = \frac{1+|S_{11} \times S_{22} - S_{12} \times S_{21}|^2 - |S_{11}|^2 - |S_{22}|^2}{2 \times |S_{12} \times S_{21}|}$. On-chip microwave measurements from 100 MHz to 30 GHz of the dual-gate MoS$_2$ RF transistors were carried out using vector network analyzers (N5225A, Agilent (Keysight), Colorado Springs, CA, USA). Before the S-parameter measurement, the on-chip measurement system was calibrated according to the short-open-load-through (SOLT) method using standard impedance calibration samples. Then S parameters of the MoS$_2$ transistors were measured, and the short-circuit current gain and the unilateral power gain can be calculated by Equations (1) and (2). As shown in Figure 5a,c, the f_T and f_{max} of the 190 nm MoS$_2$ RF transistors with back-gate floating were 4.6 and 11.9 GHz, respectively. The achieved f_T of 4.6 GHz and f_{max} of 11.9 GHz were also further verified using Gummel's method [45] and maximum available power gain (MAG) [46], as shown in Figure 5b,d. The obtained cut-off frequency and maximum oscillation frequency were consistent with our previous reported work [16], demonstrating the potential of CVD bilayer MoS$_2$ for large-scale high-frequency circuit applications [27,35].

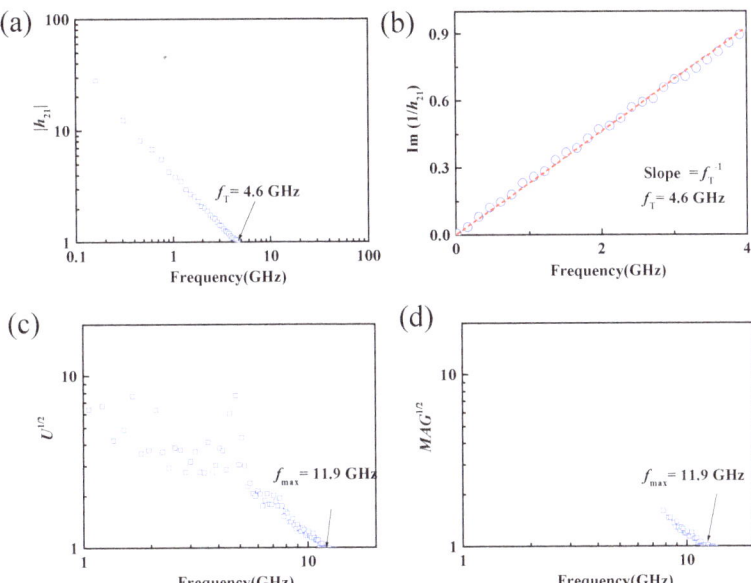

Figure 5. (**a**,**b**) Small-signal current gain $|h_{21}|$ and $\mathrm{Im}(1/h_{21})$ versus frequency. Extrinsic f_T of 4.6 GHz can be extracted. (**c**,**d**) The corresponding unilateral power gain and maximum available power gain versus frequency. An extrinsic f_{max} of 11.9 GHz can be extracted.

Although the implementation of the standard calibration method can move the measurement reference plane from the internal receiver of the vector network analyzer to the tip of the ground–signal–ground (GSG) probe, the parasitic capacitance, inductance, and resistance of the test electrodes also have a significant effect on the obtained S-parameters [27,47]. To eliminate the influence of the test electrodes on the measured S-parameters and to obtain the intrinsic RF performance of the MoS$_2$ RF transistor, this work uses the standard "open" and "short" structures for de-embedding [25]. Then, the measured S-parameters were converted to Y-parameters, and the de-embedding process was performed under the following equation: $Y_{int} = \left[(Y_{DUT} - Y_{open})^{-1} - (Y_{short} - Y_{open})^{-1}\right]^{-1}$, where Y_{DUT} stands for the Y-parameter of the measured transistors. The short-circuit current gain, unilateral power gain, and maximum available power gain versus frequency after de-embedding of the MoS$_2$ transistors with gate length of 190 nm are shown in Figure 6. Intrinsic f_T and f_{max} of 18 and 14.1 GHz were achieved, respectively.

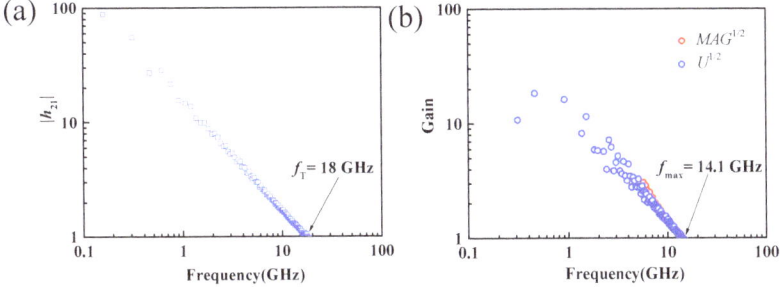

Figure 6. (**a**) Small-signal current gain $|h_{21}|$ versus frequency, (**b**) unilateral power gain and maximum available power gain versus frequency. Intrinsic f_T and f_{max} of 18 and 14.1 GHz could be extracted.

To improve the high-frequency performance of MoS$_2$ RF transistors, we can derive the dependence of f_T and f_{max} on the physical parameters of the device through the small-signal equivalent circuit model, and write them as Equations (3) and (4).

$$f_T = \frac{g_m}{2\pi} * \frac{1}{(C_{gs}+C_{gd})[1+g_{ds}(R_s+R_d)]+C_{gd}g_m(R_s+R_d)} \quad (3)$$

$$f_{max} = \frac{f_T}{2\sqrt{g_{ds}(R_s+R_d)+2\pi f_T C_g R_g}} \quad (4)$$

where g_m is the transconductance and represents the channel current controlling capability of the gate voltage, g_{ds} is the output conductance, C_{gs} and C_{gd} is the gate-to-source and gate-to-drain capacitance, respectively. R_s, R_d and R_g are the source, drain, and gate resistances. From Equations (3) and (4), we can see that g_m, g_{ds}, R_s and R_d play an important role in the high-frequency performance of RF transistors. Therefore, back-gate modulation could be an effective approach for improving the high-frequency performance of MoS$_2$ RF transistors. Figure 7 shows the intrinsic and extrinsic cut-off frequency and maximum oscillation frequency of the device as a function of the back-gate voltage. As shown in Figure 7a,c, when the back-gate voltage changes from 0 V to 3 V, the extrinsic and intrinsic cut-off frequencies before and after de-embedding increase from 4.6 to 6 GHz and from 18 to 19 GHz, respectively, demonstrating an obtained peak f_T increase as the increase of back-gate voltage. The improvement of f_T can be attributed to the reduced contact resistance thus improve transconductance and on-current with increasing V_{bg}, as shown in Figure 4. From the intrinsic f_T of 19 GHz at V_{bg} =3 V, a saturation velocity of 2.3 × 10^6 cm/s is obtained, which is comparable with previously reported works [16,25]. Similarly, when the back-gate increases from 0 to 3 V, the extrinsic and intrinsic maximum oscillation frequencies before and after de-embedding increase from 12 to 27 GHz and from 13.4 to 29.7 GHz, respectively. Because the dependence of f_{max} on output conductance is more sensitive, the increase of f_{max} with increasing V_{bg} is larger than f_T [34]. Furthermore, a comparison between reported MoS$_2$ RF transistors with comparable gate length [22–24] is listed in Table 1, below, demonstrating the advantage of dual-gate MoS$_2$ RF transistors.

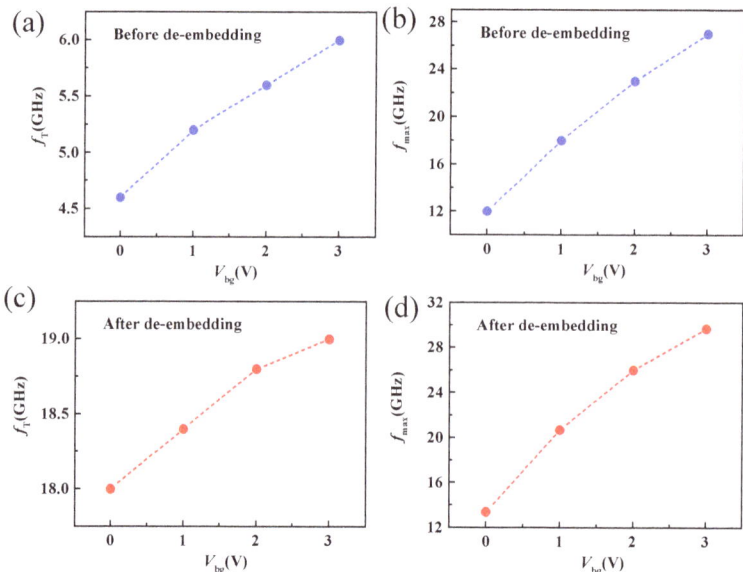

Figure 7. (a,b) Extrinsic f_T and f_{max} as a function of V_{bg}. (c,d) Intrinsic f_T and f_{max} as a function of V_{bg}.

Table 1. Comparison of reported MoS$_2$ RF transistors with comparable gate length.

MoS$_2$	Substrate	L_g (nm)	$f_{T,\text{intrinsic}}$ (GHz)	$f_{\text{max,intrinsic}}$ (GHz)	References
Exfoliated	SiO$_2$/Si	240	6	8.2	[22]
CVD	SiO$_2$/Si	250	6.7	5.3	[23]
CVD	SiO$_2$/Si	150	20	11.4	[24]
CVD	HfLaO/Si	190	19	29.7	This Work

4. Conclusions

In summary, for the first time, a systematic investigation of a dual-gate MoS$_2$ RF transistor based on CVD bilayer MoS$_2$ was performed. Improved on-current and contact resistance performance by optimizing the back-gate voltage were demonstrated. A high on-current of 278 µA/µm and a low contact resistance of 1.99 kΩ·µm were achieved at V_{bg} = 3 V. The cut-off frequency and maximum oscillation frequency can be improved by back-gate modulation. Extrinsic and intrinsic cutoff frequency of 6 and 19 GHz were demonstrated for a gate length of 190 nm at V_{bg} = 3 V. The intrinsic maximum oscillation frequency can become 2.1 times as high as the f_{max} without a back-gate bias. The results presented here indicate that tuning the back-gate voltage provides an effective way to boost f_T and f_{max} and give an insight into the high-frequency performance of MoS$_2$ RF transistors.

Author Contributions: Conceptualization, Q.G. and C.Z.; methodology, Q.G., P.L., Y.H., K.Y. and X.P.; validation, Q.G. and Z.Z.; formal analysis, Q.G., P.L., Z.Z. and X.P.; investigation, Q.G, Y.H.; resources, C.Z., Z.Y., J.Y., F.C. and L.L.; data curation, Q.G.; writing—original draft preparation, Q.G. and C.Z.; writing—review and editing, Q.G. and C.Z.; visualization, Q.G.; supervision, Q.G. and C.Z.; project administration, Q.G. and C.Z.; funding acquisition, Q.G., Z.Y. and C.Z. All authors have read and agreed to the published version of the manuscript.

Funding: This work was funded in part by the Guangdong Basic and Applied Basic Research Foundation (Grant No. 2019A1515110752), in part by the Youth Innovative Talent Project of Guangdong Education Department (Grant No. 2019KQNCX187), in part by the Outstanding Chinese and Foreign Youth Exchange Program of China Association for Science and Technology (CAST), 2019, in part by the Natural Science Foundation of China (Grant No 62071088), and in part by the Project for Innovation Team of Guangdong University (Grant No. 2018KCXTD033), in part by National Key R&D Program of China (Grant No. 2018YFB1801302), in part by Zhongshan Social Public Welfare Science and Technology (Grant No. 2019B2007), and in part by Research Project for Talent of UESTC Zhongshan Institute (419YKQN09).

Data Availability Statement: The data that support the findings of this study are available from the corresponding author upon reasonable request.

Conflicts of Interest: The authors declare no conflict of interest.

References

1. Novoselov, K.S.; Geim, A.K.; Morozov, S.V.; Jiang, D.; Zhang, Y.; Dubonos, S.V.; Grigorieva, I.V.; Firsov, A.A. Electric field effect in atomically thin carbon films. *Science* **2004**, *306*, 666–669. [CrossRef]
2. Schwierz, F. Graphene transistors. *Nat. Nanotechnol.* **2010**, *5*, 487–496. [CrossRef]
3. Radisavljevic, B.; Radenovic, A.; Brivio, J.; Giacometti, V.; Kis, A. Single-layer MoS$_2$ transistors. *Nat. Nanotechnol.* **2011**, *6*, 147–150. [CrossRef] [PubMed]
4. Desai, S.B.; Madhvapathy, S.R.; Sachid, A.B.; Llinas, J.P.; Wang, Q.; Ahn, G.H.; Pitner, G.; Kim, M.J.; Bokor, J.; Hu, C.; et al. MoS$_2$ transistors with 1-nanometer gate lengths. *Science* **2016**, *354*, 99–102. [CrossRef] [PubMed]
5. Tombros, N.; Jozsa, C.; Popinciuc, M.; Jonkman, H.T.; Van Wees, B.J. Electronic spin transport and spin precession in single graphene layers at room temperature. *Nature* **2007**, *448*, 571–574. [CrossRef] [PubMed]
6. Cho, S.; Chen, Y.-F.; Fuhrer, M.S. Gate-tunable graphene spin valve. *Appl. Phys. Lett.* **2007**, *91*, 123105. [CrossRef]
7. Schedin, F.; Geim, A.K.; Morozov, S.V.; Hill, E.W.; Blake, P.; Katsnelson, M.I.; Novoselov, K. Detection of individual gas molecules adsorbed on graphene. *Nat. Mater.* **2007**, *6*, 652–655. [CrossRef] [PubMed]
8. Ohno, Y.; Maehashi, K.; Yamashiro, Y.; Matsumoto, K. Electrolyte-Gated Graphene Field-Effect Transistors for Detecting pH and Protein Adsorption. *Nano Lett.* **2009**, *9*, 3318–3322. [CrossRef] [PubMed]

9. Cheng, Z.; Li, Q.; Li, Z.; Zhou, Q.; Fang, Y. Suspended Graphene Sensors with Improved Signal and Reduced Noise. *Nano Lett.* **2010**, *10*, 1864–1868. [CrossRef]
10. Cohen-Karni, T.; Qing, Q.; Li, Q.; Fang, Y.; Lieber, C.M. Graphene and Nanowire Transistors for Cellular Interfaces and Electrical Recording. *Nano Lett.* **2010**, *10*, 1098–1102. [CrossRef]
11. Bunch, J.S.; Van Der Zande, A.M.; Verbridge, S.S.; Frank, I.W.; Tanenbaum, D.M.; Parpia, J.M.; Craighead, H.G.; McEuen, P.L. Electromechanical Resonators from Graphene Sheets. *Science* **2007**, *315*, 490–493. [CrossRef]
12. Stoller, M.D.; Park, S.; Zhu, Y.; An, J.; Ruoff, R.S. Graphene-Based Ultracapacitors. *Nano Lett.* **2008**, *8*, 3498–3502. [CrossRef]
13. Wang, Q.H.; Kalantar-Zadeh, K.; Kis, A.; Coleman, J.N.; Strano, M.S. Electronics and optoelectronics of two-dimensional transition metal dichalcogenides. *Nat. Nanotechnol.* **2012**, *7*, 699–712. [CrossRef]
14. Yoon, Y.; Ganapathi, K.; Salahuddin, S. How good can monolayer MoS_2 transistors be? *Nano Lett.* **2011**, *11*, 3768–3773. [CrossRef]
15. Akinwande, D.; Petrone, N.; Hone, J. Two-dimensional flexible nanoelectronics. *Nat. Commun.* **2014**, *5*, 5678. [CrossRef] [PubMed]
16. Gao, Q.; Zhang, Z.; Xu, X.; Song, J.; Li, X.; Wu, Y. Scalable high performance radio frequency electronics based on large domain bilayer MoS_2. *Nat. Commun.* **2018**, *9*, 4778. [CrossRef] [PubMed]
17. Lin, Z.; Liu, Y.; Halim, U.; Ding, M.; Liu, Y.; Wang, Y.; Jia, C.; Chen, P.; Duan, X.; Wang, C.; et al. Solution-processable 2D semiconductors for high-performance large-area electronics. *Nat. Cell Biol.* **2018**, *562*, 254–258. [CrossRef]
18. Zhang, X.; Grajal, J.; Vazquez-Roy, J.L.; Radhakrishna, U.; Wang, X.; Chern, W.; Zhou, L.; Lin, Y.; Shen, P.-C.; Ji, X.; et al. Two-dimensional MoS_2-enabled flexible rectenna for Wi-Fi-band wireless energy harvesting. *Nature* **2019**, *566*, 368–372. [CrossRef] [PubMed]
19. Na, J.; Joo, M.-K.; Shin, M.; Huh, J.; Kim, J.-S.; Piao, M.; Jin, J.-E.; Jang, H.-K.; Choi, H.J.; Shim, J.H.; et al. Low-frequency noise in multilayer MoS_2 field-effect transistors: the effect of high-*k* passivation. *Nanoscale* **2014**, *6*, 433–441. [CrossRef]
20. Liu, N.; Baek, J.; Kim, S.M.; Hong, S.; Hong, Y.K.; Kim, Y.S.; Kim, H.-S.; Kim, S.; Park, J. Improving the Stability of High-Performance Multilayer MoS_2 Field-Effect Transistors. *ACS Appl. Mater. Interfaces* **2017**, *9*, 42943–42950. [CrossRef] [PubMed]
21. Chang, H.-Y.; Yogeesh, M.N.; Ghosh, R.; Rai, A.; Sanne, A.; Yang, S.; Lu, N.; Banerjee, S.K.; Akinwande, D. Large-Area Monolayer MoS_2 for Flexible Low-Power RF Nanoelectronics in the GHz Regime. *Adv. Mater.* **2016**, *28*, 1818–1823. [CrossRef] [PubMed]
22. Krasnozhon, D.; Lembke, D.; Nyffeler, C.; Leblebici, Y.; Kis, A. MoS_2 Transistors Operating at Gigahertz Frequencies. *Nano Lett.* **2014**, *14*, 5905–5911. [CrossRef] [PubMed]
23. Sanne, A.; Ghosh, R.; Rai, A.; Yogeesh, M.N.; Shin, S.H.; Sharma, A.; Jarvis, K.; Mathew, L.; Rao, R.; Akinwande, D.; et al. Radio Frequency Transistors and Circuits Based on CVD MoS_2. *Nano Lett.* **2015**, *15*, 5039–5045. [CrossRef] [PubMed]
24. Sanne, A.; Park, S.; Ghosh, R.; Yogeesh, M.N.; Liu, C.; Mathew, L.; Rao, R.; Akinwande, D.; Banerjee, S.K. Embedded gate CVD MoS_2 microwave FETs. *npj 2D Mater. Appl.* **2017**, *1*, 26. [CrossRef]
25. Cheng, R.; Jiang, S.; Chen, Y.; Liu, Y.; Weiss, N.O.; Cheng, H.-C.; Wu, H.; Huang, Y.; Duan, X. Few-layer molybdenum disulfide transistors and circuits for high-speed flexible electronics. *Nat. Commun.* **2014**, *5*, 514. [CrossRef]
26. Krasnozhon, D.; Dutta, S.; Nyffeler, C.; Leblebici, Y.; Kis, A. High-frequency, scaled MoS_2 transistors. In Proceedings of the 2015 IEEE International Electron Devices Meeting (IEDM), Washington, DC, USA, 7–9 December 2015; pp. 27.4.1–27.4.4.
27. Gao, Q.; Zhang, C.; Yang, K.; Pan, X.; Zhang, Z.; Yang, J.; Yi, Z.; Chi, F.; Liu, L. High-Performance CVD Bilayer MoS_2 Radio Frequency Transistors and Gigahertz Mixers for Flexible Nanoelectronics. *Micromachines* **2021**, *12*, 451. [CrossRef] [PubMed]
28. Li, X.; Li, T.; Zhang, Z.; Xiong, X.; Li, S.; Wu, Y. Tunable Low-Frequency Noise in Dual-Gate MoS_2 Transistors. *IEEE Electron Device Lett.* **2017**, *39*, 131–134. [CrossRef]
29. Bolshakov, P.; Khosravi, A.; Zhao, P.; Hurley, P.K.; Hinkle, C.L.; Wallace, R.M.; Young, C.D. Dual-gate MoS_2 transistors with sub-10 nm top-gate high-k dielectrics. *Appl. Phys. Lett.* **2018**, *112*, 253502. [CrossRef]
30. Lee, G.-H.; Cui, X.; Kim, Y.D.; Arefe, G.; Zhang, X.; Lee, C.-H.; Ye, F.; Watanabe, K.; Taniguchi, T.; Kim, P.; et al. Highly Stable, Dual-Gated MoS_2 Transistors Encapsulated by Hexagonal Boron Nitride with Gate-Controllable Contact, Resistance, and Threshold Voltage. *ACS Nano* **2015**, *9*, 7019–7026. [CrossRef] [PubMed]
31. Li, X.-X.; Chen, X.-Y.; Chen, J.-X.; Zeng, G.; Li, Y.-C.; Huang, W.; Ji, Z.-G.; Zhang, D.W.; Lu, H.-L. Dual-gate MoS_2 phototransistor with atomic-layer-deposited HfO^2 as top-gate dielectric for ultrahigh photoresponsivity. *Nanotechnology* **2021**, *32*, 215203. [CrossRef]
32. Li, X.; Xiong, X.; Li, T.; Li, S.; Zhang, Z.; Wu, Y. Effect of Dielectric Interface on the Performance of MoS_2 transistors. *ACS Appl. Mater. Interfaces* **2017**, *9*, 44602–44608. [CrossRef]
33. Lin, Y.-M.; Chiu, H.-Y.; Jenkins, K.A.; Farmer, D.B.; Avouris, P.; Valdes-Garcia, A. Dual-gate graphene FETs with f_T of 50 GHz. *IEEE Electron Device Lett.* **2009**, *31*, 68–70. [CrossRef]
34. Zhu, W.; Low, T.; Farmer, D.B.; Jenkins, K.; Ek, B.; Avouris, P. Effect of dual gate control on the alternating current performance of graphene radio frequency device. *J. Appl. Phys.* **2013**, *114*, 44307. [CrossRef]
35. Gao, Q.; Zhang, C.; Yi, Z.; Pan, X.; Chi, F.; Liu, L.; Li, X.; Wu, Y. Improved low-frequency noise in CVD bilayer MoS_2 field-effect transistors. *Appl. Phys. Lett.* **2021**, *118*, 153103. [CrossRef]
36. Xiong, X.; Li, X.; Huang, M.; Li, T.; Gao, T.; Wu, Y. High Performance Black Phosphorus Electronic and Photonic Devices with HfLaO Dielectric. *IEEE Electron Device Lett.* **2017**, *39*, 127–130. [CrossRef]
37. Li, S.; Tian, M.; Gao, Q.; Wang, M.; Li, T.; Hu, Q.; Li, X.; Wu, Y. Nanometre-thin indium tin oxide for advanced high-performance electronics. *Nat. Mater.* **2019**, *18*, 1091–1097. [CrossRef] [PubMed]

38. McDonnell, S.; Brennan, B.; Azcatl, A.; Lu, N.; Dong, H.; Buie, C.; Kim, J.; Hinkle, C.L.; Kim, M.J.; Wallace, R.M. HfO^2 on MoS$_2$ by Atomic Layer Deposition: Adsorption Mechanisms and Thickness Scalability. *ACS Nano* **2013**, *7*, 10354–10361. [CrossRef]
39. Kim, H.G.; Lee, H.-B.-R. Atomic Layer Deposition on 2D Materials. *Chem. Mater.* **2017**, *29*, 3809–3826. [CrossRef]
40. Wang, H.; Yu, L.; Lee, Y.-H.; Shi, Y.; Hsu, A.; Chin, M.L.; Li, L.-J.; Dubey, M.; Kong, J.; Palacios, T. Integrated Circuits Based on Bilayer MoS$_2$ Transistors. *Nano Lett.* **2012**, *12*, 4674–4680. [CrossRef]
41. Joo, M.-K.; Moon, B.H.; Ji, H.; Han, G.H.; Kim, H.; Lee, G.; Lim, S.C.; Suh, D.; Lee, Y.H. Understanding Coulomb Scattering Mechanism in Monolayer MoS$_2$ Channel in the Presence of h-BN Buffer Layer. *ACS Appl. Mater. Interfaces* **2017**, *9*, 5006–5013. [CrossRef]
42. Renteria, J.; Samnakay, R.; Rumyantsev, S.; Jiang, C.; Goli, P.; Shur, M.A.; Balandin, A. Low-frequency 1/f noise in MoS$_2$ transistors: Relative contributions of the channel and contacts. *Appl. Phys. Lett.* **2014**, *104*, 153104. [CrossRef]
43. Qing-Guo, G.; Meng-Chuan, T.; Si-Chao, L.; Xue-Fei, L.; Yan-Qing, W. Gigahertz frequency doubler based on millimeter-scale single-crystal graphene. *Acta Phys. Sin.* **2017**, *66*, 217305. [CrossRef]
44. Wu, Y.; Lin, Y.-M.; Bol, A.; Jenkins, K.A.; Xia, F.; Farmer, D.B.; Zhu, Y.; Avouris, P. High-frequency, scaled graphene transistors on diamond-like carbon. *Nat. Cell Biol.* **2011**, *472*, 74–78. [CrossRef] [PubMed]
45. Gummel, H. On the definition of the cutoff frequency fT. *Proc. IEEE* **1969**, *57*, 2159. [CrossRef]
46. Gupta, M. Power gain in feedback amplifiers, a classic revisited. *IEEE Trans. Microw. Theory Tech.* **1992**, *40*, 864–879. [CrossRef]
47. Li, T.; Tian, M.; Li, S.; Huang, M.; Xiong, X.; Hu, Q.; Li, S.; Li, X.; Wu, Y. Black Phosphorus Radio Frequency Electronics at Cryogenic Temperatures. *Adv. Electron. Mater.* **2018**, *4*, 1800138. [CrossRef]

Article

Enhanced Electrical Performance of Monolayer MoS$_2$ with Rare Earth Element Sm Doping

Shijie Li [1,2,†], Shidai Tian [1,2,†], Yuan Yao [1,2], Meng He [1,2], Li Chen [1,*], Yan Zhang [1,2,3,*] and Junyi Zhai [1,2,4,*]

1. Center on Nanoenergy Research, School of Physical Science and Technology, Guangxi University, Nanning 530004, China; lishijie@binn.cas.cn (S.L.); tianshidai@binn.cas.cn (S.T.); yaoyuan@binn.cas.cn (Y.Y.); hemeng@binn.cas.cn (M.H.)
2. CAS Center for Excellence in Nanoscience, Beijing Key Laboratory of Micro-Nano Energy and Sensor, Beijing Institute of Nanoenergy and Nanosystems, Chinese Academy of Sciences, Beijing 100083, China
3. School of Physics, University of Electronic Science and Technology of China, Chengdu 610054, China
4. College of Nanoscience and Technology, University of Chinese Academy of Science, Beijing 100049, China
* Correspondence: chenli@gxu.edu.cn (L.C.); zhangyan@uestc.edu.cn (Y.Z.); jyzhai@binn.cas.cn (J.Z.)
† These authors contributed equally to this work.

Citation: Li, S.; Tian, S.; Yao, Y.; He, M.; Chen, L.; Zhang, Y.; Zhai, J. Enhanced Electrical Performance of Monolayer MoS$_2$ with Rare Earth Element Sm Doping. *Nanomaterials* **2021**, *11*, 769. https://doi.org/10.3390/nano11030769

Academic Editor: Antonio Di Bartolomeo

Received: 21 February 2021
Accepted: 16 March 2021
Published: 18 March 2021

Publisher's Note: MDPI stays neutral with regard to jurisdictional claims in published maps and institutional affiliations.

Copyright: © 2021 by the authors. Licensee MDPI, Basel, Switzerland. This article is an open access article distributed under the terms and conditions of the Creative Commons Attribution (CC BY) license (https://creativecommons.org/licenses/by/4.0/).

Abstract: Rare earth (RE) element-doped two-dimensional (2D) transition metal dichalcogenides (TMDCs) with applications in luminescence and magnetics have received considerable attention in recent years. To date, the effect of RE element doping on the electronic properties of monolayer 2D-TMDCs remains unanswered due to challenges including the difficulty of achieving valid monolayer doping and introducing RE elements with distinct valence and atomic configurations. Herein, we report a unique strategy to grow the Sm-doped monolayer MoS$_2$ film by using an atmospheric pressure chemical vapor deposition method with the substrate face down on top of the growth source. A stable monolayer triangular Sm-doped MoS$_2$ was achieved. The threshold voltage of an Sm-doped MoS$_2$-based field effect transistor (FET) moved from −12 to 0 V due to the p-type character impurity state introduced by Sm ions in monolayer MoS$_2$. Additionally, the electrical performance of the monolayer MoS$_2$-based FET was improved by RE element Sm doping, including a 500% increase of the on/off current ratio and a 40% increase of the FET's mobility. The electronic property enhancement resulted from Sm doping MoS$_2$, which led internal lattice strain and changes in Fermi energy levels. These findings provide a general approach to synthesize RE element-doped monolayer 2D-TMDCs and to enrich their applications in electrical devices.

Keywords: monolayer MoS$_2$; CVD growth; Sm doping; electrical performance; FET

1. Introduction

In recent years, there has been an increasing interest in two-dimensional (2D) transition metal dichalcogenides (TMDCs) due to their unique properties and great potential for electronic and optoelectronic applications [1,2]. 2D-TMDCs are a kind of low-dimensional materials that have the formula of MX$_2$, where M stands for the transition-metals like Mo, W, and Ti, and X represents S, Se, and Te [3]. Nevertheless, the characteristics presented by 2D-TMDCs are extremely monotonous and limited [4]. Realizing the full potential of 2D-TMDCs in high-performance thin film transistors and to endow some new distinguishing features requires some doping strategies to effectively control their carrier type and to modulate the band gap [5]. Common doping strategies for 2D-TMDCs include substitution doping during growth, ion implantation, and surface charge transfer [6]. However, in these previous doping schemes, ion injection and surface charge transfer in monolayer 2D-TMDC doping were often not stable enough, thus limiting their application [6,7]. Substitution the doping of 2D-TMDCs has been widely explored for materials applications in electronic and optoelectronic [7], as well as room-temperature ferromagnetism, applications [8–10]. Transition elements have been used as cationic substitutes for doped 2D-TMDCs, e.g., the Nb ion-doped 2D-TMDCs achieving p-type [7] transport characteristics and the Re ion-doped 2D-TMDCs achieving nearly degenerate n-type doping [11]. Moreover, in recent studies, Fu's group confirmed ferromagnetism in monolayer MoS_2 via in situ Fe-doping at room temperature [10] and Pham's group enhanced tunable ferromagnetism in V-doped WSe_2 monolayers at 0.5–5 at% V concentrations [9]. Additionally, other transition metal elements in the in situ substitution of MoS_2-doped for electronic application studies have been demonstrated, such as for Mn [12]. The above research had demonstrated that the doping of transition metal elements is able to tune the electrical, optical, and magnetic properties of 2D-TMDCs [13]. Thus far, transition metal elements have been widely demonstrated in in situ substitution-doped monolayer 2D-TMDCs. However, the doping engineering of atomically thin TMDCs by introducing elements with different atomic valences and atomic configurations, such as RE elements, is still challenging. Currently, a range of difficult issues still exists for in situ RE element substitution-doped large monolayer 2D-TMDCs.

RE elements, which usually exist as trivalent cations, are composed of 15 lanthanides (from lanthanum to lutetium), plus scandium and yttrium [14]. In previous studies, it could be noted that RE ions were commonly doped in traditional insulator or semiconductors [15]. RE elements can also be used as efficient dopants in TMDC materials. Lanthanide (Ln) ions have a rich f-orbit configuration that allows them to absorb and emit photons from the ultraviolet to infrared region via the $4f$-$4f$ or $4f$-$5d$ transition, making them candidates for extended 2D-TMDC semiconductor luminescence [15,16]. In addition, RE dopants with unfilled $4f$ energy states and charge-transfer state structures may provide strong spin-orbit coupling to tune the semiconductor properties of the 2D-TMDC's host material [17]. Furthermore, first principle calculations confirmed the possibility of doping 2D-TMDCs with rare earth elements [18,19]. Currently, progress is being made in the study of RE element-doped 2D-TMDCs films for optical, electronic, and magnetic applications [20]. For example, Qi Zhao et al. made a breakthrough to synthesize MoS_2:Dy sheets with robust and adjustable ferromagnetic properties at room temperature by a gas–liquid chemical deposition method [17]. Gongxun Bai et al. synthesized a novel 2D system of an Er-doped multilayer MoS_2 to study NIR-to-NIR down-and up-conversion photoluminescence [16]. However, these studies were based on some thicker-layer 2D-TMDC materials. Later on, Yongxin Lyu et al. fabricated Er-embedded MoS_2 triangle islands along the in-plane size of up to around 10 µm, which apparently formed single crystals [21]. Additionally, Fu et al. used a salt-assisted sustained-release chemical vapor deposition (CVD) method to grow Eu ion-doped MoS_2 [22]. Their methods yielded smaller sized samples and tended to introduce new dopant impurities. In addition, Eu and Er element-doped 2D-TMDC research has focused on photoluminescence and ferromagnetic properties, with little reported on the electrical properties of other rare earth element-doped monolayer 2D-TMDCs. Therefore, it is unclear whether the introduction of rare earth elements into monolayer 2D-TMDCs can effectively control their carrier type and regulate carrier concentration.In this work, we demonstrate a large-sized MoS_2 film doped with the RE element Sm by an atmospheric pressure, three-zone CVD method. In addition, stable monolayer triangular Sm-doped MoS_2 films were obtained at the edge positions of the large size films.

MoS_2 was chosen as the doping host material because it is a typical example from the layered 2D-TMDC family of materials [23]. Additionally, Sm is more economic compared to Er and Eu elements when investing in the optimization conditions for rare earth element-doped monolayer 2D materials by CVD. The monolayer MoS_2 was used as a matrix material to embed Sm, as confirmed by characterization methods such as Raman, photoluminescence (PL), X-ray photoelectron spectroscopy (XPS), atomic force microscope (AFM), and energy dispersive X-ray spectroscopy (EDS) elemental mapping. As the monolayer triangle MoS_2 was found to be the most energetically stable existent morphology, we characterized the electrical properties of stable triangular MoS_2 field effect transistor (FET) before and after its doping. Electrical measurements showed that Sm element doping led to considerable changes in the electronic band structure of the host MoS_2.The doping of

Sm may lead to a non-uniform charge distribution, suppress the n-type characteristic, and change the energy band structure of MoS_2.

2. Materials and Methods

2.1. Synthesis of the Sm-Doped MoS_2 Film on a SiO_2/Si Substrate by the CVD System

The three-zone CVD system is composed of two parts—an external temperature zone heated by a heating belt and the two temperature zones of a furnace. Alcohol/isopropanol/deionized water and a 3:1 mix solution of concentrated H_2SO_4 and H_2O_2 were used in this study for the pretreatment of the 270 nm-thick, SiO_2-capped Si substrate before Sm-doped MoS_2 growth by CVD [24]. Sublimed sulfur powder (Aladdin, Shanghai, China, 99.5%; 900 mg), MoO_3(VI) powder (Alfa, Louis, MO, USA, 99.5%; 10 mg), and $SmCl_3 \cdot 6H_2O$ particles (Macklin, Shanghai, China, 99%; 5 mg) were loaded in three customized crucible lids before growth and placed in the quartz tube of the furnace, as shown in the Supplementary Materials (Figure S1).

Then, the different samples in the three-crucible lid were fed by a tool into the corresponding positions of the quartz tube. First, the SiO_2/Si (1 cm × 2 cm) substrate that was placed upside down on top of the MoO_3 powder crucible lid was placed in the second zone of the furnace. Second, the $SmCl_3 \cdot 6H_2O$ particle was put in the first zone of the furnace. Third, sulfur powder was located at the external temperature zone. The temperature and Ar gas flow control procedure for CVD-doped growth is as follows. After purging the furnace with Ar for 20 min [25], the temperature of the two temperature zones of the tube furnace itself was ramped to 100 °C in 20 min and maintained for 30 min, while the carrier gas flow rate in this process was 200 sccm. The subsequent steps in the temperature and Ar gas flow control procedure were that the first and second temperature zones of the furnace were increased from 100 to 800 and 750 °C, respectively, within 53 min and then maintained for 30 min. The Ar gas flow rate changed from 200 to 100 sccm when heating up from 100 °C. Additionally, the S powder was heated by a heating belt when the first zone of the furnace was heated to 650 °C. After the thermal growth process ended, the furnace and heating belt were allowed to naturally cool down to room temperature [26].

2.2. FET Device Fabrication

The FET device preparation is divided into two main parts: sample transfer and source and drain electrode preparation [27,28]. During the transfer process, a thin layer of poly methyl methacrylate (PMMA) was spun-coated on the CVD-grown, Sm-doped MoS_2 and then baked for 3 min at 150 °C. Next, the excess non-sample area was removed, and the remaining sample coated by the PMMA was immersed in 20% Hydrofluoric acid solution to etch SiO_2. At the end, the detached film was cleaned in deionized water several times and transferred to the heavily doped SiO_2/Si substrate. Next was the process of preparing the electrodes for the FET device. First, the residual PMMA covering the transfer sample on the target substrate was removed with an acetone solution. Second, a new thin layer of PMMA was spun-coated on the CVD-grown, Sm-doped MoS_2, and then the electrodes were exposed in the appropriate positions via electron beam lithography (EBL) according to the designed electrode pattern. Third, Cr/Au (10 nm/50 nm) of the source and drain electrodes was deposited in the corresponding position by electron beam eVaporation deposition. In SiO_2/Si substrates, Cr/Au (10 nm/50 nm) electrode plating was also required for Si as a gate voltage. Finally, the acetone solution removed the PMMA, and the corresponding device was obtained on the substrate.

2.3. Characterization

Raman and PL spectra were taken by a LabRAM HR eVolution system (HORIBA Co. Ltd., Paris, France) with a 532 nm laser. The Raman spectroscopy parameters were a diffraction grating of 1800 gr/mm, a focal length of 800 mm, a Raman frequency shift range of 50–8000 cm^{-1}, and a spectral resolution of ≤ 0.65 cm^{-1}. The morphology of fabricated devices and the morphology of as-grown Sm-doped MoS_2 were observed by a fluorescent inverted microscope (LeicaDMI6000B, Leica, Hesse-Darmstadt, Germany), and the thickness of few-layer flakes was characterized by AFM (MFP-3D-SA, Asylum Research, Santa Barbara, CA, USA) and Raman spectroscopy. The electrical properties of all the FET devices were measured using a Keithley 4200 (Tektronix, Beaverton, OR, USA) semiconductor parameter analyzer at room temperature (under dark conditions). XPS was conducted on a Thermo Scientific™ K-Alpha™+ (Thermo Scientific, Waltham, MA, USA) spectrometer equipped with a monochromatic Al Kα X-ray source (1486.6 eV) operating at 100 W. Samples were analyzed under vacuum ($p < 10^{-8}$ mbar) with a pass energy of 150 eV (survey scans) or 25 eV (high-resolution scans). All peaks would be calibrated with C1s peak binding energy at 284.8 eV for adventitious carbon. The experimental peaks were fitted with the Avantage software. TEM images were obtained with an FEI Talos F200X (Thermo Scientific, Waltham, MA, USA)

3. Results and Discussion

3.1. Fabrication of Monolayer Sm-Doped MoS$_2$

The monolayer Sm-doped MoS$_2$ film was directly synthesized by the three-zone CVD system of atmospheric pressure method on the SiO$_2$/Si substrate that was placed face down [29] on the crucible lid in a quartz tube, and the overall process of the growth system is illustrated in Figure 1a. As Figure 1a shows, sulfur powder was placed upstream, and the SmCl$_3$·6H$_2$O particle was placed in the middle of the S and MoO$_3$ powder. In the synthetic process, SmCl$_3$ has two effects: one is as a dopant, and the other is as an assistant agent for the long-distance transmission of MoO$_{3-x}$ [24]. Additionally, the SiO$_2$/Si (1 × 2 cm) substrate that was placed upside down on top of the MoO$_3$ powder crucible lid was downstream of the furnace. Figure 1b shows an enlarged growth model processes for the synthesis of monolayer Sm-doped MoS$_2$ on the SiO$_2$/Si substrate facing down on the MoO$_3$ powder. Figure 1c,d exhibits the optical images of the monolayer triangular MoS$_2$ and Sm-doped MoS$_2$, respectively. The size of CVD-grown, Sm-doped MoS$_2$ triangle islands along the in-plane was up to around 50 μm. More optical images can be seen in Figure S2. The triangle MoS$_2$ was the most energetically stable existent morphology, and the uniformity of the obtained large-size films was not as good as that of the triangle MoS$_2$. The specific analysis can be seen in the Supplementary Materials (Figure S3).

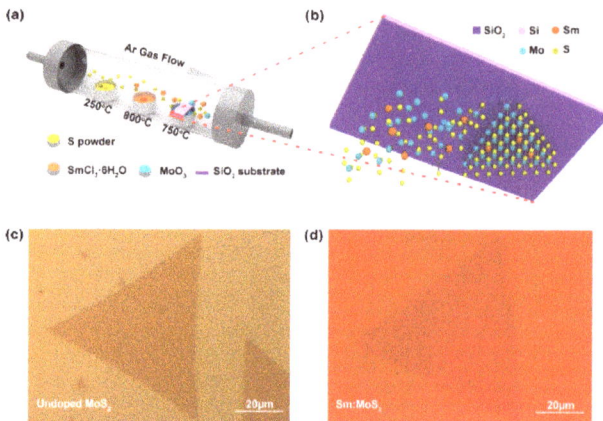

Figure 1. The growth of monolayer triangular Sm-doped MoS$_2$ film. (**a**) Schematic of the three-temperature zone chemical vapor deposition (CVD) system for the growth of the monolayer Sm-doped MoS$_2$ film on the SiO$_2$/Si substrate. (**b**) The simple growth model processes for the synthesis of monolayer triangular Sm-doped MoS$_2$ on SiO$_2$/Si substrate. Optical microscopy images of (**c**) undoped and (**d**) Sm-doped monolayer triangular MoS$_2$. Scale bar = 20 μm.

3.2. Characterizations and Analysis of Monolayer Sm-Doped MoS$_2$

3.2.1. Raman and Photoluminescence Analysis of Monolayer Sm-Doped MoS$_2$

Raman spectroscopy was performed to investigate the layers of the MoS$_2$ and Sm-doped MoS$_2$, and PL spectroscopy was employed to demonstrate the doping effect. Figure 2a shows the Raman spectra of MoS$_2$ and Sm-doped MoS$_2$, where the Raman spectrum of Sm-doped MoS$_2$ can be seen to have exhibited two typical characteristic vibration modes of layered MoS$_2$ at E^1_{2g} = 384.6 cm^{-1} (in-plane vibration of Mo and S atoms) and A_{1g} = 404.5 cm^{-1} (out-of-plane vibration of S atoms). The peak spacing between the E^1_{2g} and A_{1g} was 19.9 cm^{-1}, suggesting the MoS$_2$ and Sm-doped MoS$_2$ were monolayers [30]. Figure S4b,d shows an AFM image of the Sm-doped MoS$_2$ and undoped MoS$_2$ samples, respectively. The height profiles indicate that the thickness of a typical flake was approximately 0.83 nm, which was almost comparable to that of the single layer MoS$_2$ crystal. Additionally, both vibrational modes of Sm-doped MoS$_2$ are displayed in a small blue shift compared with the monolayer MoS$_2$, implying the possible effects of the Sm doping and/or the presence of defects on MoS$_2$ [16]. Due to the competing effects of lattice strain and Sm^{3+} charge doping on the Raman shift, the overall blue shift of the A_{1g} and E^1_{2g} peak was relatively small [31]. Furthermore, the distortion of the MoS$_2$ lattice could give rise to the optical quenching of the PL intensities [10]. It can be seen from Figure 2b that undoped MoS$_2$ had a strong PL peak at about 1.82 eV, implying the MoS$_2$ is a direct band gap semiconductor. However, the PL intensities of Sm-doped MoS$_2$ were observed to be much lower with a 30 meV blue shift than that of undoped MoS$_2$, which was consistent with previous predictions of the optical quenching of the PL intensities due to distortion of the MoS$_2$ lattice [10]. This may be ascribed to the introduction of new defects due to lattice distortion by the doped Sm ions, as well as changes in band gap width. Using the equation $\delta\omega = 2\gamma\omega_0\varepsilon$ [32] and band gap deformation potential, it was found that the lattice strains arising from the Sm doping were about 0.076% and 0.1%, respectively. This was also confirmed in the previous studies of lanthanide Er-doped [16] MoS$_2$ and Eu-doped [22] MoS$_2$. Additionally, the Raman mapping corresponding to the E^1_{2g} and A_{1g} peaks was used to confirm the uniformity growth of the monolayer triangular samples with and without Sm doping, as shown in Figure 2d,e,g,h, respectively. It was observed that the Sm-doped monolayer MoS$_2$ showed a more regular triangular shape and a more uniform peak distribution than undoped MoS$_2$. Thus, Sm doping improved the homogeneity of the sample.

3.2.2. XPS Spectrum Analysis of Monolayer Sm-Doped MoS$_2$

XPS was performed to investigate the elements and valence state information of monolayer MoS$_2$ and Sm-doped MoS$_2$. Figure 3a–c displays the comparisons of XPS results from the undoped MoS$_2$ (in black) and Sm-doped MoS$_2$ (in red). In the full spectrum (Figure 3a), there are Si, O, and C core levels in addition to S and Mo core levels. The Si and O core levels in the samples may have come from the SiO$_2$/Si substrate, so the O peak intensity was much higher than that of C. The core level of Sm was only found in the Sm-doped MoS$_2$. Additionally, the spectral shape of the S and Mo core levels after Sm-doping was nearly identical to that of the undoped MoS$_2$, which indicated that Sm-doping did not significantly chemically alter the MoS$_2$ host [33]. However, compared to the undoped sample, it was obvious that the doped S 2p and Mo 3d core level peaks were both shifted by 0.18 eV towards the lower binding energies. The specific displacement changes of the binding energy were as follows: Mo 3d$_{3/2}$ shifted from 232.64 to 232.82 eV, Mo 3d$_{5/2}$ shifted from 229.7 to 229.52 eV, S 2p$_{1/2}$ shifted from 163.74 to 163.56 eV, and S 2p$_{3/2}$ shifted from 162.54 to 162.36 eV [34]. The slight shift indicated the change of chemical microenvironment around these atoms for Sm-doped MoS$_2$ materials [22]. It can be inferred that the binding energy shifts were associated with Fermi level shifts and originated from the incorporation of Sm into MoS$_2$ single crystals [16,22]. The binding energy shift direction and magnitude of Sm-doped MoS$_2$ were also found to be consistent with the variation of p-type-doped MoS$_2$ [16]. As seen in Figure 3d, the obvious binding energy peaks related to the Sm 3d$_{5/2}$

at 1083.58 eV [35] indicated that the Sm ions were trivalent [36], but the Sm $3d_{3/2}$ did not have a significant peak. That may be attributed to the low concentration of Sm, with XPS estimating a doping concentration of about 1.1at%.

3.2.3. TEM Analysis of Monolayer Sm-Doped MoS_2

TEM was carried out to further investigate the microstructure and elemental composition of the monolayer Sm-doped MoS_2. The EDS elemental mapping images of S, Mo, and Sm in Sm-doped monolayer MoS_2, which were taken from the area shown in Figure 4a, are shown in Figure 4b–d. Though the S, Mo, and Sm elemental mapping image scans were complete, the amount of detected Sm element was small. This indicated the existence of a low doping concentration of Sm in the monolayer MoS_2. The elemental Sm doping concentration of the selected area detected by EDS (Figure S5) was about 1.42at%. In Figure S5, selected area electron diffraction (SAED) patterns indicate that Sm doping did not change the original crystal structure.

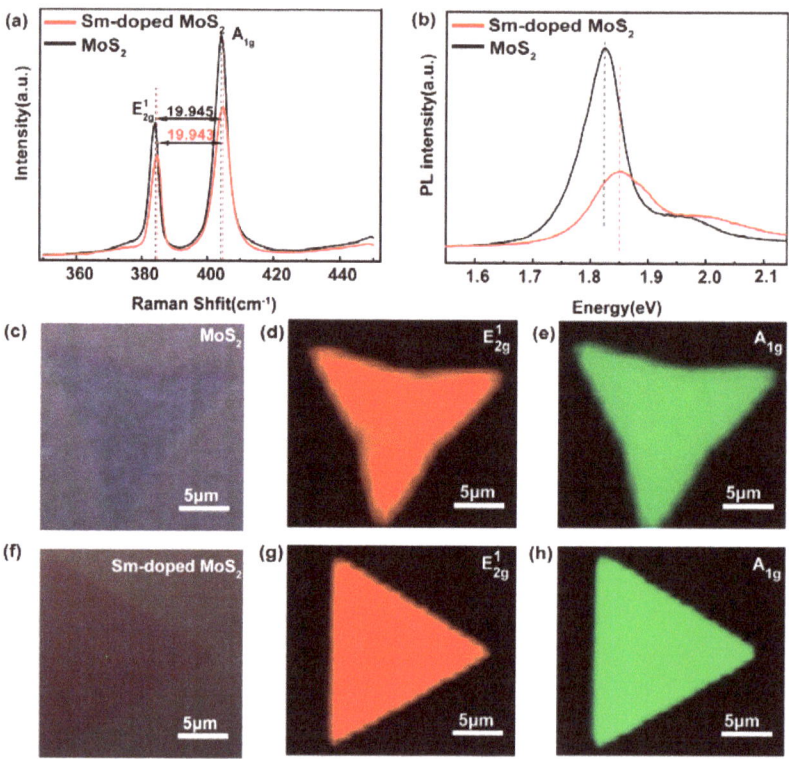

Figure 2. (a) Raman spectra and (b) photoluminescence (PL) spectra of monolayer triangular MoS_2 and Sm-doped triangular MoS_2 under 532 nm laser excitation. The (c) and (f) plots show the MoS_2 and Sm-doped MoS_2 optical microscopy images under Raman detection, respectively. (d,e,g,h) Raman mappings of the peak position corresponding to E_{2g}^1 and A_{1g} of the MoS_2 and Sm-doped MoS_2, respectively. Raman and PL spectroscopy were conducted using a confocal Raman microscope with a 532 nm laser at room temperature.

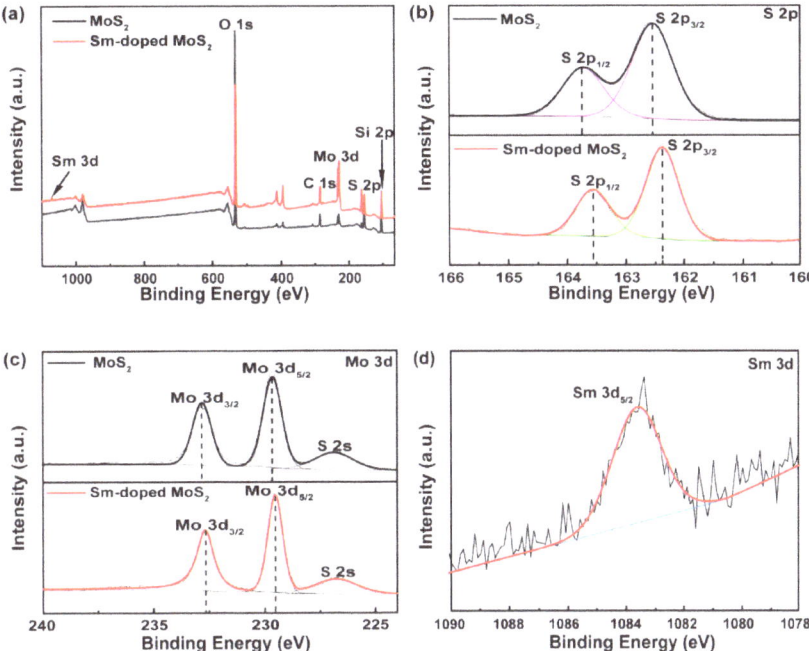

Figure 3. XPS spectrum (**a**) total scans, (**b**) S 2p, (**c**) Mo 3d, and (**d**) Sm 3d core levels.

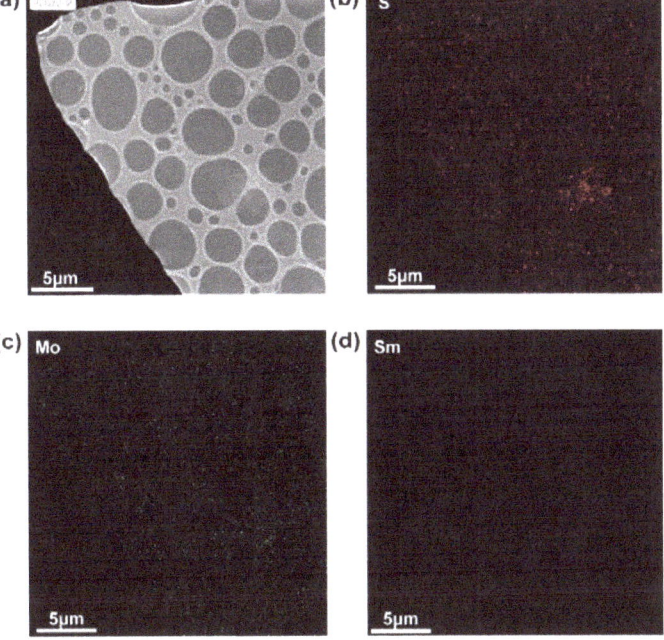

Figure 4. TEM characterizations of Sm-doped MoS_2. (**a**) Low resolution TEM area of EDS mapping. (**b–d**) EDS elemental mapping images of S, Mo, and Sm in Sm-doped MoS_2, respectively.

3.3. Electrical Properties Characterisation of Monolayer Sm-Doped MoS$_2$ FET

In order to investigate the electrical properties of the Sm-doped monolayer MoS$_2$, a bottom gate FET was fabricated on the SiO$_2$/Si substrate with Cr/Au (10/50 nm) as the source and drain electrodes as shown in Figure 5a. The SiO$_2$ layer thickness of the FET devices was 285 ± 20 nm. Specifically, the electrical performance of the FET devices was tested in the dark. Figure 5b shows the output curves of Sm-doped (red) and undoped (black) monolayer MoS$_2$ at a gate voltage of 10 V. The inset shows a microscopy image of the FET under the light microscope. It is clear that the output characteristics of monolayer MoS$_2$ were better than those of Sm doping under the same conditions, implying the restraint of electrical conductivity with Sm doping. This was due to the fact that the Sm element caused distortions in the lattice structure near the doping site, resulting in an inhomogeneous charge density distribution. Figure 5c,d shows the transfer curves of an MoS$_2$ FET with and without Sm doping. The undoped MoS$_2$ FET displayed typical n-type transport characteristics (black), as previously reported in the literature [23,37–39]. Compared to undoped MoS$_2$ (red), the threshold voltage (V_{th}) of Sm-doped MoS$_2$ moved from −12 to 0 V, as seen in Figure 5c. It can also be seen in Figure 5d that the inflection point of the transfer curve of the doped MoS$_2$ shifted to a more positive gate voltage with respect to the inflection point of the undoped MoS$_2$, implying a Fermi level closer to the valence band maximum (VBM) by Sm doping. More V_{ds} transfer characteristics of Sm-doped MoS$_2$ FET devices are shown in Figure S6 in the Supplementary Materials, where it can be seen that the V_{th} for doping all showed a tendency to shift towards a more positive gate voltage. The positive shift of the V_{th} was consistent with the p-type dopant behavior of in MoS$_2$ [40]. This was because during the Sm substitution doping process, the Sm 4f states contributed to the formation of a valence band and a hybridization of Sm 4f and Mo 4d on the edge of the valence band. This brought the Fermi energy level close to the valence band, leading to p-type doping. Furthermore, this was also coherent with the p-type doping conclusion obtained from the core energy level of XPS that shifted towards a lower binding energy. However, significant p-type (hole-transport) behavior of MoS$_2$ devices was not observed, presumably due to the Fermi-level pinning of the Cr/Au contact metal close to the conduction band of MoS$_2$ [33,41] or a smaller shift in the Fermi energy level caused by a smaller doping concentration. Figure 5e,f shows the band alignment diagrams and the formation of the Schottky barrier (SB) before and after doping. The figure shows the schematic of an energy diagram of a Cr/Au electrode and an MoS$_2$ monolayer where the work functions of Cr (Φ_{Cr}) and Au (Φ_{Au}) were 4.5 and 5.1 eV, respectively [38], and the electron affinity (χ) of MoS$_2$ was ~4.2 eV [42]. The energy band of the MoS$_2$ bended upon contact to form the SB (blue line). Sm doping in MoS$_2$ caused the Fermi energy to shift closer to the VBM and the impurity level to be close to the VBM. Additionally, an empty Sm 4f state was present at the bottom of the conduction band. All of this led to the Fermi energy level being closer to valence band and an increase the height of the SB$_{Sm}$, as well as a decrease in device current. Moreover, this corresponded to the actual measured electrical properties. The field-effect mobility (μ_{FE}) could be calculated from transfer curve (Figure 5d) according to the following equation [39]:

$$\mu_{FE} = \frac{dI_{ds}}{dV_g} \cdot \frac{L}{W} \cdot \frac{1}{C_g \cdot V_d} \quad (1)$$

$$C_g = \frac{\varepsilon_0 \varepsilon_r}{d} \quad (2)$$

where dI_{ds}/dV_g is the slope of the transfer curve; L and W are the length and width of the channel, respectively; V_d is the drain voltage; C_g is area-normalized capacitance of 280 nm-thick SiO$_2$; ε_0 is vacuum dielectric constant; ε_r is relative dielectric constant; and d is the SiO$_2$ thickness. The calculation gave mobility values of 4.35 and 3.08 cm^2/Vs for Sm-doped and undoped uncased monolayer FETs, respectively. Furthermore, the on/off current ratio for V_g ranged from −30 to +30 V, with a source-drain bias of 0.5 V for the Sm-doped monolayer MoS$_2$ FET of about 3 × 10^4, which was higher than that of the undoped monolayer MoS$_2$—5 × 10^3. This represented a 500% improvement in the on/off performance of the doped device, but the change in migration rate was not very significant. The I_{ds}–V_g curve in Figure 5c indicates that the FET made of Sm-doped MoS$_2$ showed a current density close to the MoS$_2$ FET at the "on" state but a much lower current density (1000 times lower) at the "off" state. These results suggested that Sm doping reduced the electron density in MoS$_2$ and led to a small I_{off}. As a result, both the radius difference and concentration of impurities can affect the electrical properties of monolayer MoS2. This is because the lattice distortion caused by the doped atoms can change the energy band structure of monolayer MoS$_2$ and affect the charge distribution, and the doping concentration determines the variation in band gap width and Femi energy level.

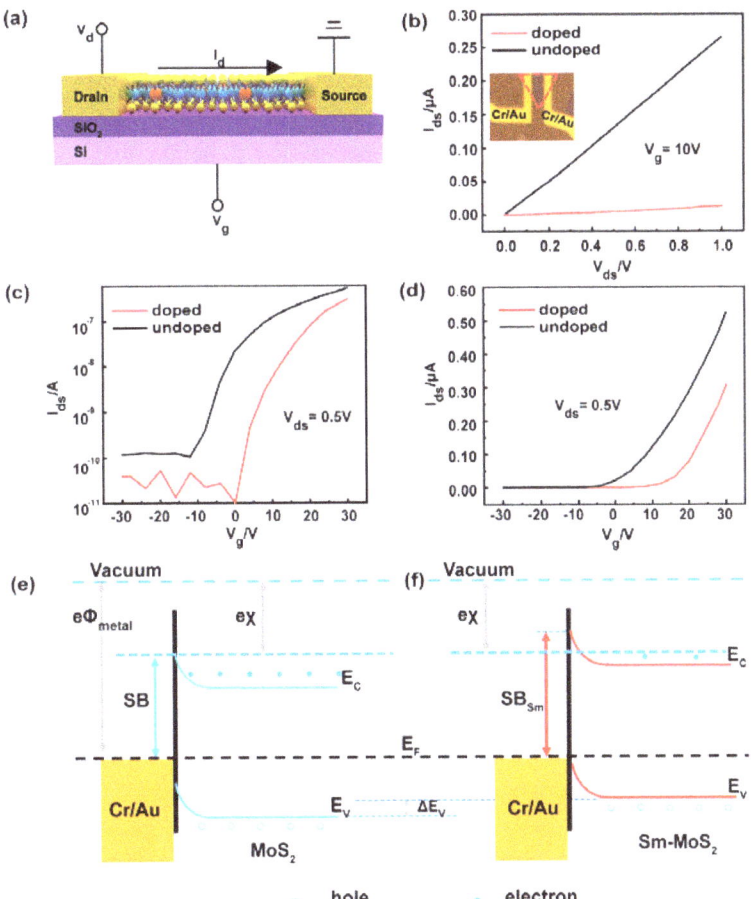

Figure 5. Electrical properties of monolayer MoS$_2$ and Sm-doped MoS$_2$. (**a**) The schematic drawing of a Sm-doped monolayer MoS$_2$ FET. (**b**) Output curves (I_{ds}–V_{ds}) of MoS$_2$ and Sm-doped MoS$_2$ devices at a gate bias of 10 V. The inset is the topography of the device. (**c**) Source-drain current (I_{ds}) vs gate voltage (V_g) characteristics of monolayer MoS$_2$ and the Sm-doped MoS$_2$ FET device at a drain voltage (V_{ds}) of 0.5 V on a log scale. (**d**) Transfer curves (I_{ds}–V_g) of monolayer MoS$_2$ and the Sm-doped MoS$_2$ FET device with a V_g from −30 to 30 V. Band alignment diagrams and the formation of the Schottky barrier after contact between the Cr/Au electrode and (**e**) pristine MoS$_2$ (blue line) and (**f**) Sm-doped MoS$_2$ (red line).

4. Conclusions

In conclusion, Sm-doped monolayer triangular MoS$_2$ was successfully grown by CVD, which was confirmed to be monolayer by Raman and AFM measurements. FET devices were fabricated with the Sm-doped monolayer triangular MoS$_2$, and its V_{th} was shifted from −12 to 0 V compared to be undoped, MoS$_2$-based FETs. The positive shift change in V_{th} was attributed to the fact that Sm acted as substitutional p-type dopant in MoS$_2$, consistent with theoretical predictions and XPS analysis. The 500% increase in the on/off current ratio of Sm-doped devices was due to the reduction of the electron density in MoS$_2$ after Sm ion doping, which also led to a small I_{off}. This was due to the lattice strain caused by Sm doping. The above results show that RE element Sm substitutional doping can tune and enhance the electrical properties of monolayer MoS$_2$. This study opens up a wide range of applications for tuning the electrical properties of monolayer 2D-TMDCs by doping with RE elements.

Supplementary Materials: The following are available online at https://www.mdpi.com/2079-4991/11/3/769/s1. Figure S1: Schematic of the CVD system for growth of monolayer Sm-doped MoS$_2$ film on SiO$_2$/Si substrate. Figure S2: Optical image of triangular monolayer Sm-doped MoS$_2$. Figure S3: Disordered and irregular films during CVD doping growth and the respective corresponding Raman spectra. Figure S4: Optical microscopy images of (a) Sm-doped and (c) undoped MoS$_2$ triangles. AFM images and the height of (b) Sm-doped and (d) undoped MoS$_2$. Figure S5. (a) Low-magnification TEM image of Sm-doped MoS$_2$ single crystal on a Cu grid. SAED patterns (b,c) collected from different sites on the monolayer triangle Sm-doped MoS$_2$. (d) Low-magnification TEM image of Sm-doped MoS$_2$; the red box shows the measured area of figure (e). EDS spectrum (e) of Sm-doped MoS$_2$ with Mo, Sm, and S labels and inset showing the atomic percent of labeled elements. Inset: partial enlargement. Figure S6: (a) Photomicrograph of the FET device. (b) Transfer curves (I_{ds}–V_g) of monolayer MoS$_2$ FET device at drain voltages (V_{ds}) of 0.1, 1, and 2 V with V_g varying from −30 to 30 V. (c) Transfer curves (I_{ds}–V_g) of monolayer Sm-doped MoS$_2$ FET device at drain voltages (V_{ds}) of 0. 1, 1, and 2 V with V_g varying from −30 to 30 V. Transfer curves (I_{ds}–V_g) comparing of monolayer MoS$_2$ and Sm-doped MoS$_2$ at drain voltages (V_{ds}) 2 V (d), 1 V (e), and 0. 1 V (f) with V_g varying from −30 to 30 V.

Author Contributions: Conceptualization, S.L., L.C., and J.Z.; methodology, S.L. and Y.Y.; validation, S.L., S.T., and M.H.; formal analysis, S.L. and S.T.; investigation, S.L. and S.T.; writing—original draft preparation, S.L.; writing—review and editing, S.L., L.C., Y.Z., and J.Z.; supervision, L.C., Y.Z., and J.Z.; project administration, L.C., Y.Z., and J.Z.; funding acquisition, L.C., Y.Z., and J.Z. All authors have read and agreed to the published version of the manuscript.

Funding: This work was supported by National Key R & D Project from Minister of Science and Technology, China (2016YFA0202703), the National Natural Science Foundation of China (Grant No. 52073032, 61904013 and 51872031) and the Fundamental Research Funds for the Central Universities.

Acknowledgments: In this section, you can acknowledge any support given which is not covered by the author contribution or funding sections. This may include administrative and technical support, or donations in kind (e.g., materials used for experiments).

Conflicts of Interest: The authors declare no conflict of interest.

References

1. Wang, Q.H.; Kalantar-Zadeh, K.; Kis, A.; Coleman, J.N.; Strano, M.S. Electronics and optoelectronics of two-dimensional transition metal dichalcogenides. *Nat. Nanotechnol.* **2012**, *7*, 699–712. [CrossRef] [PubMed]
2. Zhang, K.; Feng, S.; Wang, J.; Azcatl, A.; Lu, N.; Addou, R.; Wang, N.; Zhou, C.; Lerach, J.; Bojan, V.; et al. Manganese Doping of Monolayer MoS$_2$: The Substrate Is Critical. *Nano Lett.* **2015**, *15*, 6586–6591. [CrossRef]
3. Wang, Y.; Tseng, L.-T.; Murmu, P.P.; Bao, N.; Kennedy, J.; Ionesc, M.; Ding, J.; Suzuki, K.; Li, S.; Yi, J. Defects engineering induced room temperature ferromagnetism in transition metal doped MoS$_2$. *Mater. Des.* **2017**, *121*, 77–84. [CrossRef]
4. Li, W.; Huang, J.; Han, B.; Xie, C.; Huang, X.; Tian, K.; Zeng, Y.; Zhao, Z.; Gao, P.; Zhang, Y.; et al. Molten-Salt-Assisted Chemical Vapor Deposition Process for Substitutional Doping of Monolayer MoS$_2$ and Effectively Altering the Electronic Structure and Phononic Properties. *Adv. Sci.* **2020**, *7*, 2001080. [CrossRef] [PubMed]
5. Tang, J.; Wei, Z.; Wang, Q.; Wang, Y.; Han, B.; Li, X.; Huang, B.; Liao, M.; Liu, J.; Li, N.; et al. In Situ Oxygen Doping of Monolayer MoS$_2$ for Novel Electronics. *Small* **2020**, *16*, 2004276. [CrossRef]

6. Zhao, Y.; Xu, K.; Pan, F.; Zhou, C.; Zhou, F.; Chai, Y. Doping, Contact and Interface Engineering of Two-Dimensional Layered Transition Metal Dichalcogenides Transistors. *Adv. Funct. Mater.* **2017**, *27*, 1603484. [CrossRef]
7. Qin, Z.; Loh, L.; Wang, J.; Xu, X.; Zhang, Q.; Haas, B.; Alvarez, C.; Okuno, H.; Yong, J.Z.; Schultz, T.; et al. Growth of Nb-Doped Monolayer WS2 by Liquid-Phase Precursor Mixing. *ACS Nano* **2019**, *13*, 10768–10775. [CrossRef] [PubMed]
8. Zhang, F.; Zheng, B.; Sebastian, A.; Olson, D.H.; Liu, M.; Fujisawa, K.; Pham, Y.T.H.; Jimenez, V.O.; Kalappattil, V.; Miao, L.; et al. Monolayer Vanadium-Doped Tungsten Disulfide: A Room-Temperature Dilute Magnetic Semiconductor. *Adv. Sci.* **2020**, *7*, 2001174. [CrossRef] [PubMed]
9. Pham, Y.T.H.; Liu, M.; Jimenez, V.O.; Yu, Z.; Kalappattil, V.; Zhang, F.; Wang, K.; Williams, T.; Terrones, M.; Phan, M.H. Tunable Ferromagnetism and Thermally Induced Spin Flip in Vanadium-Doped Tungsten Diselenide Monolayers at Room Temperature. *Adv. Mater.* **2020**, *32*, 2003607. [CrossRef] [PubMed]
10. Fu, S.; Kang, K.; Shayan, K.; Yoshimura, A.; Dadras, S.; Wang, X.; Zhang, L.; Chen, S.; Liu, N.; Jindal, A.; et al. Enabling room temperature ferromagnetism in monolayer MoS_2 via in situ iron-doping. *Nat. Commun.* **2020**, *11*, 2034. [CrossRef] [PubMed]
11. Zhang, K.; Bersch, B.M.; Joshi, J.; Addou, R.; Cormier, C.R.; Zhang, C.; Xu, K.; Briggs, N.C.; Wang, K.; Subramanian, S.; et al. Tuning the Electronic and Photonic Properties of Monolayer MoS_2 via In Situ Rhenium Substitutional Doping. *Adv. Funct. Mater.* **2018**, *28*, 1706950. [CrossRef]
12. Cai, Z.; Shen, T.; Zhu, Q.; Feng, S.; Yu, Q.; Liu, J.; Tang, L.; Zhao, Y.; Wang, J.; Liu, B.; et al. Dual-Additive Assisted Chemical Vapor Deposition for the Growth of Mn-Doped 2D MoS_2 with Tunable Electronic Properties. *Small* **2020**, *16*, 1903181. [CrossRef]
13. Feng, S.; Lin, Z.; Gan, X.; Lv, R.; Terrones, M. Doping two-dimensional materials: Ultra-sensitive sensors, band gap tuning and ferromagnetic monolayers. *Nanoscale Horiz.* **2017**, *2*, 72–80. [CrossRef] [PubMed]
14. Qin, X.; Liu, X.; Huang, W.; Bettinelli, M.; Liu, X. Lanthanide-Activated Phosphors Based on 4f-5d Optical Transitions: Theoretical and Experimental Aspects. *Chem. Rev.* **2017**, *117*, 4488–4527. [CrossRef]
15. Gai, S.; Li, C.; Yang, P.; Lin, J. Recent progress in rare earth micro/nanocrystals: Soft chemical synthesis, luminescent properties, and biomedical applications. *Chem. Rev.* **2014**, *114*, 2343–2389. [CrossRef] [PubMed]
16. Bai, G.; Yuan, S.; Zhao, Y.; Yang, Z.; Choi, S.Y.; Chai, Y.; Yu, S.F.; Lau, S.P.; Hao, J. 2D Layered Materials of Rare-Earth Er-Doped MoS_2 with NIR-to-NIR Down- and Up-Conversion Photoluminescence. *Adv. Mater.* **2016**, *28*, 7472–7477. [CrossRef] [PubMed]
17. Zhao, Q.; Lu, Q.; Liu, Y.; Zhang, M. Two-dimensional Dy doped MoS_2 ferromagnetic sheets. *Appl. Surf. Sci.* **2019**, *471*, 118–123. [CrossRef]
18. Ouma, C.N.M.; Singh, S.; Obodo, K.O.; Amolo, G.O.; Romero, A.H. Controlling the magnetic and optical responses of a MoS_2 monolayer by lanthanide substitutional doping: A first-principles study. *Phys. Chem. Chem. Phys.* **2017**, *19*, 25555–25563. [CrossRef]
19. Majid, A.; Imtiaz, A.; Yoshiya, M. A density functional theory study of electronic and magnetic properties of rare earth doped monolayered molybdenum disulphide. *J. Appl. Phys.* **2016**, *120*, 142124. [CrossRef]
20. Zhang, Z.; Zhao, H.; Zhang, C.; Luo, F.; Du, Y. Rare-earth-incorporated low-dimensional chalcogenides: Dry-method syntheses and applications. *InfoMat* **2020**, *2*, 466–482. [CrossRef]
21. Lyu, Y.; Wu, Z.; Io, W.F.; Hao, J. Observation and theoretical analysis of near-infrared luminescence from CVD grown lanthanide Er doped monolayer MoS_2 triangles. *Appl. Phys. Lett.* **2019**, *115*, 153105. [CrossRef]
22. Xu, D.; Chen, W.; Zeng, M.; Xue, H.; Chen, Y.; Sang, X.; Xiao, Y.; Zhang, T.; Unocic, R.R.; Xiao, K.; et al. Crystal-Field Tuning of Photoluminescence in Two-Dimensional Materials with Embedded Lanthanide Ions. *Angew. Chem. Int. Ed. Engl.* **2018**, *57*, 755–759. [CrossRef] [PubMed]
23. Radisavljevic, B.; Radenovic, A.; Brivio, J.; Giacometti, V.; Kis, A. Single-layer MoS_2 transistors. *Nat. Nanotechnol.* **2011**, *6*, 147–150. [CrossRef]
24. Yang, Y.; Pu, H.; Di, J.; Zang, Y.; Zhang, S.; Chen, C. Synthesis and characterization of monolayer Er-doped MoS_2 films by chemical vapor deposition. *Scr. Mater.* **2018**, *152*, 64–68. [CrossRef]
25. Chae, W.H.; Cain, J.D.; Hanson, E.D.; Murthy, A.A.; Dravid, V.P. Substrate-induced strain and charge doping in CVD-grown monolayer MoS_2. *Appl. Phys. Lett.* **2017**, *111*, 143106. [CrossRef]
26. Jeon, J.; Jang, S.K.; Jeon, S.M.; Yoo, G.; Jang, Y.H.; Park, J.H.; Lee, S. Layer-controlled CVD growth of large-area two-dimensional MoS_2 films. *Nanoscale* **2015**, *7*, 1688–1695. [CrossRef]
27. Zhang, K.; Peng, M.; Wu, W.; Guo, J.; Gao, G.; Liu, Y.; Kou, J.; Wen, R.; Lei, Y.; Yu, A.; et al. A flexible p-CuO/n-MoS_2 heterojunction photodetector with enhanced photoresponse by the piezo-phototronic effect. *Mater. Horiz.* **2017**, *4*, 274–280. [CrossRef]
28. Zhang, K.; Peng, M.; Yu, A.; Fan, Y.; Zhai, J.; Wang, Z.L. A substrate-enhanced MoS_2 photodetector through a dual-photogating effect. *Mater. Horiz.* **2019**, *6*, 826–833. [CrossRef]
29. Şar, H.; Özden, A.; Demiroğlu, İ.; Sevik, C.; Perkgoz, N.K.; Ay, F. Long-Term Stability Control of CVD-Grown Monolayer MoS_2. *Phys. Status Solidi. RRL* **2019**, *13*, 1800687. [CrossRef]
30. Lee, C.; Yan, H.; Brus, L.; Heinz, T.; Hone, J.; Ryu, S. Anomalous Lattice Vibrations of Single-and Few-Layer MoS_2. *ACS Nano* **2010**, *4*, 2695–2700. [CrossRef] [PubMed]
31. Paul, K.K.; Mawlong, L.P.L.; Giri, P.K. Trion-Inhibited Strong Excitonic Emission and Broadband Giant Photoresponsivity from Chemical Vapor-Deposited Monolayer MoS_2 Grown in Situ on TiO_2 Nanostructure. *ACS Appl. Mater. Interfaces* **2018**, *10*, 42812–42825. [CrossRef]

32. Michail, A.; Delikoukos, N.; Parthenios, J.; Galiotis, C.; Papagelis, K. Optical detection of strain and doping inhomogeneities in single layer MoS$_2$. *Appl. Phys. Lett.* **2016**, *108*, 173102. [CrossRef]
33. Zhang, S.; Hill, H.M.; Moudgil, K.; Richter, C.A.; Hight Walker, A.R.; Barlow, S.; Marder, S.R.; Hacker, C.A.; Pookpanratana, S.J. Controllable, Wide-Ranging n-Doping and p-Doping of Monolayer Group 6 Transition-Metal Disulfides and Diselenides. *Adv. Mater.* **2018**, *30*, 1802991. [CrossRef]
34. Ganta, D.; Sinha, S.; Haasch, R.T. 2D Material Molybdenum Disulfide Analyzed by XPS. *Surf. Sci. Spectra* **2014**, *21*, 19–27. [CrossRef]
35. Peterson, P.F.; Olds, D.; Savici, A.T.; Zhou, W. Advances in utilizing eVent based data structures for neutron scattering experiments. *Rev. Sci. Instrum.* **2018**, *89*, 093001. [CrossRef]
36. Han, W.; Li, Z.; Li, M.; Li, W.; Zhang, M.; Yang, X.; Sun, Y. Reductive extraction of lanthanides (Ce,Sm) and its monitoring in LiCl KCl/Bi Li system. *J. Nucl. Mater.* **2019**, *514*, 311–320. [CrossRef]
37. Lopez-Sanchez, O.; Lembke, D.; Kayci, M.; Radenovic, A.; Kis, A. Ultrasensitive photodetectors based on monolayer MoS$_2$. *Nat. Nanotechnol.* **2013**, *8*, 497–501. [CrossRef]
38. Liu, B.; Chen, L.; Liu, G.; Abbas, A.N. High-performance chemical sensing using Schottky-contacted chemical vapor deposition grown monolayer MoS$_2$ transistors. *ACS Nano* **2014**, *8*, 5304–5314. [CrossRef] [PubMed]
39. Jariwala, D.; Sangwan, V.K.; Late, D.J.; Johns, J.E.; Dravid, V.P.; Marks, T.J.; Lauhon, L.J.; Hersam, M.C. Band-like transport in high mobility unencapsulated single-layer MoS$_2$ transistors. *Appl. Phys. Lett.* **2013**, *102*, 173107. [CrossRef]
40. Zhang, F.; Appenzeller, J. Tunability of short-channel effects in MoS$_2$ field-effect devices. *Nano Lett.* **2015**, *15*, 301–306. [CrossRef]
41. Kim, C.; Moon, I.; Lee, D.; Choi, M.S.; Ahmed, F.; Nam, S.; Cho, Y.; Shin, H.J.; Park, S.; Yoo, W.J. Fermi Level Pinning at Electrical Metal Contacts of Monolayer Molybdenum Dichalcogenides. *ACS Nano* **2017**, *11*, 1588–1596. [CrossRef] [PubMed]
42. Kalanyan, B.; Kimes, W.A.; Beams, R.; Stranick, S.J.; Garratt, E.; Kalish, I.; Davydov, A.V.; Kanjolia, R.K.; Maslar, J.E. Rapid Wafer-Scale Growth of Polycrystalline 2H-MoS$_2$ by Pulsed Metalorganic Chemical Vapor Deposition. *Chem. Mater.* **2017**, *29*, 6279–6288. [CrossRef] [PubMed]

Article

A Rational Fabrication Method for Low Switching-Temperature VO$_2$

László Pósa [1,2], György Molnár [1], Benjamin Kalas [1], Zsófia Baji [1], Zsolt Czigány [1], Péter Petrik [1] and János Volk [1,*]

[1] Centre for Energy Research, Institute of Technical Physics and Materials Science, Konkoly-Thege M. út 29–33, 1121 Budapest, Hungary; posa.laszlo@energia.mta.hu (L.P.); molnar.gyorgy@energia.mta.hu (G.M.); kalas.benjamin@energia.mta.hu (B.K.); baji.zsofia@energia.mta.hu (Z.B.); czigany.zsolt@energia.mta.hu (Z.C.); petrik.peter@energia.mta.hu (P.P.)
[2] Department of Physics, Budapest University of Technology and Economics, Budafoki út 8, 1111 Budapest, Hungary
* Correspondence: volk.janos@energia.mta.hu

Abstract: Due to its remarkable switching effect in electrical and optical properties, VO$_2$ is a promising material for several applications. However, the stoichiometry control of multivalent vanadium oxides, especially with a rational deposition technique, is still challenging. Here, we propose and optimize a simple fabrication method for VO$_2$ rich layers by the oxidation of metallic vanadium in atmospheric air. It was shown that a sufficiently broad annealing time window of 3.0–3.5 h can be obtained at an optimal oxidation temperature of 400 °C. The presence of VO$_2$ was detected by selected area diffraction in a transmission electron microscope. According to the temperature dependent electrical measurements, the resistance contrast ($R_{30\,°C}/R_{100\,°C}$) varied between 44 and 68, whereas the optical switching was confirmed using in situ spectroscopic ellipsometric measurement by monitoring the complex refractive indices. The obtained phase transition temperature, both for the electrical resistance and for the ellipsometric angles, was found to be 49 ± 7 °C, i.e., significantly lower than that of the bulk VO$_2$ of 68 ± 6 °C.

Keywords: phase transition; thermal oxidation; thermochromism

1. Introduction

Vanadium is a transition-metal which can coordinate to oxygen in different polyhedral structures forming a large variety of crystalline structures. Besides the single valence vanadium oxides, such as VO, V$_2$O$_3$, VO$_2$ and V$_2$O$_5$, several mixed valence states exist which can be grouped into Magneli series (V$_n$O$_{2n-1}$) between VO$_2$ and V$_2$O$_5$ phases and Wadsley series (V$_n$O$_{2n+1}$) between V$_2$O$_3$ and VO$_2$ phases. Vanadium-oxides are known by their wide range of applications from catalyst to energy storage [1–3]; however, one of their most remarkable features is the semiconductor to metal transition (SMT), due to external stimuli, i.e., temperature or electric field. The electrical conductivity of many vanadium-oxides changes several orders of magnitude as the transition temperature is crossed.

Among the series of oxides, VO$_2$ is the most studied material due to its transition close to room temperature at 68 °C, where the crystalline structure of the material reorganises from monoclinic to tetragonal rutile structure [4]. In bulk VO$_2$ besides the five orders of magnitude change in the electrical conductivity, the optical transmission also undergoes a substantial reduction, especially in the near-infrared regime. Therefore, all the optical and electrical properties of the material can be controlled through the SMT. This quality makes VO$_2$ an excellent material for optical switching [5], THz switch [6], sensors [7,8] or resistive switch [4,9]. Smart thermochromic coating on glass is also a promising application, which exploits the variation of transmission around the transition temperature [10]. The film turns opaque with respect to near-IR, without any extra stimuli or energy consumption. However, slightly lower transition temperature (20–40 °C) would be preferable. Doping of the VO$_2$ layer by W, Mo or Nb can improve this drawback [1]. Other studies demonstrated that smaller grain size [11,12] or stress stemming from substrate effect [13] can also reduce the phase transition temperature, but improvement of their reliability is still desired.

Due to the several oxidation states of vanadium, preparation of VO$_2$ film is highly challenging. Among the numerous thin film deposition techniques, such as evaporation [14], pulsed-laser deposition [15], chemical vapor deposition (CVD) [16] and atomic layer deposition (ALD) [17], the magnetron sputtering [11] is the preferred process due to its simplicity and high controllability. However, all of these methods suffer from narrow process windows, i.e., minor changes in the growth parameters can cause significant degradation in the performance of electrical/optical switching. Recently, significant progress has been achieved in the field of low temperature (250–300 °C) deposition using high-power impulse magnetron sputtering (HiPIMS) [18–20]; however, the most conventional methods still require high annealing temperatures (typically >500 °C) to improve the crystallinity and the stoichiometry of the film [21,22]. All these requirements make difficult to prepare highly reliable layers and integrate VO$_2$ into the standard CMOS process flow.

Oxidation of metallic vanadium films by thermal annealing provides a cheap and simple method for preparing vanadium-oxides; however, it also requires a precise control of the parameters to achieve the appropriate phase [23]. Since V$_2$O$_5$ is the thermodynamically most stable stoichiometry, at high O$_2$ partial pressure [24] during the oxidation, the VO$_2$ is only an intermediary phase with many other oxides towards the formation of V$_2$O$_5$. This phenomenon is most pronounced during oxidation in air, which would offer a temptingly simple approach for VO$_2$ synthesis. Therefore, reports on thermal oxidation of vanadium [12,23,25–29] also share the difficulty of a narrow process window, i.e., the pressure, the temperature and the annealing time must be adjusted very precisely to obtain the maximum fraction of crystalline VO$_2$.

The present work focuses on the preparation of VO$_2$ films with thermal oxidation of evaporated vanadium films in air. This method, combined with the measurement of electrical resistance, provides a simple, quick and sensitive optimization procedure. We found that a slightly lower than conventionally applied annealing temperature (400 °C) results in a 30 min wide process window in respect to the oxidation time. Moreover, the result of the oxidation was not sensitive to the initial quality of the metal layer; we got the same switching behavior even if the vanadium film was exposed to air for seven months. Detailed studies conducted on structural and optical properties of the optimized film revealed that the electrical and optical switching properties are maintained in case of moderate VO$_2$ content as well. This preparation approach offers a highly flexible and cost effective method to synthesise vanadium-dioxide films.

2. Materials and Methods

Metallic vanadium thin films were deposited on (100)-oriented Si wafers covered by 1.3 µm SiO$_2$. Before loading the samples into the oil free evaporation chamber, their surfaces were cleaned with cc. HNO$_3$ and DI water. Vanadium ingot of 99.5% purity was evaporated using an electron gun. The evaporation rate was between 0.2 and 0.3 nm/s, at a pressure of 3×10^{-8} Torr during deposition. The film thickness was controlled by a vibrating quartz crystal. The deposited vanadium thickness was 104 ± 4 nm according to the in situ measurement. The post deposition heat treatments were carried out in a tube furnace in air at atmospheric pressure. The annealing temperature (T_a) varied between 350 °C and 500 °C and the annealing times (t_a) were between 1 and 4 h. The annealing temperatures were measured by a small heat capacity NiCr-Ni thermocouple.

The optimization of the annealing parameters was based on temperature dependent resistance measurement between room temperature and 100 °C. The hysteresis properties (resistance contrast, transition temperature, hysteresis width) are greatly affected by the stoichiometry and the structural quality of the deposited film, e.g., grain size, stress, cleanness, which allows us a simple and sensitive characterization of the oxide layers. The resistance was acquired between two gold contacts evaporated onto the oxide surface after the oxidation, whereas the temperature was controlled by a Peltier-modul and measured by Pt1000 temperature sensor on the surface of the silicon wafer. The layer was biased by a data acquisition device, while the current was measured by a current amplifier.

The optimized oxide layers were further investigated in respect to its microstructure and optical properties. High resolution transmission electron microscopy (TEM) observation was performed by a JEOL JEM-3010 HREM instrument. Cross sectional TEM specimens were prepared by ion beam milling using a Technoorg Linda ionmill with 10 keV Ar^+ ions at an incidence angle of 5° with respect to the surface. In the final period of the milling process, the ion energy was decreased gradually to 0.3 keV to minimize ion-induced structural changes in the surface layers.

For characterizing the optical properties of the thin film at various temperatures, a Woollam M2000DI spectroscopic ellipsometer was used in a rotating compensator configuration. The sample was placed on a ceramic sample stage located in a custom-made quartz heating cell. The tube-shaped cell had a diameter of 5 cm and a length of 20 cm and it was sealed on both ends. The sample was measured prior to SMT and subsequently real time measurement was performed with a time resolution of 3 s in the available wavelength range of 265 nm to 1690 nm. During the real time measurement, a maximum temperature of 100 °C was achieved with a temperature gradient of 7 °C/min. The same gradient with the opposite sign was used for reaching room temperature again after the heating process.

3. Results And Discussion

3.1. Electrical Properties

Figure 1a shows a typical temperature dependent electrical resistance trace of an oxidized V film. The nearly two orders of magnitude changes in resistance close to room temperature anticipates VO_2 rich content. The quality of the transition is characterized by the three main parameters of the R-T curve: the transition temperature, the hysteresis width and the magnitude of the resistance change. The transition temperature (T_c) is determined by the minimum value of the derivative curve ($dlog(R)/dT$), is 56 °C during the heating and 43 °C during the cooling branch. The significant lower transition temperature compared to the pure VO_2 (68 °C) can be attributed to either the non-stoichiometric composition [30], the stress due to the lattice mismatch with the SiO_2 substrate [13] or the small grain size [11,12]. The transition temperature of our VO_x film is about 10 °C lower than layers which were oxidized in air by other groups [23,29,31]. This drop in the T_c may be ascribed to the lower annealing temperature. The hysteresis width (the difference of the heating T_c and cooling T_c) is around 10–13 °C, which is a typical value for polycrystalline thin films [23,29]. The magnitude of the transition is calculated by the resistance contrast between 30 °C and 100 °C (see blue and red dots, respectively, in Figure 1a on the heating branch) and its value for this particular sample is 68. This resistance switching ratio is in the same regime [23,29,31] or higher [12,28] than the other layers which were prepared by oxidation of metallic V under atmospheric pressure. However, all those samples were annealed at higher temperature and required a more thorough optimization process, because a few percent variation in the oxidation time leads a substantial change in the hysteresis curve.

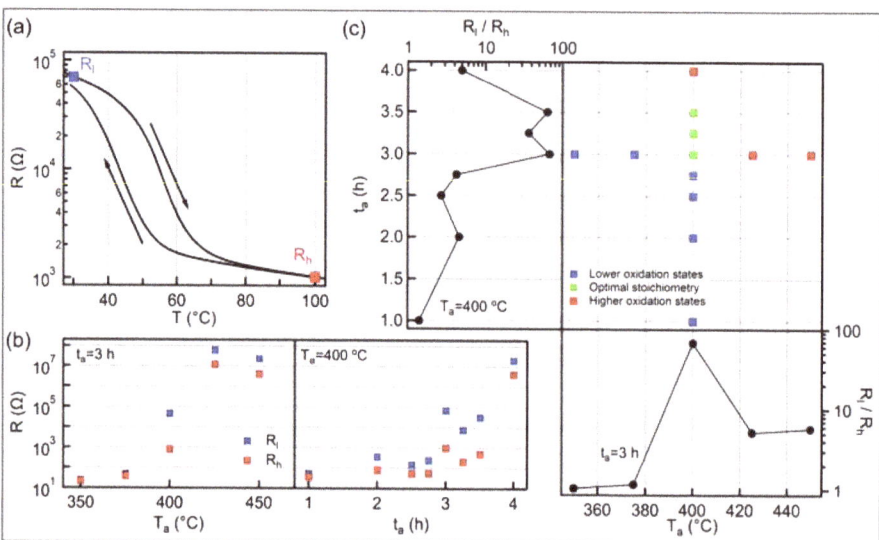

Figure 1. (a) Typical temperature dependent resistance curve of VO_x film oxidized at T_a = 400 °C for t_a = 3.0 h. The blue/red dot marks the resistance at 30/100 °C on the heating branch (R_l and R_h, respectively), whereas the arrows indicate the direction of the hysteresis curve. (b) Evolution of the low (blue dots) and high (red dots) temperature resistances as a function of annealing temperature (left panel) and annealing time (right panel), while the other oxidation parameters are fixed. The layers are considered to low oxygen content if the resistance is lower than 1 kΩ and high oxygen content if the resistance is higher than 1 MΩ during the heating cycle. (c) The applied annealing time and temperature combinations (middle panel), the colors of the dots indicate the oxidation state of the vanadium according to the electrical property. The resistance switching ratios (R_l/R_h) are also shown as a function of the annealing temperature (bottom panel) and annealing time (left panel). The films with optimal stoichiometry exhibit good electrical switching effect.

To examine the effect of annealing parameters to the SMT we varied either the annealing temperature (T_a) or the time (t_a), while the other parameter was fixed. In left panel of Figure 1b we plot the evolution of low (blue dots) and high (red dots) temperature resistance values as a function of T_a at fixed t_a = 3.0 h. Three regions can be observed as we increase the annealing temperature. Below 400 °C, the layers show metallic behaviour with low resistance (<100 Ω). This quality changes suddenly at T_a = 400 °C, where both resistances increase more than one order of magnitude, while the film exhibits resistance switching effect. Finally, above 400 °C, the resistances suddenly increase again, indicating insulator property. This tendency demonstrates well the narrow process window around 400 °C. In contrast, phase transition occurs in a wide range when varying the oxidation time (t_a) at a fixed temperature of 400 °C (see right panel of Figure 1b). The transitions between the different oxidation states are also sharp but the quality of the VO_x films does not change significantly between the annealing times of 3.0 and 3.5 h. This finding refers to a wide process window, which significantly promotes the reliable production of the VO_2 content that contribute to the phase change of the thin films. To demonstrate the robustness of the layer synthesis we created four VO_x films annealed at 400 °C for 3.0 h. Between the first and the last oxidation process seven months passed and meanwhile the metal layer was exposed to air, resulting gradually thickening native oxide layer. However, despite the different initial conditions, the electrical switching effect is always presented, whose magnitude varies between 44 and 68 and the transition temperature is in the range of 55–57 °C and 43–45 °C for heating and cooling branch, respectively.

The applied annealing temperature-time combinations during the optimization process are summarized in Figure 1c, whereas the corresponding resistance switching ratios (R_l/R_h) are shown in side panels as a function of the annealing parameters. The layers are classified into three categories according to their electrical properties. If the switching ratio is higher than 10, the oxide layer is considered to VO$_2$ content (green dots). Those samples that do not show electrical switching are denoted to low/high oxygen content if they show metallic/insulating behaviour (blue and red dots, respectively). We obtain VO$_2$ rich film, when the annealing time is between 3.0–3.5 h at T_a = 400 °C. The background of this wide process window in the oxidation time can be explained by exponential dependence on the oxidation rate from the temperature. The reaction rate of the vanadium oxidation can be described by the Arrhenius expression with activation energy between 128–177 kJ/mol [23,32]. The optimal annealing temperatures in case of 3.0 h and 3.5 h annealing time are around 400 °C and there are only a few degrees difference between them [23]. Therefore, the oxidation state must change slowly during this period, opening a wide process window in the oxidation time.

3.2. Structural Analysis

Figure 2a shows a scanning electron microscope (SEM) image about the surface morphology of a VO$_x$ film annealed at 400 °C for 3.0 h. The layer has a polycrystalline structure with anisotropic grains whose lateral size can exceed 100–200 nm, confirming the crystalline structure. The thickness variation of the VO$_x$ film as a function of the oxidation time and temperature was studied by taking cross-sectional SEM images. We found monotonically increasing tendency when the annealing temperature was raised from 375 °C to 425 °C, see Figure 2b–d. This is in accord with the theoretical considerations, since during the oxidation process the mass of the vanadium-oxide film increases with the oxidation state, while the mass density monotonically decreases. Taking into account the molar mass and the density of V and VO$_2$, we anticipate a factor of 2.18 in the film thickness expansion if the V layer transforms into pure VO$_2$. The SEM image yields an expansion ratio of 2.06 ± 0.18 in the case of optimal stoichiometry (400 °C, 3.0 h), which is close to the theoretical expectation and agree with the results of other groups [25,33,34]. In contrast, the lower/higher oxidation temperature resulted significantly different ratios (1.64 and 2.54, respectively), referring to different oxidation states. This finding indicates that the in situ thickness measurement could also act as a very simple method to optimize the oxidation parameters. Such a large difference in the thickness could not be observed when the oxidation time was varied between 3.0 h and 3.5 h, the variation of the thicknesses were within the range of 10%.

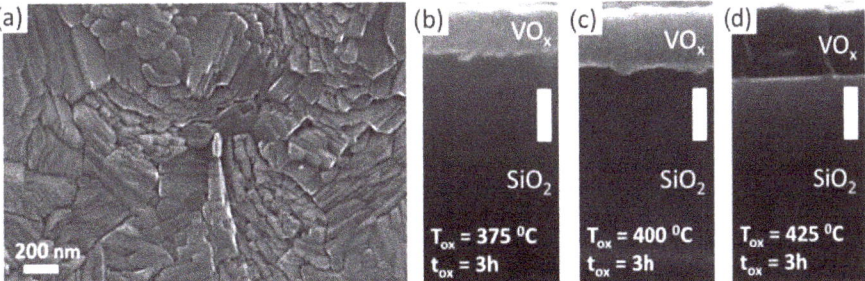

Figure 2. (a) Scanning electron microscope (SEM) micrograph of the top surface of a VO$_x$ film oxidized at 400 °C for 3.0 h. (b–d) Series of SEM images of the cross section of VO$_x$ layers oxidized at different temperatures for 3.0 h. The thickness monotonically increases with the temperature. All white scale bars on the images indicate 200 nm.

Figure 3 shows transmission electron microscope (TEM) images of the VO$_x$ film. They reveal that the ≈200 nm thick layer is not homogeneous. The bottom part of the film contains smaller particles with a typical grain size of less than 50 nm, whereas in the top part, larger grains are presented with lateral sizes of ≈100 nm (see Figure 3a). In the high resolution image, the atomic planes are clearly seen in Figure 3b. According to the selected area electron diffraction pattern (see inset of Figure 3b), the crystalline structure is consistent with simultaneous presence of monoclinic and tetragonal phases, which are characteristic to VO_2. Although the tetragonal structure should be presented only above the phase transition temperature of the VO_2 grains, its existence can be the result of the heating effect of the electron beam. The presence of other oxides, e.g., orthorhombic V_2O_5 or rhombohedral V_2O_3 are negligible in the selected area as only a few interference rings can be assigned to these phases. To exclude the effect of the electron beam irradiation, e.g., electron beam-induced crystallization, we monitored the crystalline structure in time, but no changes were observed.

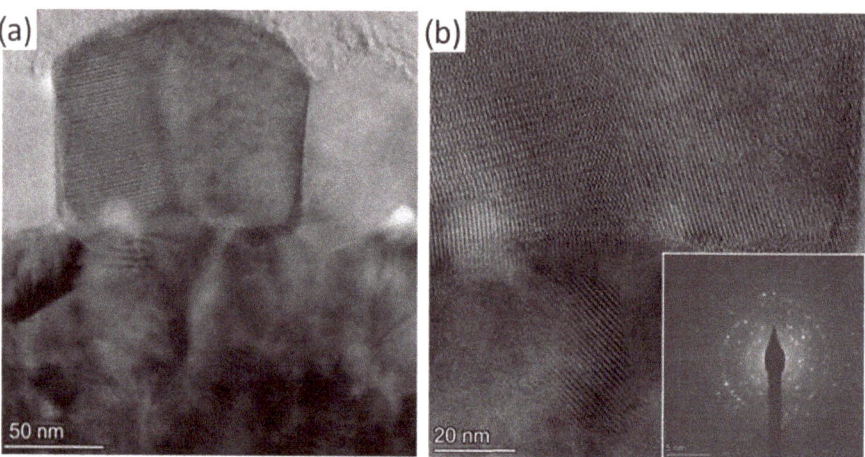

Figure 3. (a) TEM images of the VO_x film, showing around 100 nm large crytalline particle in the middle. (b) High resolution TEM image exhibiting crystalline atomic structure. The inset shows the diffraction pattern of a grain in the VO_x layer.

3.3. Optical Properties

In order to confirm that a similar low temperature switching occurs also in the near infrared optical properties, an in situ spectroscopic ellipsometry study was carried out. During the temperature dependent spectroscopic ellipsometry (SE) measurement we monitored the complex reflection coefficient (ρ) by collecting the Ψ and Δ ellipsometric angles, defined by $\rho = r_p/r_s = \tan(\Psi) \cdot \exp(i\Delta)$, where r_p and r_s are the complex reflection coefficients of the light polarized parallel and perpendicular to the plane of incidence, respectively. The annealed VO_x layer shows a reversible SMT during the heating cycle (see Figure 4a), the change in the ellipsometric angle Ψ has a maximum around 60° in the infrared wavelength range, in good agreement with previous reports [35]. The parameters of the hysteresis loop are in good accordance with the electrical characterization. The transition temperature (the maximum of $d\Psi/dT$) is around 61 °C during the heating process and 50 °C during the cooling process. The slightly higher transition temperature value in case of SE can be caused that the temperature is measured further from the sample. The optical model was set up according to the cross sectional TEM pictures where two VO_x layers (approximately 100–100 nm) were identified with different grain sizes. Thus, the model consists of a semi-infinite Si substrate, a SiO_2 layer and two VO_x thin layers. As a result of the analysis, the complex refractive index $\hat{n} = n + ik$ of the top VO_x layer was described by using three Gaussian-oscillators, whereas two oscillators were used for the bottom layer at room temperature and an additional Drude term for describing the metallic behaviour above the transition temperature (see Figure 4b).

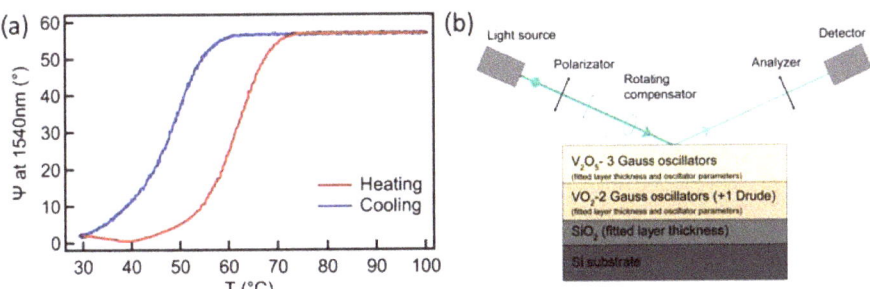

Figure 4. (a) Temperature dependent variation of Ψ during the heating cycle at the wavelength of 1540 nm wavelength in the infrared range. (b) Schematic of the applied optical model and the SE measurement arrangement.

The model fit identifies the top VO_x layer as V_2O_5 phase since the two interband transitions of pentoxide can be clearly seen near 3.0 and 4.5 eV [36,37]. The bottom VO_x layer corresponds to the VO_2 layer, the optical constants of which at the wavelength of 1540 nm at low and high temperature are (n_l, k_l) = (2.62, 0.47) and (n_h, k_h) = (2.16, 3.04), respectively, in excellent agreement with a recently reported VO_2 film, prepared by oxidation of reactive magnetron sputtered metallic V films [38]. Furthermore, our n_l/n_h and k_l/k_h ratios are in the ranges reported by other groups in the infrared wavelength range [35,38–40].

The topmost V_2O_5 layer is too thick to be regarded as a native oxide layer, therefore it had to be formed during the annealing process. The thermal oxidation of V film can be described by the Deal–Grove model [41], where diffusion and reaction are the two basic processes. If the initial V film is thick, the diffusion rate is lower than the reaction rate due to the long diffusion distance. In this diffusion-controlled regime the different valence states of V are layered after the oxidation, the highest valence state (V^{5+}, i.e., V_2O_5) is located at the top of the VO_x layer, while the lowest valence state is located at the substrate-layer interface. Both TEM and SE measurements confirmed the corresponding layered structure and accordingly below the VO_2 layer (V^{4+} valence state), there must be V^{3+} as well. The V^{3+} ions play major role in the tuning of the phase transition temperature, the oxygen vacancies reduce the T_c [26]. Our low transition temperature may arise from the high V^{3+} content. Although the T_c is still too high for smart window application, maybe it can be further reduced by using W doped V layer or V-W alloy. Recently, a new method was introduced, where the transition temperature was reduced to 22 °C by simultaneously sputtering V and W targets [42]. The V_2O_5 overlayer does not influence significantly the main character of the phase change, similar oxide layer was detected by XPS in other studies [25,26]. However, by etching the V_2O_5 layer from the surface, the magnitude of the transmission modulation can be increased a little.

Depending on the potential application, different film thickness is desired. In the case of smart window application typically 50-200 nm thick VO_2 film is applied [10,43], which matches to our layer if only the VO_2 layer is considered. However, our optimization process can be generalized to various V layer thicknesses (d), in case of diffusion-controlled oxidation, the optimal oxidation time is proportional to the square of the thickness ($t_a \sim d^2$) [44]. The lower limit of the V thickness, i.e., the transition between the reaction and diffusion-controlled oxidation, was found to be around 60 nm [26].

In conclusion, a simple and rational technique was demonstrated to fabricate VO_2 coatings. Since the oxidation of metallic vanadium is carried out at atmospheric air at a relatively low annealing temperature (400 °C), it is prosperous for mass production. Moreover, the low temperature phase transition of 49 ± 7 °C makes it a promising candidate as an infrared transmission blocking layer.

Author Contributions: G.M. performed all the sample preparations, L.P. carried out the electrical and SEM characterization. Z.C. conducted the TEM characterization. B.K. and P.P. performed the SE measurements. J.V. supervised the project. L.P., G.M., B.K. and Z.B. wrote the manuscript. P.P. and J.V. edited and revised the manuscript. All authors have read and agreed to the published version of the manuscript.

Funding: This research was supported by the National Research, Development and Innovation Fund of the Hungarian Government in the framework of KoFAH, NVKP_16-1-2016-0018 and the NKFI K128534 grant. Support from the National Development Agency grant of OTKA K131515 and European Structural and Investment Funds grant of VEKOP-2.3.3-15-2016-00002 are gratefully acknowledged.

Data Availability Statement: The data is available on reasonable request from the corresponding author (J.V.)

Acknowledgments: The authors are thankful to Noémi Szász for TEM specimen preparation.

Conflicts of Interest: The authors declare no conflict of interest.

References

1. Shao, Z.; Cao, X.; Luo, H.; Jin, P. Recent progress in the phase-transition mechanism and modulation of vanadium dioxide materials. *NPG Asia Mater.* **2018**, *10*, 581–605. [CrossRef]
2. Kamila, S.; Chakraborty, B.; Basu, S.; Jena, B.K. Combined Experimental and Theoretical Insights into Energy Storage Applications of a VO2(D)–Graphene Hybrid. *J. Phys. Chem. C* **2019**, *123*, 24280–24288. [CrossRef]
3. Wang, S.; Owusu, K.A.; Mai, L.; Ke, Y.; Zhou, Y.; Hu, P.; Magdassi, S.; Long, Y. Vanadium dioxide for energy conservation and energy storage applications: Synthesis and performance improvement. *Appl. Energy* **2018**, *211*, 200–217. [CrossRef]
4. del Valle, J.; Salev, P.; Tesler, F.; Vargas, N.M.; Kalcheim, Y.; Wang, P.; Trastoy, J.; Lee, M.H.; Kassabian, G.; Ramírez, J.G.; et al. Subthreshold firing in Mott nanodevices. *Nature* **2019**, *569*, 388–392. [CrossRef]
5. Zhao, Y.; Chen, C.; Pan, X.; Zhu, Y.; Holtz, M.; Bernussi, A.; Fan, Z. Tuning the properties of VO_2 thin films through growth temperature for infrared and terahertz modulation applications. *J. Appl. Phys.* **2013**, *114*, 113509. [CrossRef]
6. Émond, N.; Hendaoui, A.; Ibrahim, A.; Al-Naib, I.; Ozaki, T.; Chaker, M. Transmission of reactive pulsed laser deposited VO_2 films in the THz domain. *Appl. Surf. Sci.* **2016**, *379*, 377–383. [CrossRef]
7. Strelcov, E.; Lilach, Y.; Kolmakov, A. Gas Sensor Based on Metal-Insulator Transition in VO_2 Nanowire Thermistor. *Nano Lett.* **2009**, *9*, 2322–2326. [CrossRef]
8. Kocer, H.; Butun, S.; Banar, B.; Wang, K.; Tongay, S.; Wu, J.; Aydin, K. Thermal tuning of infrared resonant absorbers based on hybrid gold-VO_2 nanostructures. *Appl. Phys. Lett.* **2015**, *106*, 161104. [CrossRef]
9. Ko, C.; Ramanathan, S. Observation of electric field-assisted phase transition in thin film vanadium oxide in a metal-oxide-semiconductor device geometry. *Appl. Phys. Lett.* **2008**, *93*, 252101. [CrossRef]
10. Chang, T.C.; Cao, X.; Bao, S.H.; Ji, S.D.; Luo, H.J.; Jin, P. Review on thermochromic vanadium dioxide based smart coatings: From lab to commercial application. *Adv. Manuf.* **2018**, *6*, 1–19. [CrossRef]
11. Brassard, D.; Fourmaux, S.; Jean-Jacques, M.; Kieffer, J.C.; El Khakani, M.A. Grain size effect on the semiconductor-metal phase transition characteristics of magnetron-sputtered VO_2 thin films. *Appl. Phys. Lett.* **2005**, *87*, 051910. [CrossRef]
12. Liang, J.; Li, J.; Hou, L.; Liu, X. Tunable Metal-Insulator Properties of Vanadium Oxide Thin Films Fabricated by Rapid Thermal Annealing. *ECS J. Solid State Sci. Technol.* **2016**, *5*, P293–P298. [CrossRef]
13. Cui, Y.; Ramanathan, S. Substrate effects on metal-insulator transition characteristics of rf-sputtered epitaxial VO_2 thin films. *J. Vac. Sci. Technol. A* **2011**, *29*, 041502. [CrossRef]
14. Théry, V.; Boulle, A.; Crunteanu, A.; Orlianges, J.C.; Beaumont, A.; Mayet, R.; Mennai, A.; Cosset, F.; Bessaudou, A.; Fabert, M. Structural and electrical properties of large area epitaxial VO_2 films grown by electron beam evaporation. *J. Appl. Phys.* **2017**, *121*, 055303. [CrossRef]
15. Soltani, M.; Chaker, M.; Haddad, E.; Kruzelecky, R.V.; Nikanpour, D. Optical switching of vanadium dioxide thin films deposited by reactive pulsed laser deposition. *J. Vac. Sci. Technol. A* **2004**, *22*, 859–864. [CrossRef]
16. Vernardou, D.; Pemble, M.E.; Sheel, D.W. Vanadium oxides prepared by liquid injection MOCVD using vanadyl acetylacetonate. *Surf. Coat. Technol.* **2004**, *188–189*, 250–254. [CrossRef]
17. Prasadam, V.P.; Bahlawane, N.; Mattelaer, F.; Rampelberg, G.; Detavernier, C.; Fang, L.; Jiang, Y.; Martens, K.; Parkin, I.P.; Papakonstantinou, I. Atomic layer deposition of vanadium oxides: Process and application review. *Mater. Today Chem.* **2019**, *12*, 396–423. [CrossRef]
18. Vlček, J.; Kolenatý, D.; Houška, J.; Kozák, T.; Čerstvý, R. Controlled reactive HiPIMS—Effective technique for low-temperature (300 °C) synthesis of VO_2 films with semiconductor-to-metal transition. *J. Phys. D Appl. Phys.* **2017**, *50*, 38LT01. [CrossRef]
19. Houska, J.; Kolenaty, D.; Rezek, J.; Vlcek, J. Characterization of thermochromic VO_2 (prepared at 250 °C) in a wide temperature range by spectroscopic ellipsometry. *Appl. Surf. Sci.* **2017**, *421*, 529–534. [CrossRef]

20. Houska, J.; Kolenaty, D.; Vlcek, J.; Cerstvy, R. Properties of thermochromic VO_2 films prepared by HiPIMS onto unbiased amorphous glass substrates at a low temperature of 300 °C. *Thin Solid Film.* **2018**, *660*, 463–470. [CrossRef]
21. Ruzmetov, D.; Zawilski, K.T.; Senanayake, S.D.; Narayanamurti, V.; Ramanathan, S. Infrared reflectance and photoemission spectroscopy studies across the phase transition boundary in thin film vanadium dioxide. *J. Phys. Condens. Matter* **2008**, *20*, 465204. [CrossRef]
22. Cueff, S.; Li, D.; Zhou, Y.; Wong, F.J.; Kurvits, J.A.; Ramanathan, S.; Zia, R. Dynamic control of light emission faster than the lifetime limit using VO_2 phase-change. *Nat. Commun.* **2015**, *6*, 8636. [CrossRef]
23. Xu, X.; He, X.; Wang, G.; Yuan, X.; Liu, X.; Huang, H.; Yao, S.; Xing, H.; Chen, X.; Chu, J. The study of optimal oxidation time and different temperatures for high quality VO_2 thin film based on the sputtering oxidation coupling method. *Appl. Surf. Sci.* **2011**, *257*, 8824–8827. [CrossRef]
24. Kang, Y.B. Critical evaluation and thermodynamic optimization of the VO–VO2.5 system. *J. Eur. Ceram. Soc.* **2012**, *32*, 3187–3198. [CrossRef]
25. Guo, P.; Biegler, Z.; Back, T.; Sarangan, A. Vanadium dioxide phase change thin films produced by thermal oxidation of metallic vanadium. *Thin Solid Film.* **2020**, *707*, 138117. [CrossRef]
26. Liu, X.; Wang, S.W.; Chen, F.; Yu, L.; Chen, X. Tuning phase transition temperature of VO_2 thin films by annealing atmosphere. *J. Phys. D Appl. Phys.* **2015**, *48*, 265104. [CrossRef]
27. Liu, X.; Ji, R.; Zhang, Y.; Li, H.; Wang, S.W. Annealing process and mechanism of glass based VO_2 film from V oxidation in pure oxygen atmosphere. *Opt. Quantum Electron.* **2016**, *48*, 453. [CrossRef]
28. Liang, J.; Zhao, Y.; Guo, J.; Yang, Z.; Su, T. Rapid Thermal Oxidation of Sputtering Power Dependent Vanadium Thin Films for VO_2 Thin Films Preparation. *ECS J. Solid State Sci. Technol.* **2018**, *7*, P429–P434. [CrossRef]
29. Rampelberg, G.; De Schutter, B.; Devulder, W.; Martens, K.; Radu, I.; Detavernier, C. In situ X-ray diffraction study of the controlled oxidation and reduction in the V–O system for the synthesis of VO_2 and V_2O_3 thin films. *J. Mater. Chem. C* **2015**, *3*, 11357–11365. [CrossRef]
30. Griffiths, C.H.; Eastwood, H.K. Influence of stoichiometry on the metal-semiconductor transition in vanadium dioxide. *J. Appl. Phys.* **1974**, *45*, 2201–2206. [CrossRef]
31. Ba, C.O.F.; Fortin, V.; Bah, S.T.; Vallée, R.; Pandurang, A. Formation of VO_2 by rapid thermal annealing and cooling of sputtered vanadium thin films. *J. Vac. Sci. Technol. A* **2016**, *34*, 031505. [CrossRef]
32. Mukherjee, A.; Wach, S. Kinetics of the oxidation of vanadium in the temperature range 350–950 °C. *J. Less Common Met.* **1983**, *92*, 289–300. [CrossRef]
33. Ji, Y.X.; Niklasson, G.A.; Granqvist, C.G.; Boman, M. Thermochromic VO_2 films by thermal oxidation of vanadium in SO_2. *Sol. Energy Mater. Sol. Cells* **2016**, *144*, 713–716. [CrossRef]
34. Jiang, S.J.; Ye, C.B.; Khan, M.S.R.; Granqvist, C.G. Evolution of thermochromism during oxidation of evaporated vanadium films. *Appl. Opt.* **1991**, *30*, 847–851. [CrossRef] [PubMed]
35. Kana, J.K.; Ndjaka, J.; Vignaud, G.; Gibaud, A.; Maaza, M. Thermally tunable optical constants of vanadium dioxide thin films measured by spectroscopic ellipsometry. *Opt. Commun.* **2011**, *284*, 807–812. [CrossRef]
36. Mokerov, V.G.; Makarov, L.V.; Tulvinskii, B.V.; Begishev, A.R. Optical properties of vanadium pentoxide in the region of photon energies from 2 eV to 14 eV. *Opt. Spectrosc.* **1976**, *40*, 58–61.
37. Parker, J.C.; Lam, D.J.; Xu, Y.N.; Ching, W.Y. Optical properties of vanadium pentoxide determined from ellipsometry and band-structure calculations. *Phys. Rev. B* **1990**, *42*, 5289–5293. [CrossRef]
38. Landry, A.; Vinh Son, T.; Haché, A. Optical modulation at the interface between silicon and a phase change material. *Optik* **2020**, *209*, 164585. [CrossRef]
39. Shibuya, K.; Sawa, A. Optimization of conditions for growth of vanadium dioxide thin films on silicon by pulsed-laser deposition. *AIP Adv.* **2015**, *5*, 107118. [CrossRef]
40. Wan, C.; Zhang, Z.; Woolf, D.; Hessel, C.M.; Rensberg, J.; Hensley, J.M.; Xiao, Y.; Shahsafi, A.; Salman, J.; Richter, S.; et al. On the Optical Properties of Thin-Film Vanadium Dioxide from the Visible to the Far Infrared. *Ann. Phys.* **2019**, 1900188. [CrossRef]
41. Deal, B.E.; Grove, A.S. General Relationship for the Thermal Oxidation of Silicon. *J. Appl. Phys.* **1965**, *36*, 3770–3778. [CrossRef]
42. Bárta, T.; Vlček, J.; Houška, J.; Haviar, S.; Čerstvý, R.; Szelwicka, J.; Fahland, M.; Fahlteich, J. Pulsed Magnetron Sputtering of Strongly Thermochromic VO_2-Based Coatings with a Transition Temperature of 22 °C onto Ultrathin Flexible Glass. *Coatings* **2020**, *10*. [CrossRef]
43. Xu, F.; Cao, X.; Luo, H.; Jin, P. Recent advances in VO_2-based thermochromic composites for smart windows. *J. Mater. Chem. C* **2018**, *6*, 1903–1919. [CrossRef]
44. Mukherjee, A.; Wach, S. An investigation of the kinetics and stability of VO_2. *J. Less Common Met.* **1987**, *132*, 107–113. [CrossRef]

MDPI
St. Alban-Anlage 66
4052 Basel
Switzerland
Tel. +41 61 683 77 34
Fax +41 61 302 89 18
www.mdpi.com

Nanomaterials Editorial Office
E-mail: nanomaterials@mdpi.com
www.mdpi.com/journal/nanomaterials

www.ingramcontent.com/pod-product-compliance
Lightning Source LLC
LaVergne TN
LVHW070624100526
838202LV00012B/720